T0288813

The New Power Elite

The New Power Elite

Heather Gautney

Oxford University Press is a department of the University of Oxford. It furthers the University's objective of excellence in research, scholarship, and education by publishing worldwide. Oxford is a registered trade mark of Oxford University Press in the UK and certain other countries.

Published in the United States of America by Oxford University Press
198 Madison Avenue, New York, NY 10016, United States of America.

CIP data is on file at the Library of Congress
ISBN 978–0–19–063744–6

DOI: 10.1093/oso/9780190637446.001.0001

9 8 7 6 5 4 3 2 1

Printed by Lakeside Book Company, United States of America

Dedicated to Stanley Aronowitz

Today, as readers and writers, we must make an effort to avoid being taken in, for this is an age of the myth and the distraction. In such an age, the task of any serious book is to unmask illusion in order to define important features of social reality. The task cannot be accomplished merely through providing information, although information on the high and mighty is badly needed, we must also try to grind a lens through which we can perhaps see a little more clearly the world in which we live.

—C. Wright Mills, "Why I Wrote *The Power Elite*"

CONTENTS

ACKNOWLEDGMENTS

Thanks to Adolph Reed, Jr., Bernie Sanders, and Nina Turner for their guidance, courage, and care.

To Christian Lewelling, Anna Mesa, Samir Sonti, and Ben St. Clair for their brilliant political and editorial contributions.

To Larry Cohen, Bill DiFazio, Phil Fiermonte, Angelo Greco, Teffannie Hale, Erin Hanley, Michael Hardt, Suzanna Heller, Kathi Weeks, David Weinstein, and Cornel West for their support along the way.

To my agent William Clark and editor James Cook for their invaluable insights and for making it happen.

To my family—Spencer and Diane, Jeff and DeeAnn, Jill and Joe, Kristen, Jake, Robbie, Spencer, Olivia, Annabella, Vittoria, Hope, Hannah and Nick, Ally and Dom, Dan, and Louise. And to my loves Glenn, Lula, Sydney, and Sicily.

Introduction

Nowadays, there is a general sense among people in "democratic" societies that the world they live in is not of their own making and that someone else is pulling the strings—and in this feeling, they are quite right. Many have lost faith in basic institutions, like the legal system and news media, and distrust their political leaders. They are told that their country is the greatest on earth, a land of opportunity. But in their work lives, they are disillusioned and coerced, and only feel themselves when they are not working. When they go to the polls, if they even do, they feel the outcome has already been decided and that things are not likely to change—at least not for them. When they walk by people sleeping out in the streets and in their cars, on any given night, they are gripped by the fear that they themselves may be just one illness or layoff away from a similar fate.

On January 6, 2021, the day that the U.S. Congress was scheduled to count electoral votes and declare Joe Biden president, tens of thousands gathered in Washington, DC at a "Save America" rally to rage against the political establishment. Many of them were driven by the belief—perpetrated by political and media elites and spread through social media algorithmically designed to churn rage into profits—that the presidential election had been stolen and that their democracy was at stake. During the rally, former New York City mayor Rudolph Giuliani called for "trial by combat," and President Trump encouraged his supporters to march down Pennsylvania Avenue, confront lawmakers, and "fight like hell" or "you won't have a country anymore."[1] Then, at the U.S. Capitol, a menacing crowd broke barricades, violently attacked police officers, and smashed windows. Some, wearing Confederate flags, conspiracy group logos, and in one case a "Camp Auschwitz" sweatshirt, marauded through the opulent halls of Congress, as senators and congressmen and their staffs hid under desks and were rushed to safe spaces.

Composite sketches of January 6th rioters present a familiar picture of anomie and manipulation, the kind that shows itself when people are painfully aware of their own powerlessness and individual conscience is easily swept aside in the *jouissance* of mass defiance. Some were there to harm, even kill, legislators. But most were regular, previously law-abiding people, radicalized in a context of chronic economic instability and endemic corruption and social alienation—egged on by right-wing media and a president who thumbed his nose at the establishment and played to their fears and sense of betrayal. Liberals helped fan the flames of resentment by relentlessly painting Trump voters as losers and lowlifes.

Renowned sociologist and public intellectual C. Wright Mills wrote of these tendencies in his now-classic text *The Power Elite*, which foreshadowed January 6th and the power dynamics and erosion of social norms that it represents. Driven by a deep knowledge of the historical role that acute inequality and powerlessness played in the rise of European fascism, Mills was compelled to expose the stark realities of elite power in postwar America and warn of the country's authoritarian drift. Since then, the antidemocratic currents that he observed in his seminal book have intensified to the extreme, and the "irresponsible elites" of which he wrote now appear, through the lens of history, as relatively staid compared to those currently in power.

Despite the social inequalities and mass manipulation by the elites of his time, Mills wrote *The Power Elite* when safety nets were still in place and income and wealth gaps were at historic lows. That period witnessed a proliferation of millionaires—from 27,000 in 1953 to 90,000 in 1965—but the working class still shared in the economic gains.[2] Now, with the degraded quality of work, ruthless attacks on labor unions, and stripping of social supports, incomes have shrunk, and the average wage is no higher than it was forty years ago, despite increased productivity. Half of U.S. workers live paycheck to paycheck and incomes are so low that tens of millions rely on public assistance to get by.[3] One in five children lives in poverty, and millions of working poor battle hunger, poor health, social ostracization, and police violence on a daily basis. Life expectancy—a key measure of the health of a society—has declined. With diminishing options and a frayed safety net, millions of people have become addicted to pain medications, and in 2021 alone, over 100,000 of them died from drug overdose, mostly from opioids marketed by billionaire-owned drug companies.[4]

Meanwhile, those at the top have never been wealthier and more conspicuous in their consumption. As most Americans register negative net worth, three billionaires control more wealth than the bottom half of the entire population. Over the three decades between 1990 and 2020, when U.S. median wealth grew by just over 5 percent, billionaire wealth skyrocketed more than 1,000 percent.[5] More recently, at the height of the coronavirus pandemic, when tens of millions of people were falling ill and losing their jobs, and over a million people lost their lives,[6] 745 U.S. billionaires increased their collective wealth by $2 trillion—over just nineteen months. As the incomes of 99 percent of people around the world were falling, and more than 160 million pushed into poverty, the ten wealthiest—all multibillionaires—more than doubled their collective net worth.[7]

This condition of gross inequality and concentrated power is the result of a concerted class program, now decades in the making, to transfer wealth and political power away from ordinary people and into the hands of a few. Over the last half century, through manufactured crisis and dominance over state and corporate policymakers, "neoliberal" intellectuals—claiming the mantle of freedom against the horrors of Stalinism and fascism—elevated their fringe ideas to the status of common sense and fundamentally reconstituted the relationship between citizens, the state, and market forces. The new form of global capitalism they conceived of, and imposed, involved positioning the "free market" as an ultimate political and cultural authority and suppressing policies and rules, social movements, and political organizations that might impede profitability. In addition to economic and environmental plunder, cultural ruin, and humanitarian crisis, these "reformers" collaborated with dictators to field-test their fundamentalist theories on whole nations and instigated an ongoing War on Terror that has unleashed unspeakable violence into the world.

With governments in their pockets and billions of dollars at their backs, neoliberals legitimize their class program by demonizing the very idea of a public sphere and representative state as a threat to human freedom and the pursuit of wealth. They have worked to reduce civic and political life to consumer choice and combat sport, and enabled media monopolists to sow disinformation and desensitize people to contradiction. In keeping with the playbook of modern authoritarian regimes, they have colonized institutional pillars of political engagement—schools and universities, the media, political parties, and community organizations—to sever people's connection to their government and to each other. Pitting citizen against citizen, they have incited culture wars on a host of emotionally triggering issues, from abortion to gun ownership to gender identity to school curricula.

During and after the Great Depression, such seemingly intractable economic and social inequalities led to the rise of right-wing nationalist forces around the world. In Europe, the resultant anger and desolation were harnessed by demagogues who fused corporatism and militarism in amassing power. Those forces were also gathering in the United States—recall the mass rally in Madison Square Garden in 1939 involving tens of thousands of Nazi sympathizers—but were, at least in part, staved off by New Deal social supports and protections.[8] As those protections, rights, and supports are steadily stripped away and human despair grows, right-wing regimes around the world are once again redirecting popular anger and humiliation toward violent rage and xenophobia. Now, in the United States, when white nationalists march in the streets and fundamentalists infiltrate school boards, voting booths, newsrooms, and the U.S. Capitol, Republicans and their propagandists applaud their efforts and Democrats act as if they had no part in precipitating the decline. Standing above the fray, profiting off the misery, and driving today's authoritarian turn is a new power elite, who are not only richer and more dominant than ever before but also, as this book shows, profoundly more repressive.

THE POWER ELITE

C. Wright Mills wrote *The Power Elite* in the mid-1950s, amid the defeat of imperial fascism in Europe and the Pacific, when the United States was a nascent superpower. For the American political establishment, the Soviet Union's possession of nuclear weapons posed an existential threat, as did the Korean War and communist victory in China.[9] In response, the United States undertook a massive enlargement of its national security apparatus and consolidated its military and intelligence agencies under the executive branch.[10] Between 1950 and 1955, military allocations nearly tripled, and foreign military aid programs proliferated, along with programs and infrastructures for weapons research and development (R&D).[11]

American postwar military might was fortified by economic muscle of a similar, if not superior, order. As fascist forces gathered across Europe amid the global economic decline of the 1930s, in the United States the New Deal provided solace from the chaos of the Great Depression. It also gave wings to a new political economic paradigm, attributed to Nobel Prize–winning economist John Maynard Keynes, that rejected laissez-faire paradigms promoting unfettered markets and financial speculation in favor of state-managed capital. Keynesianism viewed full employment, good wages, and regulated capital as key factors of prosperity and growth.[12]

This state-centered approach aimed to guarantee workers consistent levels of mobility, financial security, and consumption—an honest day's work for an honest day's pay—in exchange for their productivity and social and political conformity.

Post-Depression state intervention by way of relief, safety net programs, and pro-growth policy helped to stabilize and restructure U.S. capitalism on the domestic front. But it also provided a regulatory blueprint for a new, international system—one in which the interests of the American superpower could be proffered as the interests of the world. Keynes himself helped convene the landmark meeting of 700-plus delegates from all forty-four Allied countries at the stately Mount Washington Hotel in Bretton Woods, New Hampshire in July 1944. The agreement they negotiated set rules for commercial and financial relations among participating independent nation-states and established multinational regulatory institutions headed by the United States.

The Bretton Woods system, as it came to be known, set the U.S. dollar as the global reserve currency. International loans were made by the World Bank (then the International Bank for Reconstruction and Development), debts managed by the International Monetary Fund, and trade monitored through the General Agreement on Tariffs and Trade. This new institutional framework and restructuring of the global economy expanded the reach of American corporations and helped the United States consolidate its position as the world's economic center. Governments that did not conform to the new status quo were undermined, branded "communist," or overthrown.

By the time *The Power Elite* hit bookshelves in 1956, the inferno of the Great Depression seemed but a flicker in America's rear window. Relief lines had become shopping lines and the blight of devastating joblessness and abandoned factories was alleviated by the promise of full employment and doubled wages. This period registered one of the most equitable income distributions in U.S. history.[13] Over the course of President Dwight D. Eisenhower's tenure, personal income grew by 45 percent, and for many Americans it was their first experience having discretionary income.[14] Eisenhower's large-scale government initiatives magnified the *Leave It to Beaver* image of a booming America, as the Interstate Highway program and St. Lawrence Seaway—and the system of bridges, housing, and ancillary businesses that accompanied them—stimulated the economy with well-paying jobs and increased investment in new technologies and R&D. Federal housing programs and the novel highway mobility encouraged individual homeownership, as did corporate relocations, resulting in the growth of suburbs.[15] Higher incomes also facilitated new markets for consumer products, including household goods like washing machines and color televisions, as well as automobiles and air travel. Conveniences that were once available only to the rich became middle-class staples.

Wholesale opposition to Soviet communism and desires to celebrate and safeguard the American way of life profoundly shaped the U.S. academy in those years. Liberal university education was rapidly expanding and behavioral research came into vogue. This was facilitated by generous foundation and government support, and new technologies that expanded social scientists' ability to collect and analyze larger and more complex datasets. Behaviorists perceived the central problems of modern society in terms of individual psychology—decision-making, choices and preferences, and behaviors—to the detriment of understanding human action in historical context. In political science, this methodological individualism undergirded *pluralist theory*, which eschewed class as an analytical category in favor of "interest group" dynamics. Pluralists began with the premise that the U.S. liberal-democratic state operated as a neutral space in which a plurality of interest groups (e.g., lobbyists, political parties, trade unions) could check one another's power on equal footing in a balanced system of competing interests.[16] Leading political scientist Robert Dahl described the system as a "polyarchy," in which free elections and competition among interest groups increased the variety of minority groups whose preferences could be taken into account by representative leadership, at the welcome exclusion of the apathetic masses.[17] This view was reinforced by economist John Kenneth Galbraith, who claimed that intellectuals' skepticism of corporate power was misguided, as business was already being reined in by democratic forces, like organized labor, consumers, and a regulatory state.[18]

Bypassing actual, historical dynamics allowed leading sociologists like Edward Shils, Daniel Bell, and Seymour Martin Lipset[19] to argue that the postwar welfare state had ushered in "the end of ideology"—the idea that Western societies had solved the contradictions of industrial capitalism and put an end to class and ideological struggle.[20] C. Wright Mills broke, often viciously, with this line of thought, disparaging postwar liberalism as "conformist unthinking, reason at the eager service of unreasonable kings, sophisticated apologetics for the inexcusable, social scientists as shields of orthodoxy and bellboys of authority."[21] His contempt for pluralist social science was in part informed by his engagement with pragmatist thinkers like John Dewey and William James, who viewed science as a dynamic, nondogmatic process of inquiry that should begin with practical life rather than abstractions. Pragmatism equipped Mills with a method for understanding the modern world and, importantly, the quality of mind to change it.[22]

Mills did not disagree with pluralists that postwar America was marked by political and cultural consensus; rather, he viewed their work as an elaborate fig leaf for severely undemocratic institutional arrangements driven by a consensus among elites. Indeed, Shils and Lipset were involved with the CIA-backed Congress for Cultural Freedom, whose political agenda involved fostering anti-communist sentiment among intellectuals.[23] In institutes at the University of Chicago and University of Virginia, moreover, "neoliberals" were organizing at the behest of corporate power with little pretense of academic independence.[24] Despite such obvious bias, leading academics like Bell and then-celebrated sociologist Talcott Parsons had the audacity to dismiss Mills's work and that of other left radicals as derived from passion and pathology rather than "objective" science. For Mills, the true pathology lay in how the academics of his day were intentionally obscuring the real picture of America in which power elites were silencing critical discourse and precipitating what he called a "decline of politics as genuine and public debate of alternative decisions."[25]

Behind the curtain of the "American celebration," as Mills put it, were conservative politicians and a powerful business lobby with an avowed commitment to private sector growth. In the summer of 1942—the same year the GOP won forty-seven seats in the House[26]—a cadre of "business intellectuals" assembled the Committee for Economic Development (CED)[27] for the purpose of steering the war economy toward profit-making and away from what they called (in their bylaws) "the perils of mass unemployment or mass government employment." By 1945, the CED had organized thousands of local branches across the country and some 50,000 businessmen, and had direct inroads to wartime planning agencies like the Department of Commerce. A year later, pro-capital forces played a major role in amending the Employment Act of 1946 to remove all references to "full employment" and replace them with language promoting competitive free enterprise.[28]

The American state's veering away from public sector investment helped restructure the U.S. economy to be heavily dependent on consumer spending, which itself was dependent upon income growth. Wage increases, however, ran the risk of cutting into corporate profits, spurring inflation, and enabling worker militancy. This contradiction was resolved through a confluence of decisions, manipulations, and legislative actions by power elites, none of which imply a "polyarchal" arrangement as pluralists claimed. State and corporate elites sold the compromise between capital and labor as rooted in economic growth, consumerism, and shared interests in the face of popular anxieties over Soviet communism. But draconian laws like Taft-Hartley that disciplined workers and their unions reflected the true nature of the arrangement.

For Mills, the pluralist habit of casting human behavior in an ahistorical, apolitical light obscured the collusion of state and corporate power in labor's defeat, naturalized the military worldview, and represented the liberal, capitalist order as the best of what was possible. Despite the book's rejection in the intellectual ivory towers of its day, *The Power Elite* became a veritable bible among the New Left and counterculture for having drawn back the curtain and demonstrating, in piercing prose, how elites were treading on personal freedoms and turning the United States into a mass society.

Mills derived his approach, and sense of alarm, from Franz Neumann's analysis of Third Reich power structures in his seminal text, *Behemoth: The Structure and Practice of National Socialism 1933–1944*. There, Neumann outlined the contours of the Nazis' historically distinct form of capitalism marked by a coincidence of interests among four interconnected yet competing power blocs—the state, the party, the military, and industry—that collaborated in a program of imperialist expansion and totalitarian governance. Neumann's Frankfurt School colleague Friedrich Pollock argued that Nazism constituted a kind of post-capitalist order in which business, markets, and profit-making were subordinated to the Nazis' will to power vis-à-vis an omnipotent state.[29] But for Neumann, German fascism marked a logical progression of the essential features of capitalism—profit motives, cut-throat competition, exploitation—through the cooperation of military, state, and corporate elites in pursuit of common goals. Top among those goals was a shared interest in atomizing subordinate classes by destroying or manipulating their bases of social solidarity and intermediaries with the state—civic associations, political parties, and trade unions—and, of course, intimidating them with jackboot violence.[30]

Mills took up Neumann's mantle with a critique of the increasing concentration of institutional authority in America in which elites were making "big decisions"—like building up massive military budgets or waging secret wars—that affected masses of people without their knowledge or consent.[31] Though Mills was concerned with "the quality of men" in power, he conceived of elite power not as the province of individuals, but as embedded in leadership positions of the country's top political, military, and economic institutions. Within this "interlocking directorate," leaders moved seamlessly from one top institution to the next, forming an upper crust of the American power structure from which all other social and political institutions took their cues.[32]

In the sphere of politics and the state, Mills argued that the ostensible balance of power in the U.S. government was tilted in favor of the executive branch, which he described as "the center of initiative and decision."[33] The executive could command key administrative bodies, stack the judiciary, veto laws, set foreign policy, and execute wars essentially without Congress, the governmental body positioned to represent "the people." Mills decried the executive branch as largely run by "political outsiders" who were not democratically elected or trained and socialized in the civil service, and whose loyalties lay in other kinds of institutions, like corporations and the military. Congress exercised some regulatory authority over economic and military issues, and set relevant policy, but remained locked in a purgatory of competing interests, confrontation, and compromise.

At the reins of economic power were the corporate chiefs with the modern corporation as their institutional center. They determined the shape of the national economy from employment levels and consumer activity to tax, monetary, and immigration policy; and brokered arms deals and international trade agreements. At the time, corporate monopoly and increasing private sector control over essential industries like energy, banking, housing, and insurance had expanded the reach of corporate enterprises to the point where their failure threatened social stability. As corporations consolidated power and penetrated deeper into the fabric of domestic life through work, entertainment, and consumerism, the military-industrial complex fed on the permanent war economy and greased—or forced open—markets abroad.

Mills passed away a few months before the Cuban Missile Crisis, when a small cadre of powerful men came frighteningly close to waging a catastrophic nuclear war. That such high-stakes decisions affecting the future of human and planetary life lay in the hands of "irresponsible elites" weighed heavily on his work. America's obsession with communism, he argued, was the work of "crackpot realists" who had created "a paranoid reality all their own"[34]—a reality that would legitimize a series of illegal, covert military operations in places like Cambodia, Chile, and Indonesia and justify the suppression of the labor movement and unconstitutional domestic wiretapping. That same paranoid reality would also drive an arms race that continued long after the point of mutual assured destruction while delivering arms manufacturers like Boeing and Lockheed Martin an epic windfall.

In bearing witness to the rise of mass consumerism and concentration of corporate, state, and military power, Mills developed a bitter contempt for what he viewed as a vacant triumphalism of the postwar culture, drunk on consumption and high on consensus. His theory of mass society hinged on his belief in democratic life as constituted by politically active and informed publics; and following Neumann, he understood that elite power, and fascist dictatorship, was predicated on the suppression of popular will. Such suppression could be achieved by intimidation but also through anti-intellectualism, egoist consumer culture, and patriotic consensus. *The Power Elite* exposed the power relations behind that supposed consensus and inspired others, including this author, to confront elite power and demystify its ideological justifications for generations to come.

THE NEW POWER ELITE

Since the 1970s, the military enlargement and synthesis of business and government that Mills analyzed and condemned have intensified to a degree that not even he could have imagined. As conditions worsen and elite power grows, the United States is more and more displaying the characteristics of authoritarian capitalism that he predicted, yet with less popular resistance and less of a sense of alternatives. The neoliberal program, considered fringe in Mills's time, is now the dominant paradigm of social and political life worldwide—one that is fundamentally corrupt and antidemocratic in its nature. Positioning government as an anathema to freedom, elite lawmakers, under the thumb of billionaires and corporate CEOs, have transformed the basic pillars of the social order—education, banking, housing, media and communications, infrastructure, agriculture, health care, and elections—into profit-making opportunities and ransacked rules and programs that once provided the most basic social protections and supports. The very rich dominate the electoral system and continue to attack, and in some cases severely weaken, intermediaries like trade unions and political parties. The news media and institutions of knowledge production have been privatized and politicized, and the cultural domain saturated with advertisements and superficialities.

Nowadays, extremists pulling the levers of state power are openly suppressing votes, banning books, and prohibiting teachers from discussing matters of racial injustice and gender identity in their classrooms. They have taken away women's right to bodily autonomy by banning abortion and are poised to undermine basic rights to contraception and same-sex relationships and marriage. In Texas, residents are encouraged to bring lawsuits against anyone they think may have violated the state's abortion ban—turning everyday citizens into bounty hunters and fostering a climate of suspicion and fear.[35]

The New Power Elite is a continuation of Mills's program to expose the elites driving these developments and to understand the nature of their power. Similar to his approach, it focuses primarily on policies, events, institutions, and cultural trends within the United States, but understands them as inextricably linked to the dynamics of corporate-led globalization. In that vein, it accounts for neoliberalism's imperial ambitions and supranational character, including major transformations in the political geography of corporations and labor, the rise of finance capital, and the role of U.S. imperialism in the structuring of global capitalism. The book departs from Mills on the question of whether political and military institutions should be considered as autonomous from market forces, and argues that while the American state remains an essential site of contestation—over fiscal policy or law enforcement, for example—its principal function today is to serve the interests of capital and operate on its behalf.[36] Mills himself suggested that such dynamics be assessed in historical context, and this book takes up that charge by studying the political, social, and cultural means that elites have deployed over the last half century to accumulate their incredible power and wealth.[37]

The opening chapters of this book focus on the role of the American state in the consolidation of elite power, understanding it as a vital center of class struggle over policy, ideology, means of wealth accumulation, and deployments of military power. Despite neoliberal mythologies regarding the equalities and efficiencies of self-regulating markets, really existing neoliberalism relies heavily on state forces to set legal frameworks and "conditions" for capital accumulation. Such frameworks include fiscal policy, administrative regulation, and use of the courts to facilitate capital flows as well as the disciplining of populations that might impede them.

Chapter 1 identifies the major tenets of neoliberalism and charts its rise, beginning with Pinochet's Chile, which provided the world with a preview of neoliberalism's compatibility with fascism and the consequences of elevating the free market as an ultimate authority. It assesses pivotal decisions by state and corporate elites in the 1960s and '70s that suppressed social democratic alternatives and state planning; and their use of crisis, fiscal austerity, and repression to entrench inegalitarian ideologies and institutional systems.[38]

Along with the first chapter, chapters 2 and 3 track the neoliberal advance over four presidencies, considering how each of them contributed to the gross exploitations and inequalities, and corrosion of social solidarities and liberal democratic norms, we have today. This analysis culminates in the presidency of Donald Trump, who, more than any other president, exposed the stark realities of American capitalism and the character of the elites helming it. Though Trump was in many ways singular, his ascendancy, and opportunism in exploiting popular outrage, cannot be understood apart from his predecessors' consistent betrayal of poor and working-class people—and the gaping contradictions between government elites' claims to safeguard freedom and democracy and the economic realities and political powerlessness that most people face. As these chapters show, the substance of Trump's policymaking veered little from the ongoing bipartisan commitment to a hegemonic free market and handmaiden state, whether through Democrats' brand of technocratic governance or the more openly autocratic style of the GOP.

Beginning with the Cold War and ending with the still-current War on Terror, chapter 4 examines the coercive arm of the state and reveals, in horrific detail, the sadistic face of neoliberal capitalism and its proclivity for torture and violence. For most Americans, the United States has continuously been engaged in some form of military conflict or war during their lifetimes—waving the banner of freedom while forcing "market conditions" on countries around the world and empowering police to terrorize populations and defile civil liberties at home. This chapter illustrates the processes and ideological mechanisms underlying elites' militarism—from redbaiting and inciting patriotic fervor, to bipartisan efforts to expand executive power, to the privatization of war, and enlargement of the military and security industrial complexes.

Chapter 5 studies shifts in the capitalist economy's center of gravity from production to finance over the last half century and the tremendous consolidation of elite wealth through techniques of *financialization*. It traces the global integration and unfettering of financial institutions and markets that have exponentially multiplied opportunities for wealth-making—through financial innovation, structural adjustment, predatory lending, and high-risk speculation—and the ability of "too big to fail" banks to increase their profits while externalizing risk onto the public. The chapter recalls the great wealth generated on Wall Street in the 1980s vis-à-vis leveraged buyouts and explains how private equity firms today are drawing from that playbook to extract value from corporate assets and workforces, largely through plunder. It also follows the more recent emergence of cryptocurrency and rise of asset management firms—with massive ownership stakes in nearly every major corporation—that wield immense, systemic-level power over government, public policy, and the global economy.

Chapter 6 evaluates how today's oligarchs accumulate and defend their wealth by usurping government resources, financializing business, disciplining workers, and evading taxes. As exemplars of how the very rich manipulate political and legislative systems to achieve their interests, it singles out the Koch brothers for their pioneering work in opening the floodgates of big money in politics and gutting profit-hampering federal regulations and agencies in place to protect consumers, workers, and the environment. In locating the roots of billionaire wealth in technological development and shifts in the global economy, the chapter implicates today's retail and tech giants for their monopolistic control over essential resources and institutions and shrewd exploitation of workers and global supply chains. It also implicates them for profiting off surveillance schemes that track the daily lives of masses of people, exploit their desires for connection, and stoke social and political division. Finally, the chapter looks at how the very wealthy use philanthropy to divert attention from their exploits, evade taxes, and impose their priorities and worldviews, in some cases turning public institutions into profitable industries.

Chapter 7 analyzes the role of celebrity in naturalizing social inequality and ruling class hegemony through cultural life, consumption, and the manufacturing of consent. In Mills's writing on celebrities, he positioned them in the hierarchy of elite power as subordinate to those in control of the "big three" institutional command posts. Since then, celebrities have infiltrated the highest circles of corporate power, and achieved billionaire wealth, through the increased concentration of media ownership and high-value branding enabled by the ubiquity of social media. They have also infiltrated the highest levels of political power, most notably with the presidency of Donald Trump, who not only demonstrated the culture industry's political potency, but importantly, revealed the dangers of a system in which large numbers of people are willing to accept affective stimulation and entertainment as substitutes for democratic power.

Finally, chapter 8 addresses the degraded condition of civic and political life in the United States and the ideological forces behind it, beginning with Mills's framework of *publics* and *masses*. Whereas *publics* indicate engaged, knowledgeable, autonomous agents of democratic deliberation and dissent, *masses* are anti-intellectual, uninformed, and prone to manipulation. This chapter exposes elites' efforts to politicize and banalize the news media and privatize education—both institutional pillars of civic engagement and challenging elite power—and the role of media monopolies and propaganda in the march of authoritarian capitalism. With the devaluing of political and intellectual life we have today, and lack of awareness regarding who controls the information we take as fact, everyday people are losing the ability to act as political agents and direct their own lives and communities, and fundamentally, to resist authoritarianism in its most violent, and amusing, forms.

CHAPTER 1
The State (1973–2000)

On the one hand, we have seen a decayed and frightened liberalism, and on the other hand, the insecure and ruthless fury of political gangsters.

—C. Wright Mills

In his preface to the 1982 edition of *Capitalism and Freedom*, Nobel Prize–winning economist Milton Friedman wrote, "Only a crisis—actual or perceived—produces real change. When that crisis occurs, the actions that are taken depend on the ideas that are lying around. That, I believe, is our basic function: to develop alternatives to existing policies, to keep them alive and available until the politically impossible becomes the politically inevitable."[1] True to Friedman's words, the elevation of neoliberal capitalism to the status of grand narrative and organizing principle of everyday life hinged on political elites' ability to exploit crisis, to quash egalitarian ideas, policies, and movements, and to make the politically impossible appear inevitable.

This chapter and the two that follow analyze the nature of contemporary power elitism by focusing on the political agents driving the rise of neoliberalism and the fulfillment of their class program vis-à-vis the state. Chapter 1 tracks the neoliberal march through the Carter, Reagan, and Clinton administrations, and considers how each of them contributed to the far-reaching inequalities, and corrosion of social solidarity and liberal democratic norms, we have today. This includes an assessment of the means that political elites have deployed—the policy regimes, rules and enforcement, privatization schemes, and manufactured decline of public institutions—to subordinate the American state and other elements of the world order to the interests of capital. It also involves study of how political elites and their underlings have worked to sever citizens' connection to their government and to each other by suppressing or coopting policies, social movements, and political organizations that might threaten profitability.

As this brief history shows, the success of the neoliberal class program in the United States and beyond has relied on the alignment of both major parties to wield state power for the purposes of upward wealth accumulation. Within this framework, the presidency of Donald Trump and the tribalism he engendered should be understood not as an aberration, but as a logical consequence of bipartisan powerholders' shared commitment to enlarging elite power through the neoliberal state.

NEOLIBERAL CAPITALISM

Neoliberalism's conceptual roots can be traced to a group of academic historians, philosophers, and economists who in 1947 formed the Mont Pelerin Society, named after the Swiss spa where the society first convened at a meeting financed by banks and insurance companies.[2] Members of the society—which included notables like George Stigler, Milton Friedman, Ludwig von Mises, James M. Buchanan, Karl Popper, and Friedrich von Hayek (F. A. Hayek), among others—called themselves "neoliberals" in reference to the nineteenth-century pro-market ideas that influenced them and their commitment to "individual liberty."

The Mont Pelerin Society brought together wealthy individuals and corporate leaders to advance its platform but stayed on the margins during the postwar years. As evinced by Barry Goldwater's failed 1964 presidential campaign, on which Friedman and Buchanan were advisors, neoliberal ideas were not popular with the American public. Even in the conservative South, people still looked to government as a source of economic stability and valued their public schools and federal programs like Social Security. That began to change in the 1970s and 80s with the help of conservative public officials and intellectuals in universities and think tanks. Groups like the Heritage Foundation, Hoover Institute, and American Enterprise Institute helped to transform this once-fringe system of ideas and techniques into the prevailing common sense.

In May 1981, Margaret Thatcher said during an interview with the *Sunday Times* that "What's irritated me about the whole direction of politics in the last 30 years is that it's always been towards the collectivist society. People have forgotten about the personal society." Then, in discussing her strategy, she infamously remarked, "Economics are the method; the object is to change the heart and soul."[3] In the context of the Cold War, neoliberals like Thatcher sought to change hearts and souls by associating their program with the cherished values of human dignity and freedom against the horrors of Stalinism and fascism. To them, centralized states were inefficient and easily corrupted by special interests, and majority rule posed a threat to individual liberty.

In the neoliberal worldview, the market is a neutral playing field on which anyone can realize upward mobility and personal success through hard work and competition—and that hard work and competition, they believe, are the stuff of innovation and civilizational greatness. Only through unfettered entrepreneurial pursuits can a society achieve a high standard of living and liberty and justice for all. The state's role, therefore, should be to safeguard property rights and competition, not regulate market activity or impinge on people's private property and freedom of choice.

Fundamental to this narrative are the twin concepts of *choice* and *personal responsibility*, reflected in Thatcher's oxymoronic, or just moronic, comment. Neoliberal ideology of *choice* is premised on an idea of freedom as fundamentally rooted in individuals' ability to rationally and freely pursue their private interests without interference. Personal property is protected by the rule of law, but individuals have the freedom to choose how to live and are responsible for their own well-being. In this vein, neoliberals oppose social welfare policies, and promote reduced taxes and blanket privatization of social institutions, because they believe that "forcing" people to pay into a common system that is subject to the whims of elected officials—and that "hangers-on" can exploit and abuse—is fundamentally coercive. To them, taxes are not for the common good; they are an oppressive barrier to the pursuit of happiness and wealth.

Neoliberalism is a form of authority that takes power away from people and elected officials and gives it to economists and moneyed interests. This move away from politics as a medium of citizenship and toward economic calculation, citizen-consumerism, and choice is reflected in neoliberals' anti-democratic penchant for technocratic governance and executive power. Despite their mythologies around the equalities and efficiencies of self-regulating markets, actual neoliberalism relies heavily upon state forces to set legal frameworks and "conditions" for capital accumulation. Such frameworks include fiscal policy, administrative regulation, and use of the courts to facilitate capital flows as well as the violent disciplining of populations that might impede them.

For example, political elites' brokering of "free trade" agreements involves setting legal terms for governing the global economy. But because this process requires participating countries to rescind elements of state planning, like price controls or environmental regulations, neoliberals bill it as a form of deregulation and removing "barriers" to international commerce. Removing such barriers, they argue, "levels the playing field" for all parties and fosters conditions for innovation and shared prosperity. In reality, free trade agreements remove barriers to the spread of sweatshops and exploitation of workers, and to the pillage of public institutions and indigenous lands. They have destroyed millions of jobs, lowered wages, eliminated important consumer and environmental protections, and in many places destroyed local industries.[4] Oftentimes, their enforcement mechanisms require member states to refrain from passing laws or regulations that might eat into corporate profits. Rather than create trade agreements based on how well they protect the environment or curb violations of workers' rights, rules are crafted based on how they might impact profits and capital flows.

Domestically, neoliberals justify their use of "deregulation" to discipline and control populations with rhetoric about creating opportunity and clearing away onerous rules and bureaucratic red tape (or they scaremonger about the threats of "government overreach" and communism). The officials who deregulated the banking industry, for example, justified it on the basis of expanding consumer access to credit and consumer goods and services, such as houses, cars, and college. Without government oversight, however, banks have preyed on "high risk" borrowers by imposing excessive usury rates and hidden fees, enveloping them in an iron cage of debt. That iron cage is the habitus through which masses of people now experience the world. Without other options, elderly people are using high-interest credit cards to pay for life-saving medicines, and veterans are resorting to payday loans to cover the rent and utility bills. On the other end of the lifecycle, college students are drowning in student loans that some of them will be paying off for the rest of their lives.

In the bigger picture, this unfettering of the banking system helped to shift the center of gravity in the capitalist economy from production to finance, and in the process, exponentially increased opportunities for speculation and profit-making—and crisis. For example, the relaxing of mortgage lending standards, ostensibly to expand home ownership, gave Wall Street speculators a green light to game housing markets for tens of billions of dollars and nearly tank the global economy. Despite its historical antipathy to government regulation, Wall Street welcomed the hand of the state to steady markets and bail out banks, and today, bankers continue to enjoy the moral hazard of having their profits underwritten by the U.S. taxpayer. To boot, the crisis created an opening for governors and state officials to reduce public spending and sell off public goods to compensate for fiscal budgets strained by corporate tax cuts.

In the United States, the advance of neoliberal capitalism has largely depended on bipartisan political consensus. Over the last half century, Democrats and Republicans alike have decried the dangers of "rising deficits" and importance of "fiscal responsibility," with one administration after the other imposing drastic reductions in public spending. These include cuts in critical services and institutions—such as schools, libraries, public transportation, and childcare and housing assistance—that working-class and poor people rely on and subsidize. When such cuts inevitably exacerbate social ills, lawmakers scapegoat government and public sector workers and their unions. Then they turn what were once public goods over to the private sector, where they are subject to profit motives and the vicissitudes of crisis-prone markets. As if that wasn't enough, they double down on the corporate tax cuts and subsidies that caused the "rising deficits" in the first place in the name of stimulating the economy—socialism for the rich, capitalism for everyone else.

Chile, 1973

The story of neoliberalism's ascent begins in the early 1970s with Pinochet's Chile—which provided the world with a preview of neoliberalism's compatibility with authoritarianism and the consequences of elevating the "free market" as an ultimate authority. Literary giant Eduardo Galeano spoke to this compatibility when he wrote of Uruguay: "People were in prison so that prices could be free."[5] That was indeed the dynamic in Chile, where state and corporate elites, with the help of academic economists, colluded in a genocidal "experiment" to impose neoliberal reform through extreme violence and repression.

In the 1960s, Chile was a world leader in copper mining, and a high proportion (80 percent) of its production was controlled by U.S. multinationals for whom copper was generating profits in the hundreds of millions of dollars.[6] The CIA was helping to protect those interests by funneling money to pro-U.S. business groups through the U.S. Agency for International Development (USAID). In a context of devastating income inequality and mounting resentment against American profiteers, presidential elections were held in 1970 and Salvador Allende Gossens won the popular vote on a program to nationalize major industries and cultivate ties to socialist and communist countries. Infuriated by Allende's election, President Richard Nixon and his national security advisor Henry Kissinger covertly and illegally ordered his overthrow in the name of curtailing the "domino effect" of communism, directing the CIA to "make the Chilean economy scream." In the mix was David Rockefeller, an old money power elite who lobbied on behalf of business elites with stakes in Latin America[7] to prevent the nationalization of U.S.-invested industries and other elements of Allende's platform, such as land redistribution. Since the late fifties, Rockefeller had been bankrolling a program at the University of Chicago, led by Milton Friedman, that trained Chilean students in the laissez-faire, anti-communist tradition. Once the U.S. installed Pinochet, those "Chicago Boys" returned to Chile to assume public office and implement the neoliberal market reforms they had learned.

In direct contradiction to neoliberals' claim for minimal state involvement in economic affairs—not to mention their supposed interest in human freedom—the Chilean state imposed neoliberal reforms with brutal force. Those reforms included the transfer of Chilean wealth to foreign investors and the private sector, major cuts in government spending, and the firing of tens of thousands of public sector workers. Health and pension systems were privatized and hundreds of government industries sold at bargain prices. Institutions that even hinted at public service, such as community health centers for the poor, were shut down. Pinochet also deregulated the financial sector, divested from public banking, and cut import tariffs.[8]

State repression against labor unions and resistance movements established Pinochet as one of history's most vicious dictators. According to the *Washington Post*, his government was responsible for the deaths of over 3,000 people and the torture of 29,000 more, most of which occurred when the United States was helping to establish his administration. In 2006, Chilean investigators announced that they had uncovered millions of dollars in state funds that Pinochet stored in overseas banks, including in the United States, and tons of gold worth roughly $160 million in a bank in Hong Kong.[9]

After the coup, neoliberal mooseheads—Hayek, Friedman, and Buchanan—traveled to Chile to advise Pinochet and in doing so helped to legitimize his dictatorship in the eyes of the world. During Friedman's 1975 visit, he instructed the military junta on the techniques of monetarism and austerity, and shortly after, he accepted a Nobel Prize. In May 1980, a few months after a mass purge of public university teachers, James Buchanan traveled there to provide guidance on how to manipulate the political and constitutional system so that Pinochet's "reforms" would be difficult, if not impossible, for subsequent administrations to undo.[10]

When Gerald Ford became president, he put Vice President Nelson Rockefeller in charge of a high-profile "independent" investigation into illegal CIA activities, just as evidence of the agency's unlawful wiretapping and mind-control experiments on U.S. citizens was breaking in the news. A clear case of "Jesse James guarding the banks," Rockefeller downplayed his commission's findings on CIA abuses in Chile and beyond. It was not until February 2016 that the National Security Archive at George Washington University would post a trove of evidence detailing how the Ford White House had significantly altered the Rockefeller Commission's final report, including the removal of an eighty-six-page section on CIA assassination plots.[11]

New York City, 1975

Latin America was just part of David Rockefeller's larger imperial program. The same year of the coup, he founded the Trilateral Commission, a powerful cadre of corporate, banking, and political elites from the United States, Japan, and Europe whose aim was nothing less than to consolidate ruling-class power and dictate the world order.[12] The Trilateral Commission played a leading role in getting Carter elected, and in return, he rewarded its members with top administration posts.[13] Rockefeller himself exerted remarkable influence in the Carter White House, evinced by his ill-conceived idea to bring the exiled Shah of Iran to the United States, which catalyzed the 444-day hostage crisis in Iran.[14]

Rockefeller also played a major role in the New York City fiscal crisis, which, along with the United Kingdom, is often cited as a case of "First World" neoliberal reform. Between 1970 and 1975, manufacturing employment in the Northeast had fallen by more than 10 percent, while increasing substantially in Sun Belt states with lower costs of living, cheaper land, and weaker unions. This dispersal of production by domestic business was financed with tax cuts for investment, as well as foreign direct investment in the U.S. economy, primarily by the Japanese, in addition to automation and the translation of manufacturing jobs into service work. Dispersal overseas was spearheaded by multinational corporations in what became a global production network supported by a widely distributed labor market. Highly competitive supplier pools were just forming around this time, a trend that accelerated in the 1990s with the expansion of "free trade."[15]

New York City's economic base was already ailing from deindustrialization and suburban flight in the 1960s. Riots in cities like Newark and Detroit convinced New York's leadership that strong union contracts and investment in public employment and services were necessary. As the economy sunk into a deep recession, however, and its tax base diminished through job losses, the city became increasingly reliant on federal aid. When Nixon abruptly ended federal support, Gotham was forced to increase its debt to support public expenditures. Unemployment soared, and after demanding higher interest rates, the city's creditors stopped lending entirely.[16]

The banks that refused to bail out the city were the same ones that had encouraged its excessive borrowing in the first place without regard for its ballooning debt. At the time, trading and underwriting municipal bonds was lucrative business, so the bankers had piled on: nationally, the proportion of tax-exempt municipal bonds held by banks increased from a quarter in 1960 to nearly 50 percent in 1970. These exemptions pushed effective tax rates for commercial banks down from 33 percent in 1960 to just over half of that in 1974. Because New York was in such a bind, banks were able to charge high interest rates—nearly 10 percent by the end of 1974[17]—and when they realized that municipal coffers were tapping out, they dumped their holdings and bailed out of the bond market altogether, bringing the city to the verge of bankruptcy.

The initial response of the Ford administration—steered by conservative ideologues like Defense Secretary Donald Rumsfeld and Treasury Secretary William E. Simon—was to deny federal assistance as punishment for what they described as "profligate spending."[18] In response, the *New York Daily News* published its "Ford to City: Drop Dead" cover, believed to have cost Ford the 1976 election. Financial management of New York was handed over to a committee of revanchist bankers, the Municipal Assistance Corporation, headed by legendary investment banker Felix Rohatyn, who later issued a bailout with structural adjustment terms that nearly destroyed the city.[19]

By this point, Nixon's commerce secretary, Pete Peterson, had transitioned from his cabinet post to serve as chairman of Lehman Brothers. Along with David Rockefeller, Citicorp chairman Walter Wriston (regarded as the most influential commercial banker of his time[20]) and other big hitters from Wall Street, Peterson testified before the U.S. Senate Banking Committee on October 18, 1975, at a hearing on the New York City financial crisis. While some of the bankers holding the debt simply wanted to get their money back, ideologues like Peterson used the crisis as an opportunity to attack New York's unions, social wage policies, and government regulation, and to recommend "fiscal responsibility."[21] Wriston compared the city's "financially ruinous" pension system to Uruguay's economy, in which, he said, "20 percent of the citizens ended up supporting 80 percent of the populace."[22]

Peterson and Wriston's viewpoint prevailed, and amid union and popular protest, New York City laid off masses of public sector workers and cut or froze the wages and benefits of those who remained. It ended tuition-free higher education at the City University of New York—a pipeline of upward mobility for New York's working class—and increased cutbacks in hospital and other municipal services. As David Harvey explained, "The final indignity was the requirement that municipal unions should invest their pension funds in city bonds."[23]

Secretary Simon—who would later help pioneer the leveraged buyouts of the 1980s and serve as president of the ultra-conservative Olin Foundation[24]—affirmed that under his direction the bailout conditions were intended to be "so punitive, the overall experience so painful, that no city, no political subdivision would even be tempted to go down the same road."[25] Democratic Party elites offered little resistance, spurring Alan Greenspan, then-Ford's chair of economic advisors, to remark on the apparent "convergence of attitudes" between liberals and conservatives, both of them "looking to restrain inflation, cut deficit spending, reduce regulation, and encourage investment."[26]

By 1980, New York City was using a fifth of its local revenues just to service its debts. Budget cuts in everything from firefighter rolls to hospital and sanitation services, mass transit, and public housing and education were compromising public health, depleting the safety net, and foreclosing avenues for working-class mobility. These and other factors helped force out the city's "surplus" labor force and facilitate a new demography of young professional Wall Street and advertising types, as well as midlevel managers and skilled technical workers. The transformation was legitimized with a discourse that bypassed the reality of irresponsible lending by profit-hungry bankers and, in true neoliberal fashion, blamed public sector workers, unions, and the poor, while denigrating the welfare state as a giveaway for moochers.[27]

Stagflation

The New York City fiscal crisis took place in the context of weighty deliberations over simultaneous increases in inflation and unemployment and the use of monetary policy and fiscal austerity to stem it. When Kennedy took office, he was confronted with a recession and high rates of unemployment, slumping profits, a growing balance-of-payments deficit, and sharp declines in the value of the dollar. The economic turmoil spurred debates regarding the state's role in securing full employment that tended to map onto two models of Keynesianism. In one type, the state would mitigate high unemployment through planning and direct intervention, as in a federal jobs guarantee.[28] The other model favored market-based solutions to questions of economic stability, such as using tax cuts and corporate subsidies to encourage consumer spending and private sector growth, with the expectation that business would create jobs and the stimulus would proliferate throughout the economy. Some of JFK's economic advisors recommended that he increase public spending and full employment and just accept a dose of inflation, but the president went the tax cut route and effectively took the social democratic options off the table—a key step in neoliberalism's forward march.[29]

This market-oriented form of Keynesianism promised wage increases and consumption in exchange for a productivity that outpaced worker demands, with the threat of unemployment as a means of disciplining labor. Toward the end of the 1960s, the high employment rates and economic stimulus sustained by the Vietnam War gave way to an increasing federal deficit and inflation that impelled Lyndon Johnson to retrench on some of his Great Society programs. This retrenchment exacerbated the inflationary trend into the early 1970s, which witnessed a peculiar coincidence of sharp price increases *and* high rates of unemployment—"stagflation"—that persisted over several presidencies. Stagflation undermined the prevailing assumption among mainstream economists that state intervention could achieve a functional balance between employment and inflation. While specific, short-term factors, like crop failures and the Organization of the Petroleum Exporting Countries (OPEC) oil embargo, played a vital role in spiking prices, business elites and neoliberal economists declared that Keynesianism was failing. They concluded that the stimulating effects of government spending were no longer effective in stabilizing prices and securing an adequate level of employment, and that austerity and manipulating the money supply would be.[30]

On Sunday, July 15, 1979, President Jimmy Carter appeared on primetime television before millions of viewers in a historic address to the nation. Just ten days earlier, he had planned to deliver an entirely different speech in response to OPEC oil producers announcing yet another round of bruising price increases.[31] In 1973, the first OPEC embargo quadrupled gas prices and caused major fuel shortages, forcing many Americans to queue in long lines at the pump. Since then, devastatingly high unemployment and an inflation rate at 14 percent, caused Carter's approval ratings to plummet to 25 percent—lower than Richard Nixon's in the throes of Watergate. After canceling his speech on energy, Carter repaired to Camp David, spurring rumors that he had left the country or gone into hiding.

Carter's primetime address marked his much-anticipated return from the surreptitious ten-day retreat, where he had conferred with "teachers and preachers, governors, mayors, and private citizens" on the status of his presidency.[32] Reports of him sitting on the floor scribbling notes added to media caricatures of the peanut farmer-turned-president as clueless and adrift.[33] Despite his struggles with the Middle East, for Carter, the crisis besetting America did not derive from OPEC or the Ayatollah, nor, god forbid, was it a result of his administration's misguided policies or leadership. Rather, the nation's apparent emotional breakdown was triggered by an inner "crisis of confidence" that could be healed through self-sacrifice, atonement, and spiritual rebirth. "The symptoms of this crisis of the American spirit are all around us," he lamented. "For the first time in the history of our country, a majority of our people believe that the next five years will be worse than the past five years."[34]

As his pollster Patrick Caddell predicted, Carter's "malaise speech" helped boost his approval ratings. But not for long. The day after his address, the president requested resignation letters from several cabinet officials and White House staff in a brash attempt to demonstrate his commitment to change. Treasury Secretary W. Michael Blumenthal was among the casualties of the shake-up. Then-chairman of the Federal Reserve G. William Miller assumed Blumenthal's post, leaving a conspicuous vacancy at the Fed—which not only rattled financial markets but also sent the value of the dollar on a downward trend. Carter calmed the markets by appointing Paul Volcker to replace Miller as Fed chairman, despite his reservations about Volcker's conservatism and reputation as a maverick.[35]

Not only was Volcker Wall Street's pick, but his appointment carried political value. He came highly recommended by David Rockefeller, and his appearance as an autonomous thinker had the potential to help restore the Federal Reserve's tarnished reputation left by Nixon and his Fed chairman Arthur Burns. Under pressure by Nixon, Burns had manipulated the money supply to help the president's re-election, which stimulated the economy but also spurred inflation.[36] Carter believed that his new Fed chair would restore independence to the Federal Reserve and stability to the country. He could not have been more wrong.

Two months after Carter's malaise speech, Volcker delivered his own landmark address, aptly called the "Saturday Night Massacre." While Carter's speech beckoned Americans to self-sacrifice, Volcker's forced it on them mercilessly. Despite tensions within the Federal Reserve leadership regarding the fitness of monetarist solutions to stem runaway inflation (solutions that Volcker himself had previously opposed), a series of closed-door meetings helped foster consensus among decision makers that drastic measures were in order. Years later, economists would counter that these inflationary trends were likely overestimated. Putting aside the dramatic and temporary increases in oil and food prices, they argued that the core inflation rate was actually much lower, suggesting that the more prudent response would have been to wait it out.[37]

But the "Volcker Shock" was more than a market correction.[38] It was meant as a disciplinary measure to impose fiscal austerity and subordinate workers by creating a deep recession and driving up unemployment.[39] An admirer of F. A. Hayek, Volcker had a long-standing preoccupation with inflation and belief in austerity and "self-discipline." He viewed wage demands as a leading cause of rising prices and even carried around in his pocket an index card of union contract negotiation schedules.[40] With large numbers of people out of work and too broke and afraid to spend money, Volcker would not only break inflation, he would break unions and worker power as well. No one was more shocked by the Volcker Shock than President Carter, who had been preparing his own anti-inflation strategy, formed in consultation with business executives and labor leaders. Volcker's plan undercut the president's plan and likely cost Carter re-election. But for neoliberals, it created the crisis conditions for what Milton Friedman called "real change."

In many ways, Carter was already well down the road of neoliberal reform. As Georgia's governor, he dedicated himself to ending government inefficiency and linked inflation to budget deficits and public spending.[41] In a televised speech on October 24, 1978, he named inflation America's "most serious domestic problem" and announced his top priorities: "We are going to hold down government spending, reduce the budget deficit, and eliminate government waste. We will slash Federal hiring and cut the Federal work force. We will eliminate needless regulations." That same day, he signed into law the Airline Deregulation Act of 1978, which he claimed was vital to the "fight against inflation." But in removing price controls and allowing small carriers to go belly-up, the act reduced airline workers' wages and undercut their benefits.[42] That year, Carter also invoked the anti-labor Taft-Hartley Act to force wildcat striking coal miners back to work so they could help make the country "energy independent."[43]

Carter proposed cuts to Social Security while increasing defense spending, and his tax cuts largely benefited corporations and the wealthy.[44] He suppressed the Humphrey-Hawkins bill that would have required the Federal Reserve to make a low unemployment rate an explicit objective, and instead elevated business's anti-inflation agenda to the forefront of employment policy. In addition to the deregulation of airlines, trucking, and railroads, he removed New Deal "Regulation Q" interest rate ceilings, creating new opportunities for financial exploitation, including subprime mortgage lending and car and payday loans used to fleece poor and vulnerable people.[45]

In this context, the Volcker Shock effected a sharp increase in interest rates to nearly 20 percent, grueling levels of (double-digit) unemployment, near 15 percent inflation,[46] and cuts in public spending that severely curtailed the ability of working people to stay afloat.[47] Larger corporations and financial institutions survived the shock through selective bailouts issued by Volcker and the Federal Reserve that foreshadowed the 2007 Wall Street bailout and the many less conspicuous bailouts in the years between and after—none of which involved bailouts for the people. With over a tenth of the country out of work, prices for vital commodities like food and fuel going through the roof, and lack of access to mortgages and automobile loans, middle-class Americans' standard of living dropped to a degree not felt since the Great Depression. As Robert J. Samuelson described in *The Great Inflation and Its Aftermath*, "Evidence of economic carnage was everywhere. By Spring, bankruptcies were running at 280 a day, a post-World War II high. . . . The Fed's staff economists had expected a recovery by mid-1982, so had many private economists. But it wasn't happening."[48] What did happen in the years to come is that neoliberal monetarists and inflation hawks would continue to lay the blame for inflation on public spending and wage increases, despite stagnant and declining wage trends, and the obvious role of other causes, like a global pandemic and supply-chain disturbances associated with war.

THE REAGAN REVOLUTION

Ronald Reagan was neoliberals' first president, uniquely suited to deliver the gospel of Friedman with authentic conservatism, plain-spokenness, and an overriding commitment to U.S. hegemony—and to making some people very rich. Between 1979, the year of Volcker's decision, and 1989, the close of Reagan's presidency, the proportion of the nation's wealth held by the top 1 percent nearly doubled from 22 percent to 39 percent—one of the fastest escalations in U.S. history.[49] Telegraphing this deliberate class program, Reagan hung a portrait of Calvin Coolidge in the White House Cabinet Room and during his first inaugural speech declared "government is the problem."[50] Regarding the portrait, Reagan's treasury secretary, Donald T. Regan, explained: "We're not going back to high-button shoes and celluloid collars. But the President does want to go back to many of the financial methods and economic incentives that brought about the prosperity of the Coolidge period." That meant passing massive tax cuts for corporations and top income earners and "permissive regulation" of the financial sector—and on the flipside, steady attacks on workers, unions, and the poor.[51] It also meant eliminating New Deal anti-monopoly frameworks and allowing the kind of large concentrations of corporate power that abetted the rise of European fascism, as Franz Neumann laid bare in *Behemoth*.

Early in his administration, Reagan assembled a neoliberal "dream team" of economic advisors, led by Nixon treasury secretary George Shultz, that included Friedman and Stigler as well as Alan Greenspan, Walter Wriston, Jack Kemp, Arthur Laffer, and others.[52] Reagan's "trickle-down" agenda relied heavily on Laffer's claim that revenues would rise if tax rates were lowered ("the Laffer Curve") and the idea that feeding corporations and the wealthy with tax cuts and subsidies would foster investment, expand the nation's overall productive capacity, and "naturally" benefit all.[53] Toward that end, Reagan's tax reforms in 1981 and 1986 reduced the top marginal tax rate from 70 percent to 28 percent—in both years, with the support of congressional Democrats. He adjusted for "bracket creep" to prevent inflation from pushing workers into higher tax brackets and made the Business Roundtable happy by fulfilling its desire for a more generous depreciation allowance.[54]

In 1976, Reagan ran for and lost the GOP nomination on an unsuccessful program of "voluntary Social Security" in which workers could "choose" to make their own retirement investments—a scheme to privatize Social Security by allowing the rich to opt out and starve the system of critical revenue. As president, he appointed a blue-ribbon commission, headed by Alan Greenspan, to address the program's future solvency. The "Greenspan Commission" recommended an increase in payroll taxes to cover payouts when the Trust Fund started to run a deficit, which passed in 1983 through a series of amendments. The tax was particularly regressive, as earners in middle brackets paid a much larger share of their income than those at the top due to a low-income ceiling. In an audacious show of state-facilitated wealth transfer, the surplus revenue generated by Reagan's tax on working people was used to offset the costs of his extensive tax cuts for corporations and the wealthy.[55] In 1987, Reagan rewarded Greenspan for his work on Social Security with an appointment to Fed chair. Emblematic of the bipartisan neoliberal consensus, Greenspan was reappointed by both Republican *and* Democratic presidents until he retired from public office in 2006.

Tax incentives meant to help businesses innovate and create jobs went mostly for factory plant updates, expansion, and deindustrialization. Core industries of the postwar era, like steel, cars, and machinery, lost jobs to rising imports and dislocation to southern states with weaker labor controls and cheaper real estate. Nondurables, like textiles, moved out of the country entirely to locations in Mexico or Asia. The auto industry lost a quarter of a million jobs between 1979 and 1983, and by the end of the 1980s, foreign producers dominated half of the market. Employment in steel halved between 1980 and 1984 and continued to fall afterward. In Reagan's free market promised land, the corporate chiefs, and not the state, managed the labor market, and the innovation and growth of what Robert Gordon has called the "special century" (from 1870 to 1970) came to a screeching halt—a trend exacerbated by increases in speculative trading, stock buybacks, and corporate mergers in the decades that followed.[56]

With corporate and financial interests at the helm, the Reagan administration waged a vigorous assault on workers. It populated federal courts and the National Labor Relations Board (NLRB) with conservative judges and officials and aggressively busted labor unions. The infamous firing of over 10,000 Professional Air Traffic Controllers Organization (PATCO) workers (who supported him in 1980) using military personnel and middle managers as scabs put "the threat of the sack" in the hands of employers, which some already had in light of trade policies incentivizing them to ship jobs offshore. Workers were fired for trying to unionize and replaced with temporary staff willing to accept lower wages and no benefits.[57] Nearly a quarter of American workers belonged to unions when Reagan took office. When he left, the rolls had been reduced to 17 percent. By 2013, that number had shrunk even further, to just 11 percent, and remains around that low today despite evidence that union workers are more likely than non-union workers to have pensions, employer-provided health benefits, and higher wages.[58] During Reagan's presidency, moreover, the federal minimum wage—on par with the poverty level in 1980—fell 24 percent by 1990.[59]

Reagan also waged a vigorous assault on the poor. He publicly characterized unemployment and homelessness as matters of choice and personal responsibility and stigmatized poor Black women using the racially coded language of "welfare queens."[60] (This was in keeping with his Goldwater-inspired record of siding with Southern white supremacists in opposing school integration, affirmative action, and the 1964 Civil Rights Act, and launching his 1980 campaign on the site of the 1964 "Mississippi Burning" murder of civil rights activists.) High unemployment meant that some sixteen million lost their health insurance, and cutbacks in funding for school lunch programs increased child hunger. Homelessness rates soared as a result of drastic cuts to public housing and Section 8 assistance.[61] The Housing Act of 1968 committed the country to producing 2.6 million housing units a year, 600,000 of which were for low-income families. By 1979, Congress had authorized 55,000 new public housing units, but under Reagan, it authorized none and instead promoted rental vouchers.[62] In his systematic dismantling of the New Deal, Reagan abandoned the federal government's commitment to public housing and said it would leave affordable housing to the private sector. As an administration official explained: "The whole attitude that the Federal Government can solve all the housing problems of this country—those days are over."[63]

Across the Atlantic, the neoliberal assault on the public sector and working class and poor was in full swing. Margaret Thatcher's electoral success was largely due to her antagonism toward trade unions, which, by the time of her election, had fallen into disrepute with voters. As in the United States, "stagflation" had thrown the British economy into a tailspin, and when the Labour Party government turned to the International Monetary Fund (IMF) for relief, the IMF stipulated cuts in welfare expenditures as a precondition for the loan. When the Labour Party still failed to control stagflation, everyone from gravediggers to hospital and sanitation workers went on strike during the 1978 Winter of Discontent. Trash piled in the streets and bodies that went unburied helped turn the media, then the public, against the unions, opening the door for Thatcher's victory.[64]

Influenced by Popper and Hayek, Thatcher's fanatical dedication to neoliberal dogma was reflected in her shrewd and tireless attacks on union bureaucracy and the welfare state and dramatic appeals to the virtues of individual freedom—"there is no such thing as society, only individual men and women . . . and families," she said. In privatizing and selling off state-owned industries—from airlines to telecommunications to energy services—she "streamlined" operations (fired workers) to render state assets more attractive to investors. In the purge, much of the country's public housing was sold at low prices, encouraging private home ownership and feeding into the middle-class dream of owning a home. During the Thatcher ministry, unemployment rose to 10 percent and trade unions were nearly wiped out.[65]

THE NEW DEMOCRATS

When Thatcher was asked in 2002 about her greatest achievement as prime minister, she replied, "Tony Blair and New Labour. We forced our opponents to change their minds."[66] The same can be said of neoliberals' achievement in Bill Clinton and the New Democrats. From the early 1990s onward, Democrats sought political power by leaving behind their traditional alliance with the AFL-CIO and working class and aligning themselves with Walmart, Goldman Sachs, Big Pharma, and other bastions of corporate power—becoming the party of fiscal austerity, deregulation, and free trade, and usurping the GOP's "law and order" agenda and war on the poor, as well as its imperial ambitions abroad.

That rightward drift—of Democrats and the political horizon more generally—was apparent during the 1984 presidential race, when Democrats' strategy of "fiscal responsibility" inspired the *New York Times*'s Peter T. Kilborn to write, "Close your eyes, listen to what they're saying and you'd think it was the G.O.P. Good government, the Democrats are saying in New Hampshire, need not be big government."[67] In 1984, Walter Mondale did run for president on a deficit reduction platform, but he also called for increased taxes, reduced defense spending, and regulating health care costs, rather than cutting social programs, as Reagan did. Other Democrats, however, such as then-senator Joe Biden, attempted to outflank Reagan from the right by cosponsoring Republican legislation to freeze Social Security and raise the retirement age.[68] The Biden way prevailed, and on the heels of three painful electoral losses—by Carter, Mondale, and Dukakis—a corps of neoliberal Democrats founded the Democratic Leadership Council (DLC) to shift the party further toward "the center," where they believed elections could be won.

With Republicans having more than quadrupled the national debt by 1992, Democratic presidential candidate Senator Paul Tsongas brought to the national stage his conservative manifesto, *A Call to Economic Arms*, which painted a doomsday picture of "crushing and unsustainable debt" that, he argued, necessitated entitlement reform and a cut in the capital gains tax to encourage long-term investment.[69] Also in the 1992 presidential race was folksy information-technology titan Ross Perot, who claimed that he could save $20 to $100 billion by means-testing Social Security.[70] Five-term Arkansas governor Bill Clinton called Perot's plan "a full-scale assault on the Social Security system, undermining the universality of the program."[71] But he too had run on a program of "leaner, not meaner government" and "no more something for nothing." During his acceptance speech for the Democratic Party nomination, Clinton foreshadowed how his "new covenant" would cut social spending, facilitate school choice, and promote "a new approach to government . . . that understands that jobs must come from growth in a vibrant and vital system of free enterprise."[72]

As president, Clinton championed a "Third Way" of social liberalism and fiscal conservatism—with the former buttressing the latter. Identity politics served Clinton's (and later, his wife's) political ambitions but also offered New Democrats a means for coopting racial and gender liberalism to justify their class program using pluralist terms of inclusion and recognition rather than redistribution. Clinton's cabinet included Attorney General (AG) Janet Reno and Secretary of State Madeleine Albright, the first women to occupy such high executive posts—which was historic, but not progressive. As AG, Reno advocated tough policing and oversaw the dawn of mass incarceration that predominantly affected poor Black and Hispanic men. As the country's lead diplomat, Albright remarked, "This is a very hard choice, but the price, we think the price is worth it," when asked about U.S. sanctions on Iraq costing the lives of 500,000 children.[73] The New Democrats' hijacking of anti-racism was also apparent in the contradiction between their claims to racial justice and their actual treatment of poor and working-class people. Clinton may have worked southern Black churches with songs of uplift, but his welfare reform rhetoric brutally echoed Reagan's shaming of poor Black men and women to justify a war on the poor and entrenchment of the carceral state.

Clinton's first budget, the Omnibus Budget Reconciliation Act of 1993 (otherwise known as the Deficit Reduction Act), laid out his plan to use spending cuts to reduce the deficit. This followed on the heels of George H. W. Bush's historic compromise with moderate Democrats to cap discretionary spending (read: cut social spending) by way of "pay as you go" (PAYGO) rules. PAYGO mandated that all legislative change regarding taxes and public spending be deficit-neutral or -reducing. If not, across-the-board cuts in nonexempt mandatory programs—like Medicare and block grants for low-income people—would be triggered to offset the deficit increase.

Despite its fiscal conservatism, it was not clear at the time whether Clinton's inaugural budget had the votes to pass. To secure the deciding vote of Democratic senator Bob Kerrey—who thought the budget was too soft on the deficit—Clinton assembled a bipartisan commission to study entitlements. Among the commission appointees was Pete Peterson, one of the few to support Kerrey's proposed cuts and privatization schemes.[74] Though the group failed to reach a consensus, conservative economist Martin Feldstein noted its profound impact:

> The Clinton speeches and the official national education campaign that he launched moved the discussion of investment-based Social Security reform away from an ideological debate about the merits of government versus private systems to the more technical issues of how to design a mixed system that includes both pay-as-you-go benefits and investment-based defined contribution annuities.[75]

Clinton's 1993 budget also included spending on "empowerment zones," a concept touted by the likes of Margaret Thatcher and Jack Kemp that involved using tax breaks and regulatory relief to incentivize business-driven development in low-income areas. Empowerment zones were a market-based solution to urban decay and regional development that not only opened doors for profit-making, but also performed the important ideological work of painting taxes and regulation as impediments to the well-being of low-income people. These kinds of technocratic public-private partnership solutions are now commonplace among both Democratic and Republican policymakers looking to curb public spending by offering highly favorable terms to investors: they glean the profits while taxpayers absorb the risk.

Disciplining the Working Class and Poor

During Reagan's tenure, hundreds of thousands of manufacturing jobs were lost to deindustrialization, contributing to a crack epidemic across working-class inner-city neighborhoods. Crime rates soared, and according to polls, a majority of Americans favored harsh policies on crime—a disposition largely cultivated through media propaganda portraying the poor as criminals instead of oppressed human beings. Clinton built his career exploiting such fears and adopted Republicans' disciplinary approach to poverty and crime, using racist discourse to exploit cultural anxieties.

In the lead-up to the 1992 New Hampshire primary, as Clinton was neck and neck with opponent Paul Tsongas and mired in scandal over his long-term affair with Gennifer Flowers, he sought to gain a political edge by demonstrating his toughness on crime. He flew to Arkansas to oversee the state murder of Ricky Ray Rector, a Black man who had been sentenced to death by an all-white jury for fatally shooting a white policeman. After the shooting, Rector shot himself in the head, but doctors saved his life by performing a lobotomy that left him with a significantly reduced mental capacity. This severe impairment should have exempted Rector from capital punishment on the grounds that it would have violated the Eighth Amendment's ban on cruel and unusual punishment.[76] But in Clinton's political calculation, cruel and unusual punishment was exactly what he needed to win the support of law enforcement and other moderate constituencies, and position him to out-law-and-order the GOP, which is exactly what he did.[77]

When in power, Clinton's law-and-order crusade intensified. His 1994 Violent Crime Control and Law Enforcement Act—the Crime Bill—included provisions for expanding the death penalty to cover more than fifty federal crimes and mandating life sentences for three-time offenders.

It eliminated federal higher education grants for prisoners, denied financial aid to students with drug convictions, and imposed a lifetime ban on food stamps for those convicted of a felony drug offense.[78] During a 1996 campaign speech for her husband, First Lady Hillary promoted these measures, calling Black teens "super-predators" and saying they needed to be "brought to heel."[79]

Instead of using government programs to stimulate youth employment and stem the downward spiral of poverty and incarceration, the Clintons spoke of personal responsibility and free markets as keys to social mobility.[80] They transferred billions of taxpayer dollars from public housing and child welfare budgets to jumpstart this newly emerging carceral state. Public housing funding was cut by 61 percent, while funding for corrections was boosted by 171 percent.[81]

The Crime Bill propelled U.S. incarceration rates to the highest in the world—Gulag levels—doubling the number of federal prisoners, 58 percent of whom were in for drug-related offenses. The bill's 100-to-1 sentencing disparity for crack versus powder cocaine produced staggering racial disparities.[82] By the end of Clinton's presidency, more than half of working-age African American men in many large urban areas were saddled with criminal records and restricted voting rights, and subject to legalized discrimination in employment, housing, education, and access to basic public benefits. While whites saw historic reductions in unemployment, the rate among Black men in their twenties without a college degree rose to an all-time high—42 percent in 2001, when Clinton left office—largely because of skyrocketing rates of incarceration.[83]

Clinton also went toe to toe with Republicans in disciplining the poor. Republican Speaker of the House Newt Gingrich addressed U.S. poverty by trivializing the needs of poor people and spouting hate speech about immigrants and "illegitimate" children. He said that he would stop welfare benefits for teen mothers and take their children away and put them in orphanages, ban benefits for all immigrants, and block-grant school lunches and Medicaid.[84] Clinton did not go that far, but he did echo Gingrich and Reagan's racist invectives against "welfare queens" and ran his campaign on a program of "ending welfare as we know it." His Personal Responsibility and Work Opportunity Reconciliation Act eliminated decades-old safety net protections for poor families by replacing the New Deal–era Aid to Families with Dependent Children (AFDC) with a Temporary Assistance to Needy Families (TANF) block grant. The block-grant structure was a way to cut government spending by transforming welfare and poverty relief from a federal support that automatically increased when need arose (like during a recession) to a fixed amount of grant funding that states could renew annually. In other words, it ended the very idea of a federal safety net for the needy.[85]

TANF cut spending on food stamps and disability benefits and barred hundreds of thousands of legal immigrants—many of whom had worked and paid taxes in the United States for decades—from receiving disability and retirement assistance. It added punitive work requirements and created caps for how long a person could be on welfare and how much they could receive. Predictably, without offering daycare provisions or addressing barriers to employment, the law put many children at risk. A high-level official in Clinton's Department of Health and Human Services, Peter Edelman, wrote in a scathing opinion essay—titled "The Worst Thing Bill Clinton Has Done"—that "[t]he bill closes its eyes to all the facts and complexities of the real world and essentially says to recipients, find a job." Edelman had served in government for decades, but he publicly resigned in protest against the legislation because, he said, Clinton and congressional lawmakers knew that it would catapult some two million children into poverty, but they passed it anyway. Voting against the bill, Senator Edward Kennedy called it "legislative child abuse."[86]

"Workfare" created an indentured workforce that was used to drive down wages for other workers and undermine their unions. It forced people in need, including women with newborns, to work for next to nothing in heinous working conditions—collecting trash in city parks, cleaning offices, gutting chickens in rural poultry factories—and treated them like criminals, monitoring their every move. Mothers were asked to provide the name of their child's father to authorities, and if they did not, they could be dropped from the welfare rolls.[87] Clinton justified this moralism and cruelty with talk of "family values" despite his regular practice of deceiving and degrading his own family.

An extension of welfare reform, Clinton's HOPE-VI program—lifted from the Reagan-Kemp playbook[88]—razed low-income public housing complexes and replaced them with "mixed use" housing that combined market-rate owner-occupied units with subsidized rentals. Under HOPE-VI, tens of thousands of low-income people in cities across the country were displaced from their homes (sometimes forcibly) and issued rental vouchers to use on the open housing market. Others were evicted under Clinton's "one strike and you're out" rule, which mandated that families could be evicted from public housing if one member (or a guest) committed even a minor offense.[89] Under this brutal privatization scheme, people released from prison, with no money, no job, and nowhere to go, could not return home without putting their families at risk. This law made it easier for public housing agencies to deny shelter to anyone with a criminal history, even just an arrest, while greasing the wheels of gentrification.

Not surprisingly, Clinton's efforts to force people "from welfare to work" fueled the expansion of deep poverty.[90] During the 2007 global financial crisis, which Clinton's banking deregulation program helped trigger, the number of very poor Americans surviving on incomes of $2.00 a day doubled to 1.5 million. With TANF administered as a block grant, states had "free choice" to cut their poverty relief programs to close budget shortfalls and thus leave millions of people without access to the most basic of needs at a time of national crisis.[91]

The New Economy

As if disciplining poor and working-class people in the United States was not enough, Clinton exported his war on the poor to other parts of the world. After the fall of the Berlin Wall and supposed triumph of capitalism and liberal democracy, his administration branded its economic agenda "the new economy"—tinseling it with futuristic rhetoric about growth, free enterprise, and globalization. This agenda involved removing regulations fighting trusts and governing finance, telecommunications, and a host of other institutions, to unfetter markets and facilitate corporate profits and mega-mergers. It also significantly expanded free trade and weaponized the IMF, World Bank, and World Trade Organization (WTO) to force various countries' economies into a world system dominated by transnational capital.

Whereas the IMF and World Bank used debt to exert imperial power, the WTO set an enforceable legal foundation for corporate-friendly trade agreements that privileged profit-making and "favorable market conditions" over human and environmental protection. Free trade extended supply chains across the globe, which made it easier for corporations to source workers and materials in regions with lax labor and environmental controls. It eliminated so-called trade barriers by compelling countries to rescind control over their domestic economies, and cut regulations, subsidies, and price controls in place to protect their economies and populations. Moreover, in opening domestic markets to global competition, it destroyed local industries and indigenous businesses. In India, for example, the cotton industry was decimated by a combination of low-priced cotton imports and Monsanto's monopolization of the seed market (Monsanto's seeds were designed to self-destruct, forcing buyers to repurchase them annually). This situation triggered waves of farmer suicides, numbering in the hundreds of thousands over two decades.[92]

In the United States, free trade devastated the country's manufacturing base by moving good-paying jobs to low-wage countries where workers were paid a fraction of what their U.S. counterparts made. The North American Free Trade Agreement (NAFTA) alone is estimated to have cost the country some 850,000 jobs over a ten-year period. Such a flight disempowered workers whose jobs became disposable.[93] When Clinton tried to convince workers that NAFTA would be positive for them and the environment, he was confronted with stiff and unusually unified resistance from labor and progressive Democrats, who rightly pointed out that NAFTA would weaken worker power and put downward pressure on wages. Clinton remained unmoved, as his party's New Democrat faction was already untethering itself from labor and tying itself to corporate power. In fact, by the end of his presidency, when trade relations with China took center stage, the DLC executive council had become a who's who of corporate elites—including those from Enron, Microsoft, AIG, Phillip Morris, and, astonishingly, Koch Industries.[94]

In Mexico, privatization and fiscal austerity imposed by the World Bank in the 1980s resulted in severe lack of government spending on basics such as trash removal, health care, water, and transportation. In the 1990s, public sector industries were sold off to foreign investors, which starved the peasant population while producing some twenty-four billionaires.[95] Under NAFTA, Mexican farmers without government subsidies were forced to compete on the open market with large-scale producers sponsored by the U.S. government. NAFTA prohibited price controls, so when U.S. exports substantially increased, prices were driven down to such untenable levels that local producers could not make a profit on their products. U.S. companies exploited the situation by buying up land and entire industries and further abusing the stressed, low-wage workforce—all while killing U.S. jobs and disempowering workers.[96]

By the numbers, between 1989 and 1997, 86 percent of stock market gains went to the top 10 percent of households, and about half that went to the top 1 percent. Income for the top 1 percent and .01 percent grew at a much faster clip than for everyone else.[97] And for many Americans, debt outgrew assets and their net worth declined. Those in the welfare system were forced into indentured servitude, and tens of millions of people, disproportionately Black and brown, were locked up and denied the right to vote for the rest of their lives. Meanwhile, Wall Street and the Fortune 500 were given a freer hand to amass formidable monopoly power, manipulate financial markets (see chapter 5), and exploit workers, indigenous communities, and the environment.

Rather than reverse the tide of neoliberal reform under Reagan, Clinton fortified it. He further subordinated the state to elite interests by demonizing public spending under the guise of "balancing budgets" and greasing the wheels of privatization in the name of growth and free enterprise. He debased and punished poor people under the banner of "personal responsibility" and offshored millions of good-paying jobs held by U.S. workers. For the sake of political expediency, he adopted draconian law-and-order policies and chose to ally himself with corporations rather than unions. With all of this and more, Clinton effectively foreclosed progressive alternatives and lurched the country's political horizon rightward, which as the following chapters show, fostered the dangerous conditions of inequality and popular resentment that today plague political and social systems worldwide.

CHAPTER 2

The State (2000–2017)

Understanding the roots of the acute social inequalities of our time and the ongoing rise of reactionary forces requires an accounting of the policy regimes and ideological manipulations that U.S. political elites have deployed over the past few decades to realize their interests. Accordingly, this chapter picks up where the last one left off, with the administrations of George W. Bush and Barack Obama. It tracks the neoliberal advance through their presidencies and looks at how they and other political elites exploited the American state and various crises to serve the interests of elite powerholders. In the case of George Bush, it recalls how he used the attack on the World Trade Center to garner support for his agenda to redistribute wealth through tax cuts, corruption, financial deregulation, privatization schemes, and, of course, war. Regarding Obama, it analyzes how his administration took up Bush's mantle of tax cuts, public-private partnerships, free trade, and balanced budgets, and importantly, how he provided cover for Wall Street when it was on the ropes during the 2007 global financial crisis. The chapter also assesses the ideological means through which each president reproduced their class program, from Bush's appeals to neoconservative values and American exceptionalism to Obama's cooptation of anti-racism to promote self-help, personal responsibility, and fiscal austerity over safety nets and public investment.

BUSH AND THE NEOCONS

For the 2000 presidential election, the Republican Party chose as their nominee George W. Bush, a son of party royalty. Bush's grandfather, Prescott, was Connecticut's revered senator; his brother Jeb was governor of Florida; and his father George H. W.—"Poppy"—was a war hero, a former UN ambassador, a Republican National Committee (RNC) chairman, Ford's CIA director, Reagan's vice president, and the nation's forty-first president. Living in Poppy's shadow, Bush downplayed his father's New England stodginess while living off the fat of it. Despite the family's low expectations, and his conspicuous lack of attention span, he was propelled to high office by his many social advantages as well as his good-ol'-boy charm and born-again Christianity. In a major upset, Bush unseated incumbent Ann Richards, a Democratic icon, to become governor of Texas, then went on to defeat Arizona senator John McCain in the GOP primary. Upon winning the nomination, Bush characteristically said of his party establishment, "They misunderestimated me."[1]

Without a majority in either chamber of Congress, Democrats selected Democratic Leadership Council (DLC) founder and Bill Clinton's vice president, Al Gore, as their nominee. As his running mate, they selected a devout neoconservative, Senator Joe Lieberman, whose sterling credentials included support for school vouchers and Social Security privatization. The choice of Gore-Lieberman signaled not only the party's commitment to neoliberal reform but also its intent to accelerate it. For his policy platform, Gore stayed Clinton's course, emphasizing free trade and some public spending within the framework of market-based solutions to social problems and public-private partnerships. On the campaign trail, however, he distanced himself from the president amid revelations of Clinton's lascivious behavior, chronicled in the *Starr Report*—independent counsel Kenneth Starr's excessively detailed account of Clinton's sexual relationship with twenty-two-year-old intern Monica Lewinsky. Despite the more than forty romantic encounters Clinton had with Lewinsky in the Oval Office alone, he repeatedly denied his involvement with her, opening the door for impeachment on charges of perjury and obstruction of justice. Although he was acquitted by the Senate, the ordeal left an indelible mark on his legacy, already tarnished by other extramarital affairs and allegations of sexual harassment and assault.[2]

Bush's domestic agenda was straightforward: corporate deregulation, tax cuts for corporations and the wealthy, and "entitlement reform" (read: privatizing Social Security, Medicare, and Medicaid). Beyond free trade, Bush put forth a milquetoast foreign policy agenda and was critical of Clinton's attempts at regime change in Somalia and the Balkans. On the issue of character, with Clinton's lurid infidelities looming so large over the country, Bush handily deflected from his own checkered past—his drinking, bad grades, and general unseriousness—with promises to restore honor and dignity to the White House.

The presidential election took place on November 7, 2000. To the Democrats' surprise, Green Party candidate Ralph Nader captured three million votes running on a program that was critical of free trade, corporate welfare, and the two-party duopoly—against a backdrop of mass international protests against corporate-led globalization. Democrats scapegoated him for their loss, and still do, despite the glaring weakness of the Gore-Lieberman ticket, along with the party's blatant disregard for its progressive wing and for working-class and poor people more generally.

There was also the matter of Republicans outsmarting and outspending them when a small vote margin in Florida necessitated a recount and threw the entire election into chaos. Florida was a stronghold for the Bushes, with Jeb as governor, and right-wing Cubans were still seething from the drama around the Clinton administration's return of six-year-old Elián González to his father in Cuba. After a month of legal battles, protests, and poll worker intimidation—on which Republicans spent $13.8 million to Democrats' $3.2 million[3]—the U.S. Supreme Court controversially decided to terminate the recount and call the election. At least 10,000 ballots in Miami-Dade County had not been counted, but that did not stop Jeb's secretary of state, Katherine Harris, from calling Florida in Bush's favor by just 537 votes, clinching the presidency for him. In the end, Gore won the popular vote, but Bush bested him in the Electoral College 271 to 266. Down-ballot, Republicans retained a narrow majority in the House but lost five seats in the Senate, leaving a fifty-fifty partisan balance with newly minted Vice President Dick Cheney as the tiebreaker.

For his cabinet and team of advisors, Bush brought in confidant and kingmaker Karl Rove and other members of his close-knit Texas team. He kept Clinton appointee George Tenet as CIA director and made evangelical favorite John Ashcroft attorney general. He also installed trusted hands from his father's administration, including Poppy's chairman of the joint chiefs of staff, Colin Powell, as secretary of state; National Security Council member Condoleezza Rice as national security advisor; and of course, Poppy's secretary of defense, Dick Cheney, as vice president. As the head of the transition effort, Cheney populated the administration with loyalists and neoconservatives, most notably Donald Rumsfeld as secretary of defense and Paul Wolfowitz as Rumsfeld's deputy. In an attempt to delineate an official neoconservative agenda, Wolfowitz had coauthored the 1992 Defense Planning Guidance,[4] which was so extreme that both Bush Sr. and Clinton had disavowed it. The agenda appeared again in the Project for a New American Century's 1997 Statement of Principles[5] that served as the basis for the infamous "Rebuilding America's Defenses" report[6] that Bush Jr., unlike his father, adopted as the blueprint for his War on Terror.

The neoconservative worldview, in broad strokes, eschewed international organizations and treaties and insisted on American exceptionalism—hence Bush's decision to pull the United States out of six international agreements, including the Kyoto Protocol. Neocons rejected isolationism, not because they were interested in international cooperation, but because they believed that brazen shows of unilateral force without regard for other states' sovereignty were necessary to achieve their ultimate goal: world domination. They used catchphrases like "American greatness" and "American values" and fearmongered about terrorism and communism to justify their imperial adventures and advance dominance as a precondition for the security of the post–Cold War world order. They also used concepts like patriotism, democracy, and defense of the free market to build legitimacy and solidarity at home. That social solidarity around perceived threats, war, and exceptionalism played an important role in elevating Bush's agenda, but also in mitigating neoliberalism's tendency toward egoism and privatism.

The War on Terror

On September 11, 2001, President Bush was in the middle of a No Child Left Behind photo op at Emma E. Booker Elementary School in Sarasota, Florida, when his aides informed him that the World Trade Center (WTC) had been attacked. That day, members of al-Qaeda, a group led by Osama bin Laden, hijacked four airliners and flew two of them into the Twin Towers and one into the Pentagon. A fourth was brought down in Pennsylvania following a struggle between the hijackers and passengers. Among U.S. intelligence agencies, the attacks were not unexpected. In 1998, the CIA knew that bin Laden had been planning to hijack U.S. aircraft, and in January 2001, both White House counterterrorism coordinator Richard Clarke and CIA director George Tenet alerted National Security Advisor Condoleezza Rice to the threat. A few months later, intelligence officers again warned Rice and others that an attack from al-Qaeda was imminent. According to Clarke's recollection, Rice did not seem to know what al-Qaeda even was.[7]

The night of 9/11, Bush addressed the nation from the Oval Office and laid out his neocon-inspired Bush Doctrine: "We will make no distinction between the terrorists who committed these acts and those who harbor them," he threatened. That night, he told his National Security Council that the attack posed "an opportunity to go beyond Afghanistan" and "shake terror loose" in places like Syria, Iraq, and Iran. Saner members of his team advised the president that, legally, the United States could only use war to *defend* against attacks, to which Bush responded that he didn't care "what the international lawyers say" and that he was going to "kick some ass."[8] The following day, Bush called the WTC attack "an act of war" and escalated the conflict by declaring a "War on Terror"—repackaging himself as a wartime president, and the conflict as one between good and evil.

When Bush met with members of his administration on September 12, Deputy Defense Secretary Paul Wolfowitz brought up Iraq and questioned its role in the attacks, despite the known antagonism between bin Laden and Saddam Hussein. Wolfowitz had long advocated for assassinating the Iraqi leader, dating back to his service in Bush Sr.'s administration, when Hussein allegedly plotted to kill his boss—a claim that Iraqi officials have consistently denied and Pentagon reports have called into question. Bush Jr. responded to Wolfowitz's suggestion of Iraq by emphasizing that "the enemy" was not just bin Laden but any country that supported terrorists. After the meeting, Bush asked Clarke to look for links between 9/11 and Iraq. When Clarke responded that the CIA had already investigated and found nothing, Bush ordered him to keep looking. The next day, the president asked Rumsfeld whether it was possible to attack both Afghanistan and Iraq at the same time, to which his hawkish defense secretary responded that yes, he could.

On September 13, Bush made a spectacular appearance at Ground Zero of the WTC site to show his support for the shellshocked firefighters and rescue workers there. Standing with a bullhorn atop the smoldering rubble, he spoke of American greatness and vowed revenge. That same day, Congress passed the 2001 Authorization for the Use of Military Force (AUMF), giving the president far-reaching martial powers. It also denied his requests to declare preemptive wars, strip domestic suspects of constitutional rights, and engage in unlimited domestic surveillance—all of which Bush ended up doing anyway. That week, he blustered to the press, "We will smoke them out of their holes," and in a private meeting with his war council, he authorized CIA renditions.

Early in October, Bush issued an ultimatum to the Taliban to hand over bin Laden, and shortly after, authorized the U.S. attack on Afghanistan. Congress signed the U.S. Patriot Act—expanding the government's authority to Big Brother levels of domestic surveillance—and Bush authorized the National Security Agency (NSA) to conduct warrantless surveillance of communications in and out of the United States. A year later, in November 2002, he established a powerful new cabinet-level agency—the Office of Homeland Security (OHS)—and charged it with overseeing customs, immigration, and coastal and border control; the Federal Emergency Management Agency (FEMA); and the newly established Transportation Security Administration (TSA).

Kabul fell in short order, and Bush installed Hamid Karzai as the new president of Afghanistan. Karzai remained in power for the duration of Bush's presidency, but his jurisdiction was limited to the area around Kabul, as warlords controlled the rest of the country. Buoyed by the global outpouring of solidarity around 9/11, Bush began to obsessively promote a war with Iraq as part of his War on Terror, threatening allies that neutrality was not an option. Finally, during his January 2002 State of the Union speech, he accused Saddam of harboring weapons of mass destruction (WMDs) and argued for expanding the war to Iraq—which, along with Iran and North Korea, he called the "axis of evil."

Holy War

When it came to his War on Terror, George W. Bush viewed America as an instrument of God, a virtuous and exceptional liberator called to rid the world of "evildoers." French president Jacques Chirac got a taste of this militarist evangelicalism during a phone call with the president in the lead-up to the Iraq War: "Gog and Magog are at work in the Middle East," Bush warned him. "Biblical prophesies are being fulfilled. This confrontation is willed by God, who wants to use this conflict to erase His people's enemies before a New Age begins."[9] After that, Chirac became a leading voice of dissent against Bush's holy war.

On top of his otherworldly approach to national security, Bush harbored grandiose ideas of his own office. To him, the U.S. president was inherently above the law, a lone executive and ultimate "decider." Building on Reagan's use of *unitary executive theory*—the idea that the president has ultimate authority over the executive branch, especially on matters of war and security—Bush used the concept in his signing statements to cherry-pick which parts of any given piece of legislation he wanted to follow. This concept of an imperial executive was encouraged by Bush's Office of Legal Counsel (OLC) led by Deputy Assistant Attorney General John C. Yoo. Yoo issued a series of now-infamous memos justifying Bush's blatant overreaches of presidential power, from warrantless domestic wiretapping to authorizing renditions and torture. It was also reinforced by those in the president's inner circle, including Rove, who allegedly claimed, "We are an empire now, and when we act, we create our own reality."[10]

The *New York Times* helped to turn up the volume on Bush's war with Michael Gordon and Judith Miller's reporting on Saddam's alleged possession of WMDs,[11] as did the fearmongering of Attorney General Ashcroft, who issued a "code orange" just a day before 9/11's one-year anniversary.[12]

On that anniversary, Bush appeared before the UN Security Council to make the case for his illegal, preemptive war. He cited Saddam Hussein's supposed possession of WMDs and warned the international body that not acting was akin to abetting terrorists and that the United States was ready to go it alone. No one in the audience clapped during the intended applause lines. The speech, pardon the pun, bombed.

On the eve of the midterm elections and in the wake of a major media offensive by Bush cabinet officials—in which they spread falsehoods about yellowcake uranium and mushroom clouds—Congress authorized Bush to use military force against Iraq, abdicating its oversight responsibility and giving a battle-hungry president a free hand.[13] In the House, a majority of Democrats opposed the war, but in the Senate, a majority supported it—notably, then-senators Joe Biden, Hillary Clinton, and John Kerry, who, despite their inconceivably poor judgment, would go on to occupy high posts in the White House.

UN weapons inspectors led by Hans Blix continued to report no evidence of WMDs in Iraq and discredited the British intelligence that Bush was using to justify his war. On February 2, Colin Powell, the most credible member of the Bush administration, presented the case to the UN Security Council with a speech that was rife with falsehoods. The *Washington Post* and *New York Times* described it as a "powerful case and irrefutable evidence," but the UN Security Council did not agree. Turkey denied the United States' petition to pass through its territory for military operations, and France, Germany, Russia, China, India, and many others stated their opposition. After Chirac declared his dissent, government officials and the U.S. media spouted adolescent harangues, calling French people "cheese-eating surrender monkeys" and renaming French fries "freedom fries."[14]

Key members of the U.S. religious, military, and diplomatic establishments registered their dissent. George H. W. Bush's national security advisor, Brent Scowcroft, penned a *Wall Street Journal* op-ed titled "Don't Attack Saddam,"[15] and revered four-star general Norman Schwarzkopf raised red flags about the war's aftermath. The U.S. Conference of Catholic Bishops signed a letter to the president stating that any preemptive use of military force was not justified. The Vatican spoke out, soldiers refused to deploy, and career diplomats resigned.

On February 15, 2003, ten to fifteen million people in over 600 cities around the world took to the streets to protest Bush's war. At the time, these were the largest street demonstrations in history, a Guinness World Record. A CBS News/*New York Times* poll found that a majority (63 percent) of Americans wanted Bush to find a diplomatic solution and just 31 percent favored military intervention.[16] In response to the protests, the *New York*

Times front page read: "The fracturing of the Western alliance over Iraq and the huge antiwar demonstrations around the world this weekend are reminders that there may still be two superpowers on the planet: the United States and world public opinion."[17] When asked about the protests during a press conference, Bush responded that he was not going to decide military policy based on "a focus group."[18]

A few weeks later, the UN Security Council was called into session to hear the final reports of the weapons inspectors in Iraq. They reported without caveat that WMDs could not be found. Bush continued to insist that there was "no doubt" Iraq possessed WMDs, and without Security Council sanction, he authorized Operation Iraqi Freedom—sweeping aside any pretense of an international legal order and imposing new rules of engagement that he alone decided.[19]

On March 20, 2003, U.S. forces led by General Tommy Franks launched an offensive against Iraq that the U.S. media sensationalized as "shock and awe." The 145,000-person ground force quickly overcame Iraqis' resistance and thousands of Saddam's soldiers deserted. When Baghdad fell in early April, an iconic statue of Saddam Hussein was toppled and dragged through the city. In a video broadcast directed to the Iraqi people, Bush spoke of Americans' respect for Iraq's "great religious traditions" and how U.S. troops would work with them to restore peace, security, and economic prosperity. That same day, as Baghdad erupted, international media broadcast footage of U.S. soldiers standing by as ancient artifacts from the National Museum of Iraq were looted. When asked about the postinvasion chaos, Rumsfeld glibly replied, "Stuff happens" and said that freedom is "untidy."[20] Then on May 1, Bush made a spectacular landing on the aircraft carrier *USS Abraham Lincoln*. After making two theatrical fly-bys, he arrived in the co-pilot's seat of a Navy S-3B Viking dressed up in a green flight outfit and white helmet. The jet's exterior was marked "Navy 1" in the back and "George W. Bush, Commander in Chief" below the cockpit. Following a costume change, Bush addressed the troops in front of a banner that read "Mission Accomplished" and trumpeted about how America was bringing democracy to Iraq. Believing that the invasion had been a resounding success, and only a minimal residual force was needed, Bush and Franks set an August deadline for a 30,000-troop drawdown. But the insurgency was just beginning.

As part of U.S. efforts "to transition Iraq to self-government," Bush appointed ambassador Paul Bremer as the presidential envoy to Iraq. Bremer imposed a policy of "de-Ba'athification," removing tens of thousands of Iraqis from government service who were holding the country together amid food shortages, shuttered schools, and devastated infrastructure.

He also disbanded the Iraqi military and police in charge of domestic security, leaving hundreds of thousands of government employees and *armed* Iraqi soldiers without jobs. These and other disastrous decisions nourished a potent insurgency and one of the longest wars in world history. Between the start of the invasion in March 2002 and the end of 2003, some 580 U.S. soldiers were killed, two-thirds of them after Bush's "Mission Accomplished" speech. By 2020, that number would quadruple, without counting the thousands of mercenary-contractor casualties.[21] A survey conducted in 2018 produced the horrifying estimate that the war had taken the lives of roughly 2.4 million Iraqis.[22]

BUSH'S DOMESTIC AGENDA

Bush's domestic agenda to remake America into what he called an "ownership society" (a Cato Institute slogan) focused on shredding the New Deal, privatizing public institutions, and fraying safety nets. Rather than use futuristic slogans like "the new economy," Bush cloaked his policy platform in the red, white, and blue of a wartime president and equated patriotism with free markets. Those who opposed this program were deemed disloyal: "The terrorists not only attacked our freedom, but they also attacked our economy. And we need to respond in unison," Bush said.[23]

Among Bush's first legislative victories was his $1.7 trillion tax cut, which passed with the support of a key minority of Democrats. Billed as a stimulus during that year's recession, the cuts were an obvious handout to the wealthy, especially his efforts to phase out the estate tax (which, on an official White House factsheet, he called a "death tax").[24] To legitimize the massive giveaway, the administration echoed Heritage Foundation rhetoric about how the tax cuts would spur growth, create jobs, and pay for themselves. When Treasury Secretary Paul O'Neil warned that the cuts would swell the deficit, Bush insisted that this was "the people's money" and Cheney replied candidly that "deficits don't matter."[25]

In 2003, Bush passed another round of tax cuts—an additional $350 billion over ten years—this time for the investor class. He reduced taxes on long-term capital gains and dividends and called for a tax holiday for companies that stashed their profits offshore.[26] In 2005, corporations repatriated nearly $300 billion in profits, a major increase from the average $62 billion between 2000 and 2004. The law mandated that the repatriated profits be used for creating jobs and not stock buybacks, but the tax holiday—which cost the Treasury billions in revenue—did not create jobs, and was in fact widely used for stock buybacks.[27]

The "Bush tax cuts" included a 2010 expiration date that Obama, as a candidate, promised he would let expire for those making over $250,000 a year. As president, though, Obama extended the cuts and made most of them permanent, rolling back some for top earners. The year the cuts were fully phased in, the top 1 percent of households saw their after-tax income grow by 6.7 percent, while the middle 20 percent saw only a 2.8 percent increase. For the bottom 20 percent, after-tax income grew by just 1 percent.[28]

Bush's ownership society also included attempts to privatize Medicare and Social Security. During his first term, he passed legislation that he said would lower prescription drug prices by having Medicare cover the cost of prescription drugs through the expansion of private health plans. His goal was that all forty-million-plus Medicare beneficiaries would receive prescription drug coverage through private insurance companies, incentivized by increased payments from the federal government—a clear transfer of public wealth into private hands. The legislation prohibited the federal government from negotiating price discounts from drug companies and forbade the importation of lower-priced prescription drugs from Canada and other countries. As a result, drug prices under Medicare Part D were 80 percent more expensive than the prices negotiated by Medicaid and Veterans Affairs and 60 percent more than what Canadians paid for the same medicines.[29]

As part of his "freedom agenda" to privatize Social Security, Bush proposed restructuring the program so that people could put their retirement savings in personal investment accounts (notably, Al Gore put forward a similar plan). Social Security was expected to be solvent for decades, but Bush told the American people that "the program was going bankrupt" and "the crisis is now." When Bush talked about Social Security reform during the first State of the Union speech of his second term, the Democrats booed him. Senator Max Baucus of Montana had been Bush's go-to Democrat on tax cuts and other programs, but Bush made the mistake of visiting Baucus's state to sell his Social Security plan without notifying the senator. Baucus declared war, and congressional Democrats as well as moderate Republicans refused to back the plan. Social Security once again survived, but just barely.

No Child Left Behind

Bush's other major domestic accomplishment early in his presidency was No Child Left Behind (NCLB)—an education reform policy on which he campaigned as a "compassionate conservative" to save poor children, he said, from "the soft bigotry of low expectations." Central to NCLB were principles of "accountability" and "achievement," operationalized through high-stakes standardized tests. The tests were "high stakes" in that schools were required to demonstrate student progress, or they would lose federal funding, be shut down, and their teachers and administrators fired. Instead of confronting the problems of social inequality and underinvestment in the public sector that directly shape educational opportunities, NCLB scapegoated students, teachers, and the entire system of public schooling.

In Bush's initial plan, children in schools that were shuttered due to underperformance would be issued vouchers to attend private schools of their choice. Democrats strongly opposed vouchers, but New Democrats did encourage "injecting more market forces and competition within our public education system."[30] In the final version of NCLB, legislators included a compromise "school choice" option that permitted transfers to charter schools—a public-private partnership model of policymaking that Republicans and Democrats alike use to grease the wheels of school privatization. Studies have shown that charter schools, some of them managed by for-profit entities, siphon funds away from public schools, are correlated with racial segregation, and lack accountability.

In the wake of the WTC tragedy, NCLB passed with majority bipartisan support. Massachusetts senator Ted Kennedy and House Speaker John Boehner had been part of the policy development process early on when Bush was still president-elect and they continued to serve as NCLB's chief sponsors. Boehner was an unlikely proponent of the legislation, having once called for the elimination of the Department of Education entirely, but his greater priority was to cement Bush's questionable electoral victory with a solid legislative win—which NCLB achieved.

Soon after NCLB passed, it became clear that Republicans did not plan to fund it at the agreed-upon levels, which incensed Kennedy and other Democrats. Nonetheless, states were required to comply with NCLB provisions, and without adequate funding, had to trim their budgets for things like school supplies, books, and field trips. Some also had to suspend or deprioritize instruction in subjects that were not included in federal and state testing mandates, such as art and music, social studies, science, and foreign languages—despite the wealth of evidence that those subjects increase academic performance and students' social and emotional well-being.[31]

NCLB set rigid and unreachable goals, then punished schools and teachers for not meeting them. It transformed classrooms into standardized testing factories, creating anxiety among students and robbing them of the joy of learning. In addition to undermining the profession of teaching by forcing teachers to "teach to the test," the pressure of high-stakes testing burnt teachers out and, along with cuts in pay and benefits, resulted in still-ongoing teacher shortages. NCLB rules mandated that every student be tested, including those with acute disabilities. Horror stories abound of teachers being forced to administer standardized tests to children who were severely, and fatally, disabled.[32]

Interviews with former administration officials reveal that NCLB was a wrecking ball by design, with the ultimate goal of fully privatizing the education system.[33] It somewhat worked. The NCLB-induced myth of public schools and teachers as failing helped to facilitate the bipartisan "school choice" agenda to expand charter schools—many of which are nonunion and some of which are for-profit and funded by ultra-conservative billionaires.[34]

Enron

Early in Bush's presidency, the bankruptcy of energy industry giant Enron exposed a shocking and complex web of price manipulation, accounting fraud, and corruption that would become the norm in the United States' increasingly deregulated and financialized economy. Founded in 1985, Enron was one of the world's largest electricity, natural gas, pulp and paper, and communications companies, claiming revenues of over $100 billion in 2000. The company enjoyed a blue-chip stock rating, and for six years in a row *Fortune* voted it "America's Most Innovative Company." While Enron initially operated as an energy supply company, it was on the forefront of neoliberal financialization, expanding its portfolio to include financial products, and not only trading energy, but speculating on bandwidth and weather derivatives as well.

Bush and the Republican Party were directly implicated in the scandal. Enron and its CEO Kenneth Lay were among Bush's largest campaign contributors dating back to his gubernatorial campaign. Lay lent Enron's private jet to Bush's campaign, served on his transition team, and was tight with Vice President Cheney, an old friend of Big Oil. After assuming office in 2001, Bush immediately waged a legislative and public relations campaign against federal price controls in the electricity market and abandoned plans to limit tax havens.[35] This lack of oversight enabled Enron to drive up prices on electricity, an essential service and basic need. It also allowed the company to conceal its balance sheet in offshore subsidiaries and continue to inflate the value of its assets and profits, such that Enron's prized stock value was always much larger than the actual value of its assets.

Republican congressman Phil Gramm and his wife, Wendy, were also major players. Wendy Gramm served as chair of the federal Commodity Futures Trading Commission, but after issuing a positive ruling for Enron, she resigned from the commission and was appointed to Enron's board of directors. In 1996, California's electricity utility was deregulated under Republican Governor Pete Wilson, but it still operated under a complex system of rules meant to protect consumers from price increases. In 2000, Enron spent $3.45 million lobbying to deregulate energy trading, and in December of that year Senator Gramm fast-tracked a bill allowing the company to gain control over a significant share of California's electricity and natural gas market. Gramm's legislation conflicted with recommendations put forth by President Clinton's Working Group on Financial Markets, which warned against deregulating energy commodity trading because they knew that it would enable traders to manipulate prices and supply—which is exactly what they did.

In 2000 and 2001, Enron traders created fake energy shortages and increased prices for California utility companies. They manipulated the demand for energy by creating an appearance of scarcity, then raised prices through the roof and booked record profits. The bogus shortages and price increases bankrupted local utility companies, and the rolling blackouts left many people, not to mention schools, hospitals, and other essential institutions, without electricity.[36] Tapes of phone transactions released in May 2004 revealed Enron traders joking about how they stole millions from California and elderly people like "Grandma Millie."[37] The energy crisis that Enron manufactured, with the help of the Gramms, Bush, and other political elites, lasted for an entire year and cost California $40 to $45 billion.[38] When federal regulators finally imposed price controls, Enron lost its ability to price-gouge, and the losses that ensued made it difficult for the company's executives to hide their accounting manipulations and offshore accounts. Deregulation made Lay and a host of others very rich, but when the bubble burst, 15,000 rank-and-file Enron employees lost their jobs along with $1.3 billion in retirement funds.[39] For their part, Bush and Cheney continued to push deregulation and distanced themselves from Enron's "few bad apples."

Twin Disasters

One of Bush's most ominous domestic challenges—and failures—involved the hurricane that decimated New Orleans and much of the Gulf Coast on August 29, 2005. At the time, Bush was vacationing at his ranch in

Crawford, Texas, and though he had been briefed on the magnitude of the storm, he decided to maintain his regular schedule and leave the matter to state and local government. This was in keeping with the neoliberal program of big government for wars and corporate subsidies, and small government for the people. As the storm hit and bodies piled up in the streets of the Crescent City, Bush was caught clowning for cameras backstage at an event at a naval base outside of San Diego. Two days after landfall, with the city in shambles, he flew over New Orleans in Air Force One as a photo op, looking down on the city like a detached tourist.

Like the WTC attacks, Bush had been warned. In 2001, FEMA predicted that a hurricane hitting New Orleans was one of the three most likely disasters threatening the United States, but the Bush administration cut the city's flood control funding almost in half to bankroll his holy war. The year before the hurricane hit, Army Corps of Engineers funding for New Orleans hurricane protection was also cut, forcing the New Orleans district of the corps to impose a hiring freeze. The Bush administration, despite promising to maintain the wetlands, turned them over to private developers in 2003, compromising a major buffer between the city and the deadly storm surge.[40]

At nearly all layers, the federal response was poorly coordinated and marred by incompetence, political maneuvering, and the neoliberal tendency to oppose government assistance for the working class and poor. Louisiana's governor and New Orleans' mayor delayed ordering a mandatory evacuation until just nineteen hours before landfall, with no provisions for homeless, low-income, or sick people. Most of those stranded in the city had few to no resources, and the conditions for sheltering them were abysmal. As the storm abated, survivors were found sleeping in the streets next to dead bodies, feces, and urine, and there was garbage everywhere. FEMA was nowhere to be found.

Once the government did act, cleanup proceeded at a glacial pace, and years later whole parts of the city remained uninhabitable. Millions of longtime residents were displaced for months, if not years, sharply reducing the size of its population by 60 percent in 2006 (and still, by about 15 percent in 2021).[41] Politicians and members of the media had the audacity to refer to displaced New Orleanians as "refugees," and in a stunning show of ignorance and power elitism, the president's mother, Barbara Bush, said of the evacuees in Houston, "What I'm hearing, which is sort of scary, is that they all want to stay in Texas. Everyone is so overwhelmed by the hospitality. And so many of the people in the arena, here, you know, were underprivileged anyway, so this is working very well for them."[42] Topping Barbara Bush, Louisiana representative Richard H. Baker remarked, "We finally cleaned up public housing in New Orleans. We couldn't do it. But God did."[43]

As in Iraq, the Bush administration hired private contractors to handle the recovery, compounding the disaster with waste, mismanagement, and corruption. No-bid rebuilding contracts were doled out to companies with ties to local officials. These contractors didn't hire locals desperately in need of jobs, and some didn't pay their workers. When congressional Democrats demanded accountability, Bush responded: "We'll make sure your money is being spent wisely. And we are going to make sure that the money is spent honestly."[44] Just like with Iraq, the response to congressional oversight was, "I'm the president, just trust me."

The same dynamic beset the rebuilding of New Orleans' education system. Before the storm hit, the city's public schools were in a state of decay due to severe mismanagement and neglect, which school choice advocates used as an excuse to "reform" the public school system.[45] "Reform" meant that mostly Black unionized teachers would be replaced by young, mostly white college grads from Teach for America, and all of the city's public schools converted to charter schools, with little to no oversight. Many special needs students fell through the cracks, and students were being selected out of schools based on their expected performance on standardized tests, according to a lawsuit filed by the Southern Poverty Law Center.[46] Meanwhile, school choice advocates falsely claimed that student performance at charters exceeded that at public schools, despite evidence to the contrary.

Thousands of people died because of the indifference and incompetence of government officials, and billions were wasted on their corrupt recovery effort. After Katrina, Bush's approval rating fell below 40 percent and remained there for the rest of his term. During his 2006 State of the Union address, he focused on Iraq and said nothing about the human suffering caused by the hurricane and his administration's poor response. He did not mention Katrina in his 2007 State of the Union address either, despite the fact that the recovery was far from complete.[47]

Toward the end of Bush's second term, reckless lending in the housing market—enabled by financial deregulation dating back to Carter and accelerated by his successors—came to a head. Home prices started to drop in 2006, but instead of putting on the brakes, Fannie Mae and Freddie Mac, along with a host of other lenders, lowered standards even further and backed riskier mortgages. In the second quarter of 2008, for example, half of Fannie and Freddie's losses were from home loans that did not require proof of income.[48]

When the housing bubble burst, the country witnessed astronomical rates of foreclosure that threatened the stability of the country, and ultimately, the world economy. In a context of widespread layoffs, depleted pensions, and the potential extinction of major U.S. industries, the Bush administration arranged for a bailout of the largest banks and put Fannie Mae into conservatorship. A newly elected Obama is often credited for saving the auto industry, but it was Bush who spearheaded the bailout to car manufacturers. The debacles surrounding the Wall Street bailout—on both Bush's and Obama's watch—are discussed further in chapter 4.

In the opening line to his superb biography on George W. Bush, Jean Edward Smith wrote, "Rarely in the history of the United States has the nation been so ill-served as during the presidency of George W. Bush."[49] By the numbers, on Bush's watch, corporations and the wealthy received a multi-trillion-dollar tax cut that nearly doubled the national debt and facilitated a massive upward wealth transfer by falsely justifying cuts in public spending.[50] The country was left in a deep recession with hundreds of thousands of jobs lost per month. Median household income declined. More than eight million Americans went from middle class to poverty, 7.9 million Americans lost their health insurance, and millions lost their pensions.[51] Due to draconian high-stakes testing, the shuttering of schools affected more than 200,000 children annually.[52]

Bush further consolidated executive power, expanded unlawful wiretapping, and normalized corruption. Instead of supporting the workers and families afflicted by 9/11 or Katrina, he swelled the defense budget, spent trillions on unnecessary wars, and sanctioned war crimes and torture. By the end of his term, Americans seemed to believe that the Bush presidency was just an aberration—a low from which the country could only rise. They were wrong: it was just the beginning.

BARACK OBAMA

America broke a seemingly impenetrable racial barrier when it elected Barack Obama the country's first Black president. While that Democratic primary cycle was complicated by the possibility of the first woman president, the general election was a relative layup for Obama given George W. Bush's unpopularity and the ill-conceived, and often buffoonish, Republican ticket of John McCain and Sarah Palin. Obama's public relations team sought to bolster these advantages by portraying him as a youthful and progressive visionary who represented the promise of a new, postpartisan era. As it turned out, Obama's election was a major victory for his Wall Street and corporate donors, who viewed his Camelot image as an effective means for rendering their elite agenda palatable, especially when it was being tested by a major financial crisis.

It also became a victory for the Far Right. In the years leading up to Obama's win, right-wing political forces that had been gathering since the early 1970s—many of them associated with the Mont Pelerin set—were expanding their reach through deep-pocketed donor networks and fundamentalist think tanks. In 2010, ultra-conservatives gained significant political ground in state and local elections by painting Democrats as "liberal elites" and blaming them for the country's declining living standards and lack of upward mobility. Those wins—and the Right's obstructionist grip on the Obama presidency—were made possible by the New Democrats' betrothing of their party to Wall Street and the Fortune 500 and their severe neglect of, and open disdain for, poor and working-class people.

Obama's fealty to this class program was on gross display during his 2007 campaign when he used his bully pulpit to openly lecture poor and working-class Black people about good personal habits and parenting—echoing conservative mantras about "tough love" and "personal responsibility." Pedigreed in the Ivy League, the Illinois senator mocked uneducated poor people with quips like "don't get too carried away with that eighth-grade education," and he scolded parents for supposedly feeding their kids "cold Popeye's for breakfast" and "eight sodas a day." As a metaphor for poor and working-class whites, Obama spoke of shiftless "Uncle Jethro" sitting on the couch watching SportsCenter, and feigned empathy for the unemployed in small midwestern towns who "cling to guns or religion" and express "anti-trade sentiment as a way to explain their frustrations."[53] This was despite the fact that free trade *had* eliminated their jobs and decimated their communities, while enriching multinationals like the ones bankrolling his campaign.

Once in office, with the country reeling from foreclosure and rising unemployment, Obama hired Wall Street insiders for top posts in his administration: Tim Geithner, Peter Orszag, Rahm Emanuel, Larry Summers, and others. To lead his Justice Department, he appointed Eric Holder from Covington & Burling, a high-end legal firm that represented big banks like Wells Fargo, JPMorgan Chase, Citibank, and Goldman Sachs.[54] The banks returned the favor by greasing the revolving door to their offices and making major contributions to Obama's Victory Fund. With the wolves of Wall Street guarding the henhouse, it was no surprise that Obama's Treasury Department failed to rein in the banks' criminal behavior and forced taxpayers to spend trillions bailing them out.[55] Behind his progressive facade, the big banks got bigger, as did their confidence in the state to protect their interests unconditionally.

In the wake of the 2007 global financial crisis, Obama passed a $787 billion stimulus bill—the Troubled Assets Relief Program (TARP)—to jump-start the economy. It included funding for jobs, infrastructure, small business, education, health services, unemployment compensation, and more. At the time, it was the largest stimulus in peacetime history and likely saved the country from a full-blown economic depression. Economists inside his administration argued that the $700-billion-plus figure was inadequate and should have been doubled, but they were overruled by Summers and other resident deficit hawks who had much more power and influence in and outside the administration.[56] Included in the stimulus was a doubling down on George W. Bush's NCLB—aptly named "Race to the Top"—which forced underfunded public schools to compete against each other for federal funds and incentivized a proliferation of charter schools. As a compromise with Republicans, it also provided tax cuts that yielded little political currency with most Americans for whom the reductions were hardly noticeable.

For homeowners in distress, Obama's stimulus legislation was, as TARP Special Inspector General Neil Barofsky put it, "a colossal failure,"[57] spending only a fraction of what was needed. That did not stop the right wing from waging an all-out, anti-government offensive, labeling Obama a "socialist" and making racist innuendos about his middle name, Hussein. This reaction was led in part by the Tea Party, whose emergence is often credited to Rick Santelli, a CNBC on-air editor who melted down on live TV criticizing the bailout and calling people who were struggling with foreclosure "losers."[58] In reality, the Tea Party was funded by the Koch network to create the appearance of a grassroots movement dedicated to their cause. Had Obama provided a proper bailout for the American people, the Right still would have smeared him, but with a strong recovery, their red-baiting would have been more likely to fall on deaf ears.

2010

2010 was a particularly consequential year in American politics, beginning with the U.S. Supreme Court's decision in *Citizens United v. Federal Election Commission (FEC)*. Two years prior, the conservative lobby group Citizens United had planned to air an anti–Hillary Clinton film on cable TV right before the Democratic primaries, but doing so would have violated existing laws governing elections.[59] The group challenged the constitutionality of the law, and the case went all the way to the Supreme Court. In 2010, the Court decided in favor of the group that restrictions on independent expenditures by corporations, associations, and labor unions constituted a violation of their First Amendment rights.

By conferring "personhood" on these entities, the courts granted them the right, as a matter of free speech, to spend unlimited money on political campaigns without having to disclose it to their shareholders or to the public, provided that they did not donate directly to candidates or coordinate with them. The history of corporate personhood traces back to a memo penned by Justice Lewis Powell on behalf of the U.S. Chamber of Commerce before Richard Nixon appointed him to the Supreme Court. In it, Powell warned of a growing movement of far leftists and "statists"—in university classrooms, church pulpits, and anchor desks—who, in his view, posed a dire threat to American free enterprise and greatness. In his blueprint for a new, corporate rights movement, he encouraged his comrades to deploy conservative intellectuals in courts and universities, censor (intimidate) academics, cultivate their own politicians, and wage a comprehensive propaganda campaign around American liberty and free enterprise.

As part of his crusade, Powell targeted Ralph Nader for his consumer protection activism and challenges to corporate power, which included a successful campaign to require automobile manufacturers to install lifesaving seat belts. Powell's disregard for public health and safety, in favor of corporate interests, would appear again in his legal defense of Big Tobacco's supposed First Amendment right to counter public health warnings on the dangers of smoking—which, incidentally, posed a clear conflict of interest given that Powell was a former director at Philip Morris and advisor to the seedy Tobacco Institute. Though he ultimately lost on tobacco, Powell's theory of corporations having constitutional rights and his work to foster "activist" courts gained consensus among conservatives seated on the highest courts of the land. Now, various industries—from coal and oil to banks and pharmaceuticals—can use the concept of corporate personhood to invalidate legal protections, along with consumer, labor, and environmental rights, and effectively usurp the power of the legislature.

Citizens United opened the floodgates for millionaires, billionaires, and large corporations to exert extraordinary influence over U.S. elections by spending huge sums of money up and down the ballot. This allowed ultra-rich people like the Koch brothers, whose resources exceeded those of both major parties, to sponsor their own candidates in primaries, in some cases against the Republican Party's chosen candidate. Obama spoke out against *Citizens United*, but he and the Democrats continued to take campaign contributions from big money donors. It was not until 2015 that a major presidential candidate—Vermont senator Bernie Sanders, an Independent—would refuse to take big money and run a competitive national campaign on small donations.[60]

The year 2010 also witnessed an overhaul of the U.S. health care system with the signing of Obama's Patient Protection and Affordable Care Act ("the ACA" or "Obamacare"), which was derived from a Heritage Foundation plan that Mitt Romney implemented as governor of Massachusetts. The ACA cut the number of uninsured in half by: (1) significantly expanding Medicaid; (2) allowing young people to stay on their parents' insurance until age twenty-six; (3) prohibiting insurance companies from discriminating against people with pre-existing conditions; and (4) mandating that people sign up for health insurance or face financial penalty.[61] Republicans attempted to undermine the ACA in innumerable ways, including obstructing Medicaid expansion in their states and thus callously blocking their most vulnerable constituents from accessing health care.

What the ACA did not do is prevent businesses from dropping coverage for their employees or cutting their hours to reduce benefits. Health care costs remain exorbitantly high, and people in the United States still pay thousands of dollars a year for health insurance, in addition to steep deductibles and copays, leaving tens of millions underinsured and undertreated. According to the Institute of Medicine, "The uninsured have poorer health and shortened lives."[62] In the United States, an estimated 26,000 people die each year due to lack of coverage.

The ACA did provide a windfall for the health insurance and pharmaceutical industries and, in the bigger picture, signaled the Democratic Party's rejection of the idea of health care as a fundamental human right. Obama talked a good game about providing health care to all, but as members of his administration were reassuring the public that the ACA would include a public option, he was in a back room with hospital and insurance lobbyists promising that the final legislation would not include a government-run health plan.[63] On the campaign trail, he excoriated drug companies and their lobbyists and ran a TV ad targeting former Louisiana congressman Billy Tauzin, the industry's chief lobbyist. Once Obama took office, however, Tauzin had his seat at the table, and the president negotiated away many of his promises.

Most countries' governments negotiate drug pricing to protect citizens from price gouging on lifesaving medicines. Obama nixed that idea, and even prevented drug importation from other countries, which would have dramatically reduced prices. His duplicitous and evolving rhetoric went from lambasting the greed of pharmaceutical companies to praising them for their "service," which included a multimillion-dollar advertising campaign touting Obama's signature health care policy. In the end, the drug companies secured their profits, Obama advanced his political agenda, and Democrats enjoyed an influx of campaign donations from Big Pharma. Disabled, sick, and elderly people paid the price.[64]

On the right, "Obamacare" became a lightning rod for Republican opposition, fueling their anti-big-government narrative, particularly after a botched rollout and broken promises regarding whether people could keep their current physician. On the left, the ACA became a symbol of shameless profiteering and proof that Obama was not the progressive champion many thought him to be. Under his health care reform, Mylan Pharmaceuticals, which held a virtual monopoly on the EpiPen, jacked prices up 400 percent;[65] and Turing Pharmaceuticals' "Pharma bro" Martin Shkreli had a free hand to raise the price of a standard treatment for parasitic infection from $13.50 to $750 per tablet—an increase of 5,000 percent. Remarkably, Shkreli was jailed for defrauding his hedge fund investors but not for his criminal price gouging. Today, under the ACA, sick and elderly people are rationing the prescription drugs they need to stay healthy and survive and are even fundraising online to scrape by. Some of them are dying, lacking the medicines they need. Meanwhile, drug and health insurance company CEOs rank among the highest-paid people in the world, making tens of millions annually.

A few months after passing the ACA, Obama signed into law the Dodd-Frank Wall Street Reform and Consumer Protection Act, which he presented as "a set of reforms to empower consumers and investors, to bring the shadowy deals that caused this crisis into the light of day, and to put a stop to taxpayer bailouts once and for all."[66] The bill went into effect in July 2010, but the reforms aimed at restricting banks' speculative activity took much longer and lacked teeth.[67] Nonetheless, Obama promised the American people that Dodd-Frank would prevent another financial crisis and taxpayer bailout.[68] According to the Levy Institute, however, his White House would issue tens of trillions more in bank bailout funds,[69] tax deferrals, and secret loans (see chapter 5).[70]

With the emptiness of Obama's "hope and change" rhetoric revealing itself, Republicans "shellacked" Democrats in the November 2010 midterms.[71] They retook control of the House, narrowed Democrats' majority in the Senate, and even won "blue state" Massachusetts following Senator Ted Kennedy's death. Since it was a census year, conservatives targeted posts in state legislatures where newly elected officials could gerrymander districts in their favor. Under the name Project RedMap, those efforts turned "purple" states—like Wisconsin, Michigan, Pennsylvania, and Florida—"red," and far right-wing Republicans came to dominate local legislatures and governors' mansions. The policy agendas of these local officials were conspicuously similar, designed by the American Legislative Exchange Council (ALEC) and backed by the Kochs and other rich, like-minded donors.

Founded in 1973, the year Lewis Powell penned his infamous memo, ALEC has become a potent political force in U.S. politics. Bringing together corporate chiefs and conservative public officials, the group forges policy platforms and legislative templates to be distributed widely at all levels of government. ALEC's raison d'être is to advance a class agenda to consolidate corporate power through legislation that undermines labor unions, strips environmental and other regulations, eliminates safety nets and minimum-wage laws, and privatizes public services—self-perpetuating their agenda by suppressing the vote through partisan gerrymandering and dark money.

The combination of budget shortfalls rendered by the financial crisis, the rise of the Tea Party, and the success of Project RedMap, among other factors, created an opening for ALEC in states across the country. As conservative governors and state legislators cut taxes for corporations and the wealthy, they made Pinochet-like cuts in public services and institutions. They laid off public school teachers and librarians, ballooned class sizes, and shortened school weeks. In Florida, schools increased their thermostat settings beyond the legal limit to save money; and in Arizona, preschool was eliminated entirely.[72] They reduced health and pension benefits for public sector workers and cut budgets for local health departments, forcing them to stop providing immunizations and child health care. Food safety inspections were cut back. Even in "blue state" New York, the state's first Black governor, David Paterson, called the social safety net an "addiction to spending"[73] and blamed some of his state's fiscal problems on the supposedly excessive pay of teachers and other public employees.[74]

Backed by the Koch network, Governor Sam Brownback passed one of the largest tax cuts in Kansas' history, designed by ALEC and "trickle down" economist Arthur Laffer. Brownback ran his state so far into the ground that it was twice downgraded by bond rating agencies within a two-year period. The massive revenue loss was used to justify savage cuts in health care, transportation, and infrastructure. Education cuts were so deep that some schools could only stay open four days a week.[75] Rivaling Brownback's sociopathic governance were Wisconsin governor Scott Walker and Congressman Paul Ryan, also funded by Koch. Walker rolled back collective bargaining rights to such a degree that within five years, the state's share of public sector workers who belonged to unions was cut in half.[76] Ryan, as chairman of the House Budget Committee, relentlessly called for punishing cuts to the federal budget, once telling an American Israel Public Affairs Committee (AIPAC) audience that school lunches leave kids with "a full stomach—and an empty soul."[77] Without school lunches, millions of children in the United States would go hungry.

The Bush Tax Cuts

On the campaign trail, Obama promised that he would let the Bush tax cuts expire for those making more than $250,000 a year. But in 2010, nearly every Republican, and some Democrats, argued that tax hikes on high-income earners would produce job losses and economic suffering. Once in power, Obama acquiesced and responded to the worst economic crisis since the Great Depression by issuing more tax cuts for the wealthy and passing a 2 percent cut in the payroll taxes that fund Social Security. In a now-famous nine-hour filibuster, Senator Bernie Sanders protested the tax cuts, warning that conservatives on both sides of the aisle would use the rising deficit—a product of the Bush tax cuts!—as an excuse to cut social programs. Which is exactly what they did.[78]

Obama shamelessly lauded his compromise as "a substantial victory for middle-class families across the country" and said that it would create jobs and boost the economy.[79] House Speaker John Boehner was at least more candid: "If we want to . . . begin creating jobs, we need to end the job-killing spending binges" by the federal government and "provide more certainty to business."[80] Soon after extending the tax cuts, Obama renewed the statutory "pay as you go" (PAYGO) provision that required all new spending to be offset with either budget cuts or tax increases (recall that PAYGO was a Republican policy aimed at curbing public spending).[81] He also signed an executive order to create a bipartisan National Commission on Fiscal Responsibility and Reform[82]—led by Alan Simpson (R-WI) and former White House chief of staff Erskine Bowles—charged with developing ways to "balance" the budget. In its final report, the Simpson-Bowles commission recommended increases to the retirement age and cost-of-living adjustments for Social Security. It also suggested cuts in student loan subsidies and making workers pay taxes on their health benefits, while rewarding companies that outsourced jobs abroad with tax cuts. Moreover, it proposed shifting the costs of Medicare and Medicaid on to patients—including the elderly, disabled, and poor—and imposing spending caps that would force a 14 percent cut in domestic programs by 2013, and a 22 percent cut by 2022.[83]

In the mix were Bill and Hillary Clinton, who partnered with billionaire Pete Peterson's foundation that year to launch a propaganda campaign called "Up to Us"—a year-long competition judged by Simpson, Bowles, and Chelsea Clinton in which students from major universities ran campaigns to "raise awareness about fiscal sustainability." The campaign's name derived from the neoliberal mantra of "choice"[84] and "personal responsibility" emphasized in Obama's 2009 D-Day speech: "Our history has always been the sum total of the choices made and the actions taken by each individual man and woman. It has always been up to us."[85]

That summer, Obama warned the American people, "Government has to start living within its means, just like families do. We have to cut the spending we can't afford so we can put the economy on sounder footing, and give our businesses the confidence they need to grow and create jobs."[86] With the threat of a credit downgrade and obtuse chatter about how the United States might default "like Greece," Obama struck a "grand bargain" with Boehner that included both raising taxes and cutting spending. While Obama and Boehner agreed, Minority Whip Eric Cantor and the Tea Party–dominated GOP held the debt limit hostage, demanding deep spending cuts while reveling in having duped Obama.[87] Democrats were not happy either, with Obama having agreed to cut Social Security, Medicare, and Medicaid and spending more time courting Republicans than those in his own party.

Democrats eventually came to a deal with Republicans in the form of the Budget Control Act of 2011, which allowed for raising the debt ceiling in exchange for immediate $1 trillion spending cuts (over ten years) and the formation of a bipartisan "supercommittee" charged with reducing the deficit by another $1.2 to $1.5 trillion—about the same figure as the Bush tax cuts. If the supercommittee failed to reach a deal, the legislation would trigger $1.2 trillion in across-the-board spending cuts, aka "sequestration," over the next decade. Democrats entered the process assuming no one wanted that, but when the supercommittee predictably failed, Obama struck yet another deal to stave off the sequester, making the Bush tax cuts permanent.

For his 2014 budget, Obama doubled down on the neoliberal "enterprise zone" concept in the form of what he called "promise zones," and resurrected the Simpson-Bowles recommendation to cut Social Security by changing the way cost-of-living adjustments were calculated. In protest, Bernie Sanders, Social Security Works, and about a hundred other groups delivered to the White House a petition signed by 2 million people demanding an expansion of Social Security benefits.[88] Sanders also led a congressional coalition to pressure Obama to abandon the cost-of-living adjustment manipulations, which he eventually did.

FREE TRADE

Obama followed in the footsteps of both Republican and Democratic presidents before him in his unwavering commitment to free trade, and to the Trans-Pacific Partnership (TPP) in particular—which his administration billed as his signature achievement. Initiated by George W. Bush, the TPP was a massive, corporate-driven free trade deal that involved the United States and eleven other countries along the Pacific Rim in what would have been the world's largest free trade area, accounting for 40 percent of the global economy.[89] Like other free trade agreements that preceded it, the TPP was expected to reduce wages, offshore good-paying U.S. jobs, and deregulate critical industries—all of which would have reduced tax revenue for local and state governments at a time when their budgets were already strained by profligate tax cuts and increased demand for social services.[90]

The TPP's Investor-State Dispute Settlement system of secret tribunals would have allowed multinational corporations to circumvent countries' legal systems and challenge any domestic law, court decision, or regulation that might negatively affect their bottom lines, including safety standards, banking regulations, pollution protections, and so on. This juridical framework stood in stark contrast to the weak grievance process for environmental, labor, and consumer violations.[91] Instead of disputing an action based on its harm to the environment or violation of workplace rights, under the TPP the measure of a law or regulation was how it impacted corporate profits.

The TPP, and free trade more generally, was a major factor in Democrats' shocking loss in the 2016 election. By the end of Obama's presidency, it was widely known, and felt, that free trade agreements were causes of America's widening wealth gap and middle-class decline. As a result of the North American Free Trade Agreement (NAFTA) and Permanent Normal Trade Relations with China (PNTR), thousands of U.S. factories had been boarded up, and once-vibrant manufacturing towns decayed into sites of deep poverty, home foreclosure, low graduation rates, and opioid addiction. Given that the TPP would have accelerated this downward spiral, consumer rights advocates, family farmers, and social justice groups worldwide vocally opposed it. Labor unions of all stripes were united in their opposition, and environmental groups cautioned that it would accelerate climate change and harmful resource extraction in the Pacific Rim. Doctors warned that it would thwart developing countries' access to medicine, since under the TPP drug companies would have the power to prevent price controls, drug importation, and the development of low-cost generic drugs—and any other policy that threatened to eat into their profits.[92]

Despite this broadening opposition, Obama used his 2015 State of the Union speech to stress the importance of being economically dominant in the Asia-Pacific and promised that the TPP would create more and better jobs. He beckoned Congress for executive "fast track" authority to broker the deal, which would have sidelined elected lawmakers from negotiations that already had included about 600 corporate "trade advisors."[93] As the next chapter shows, before shutting the TPP down as president, Donald Trump used it to needle divisions between progressive and corporate Democrats, highlighting the latter's disregard for how the TPP would impact workers. In the process, he forced Hillary Clinton to go against her party, and her own record, in rejecting the TPP to win over working-class voters—who, frankly, saw right through her.

During an interview with Univision in December 2012, Obama told a reporter, "The truth of the matter is that my policies are so mainstream that if I had set the same policies that I had back in the 1980s, I would be considered a moderate Republican."[94] Obama *did* reduce unemployment and modestly increase real median income, and he helped to save the U.S. auto industry. But Democrats occupied the White House for sixteen of the twenty-four years before Trump's election, and, for four of those years, both chambers of Congress. During that time, wealth inequality and corporate power increased, labor unions were weakened, and forty-three million people lived in poverty.[95] Under Obama, domestic fossil fuel production reached its highest historical levels, and student and consumer debt skyrocketed.[96] Over twenty-six million Americans remained without health insurance, and millions more were underinsured.[97] Wall Street, alternatively, became more powerful than ever, as did the radical Right. The surveillance/police state grew, executive branch power further consolidated, and the United States' military adventures became more deadly, torturous, and covert.

Obama got elected by building a historic coalition that brought together the progressive and neoliberal wings of his party. However, his biggest accomplishment involved providing major cover for Wall Street and corporate forces when they were on the ropes, and renewing policies like the Bush tax cuts that served elites' interests. Had Obama lived up to his promises to substantively address problems of wealth and income inequality, end U.S. wars, and guide the state toward the interests of the many rather than the few, he might have helped to mitigate America's livability crisis and stave off the Far Right's rising tide. In doing just the opposite, he handed the keys to the White House over to reactionary forces, the kind that emerge when people feel talked down to, misled, and desperate.

CHAPTER 3

The State (2017–2022)

When billionaire real estate mogul and reality TV star Donald Trump announced his 2015 run for president, he staged it at Trump Tower—descending down a gold escalator with his trophy wife as a crowd wearing "Make America Great Again" T-shirts cheered him on, many of them paid actors.[1] A frequent subject of tabloids and Page Six, Trump was known to exaggerate his wealth and exploits, peddle conspiracy theory, and associate with mafia types and conmen. Though invested in anachronisms like beauty pageants and Atlantic City casinos, and mired in bankruptcy, Trump resurrected his brand on the cutting edge of the reality TV boom. The hit series *The Apprentice* brought him into the homes of tens of millions of people, boosted his image as dogged and self-made, and ultimately helped propel him into the White House.

During his announcement speech, Trump bragged about being "really rich" and called U.S. politicians "stupid" and "morally corrupt." He bemoaned exorbitant health insurance deductibles and the trillion-dollar price tag of the Iraq War, and how, as a country, "we don't have victories anymore." He warned that the United States was in "serious trouble" because China and Japan were "killing us" on trade—though as a shrewd dealmaker he himself "beat China all the time." With regard to the complex issue of southern border immigration, he claimed that the United States had become "a dumping ground for everybody else's problems." If elected, he would build "a great wall" to protect the country from "illegal" Mexican "rapists and drug dealers"[2] and get Mexico to pay for it.

Such unscripted bombast and incendiary rhetoric are rare in presidential campaigns. But Trump's trash talking was not entirely out of place given the rise of the nativist Far Right in the media and U.S. Congress, and the U.S. electorate's mass apathy and bitterness. Just a few years before Trump was elected, pollster Patrick Caddell conducted a study of establishment Republicans' waning popularity and found an extraordinarily high level of discontent among U.S. voters and desires for "an outsider" to fix Washington. Similar trends could be seen in Europe, Turkey, the Philippines, Brazil, and elsewhere: reactionism was on the rise as quality of life and access to basic needs were on the decline and the contradictions of neoliberal capitalism deepening.

Trump won his seat in the Oval Office by playing to those resentments. While Obama Democrats peddled untruths about how the Trans-Pacific Partnership would be "good for workers," Trump appeared to tell it straight, calling out the disastrous effects of free trade on labor and working-class communities. When Republican candidates stressed the urgency of "entitlement reform," Trump pledged to protect Social Security and Medicare and lower the cost of prescription drugs at a time when one out of five Americans could not afford them.[3] In a GOP field bankrolled by Wall Street and billionaires—recall the "Adelson primary" of casino mogul Sheldon Adelson—Trump bragged about his ability to self-fund his campaign and made fun of his opponents for kowtowing to wealthy donors. When asked about extreme partisanship inside the DC beltway, he promised to "drain the swamp." For those whom Hillary Clinton dismissed as "deplorables,"[4] Trump vowed, "I will be your voice."[5]

In his analysis of World War II Germany, philosopher Theodor Adorno theorized how fascist dictatorship relies on identification with, and idolatry of, an authority figure who disinhibits the worst of humanity's tendencies and destabilizes political and social life through disinformation. Trump's techniques of disinhibition involved using vulgar humor and juvenile entertainment to take down his opponents, which was enabled by his dominance over news cycles.[6] He defied the Republican aristocracy by mocking "low energy" Jeb Bush and claiming that Senator John McCain, a Vietnam POW, was not a war hero because he had been captured. "I like people who weren't captured," Trump said.[7] After Senator Lindsey Graham called him a "jackass," Trump retaliated by announcing the senator's personal cell phone number on national TV.[8] When the race had been pared down to just him and Senator Ted Cruz, Trump claimed that Cruz was not eligible to be president because he was born in Canada. He also tweeted an unflattering photo of Cruz's wife juxtaposed with a glamor shot of his own wife, a former model, with the caption: "A picture is worth a thousand words."[9]

In addition to debasing his political rivals, Trump fanned the flames of working-class resentment with Nixonian appeals to "the silent majority" and scapegoated immigrants for a variety of problems—from high crime rates to middle-class job losses to the alleged insolvency of Social Security. On the campaign trail, he threatened to deport millions of undocumented immigrants and fearmongered about Syrian war refugees, saying "they could be ISIS."[10] He vowed to create a database to track Muslims in the United States, and following the horrific 2015 mass shooting in San Bernardino by two *American-born* Pakistanis, he called for a temporary ban on Muslims entering the country.

In response to a lawsuit charging Trump University with defrauding students, Trump deflected by attacking the presiding judge in the case, Judge Gonzalo Curiel, on the basis of his ethnicity. Curiel was born in Indiana, but Trump insisted that his Mexican heritage was a "conflict of interest" given Trump's extremist views regarding the southern border.[11] Once in office, Trump signed a series of hardline executive orders banning Muslims from entering the United States, accelerated gestapo-like roundups of undocumented immigrants, and, with extreme cruelty, forced family separations at the border. White supremacists and the "alt-Right"[12] received his racist comments as a wink of approval. With hate crimes on the rise, a neo-Nazi in Charlottesville, Virginia, drove his car into a crowd of anti-racism protesters, killing a young woman and injuring two dozen people. Trump defended the Nazis at the demonstration as "very fine people."[13]

In addition to disinhibiting hatred and xenophobia, Trump brewed mistrust by proliferating falsehoods and disinformation. He politicized what was left of "straight journalism" and incited violence against reporters who challenged his often-cockamamie narratives, branding the press "fake news." His prolific use of Twitter—a perfect conduit for inflammatory speech—earned him tens of millions of followers and continuous controversy. Fringe right-wing radio shows, internet sites, and the widely viewed Fox News channel served as an echo chamber for his untruths to such a degree that Trump had large portions of the country believing that Obama was not a U.S. citizen, that windmills cause cancer, that Ted Cruz's father shot JFK, and that a deadly coronavirus was "like the regular flu."[14] Trump supporters waving signs that read "Get your government hands off my Medicare" epitomized the depth of his distortions.

Though singular in the flagrancy of his bigotry and opportunism, and lack of regard for social and governmental norms, Trump's presidency is a clear exposition of the endemic corruption and anti-democratic nature of neoliberal capitalism. As such, his ascendancy should be evaluated in context, as a progression of political elites' decades-long, bipartisan commitment to a mythical yet hegemonic free market, and as a consequence of their contradictory claims to freedom and democracy against most Americans' lived experience of powerlessness and insecurity.

This chapter takes up from the previous two in tracing Trump's part in the ongoing consolidation of elite power vis-à-vis the neoliberal state. That includes analysis of the policies and bureaucratic manipulations that his administration employed in the service of expanding elite power—his tax cuts, privatization schemes, corporate deregulation, and expansion of executive authority—and Trump's branding of such techniques in narratives that associated unfettered markets with American greatness.

EXECUTIVE POWER

The executive branch of the U.S. government is a gigantic bureaucracy, consisting of over two million civilian employees across hundreds of agencies, charged with keeping people safe, minimizing risk, and, on a good day, fostering social, scientific, and technological progress.[15] In addition to defense and national security, to which 70 percent of this mammoth workforce is dedicated,[16] the federal government provides services that the private sector cannot or will not offer, such as air traffic control or guaranteeing food safety. Given the importance of these federal agencies, changes in their personnel and operations can have profound effects on the government's ability to function, which is why presidential transitions and competent staffing and management are so important.

As president, Trump achieved parts of his policy agenda by manipulating the bureaucratic administration of the executive branch and defunding and reorganizing agencies in ways that altered their regulatory and enforcement capacities. For years, Koch-style libertarians and ultra-conservatives have called for the dissolution of government agencies and the elimination of taxes and all fetters on corporate power, arguing that such moves are vital to human liberty. Right-wing media executive and former White House chief strategist Steve Bannon termed it "the deconstruction of the administrative state"—though in reality, the goal is to co-opt government, not simply dismantle it.[17]

During the Obama presidency, sequestration forced by austerity hawks marked a major step in achieving that "deconstruction" as across-the-board spending cuts neutered various public programs and significantly reduced the federal workforce. Trump continued in that vein, intentionally botching the transition, purging career civil servants who might undermine him, and defunding agencies charged with overseeing the country's banks, workplaces, environment, transportation, postal systems, elections, consumer protections, and emergency preparedness. He left hundreds of positions in executive branch agencies unfilled, or politicized them, while firing hundreds of people and replacing them with loyalists who had no relevant or government experience at all. These maneuvers deepened public distrust of government and led tens of thousands of dispirited career civil servants to resign from their posts or remain on staff and leak evidence of the administration's malfeasance to the press.[18]

Trump's gutting of the federal workforce reduced caseloads, penalties, and enforcement actions across nearly every government agency, opening the door for catastrophe. For example, the Boeing 737 Max plane crashes, taking the lives of hundreds of people,[19] were in part the result of a poorly funded Federal Aviation Administration (FAA) that allowed Boeing and other air carriers to self-regulate (during both the Obama and Trump administrations).[20] The crash of the hospital system during the coronavirus pandemic can be traced to states' lack of access to the national stockpile of medical supplies, as well as understaffing and defunding at the Centers for Disease Control and Prevention (CDC). The Trump administration's efforts to weaken the Environmental Protection Agency (EPA)—which included issuing thousands of waivers to corporations—resulted in pollution levels that experts say will be responsible for "countless deaths."[21]

If "personnel is policy," as they say inside the DC beltway, Trump's official policy was bold-faced cronyism and corruption. Trump called on media personalities like Lou Dobbs and Sean Hannity to serve as senior advisors and installed former lobbyists, corporate insiders, and right-wing ideologues at the highest levels of government, including some known white supremacists. Despite existing norms and legal constraints against nepotism,[22] among the most powerful people in the Trump White House were his daughter Ivanka and her husband, Jared Kushner—both self-dealing opportunists whose attachments to their indecent, cutthroat fathers went far beyond those of normal adults. The couple, especially Jared, assumed portfolios far afield of their competency—including Israel-Palestine relations, immigration reform, and pandemic response—spurring the *New York Times*'s Michelle Goldberg to describe their roles as "dilettantism raised to the level of sociopathy."[23]

A poster child of Ivy League corruption, Kushner's Harvard pedigree was bought through his father's generous gifts to the school's endowment. As owner of the *New York Observer*, he ran hit jobs on opponents,[24] and upon entering government service, he brazenly lied on his legal financial disclosures. Kushner used his White House position to secure a bailout for his ill-conceived $1.8 billion real estate purchase of 666 Fifth Avenue in Manhattan. And he befriended and made business deals with the notoriously brutal Saudi crown prince, Mohammed bin Salman (MBS), known to have ordered the murder and dismemberment of *Washington Post* journalist Jamal Khashoggi.[25] Despite his perception of MBS as a business partner and chum, the Saudi prince boasted to his confidants that Kushner was "in his pocket."[26] At the White House, photojournalists nicknamed Kushner "the man witch," given his sinister manner and bloodless complexion.

Ivanka's résumé for serving as a senior official in the White House included working as a pageant spokesmodel, founding her own jewelry line and fashion label (sewn in sweatshops), making cameos on her father's reality TV show, and overseeing his real estate holdings, which included shady dealings with the Russian mafia, the Gambino crime family, and a Brazilian money launderer.[27] Amid public snickering, Trump called Ivanka "baby" in official meetings, positioned her alongside foreign heads of state and world business leaders at high-level events, and seriously considered nominating her for World Bank president because, he said, "she's very good with numbers."[28]

Trump's unlikely pick for vice president was Indiana governor Mike Pence, "a Christian, a conservative, and a Republican, in that order," as Pence liked to say. His choirboy demeanor and extreme traditionalism—he allegedly calls his wife "mother" and forbids her from being alone with other men[29]—balanced Trump's lasciviousness and lack of piety. Selecting Pence was also a nod to the Koch brothers, who had long bankrolled him and guided his gubernatorial agenda of tax cuts for the rich and austerity for the rest.[30] Several others in Trump's cabinet had strong Koch ties, including Mike Pompeo, the Kansas congressman who Trump first named CIA director, then appointed as secretary of state to replace former Exxon CEO Rex Tillerson (who Trump fired by tweet). Known as "the congressman from Koch," Pompeo advanced a far right libertarian agenda laced with post-9/11 Islamophobia and spent nearly $65,000 in taxpayer money on lavish State Department dinners attended by his campaign donors, then tried to cover it up in his reports to Congress.[31]

Trump's cabinet was largely composed of ideologues who had spent their careers battling the very agencies they were hired to lead. For example, to head the Consumer Finance Protection Bureau (CFPB), the agency in charge of protecting consumers from being defrauded by banks, Trump appointed Tea Party favorite Mick Mulvaney, a former South Carolina congressman who once described the CFPB as a "sick, sad joke."[32] Mulvaney dismantled the CFPB's offices, fired its advisory board, and proposed an operations budget of zero. Under his watch, the number of CFPB enforcement actions plummeted, including those involving predatory payday lenders—an industry defined by its wanton greed—who had donated tens of thousands to Mulvaney's congressional campaigns and millions to Trump's presidential run.[33]

To helm the EPA, Trump nominated Oklahoma attorney general Scott Pruitt, who had made a career out of undermining pollution standards and who described himself as "a leading advocate against the EPA's activist agenda."[34] A notorious climate denier, Pruitt once claimed that global warming could be a good thing and help "humans flourish."[35] During his short stint as EPA chief, Pruitt faced more than a dozen inquiries into his use of government funds, which included installing biometric locks on his office door, a $43,000 soundproof phone booth, twenty-four-hour guards, and first-class travel.[36] According to a former aide, Pruitt and his staff also regularly—and illegally—"scrubbed" meetings from his official calendar that might "look bad," such as those with industry CEOs.[37] Eventually, bad press and congressional inquiries pressured Pruitt to resign. In his resignation letter, he lathered Trump: "I believe you are serving as President today because of God's providence."[38]

For the Department of Health and Human Services (HHS), Trump appointed Tom Price, an orthopedic surgeon turned Georgia congressman who led House Republicans' attempts to repeal the Affordable Care Act and privatize Medicare, and who spearheaded legislation that directly benefited drug companies in which he was heavily invested. Price resigned from HHS after making headlines for amassing almost half a million dollars in bills for chartered flights on taxpayers' dime.[39] Trump replaced him with Big Pharma's Alex Azar,[40] who as CEO of Eli Lily oversaw a sharp increase in the price of insulin and received a more than $2 billion fine for fraudulently promoting a treatment that was not approved by the Food and Drug Administration (FDA).[41]

Despite his image as an advocate for the "silent majority," Trump appointed more billionaires to his cabinet than any other president in U.S. history. For commerce secretary, he appointed billionaire investor Wilbur Ross, a known vulture capitalist who made his fortune off the backs of workers and retirees. Rudy Giuliani called Ross his "privatization advisor" and *Fortune* christened him the "king of bankruptcy" and "dean of distressed investing."[42] To head the Small Business Administration, he appointed billionaire Linda McMahon, cofounder of World Wrestling Entertainment. And as education secretary he installed Betsy DeVos, a religious ideologue whose family made billions off the cultish pyramid scheme Amway. In keeping with her family's fundamentalist history, DeVos supported creationism, advocated for school vouchers and privatization, worked to reduce the federal government's role in protecting civil rights in schools, and defended for-profit universities like Trump's that openly defrauded students.[43] Also in the mix was DeVos's brother Erik Prince, the Islamophobic[44] founder of the security and mercenary outfit Blackwater—a firm notorious for having massacred hundreds of innocent people during the Iraq War, including young children.[45]

Utilizing the revolving door between the White House and Wall Street that bipartisan presidents before him had well oiled, Trump appointed Goldman Sachs CIO Steve Mnuchin as his treasury secretary, and at least half a dozen other Goldman executives, including its former president, Gary Cohn, as chief economic advisor. During the 2007 global financial crisis, Mnuchin was a lead investor for IndyMac, a failed subprime lender that he transformed into a "foreclosure machine" under the name OneWest Bank.[46] For transportation, Trump appointed George W. Bush's labor secretary, Elaine Chao, a shipping heiress and wife of Senate Majority Leader Mitch McConnell. In her home state of Kentucky—one of the poorest in the nation—Chao had a reputation for mistreating "the help" and riding around in chauffeured vehicles. Together, she and McConnell were a driving force in Kentucky big-donor politics, known for shielding their Big Coal donors from liability in cases of gross malfeasance and devastating pollution.[47]

Trump exploited the status-honor of military officials, appointing more generals to top posts than any president since World War II—though none of his generals made it through his presidency.[48] Neither did his first five communications directors, nor his first three chiefs of staff. Trump's Veterans Affairs chief, David Shulkin, was let go after using taxpayer funds to bankroll a European vacation for himself and his wife.[49] Chief strategist Steve Bannon also left within the first year due to conflicts with White House staff. Nicknames like the "Prince of Darkness" and "Shadow President" captured Bannon's diabolical nature and his leading role in the ideological design of Trumpism. Three years after leaving the White House, Bannon was arrested by federal agents—while lounging on a $30 million, 150-foot superyacht belonging to an exiled Chinese billionaire—for defrauding donors through a fundraising campaign for a border wall.[50] In their investigation of the swindle, prosecutors revealed that some of the raised monies had been spent on jewelry, a golf cart, a luxury car, and cosmetic surgery.[51]

Some of Trump's cabinet nominees were never confirmed, even with a Republican majority in the Senate. Trump tried to replace Shulkin with his White House physician Ronny Jackson, but Jackson withdrew his name after Congress discovered allegations that he drank on the job and dispensed prescription drugs like Halloween candy, earning the nickname

"Candyman."[52] Trump's first choice for labor secretary, CEO of CKE Restaurants Andy Puzder, withdrew his name from consideration due to controversy surrounding his company's poor treatment of workers, which included paying low wages, forcing employees to forgo legally mandated breaks, lawsuits stemming from discriminatory practices, and sexual harassment.[53] He was also the subject of allegations of domestic abuse by his wife, who did a "tell all" about her relationship with Puzder on Oprah Winfrey's popular talk show.[54] Instead of Puzder, Trump appointed former Florida district attorney Alexander Acosta, but he too resigned after it was revealed that he had awarded billionaire pedophile Jeffrey Epstein a nonprosecution deal that allowed him to serve only thirteen months in jail, during which he was given daily leave off the grounds "for work."[55] Acosta also granted immunity to Epstein's "potential co-conspirators" rumored to include Bill Clinton, Prince Andrew, and other power elites. In granting the plea deal, Acosta effectively shut down an ongoing investigation that, by that time, had identified thirty-six of Epstein's hundreds of underage victims, some as young as eleven years old.[56]

Trumpian Justice

Trump was not the first U.S. president to blow past the limits of presidential power and position himself above the law—though he was, most certainly, the most extreme.[57] Even before becoming president, Trump operated as if the rules didn't apply, his career overseasoned with bunk lawsuits and shady contracts. As the institutional bedrock of the rule of law, the Department of Justice (DOJ) is supposed to operate independently of presidents and the executive and legislative branches. Previous DOJs and attorneys general (AGs)—like Bush Jr.'s Alberto Gonzales or Obama's Eric Holder—have violated this norm in providing legal cover for their bosses. But Trump's Justice Department was far more brazen and, in some instances, his AGs' rhetoric and policies were openly dictatorial.

As his first attorney general, Trump selected Alabama senator Jeff Sessions, a conservative hardliner and former federal prosecutor with a reputation for being openly racist. Sessions was an early supporter of Trump's candidacy and the only sitting U.S. senator to support his longshot campaign. As AG, Sessions exacerbated mass incarceration by instructing prosecutors to impose the harshest sentences possible for drug offenses.[58] He rolled back restrictions protecting low-income defendants from excessive fines and rules aimed at checking police misconduct. He advised the death penalty for major drug offenders and brought back civil asset forfeiture, which allowed police to seize the property of those suspected (but not charged) of crimes, and thus gave them an incentive to do so.[59] He rolled back Obama-era policies to end discrimination against transgender students.[60] And he closed the Office for Access to Justice, charged with mitigating severe inequalities in the criminal justice system by expanding access to legal counsel. For Wall Street and the Fortune 500, on the other hand, he neutered DOJ's fraud division overseeing white-collar crime and stopped enforcing banking regulations altogether. He also shelved ongoing investigations or settled them for minimal fines, including a probe into a multinational bank's involvement in drug-money laundering, and another case in which a major bank was caught discriminating against minority borrowers.[61]

As Trump's lead advisor on border enforcement, Sessions cracked down on immigrants. He threatened to cut federal funding for sanctuary cities and prosecute their local officials. He ruled that victims of domestic abuse or gang violence would no longer qualify for asylum, and for months, stopped refugees from entering the country, banning those from war-torn Syria indefinitely. Sessions also supported Trump's xenophobic "Muslim ban," which suspended the entry of immigrants from seven Muslim-majority countries: Syria, Iran, Iraq, Libya, Sudan, Yemen, and Somalia. More than 1,000 U.S. diplomats officially condemned the order and tens of thousands of people flooded into airports across the country to protest its implementation.[62]

To justify its crackdowns, the Trump administration mandated the creation of a public list delineating crimes committed by undocumented people. It increased the number of agents at the Mexico-U.S. border by the thousands and directed federal funding to construct a medieval border wall and additional detention facilities, often for profit. While Bill Clinton had schemed to use private prisons as a way to reduce government spending, the Obama administration tried to phase them out due to numerous reports of corruption and heinous living conditions.[63] Trump campaigned on expanding them and in doing so helped their stock values soar. His most cruel and controversial policy, however, involved separating children from their parents as a supposed deterrent to illegal immigration, an idea that Attorney General Sessions justified through a mix of scare tactics and Bible thumping.[64]

Before Trump took office, a wave of unaccompanied children had arrived at the southern U.S. border, some as young as three years old. The Obama administration responded by increasing deportations and holding some of the children in cages with concrete floors.[65] Between 2011 and 2013, some 2 million immigrants were put in detention, compared to 1.57 million during the entire Bush presidency.[66] Despite this cruelty, the coherence between the Obama and Trump administrations' immigration policies should not obscure their fundamental differences. Among Obama's important accomplishments was the humane and popular Deferred Action for Childhood Arrivals (DACA) program and the pathway to citizenship that he attempted to create for undocumented immigrants through the Development, Relief, and Education for Alien Minors (DREAM) Act. Critics contend that had Obama pushed for stronger immigration reforms at the start of his presidency, when Democrats controlled both chambers of Congress, the country might have avoided the Trumpian horrors to come. Nonetheless, Obama's hawkish approach paled in comparison to that of Trump's, whose family separations were not just a matter of militarism and overpolicing, but overt expressions of brutality hatched by unapologetic white supremacists.

Leading the administration on immigration policy was Sessions's former communications director, Stephen Miller, an avowed white nationalist who sought to not only bar and deport immigrants from entry but also to punish them. According to one official, "Miller made clear to us that, if you start to treat children badly enough, you'll be able to convince other parents to stop trying to come with theirs."[67] Their sadistic plan hit a roadblock, however, after a recording from a detention center leaked to the public in which small children could be heard sobbing for their parents, crying so hard they can hardly breathe. Also on the recording, a Border Patrol agent can be heard mocking the weeping children, saying, "Well, here we have an orchestra."[68] The leaked recording spurred a federal judge to order the by then thousands of imprisoned children to be reunited with their families. Because of the administration's malice and incompetence, however, it took months to locate some of the parents, many of whom had been deported and may never see their children again.[69]

Sessions's tenure came to an end after months of conflict with Trump regarding his decision to recuse himself from a DOJ investigation into Russian interference in the 2016 election. After lying about his interactions with Russian officials during his Senate confirmation hearings, Sessions tried to save face by removing himself from the investigation and allowing his deputy Rod Rosenstein to appoint former FBI director Robert Mueller to lead it. Sessions's recusal provoked Trump to ask, "Where's my Roy Cohn?"—a reference to his former mentor and fixer, the viperous New York City lawyer who began his legal career red-baiting Americans alongside Senator Joseph McCarthy. Trump repeatedly pressured Sessions to reverse his decision, calling him "an idiot" and publicly humiliating him with bigoted insults like "mentally retarded" and "dumb southerner."[70]

In response to Trump's pressures, Sessions asserted that as attorney general he would "not be improperly influenced by political considerations."[71] Eventually, Trump replaced Sessions with William Barr, Bush Sr.'s attorney general, who also had been involved in the Russia probe but chose *not* to recuse himself. Before assuming his post atop Trump's DOJ, Barr had sent a long, unsolicited legal memo to Rosenstein and, without knowing the facts of the case, argued that the president's Article II powers rendered him incapable of obstructing justice.[72] The Senate Democrats who confirmed him hoped—or, better, fantasized—that Barr would be a moderating force. That was despite his widely known extremist views on presidential power, including his career-long devotion to *unitary executive theory*—the belief that the president is the ultimate authority over the executive branch and its agencies.[73] Given this belief, Barr was a likely candidate to help absolve Trump from any illegal doings and undercut investigations into them, which is exactly what he did. With his AG's blessing, Trump fired inspectors general, intimidated whistleblowers, and obstructed probes into his business dealings. When investigators requested documents or testimony, sometimes under subpoena, DOJ officials often refused, invoking "executive privilege" and "national security."

The Mueller investigation did not end with legal action against Trump, as many had hoped, but it did expose the criminal shadiness of his associates. Campaign chairman Paul Manafort was charged with financial crimes related to his lobbying work in Ukraine; former national security advisor Army Lt. Gen. Michael Flynn was caught lying to the FBI about his contact with Russian officials; and longtime friend Roger Stone was charged with obstruction of an official proceeding, lying to Congress, and witness tampering. Trump's personal attorney and fixer Michael Cohen pled guilty to making false statements to Congress regarding hush money he paid to porn actress Stormy Daniels, with whom Trump had an affair. AG Barr trod far outside the ethical boundaries of his office by intervening in the conviction and sentencing of Stone and Flynn, both of whom, along with Bannon, Trump pardoned on his way out the door.

The other fault line of judicial power that Trump sought to exploit, and that may go down as his most significant achievement, involved reshaping the country's legal system by placing far-right judges on the federal bench—Senator Mitch McConnell's legacy project. McConnell infamously obstructed Obama's appointment of Merrick Garland to the Supreme Court with 342 days still left in the president's second term, disingenuously arguing that since it was an election year, the nomination should be "up to the people." This posture flew in the face of precedent, as seventeen Supreme Court nominees had previously been confirmed during election years. Nonetheless, McConnell resented Obama's high-brow professorial, even lecturing, ways—once asserting that Obama "talks down to people"—and was happy to stick it to him. That he did, using the Supreme Court nomination process and his promise to overturn *Roe v. Wade* to help a godless Trump secure the evangelical vote that was so decisive to his longshot victory.

Trump openly outsourced the selection of judges to right-wing groups like the Federalist Society, installing more than 230 on the federal bench. That included appointing three new justices to the U.S. Supreme Court of the United States (SCOTUS), giving it a six-to-three conservative majority. Ten of Trump's federal court nominees were deemed unqualified by the American Bar Association; seven were nonetheless appointed. Some of his nominees had never argued a motion, tried a case, or taken a deposition. One of them wandered cemeteries hunting for ghosts and blogged positively about the KKK; another claimed that transgender children were all a part of "Satan's plan."[74] Among those who made it through confirmation, a significant number were young and markedly more conservative than those appointed by previous presidents.[75]

In terms of his SCOTUS appointments, both Justices Neil Gorsuch and Brett Kavanaugh were known for writing pro-business opinions and for their fidelity to the far-right agenda, including on voting and abortion rights.[76] Kavanaugh's confirmation process was especially bruising, in part because of a highly credible and public accusation of sexual assault by psychology professor Christine Blasey Ford[77]—but also because Kavanaugh had argued in writing that presidents should not be subject to investigation while in office. In advance of his confirmation hearing, the White House refused to hand over documents that Congress requested regarding Kavanaugh's work in the Bush administration, citing "constitutional privilege"—which members of Congress said was a blatant bunk-assertion of an actual legal privilege.[78]

With the death of Justice Ruth Bader Ginsburg, Trump confirmed his third nominee, Amy Coney Barrett, right before the November election, before Ginsburg was even buried. Barrett had no trial experience, and until Trump appointed her to the Seventh Circuit of Appeals in 2017, she had never worked as a judge or counsel. What did she have was a household of seven school-age children and the kind of "soccer mom" image that conservatives relish. She also had a demonstrated commitment to the militant and inhumane agenda of the Federalist Society, which helped to underwrite her campaign for the SCOTUS seat by sponsoring a multi-stop speaking tour for her.[79] The effects of Trump's SCOTUS appointments, and those of his predecessors', will have far-reaching consequences on all aspects of American life. During the 2021–2022 session alone, this Right-dominated Court severely restricted the EPA's power to perform oversight, made it easier to carry a gun, and undermined women's decades-old right to bodily autonomy by overturning *Roe v. Wade*.[80]

HEALTH CARE AND TAX CUTS

Hours after being sworn in as president, Trump signed an executive order aimed at reversing the Affordable Care Act (ACA), which GOP lawmakers had vowed to "repeal and replace." Prior to that, Republicans had made several attempts to undo the legislation, through amendments to the federal budget and other means, but had not offered an official policy alternative. After Trump's election, "repeal and replace" proposals by individual senators came flooding in, all of which would have thrown tens of millions of people off their health insurance. Most of the proposals targeted Medicaid, which provides two-thirds of all funding for nursing homes and is a lifeline for tens of millions of low-income and disabled people. Behind closed doors, Democrats gave Trump foe Senator John McCain a thumbs up on increased defense spending in exchange for his dramatic thumbs down on a much-anticipated vote to repeal the ACA, breaking party ranks and denying Trump an early win. Republicans recovered from the setback by passing the largest tax cut in U.S. history, one that once again grossly favored corporations and the wealthy.

During his presidential campaign, Trump stated with regard to taxes, "I am willing to pay more, and you know what, the wealthy are willing to pay more."[81] But right after the election, at Manhattan's exclusive 21 Club, he assured wealthy patrons, "We'll get your taxes down, don't worry."[82] Trump sold his tax cut plan as a gift to "the folks who work in the mail rooms and the machine shops of America," but nearly all of its benefits—more than 80 percent—went to the wealthiest individuals. For those in middle- and lower-income brackets, their taxes would increase over time.[83]

Trump reduced the corporate tax rate from 35 percent to 21 percent, with most of the windfall going to investors in the form of dividends and stock buybacks. He justified the reduction using the talking points of lobbyists and corporate-friendly politicians, claiming that U.S. companies were among "the highest-taxed in the world." It was common knowledge, however, that the *effective* tax rate paid by many U.S. corporations was far less than 35 percent because of special breaks and loopholes in the tax code. In fact, dozens of Fortune 500 companies still do not pay any income taxes and some get rebates, despite the fact that corporate profits are at an all-time high and CEOs earn hundreds of times more than the average worker.[84] For the investor class, Trump lowered taxes on capital gains, and for the unspeakably rich, he reduced the estate tax—a multi-billion-dollar giveaway to the wealthiest 0.2 percent, including an estimated $4 billion for his own family. He also proposed a new tax system for corporations stashing their profits overseas that allowed them to avoid paying hundreds of billions to Uncle Sam. In 2020, the Tax Justice Network estimated that multinational corporations and the wealthy are costing governments over $427 billion each year due to international tax abuse.[85]

Republicans paired their $1.9 trillion tax cut legislation with a budget proposal to cut $5 trillion (over ten years) in programs that working-class Americans rely on and desperately need. At a time when more than fifteen million families did not have enough food to eat and more than half a million were without shelter, Republicans proposed cuts to nutrition assistance and affordable housing programs. Despite the fact that twenty-eight million people did not have health insurance, they put forth policies that would block or restrict access to care.[86] And although Trump promised that he would "do everything within my power not to touch Social Security," his budget proposals for 2018, 2019, and 2020 all included cuts to Social Security programs and Medicare.[87]

COVID-19

In late January 2020, health officials raised red flags that a novel coronavirus plaguing mainland China was spreading to the United States. As a senior medical advisor at the Department of Veterans Affairs put it in an email to a group of public health officials, "Any way you cut it, this is going to be bad."[88] By then, the Trump administration had "deconstructed" parts of "the administrative state" charged with training field epidemiologists in China on how to respond to disease outbreaks and ended funding for pandemic early-warning programs there.[89] After the first U.S. case of COVID-19 was recorded that month, Trump's only solution was to restrict flights arriving from China and spout xenophobic quips about "the Chinese virus" and "kung flu," provoking a sharp rise in anti-Asian hate crime and speech. HHS secretary Alex Azar, among others, warned him of the coming calamity, but the president accused Azar of being "alarmist," and to a crowd of supporters in South Carolina, he described the coronavirus as Democrats' "new hoax."[90] Toward the end of February, when Democrats demanded funding for pandemic relief, Senator Mitch McConnell accused them of "performative outrage."[91]

Trump appointed a Coronavirus Task Force headed by Mike Pence, who as Indiana's governor promoted prayer as a policy for mitigating a major HIV outbreak in his state instead of a proven needle exchange program. Trump continued to politicize and downplay the threat, assuring the public that the pandemic was under control, and by springtime, it would just go away.[92] He did not call a national health emergency until mid-March, by which time COVID-19 had spread to all fifty states. With the massive influx of deathly ill patients, hospitals were buckling under the pressure to such an extent that the military had to be called in to construct emergency facilities. New York was especially hard hit. By early April, the city was seeing about 10,000 new cases a day (that number would peak above 50,000 cases per day in January 2022).[93] With fatalities accumulating beyond the capacity of hospital morgues, refrigerated trucks lined the streets to transport the dead.

Trump's pandemic management plan was a free market disaster with all the ideological trappings of "states' rights" and attacks on "big government," as well as the grifting of federal resources and utter neglect of everyday people. As hospitals across the country experienced major shortages of tests, ventilators, and personal protective equipment (PPE) for frontline workers, states were forced to outbid each other in a scramble for supplies at inflated prices. In some cases, the Federal Emergency Management Agency (FEMA) or foreign governments outbid states, whose orders for medical supplies were then confiscated and diverted to other locations. Governors were forced to work their personal networks and call in favors to access lifesaving equipment.[94]

At a White House briefing in April, Jared Kushner announced that "the notion of the federal stockpile was it's supposed to be our stockpile. It's not supposed to be states' stockpiles that they then use."[95] But supporting states is exactly what the stockpile is meant to do. The White House's own website said as much until the administration scrubbed it after Kushner's comments were widely panned. Way out of his depth, Kushner had been running a shadow coronavirus task force with a team of about a dozen young volunteers drawn from venture capital and private equity firms. With no experience in supply chains or equipment procurement—much less in emergency and pandemic preparedness—Kushner's Wall Street youth were instructed to prioritize tips from Trump's political allies and business associates, resulting in billions of dollars in no-bid contracts for questionable and unvetted businesses.[96]

In late March, the White House called a meeting of heavy-hitter corporate advisors to help figure out how the private sector could help disseminate protective gear and medical equipment throughout the country.

The group recommended that the administration invoke the Defense Production Act, a World War II–era law that gives the president the authority to expedite the supply of materials from the U.S. industrial base to serve the national defense. Sitting at the head of the conference table, in an oversized chair like Trump's on *The Apprentice*, Kushner responded that, "The federal government is not going to lead this response. It's up to the states to figure out what they want to do." When the group recommended they focus on hard-hit New York, Kushner said of the state's Democratic governor, "His people are going to suffer and that's their problem." One of the attendees pointed out that Americans were being forced to bid against each other for supplies, which was driving up prices, to which Kushner replied, "Free markets will solve this. That is not the role of government."[97]

Around this time, Trump directed the FDA to test certain medications for treating COVID-19, including hydroxychloroquine, which is used to treat malaria. Studies found that hydroxychloroquine did not have significant effects for COVID-19 treatment and in some patients caused heart problems.[98] That did not stop a handful of quack doctors, Rudy Giuliani, and Fox News's Laura Ingraham from promoting the drug—parroting the president, who claimed that he himself was taking it. After Trump urged, "What do you have to lose? Take it," a slew of overdoses and lethal misuses of chloroquine and hydroxychloroquine were reported across the country.[99] Worse, at a White House press conference at the end of April, Trump suggested that the virus could be combated by injecting disinfectants into the body.[100] "Is there a way we can do something like that by injection, inside, or almost a cleaning?" he asked. The following day, the manufacturer of household disinfectants Dettol and Lysol issued a statement warning the public not to ingest or inject their products.[101]

With much of the country in disarray and locking down, Congress bickered over how to provide relief and contain the rapidly spreading virus. This came after four U.S. senators were exposed for insider trading, using their privileged knowledge about the coming pandemic to shore up their own financial interests while publicly downplaying the threat. Republican North Carolina senator Richard Burr sold more than $1 million in stock before the market crashed, just as he was assuring his constituents that the pandemic was under control.[102] Congress passed a $2.2 trillion bill, the Coronavirus Aid, Relief, and Economic Security (CARES) Act, that included expanded unemployment benefits, a one-time direct payment to U.S. citizens, student loan forbearance, and a moratorium on evictions to prevent thirty to forty million people from losing their homes. Those provisions, among others, barely kept middle-class and low-income Americans afloat, and like so many bailouts before it, the greatest benefits went to big business and the wealthy.

Large parts of the CARES Act had nothing to do with the virus and were simply handouts to corporate and Wall Street lobbyists and donors, including hundreds of billions in tax breaks tailored specifically to benefit large companies.[103] The act included a program to support small businesses and protect workers from layoffs, but as usual the banks put in charge prioritized their friends over underserved people and small businesses. Medium-sized businesses with strong banking relationships were much better positioned to access the program, and for already-flush private equity firms, universities, charter schools, and even celebrities, COVID relief was a veritable gold rush.[104]

From January through March 2020, the U.S. economy contracted nearly 5 percent, and by April the unemployment rate had risen to almost 15 percent. Instead of acknowledging the necessity of shutting down the economy to save lives, Trump and Attorney General Barr threatened governors with legal retribution for authorizing lockdowns.[105] Against clear scientific advice, and with the death toll rising, *New York Times* columnist Thomas Friedman, a reliable mouthpiece of neoliberal propaganda, wrote in his March 22, 2020, opinion column, "But as so many of our businesses shut down and millions begin to be laid off, some experts are beginning to ask: 'Wait a minute! *What the hell are we doing to ourselves?* To our economy? To our next generation? Is this cure—even for a short while—worse than the disease?' "[106] That night, Trump tweeted: "WE CANNOT LET THE CURE BE WORSE THAN THE PROBLEM ITSELF."

As the rates of infections skyrocketed, Trump stoked right-wing resistance to scientific guidance on social distancing, mask wearing, quarantines, and the lifesaving lockdowns. In mid-April, conservative groups across the country staged public, and sometimes violent, protests against state governments, arguing that the lockdowns and mask-wearing requirements infringed on their personal freedoms. In Michigan, pro-Trump supporters rushed the state house to intimidate Governor Gretchen Whitmer, many of them carrying guns. Some plotted to kidnap and assassinate her, but were apprehended. In late May, a very different set of protests broke out in more than two hundred cities in response to the murder of George Floyd, a Black man who was choked to death by a police officer kneeling, for nearly nine minutes, on his neck—one of many such killings by police over the last several years. In some parts of the country, armed Trump supporters counterprotested the anti-racism demonstrations, creating a whirlwind of chaos in what appeared to be an elite-manufactured civil war.

As the country erupted in civil unrest, the number of coronavirus cases passed two million and the death toll reached more than 100,000. In response to those devastating numbers, Trump argued that COVID-19 testing was to blame and bragged to attendees at a rally in Oklahoma that he had ordered a slowdown in testing. In July, he called the rise in COVID-19 cases "fodder for the fake news" and said that he was "okay with testing" even though it "makes us look bad."[107] In place of actual health and infectious disease experts, he took advice from crackpots like neuroradiologist Scott Atlas, a fellow at Stanford's conservative Hoover Institute who became a White House pandemic advisor without having any background in infectious disease or epidemiology. Along with radical market libertarian Senator Rand Paul, an ophthalmologist, Atlas promoted "herd immunity"—the idea that mass immunity could be achieved by just allowing the coronavirus to spread—to justify keeping businesses open and workers working. This, despite the reality that such a laissez-faire approach would have exponentially increased the death roll and likelihood of more deadly and contagious variants, not to mention the unspeakable strain on the health care system. Months later, Paul would lead, and fundraise over, an anti-science crusade against renowned infectious disease expert Dr. Anthony Fauci that resulted in multiple death threats against the doctor and his family.

With elements of the CARES Act set to expire and COVID cases topping the five million mark, Democrats called for another stimulus to aid states and cover the costs of mail-in voting for the November election. Republicans resisted, at first delaying, then arguing for a smaller expenditure. As some states teetered on the verge of insolvency, Mitch McConnell said, "Let them go bankrupt." Importantly, Trump also started promoting the idea that mail-in voting was "corrupt," even though the last time he himself had voted, it was by mail.[108] With the possibility of an all mail-in ballot election on the near horizon, Trump appointed as postmaster general Louis DeJoy, a big-money campaign donor with no relevant experience, and who had major investments in companies that would directly benefit from privatizing the U.S. Postal Service.[109] Once installed, DeJoy made a series of operational changes, such as forbidding overtime for postal workers and dismantling mail-sorting machines, that would have prevented the Postal Service from meeting the demands of a largely vote-by-mail election. After these changes predictably plunged the postal system into chaos—veterans and seniors' prescription drugs were not being delivered on time—outrage crossed party lines and the Trump administration ceased its assault on this vital governmental service.

As Trump sowed suspicion around electoral integrity, Congress continued to falter in its efforts to provide relief. Playing "hardball" before the 2020 elections under the assumption that Democrats would win additional seats in both chambers, House Speaker Nancy Pelosi refused relief proposals just under $2 trillion. Trump lost the election, but he won some seventy-four million votes, and his party nearly took back the House, both of which gave Republicans unexpected leverage in relief negotiations. Among their priorities was liability relief for corporations, which was of paramount concern to their corporate donors in light of horrific worker abuses associated with the pandemic. At the Tyson pork processing facility in Waterloo, Iowa, for example, managers had been forcing workers to stay on the job and laying bets on which of them would get infected with the deadly virus.

As COVID vaccines rolled out, more people were dying *daily* than the total lives lost on 9/11, but Trump continued to politicize masks, lockdowns, and vaccines as a matter of states' and individuals' rights. His disinformation cost untold numbers of people their health or their lives, while he and his staff received the highest level of care and experimental treatments. Trump's own bout with COVID was sensationalized vis-à-vis the image of a strongman battling and defeating the virus. That included a spectacle surrounding his return from Walter Reed to the White House in which Trump performed a dramatic salute to Marine One, then—up-lit and with caked-on make-up—bragged about being "cured" (while trying to suppress his COVID-induced panting). The intent was to portray Trump's recovery as evidence of his superior strength and the virus's triviality and "weakness." This, despite the fact that hospitals at the time were resembling war-time medical centers and thousands of COVID-19 patients were gasping for their last breaths as traumatized hospital workers struggled to care for them. Essential workers and the sick did not make it into Trump's narrative of the pandemic. His America was all brute strength, states' rights, and market freedom.

By the numbers, Trump passed a $1.9 trillion tax cut for the wealthy, and *Forbes* estimated that his corrupt dealings while in office helped his businesses earn $2.4 billion.[110] He was impeached twice, a historical first, and made tens of thousands of false statements. He spent one out of five days of his presidency on the golf course.[111] His administration was responsible for more executions than any U.S. president in the last seventy-five years.[112] Hate crimes surged by over 20 percent and thousands of children were separated from their parents.[113] Poverty increased, and COVID-19 killed hundreds of thousands—many of whose deaths, experts say, could have been avoided.[114]

On his way out the door, Trump forced vote recounts and brought lawsuits to have his election loss overturned, including strongarming a

Georgia official to "find" him enough votes to win the state.[115] He proliferated conspiracies that the election had been stolen and urged his supporters to "stop the steal." In protesting the election results, some of his followers went so far as to terrorize poll workers and election officials outside their homes.[116] Some issued death threats, and the speaker of the House and senate majority leader's residences were vandalized. In states across the country, brazen intimidation and disruption of voting processes—and growing Republican dominance on election boards and in state and local governments—suggested that the U.S. electoral system, and even the semblance of democracy, was in peril and would likely be for some time.

A few months before the 2020 election, during a presidential debate, moderators asked Trump about his association with militia and white supremacists. When asked specifically about a group called the Proud Boys, Trump replied, "Proud Boys stand back, and stand by," which many, including the Proud Boys themselves, viewed as an unambiguous call for readiness. With the country unsure that he would follow through on a peaceful transition of power, Trump staged a "Save America" rally on January 6, 2021, the day Congress was scheduled to count the electoral votes and declare Joe Biden the winner. The chatter on social media and right-wing outlets indicated that the crowd would be armed and violent. Some said that it was a cause they would die for, and others went so far as to threaten the lives of police and members of Congress in the name of "saving the country." The threats were so intense that even the right-wing social media outlet Parler reported it to law enforcement.

During the rally, Trump encouraged his supporters to march to the Capitol and "fight like hell" or "you won't have a country anymore."[117] The crowd did as they were told, storming the Capitol and clubbing and severely injuring journalists and police as they invaded the building. While rampaging through the stately halls of Congress, some waved Confederate flags and looted offices. They also called out to "hang Mike Pence" for not bending to Trump's pressures to disrupt the election certification process over which the vice president presided. Capitol police on site were woefully unprepared—despite the deluge of intelligence that law enforcement, security agencies, and social media companies had reported—and some of them were severely injured or killed. One photojournalist was dragged down stairs and thrown over a wall. In the offices and on the House floor, elected officials and their staffs hid under tables and behind chairs.

Pictorial postmortems of January 6 show rioters dressed in gear indicating membership in QAnon and paramilitary groups like the Oathkeepers that had gathered steam during Trump's presidency. An online conspiracy group, QAnon adherents claim that a cabal of liberal elites, who worship Satan and traffic children for sex, had infiltrated Trump's White House. Some of them believe that members of this cabal are part of a reptilian alien race disguised as humans. In December 2020, an NPR-Ipsos poll found that 17 percent of Americans believe this conspiracy theory to be true, and the year Trump became president, two members of QAnon were elected to Congress.[118]

In the months following January 6, Republican Party officials, some of whom had hidden under desks and run for cover that day, echoed Trump's claims of widespread election fraud and elevated it as a central issue. Even Mike Pence downplayed the threats to his person. GOP propaganda of a stolen election was so effective that by the end of October 2021, a poll found that 35 percent of voters said they believed that the 2020 election should be overturned.[119] Bowing further to the Trumpian winds, in February 2022 the Republican National Committee voted to censure Representatives Liz Cheney and Adam Kinzinger for serving on a Democrat-led congressional committee to investigate the events of January 6. In their resolution, Republicans accused Cheney and Kinzinger of participating in the "persecution of ordinary citizens engaged in legitimate political discourse"—a clear and open endorsement of hooligan violence.[120]

In addition to political violence and false claims of a stolen election, pervasive disinformation around the coronavirus vaccine profoundly impacted newly elected president Joe Biden's ability to calm the country and mitigate the pandemic. By summer 2021, over eighty million people in the United States were refusing vaccination out of fear or in the name of "liberty" and "freedom." In Florida, Governor Ron DeSantis, a hardliner, forbid mask mandates in schools despite drastic increases in deaths associated with the COVID-19 Delta variant, including among infants and young children. Instead, he recommended a monoclonal antibody treatment sold by the drug company Regeneron, in which one of his major donors, Citadel CEO Ken Griffin, was heavily invested. Anti-vaxxers also spread flawed and fraudulent medical studies about treating COVID-19 with ivermectin, a drug used to treat animals.

Against this tumultuous backdrop, Biden attempted to implement a legislative program that included some reassertion of federal government oversight in matters of environmental, banking, and labor regulation and limited public investment in social programs and infrastructure. His model involved using government to stimulate investment by the private sector and expand its infrastructural role, rather than actually center the public sector and state planning.

Biden did emphasize unions in a context of growing worker empowerment and strike activity that the ever-tightening labor market was providing. And he proposed tax increases on the wealthy, corporate profits, and capital gains to fund public spending, including an agreement among major countries to implement a global minimum corporate tax. But with his approval ratings in free fall by November 2021—amid rising crime rates, a botched troop withdrawal in Afghanistan, flawed immigration policies, and importantly, mounting inflation—Democrats found themselves in a panic to pass *something* into law.

Despite having control of both chambers and the presidency, Democrats were embarrassingly divided over two bills reflecting the president's major priorities—one on infrastructure and the other on social spending (called "Build Back Better"). Biden's corporate-friendly infrastructure bill had already passed in the Senate with bipartisan support, but the party's progressive wing—which had grown, tenuously, into a majority coalition—wisely used infrastructure as a bargaining chip to pass the social spending legislation. For them, the infrastructure bill—with its tens of billions in new subsidies for the fossil fuel industry masked as climate solutions—represented the corporate wing of the party, while social spending, paid for with taxes on the wealthy, was theirs (even though the bill was laden with means testing, tax credit frameworks, and hybrid private sector-state-federal funding).[121]

As Democrats flip-flopped all over the cable news, a "problem solver's caucus," headed by Democratic New Jersey congressman Josh Gottheimer, pushed back in favor of the infrastructure bill and against social spending—raking in major fundraising hauls from donors whose taxes would have increased under the social spending bill.[122] Those efforts were echoed in the Senate by Democrats Joe Manchin of West Virginia and Kyrsten Sinema of Arizona, who had already opposed Biden's COVID-19 stimulus checks for the poor and middle class and blocked his efforts to raise the minimum wage, lift the Senate filibuster, and thwart partisan gerrymandering. A lifelong deficit hawk, Manchin told reporters, "I cannot accept our economy, or, basically, our society, moving towards an entitlement mentality."[123] He also claimed that parents were using the child tax credit to buy drugs and accused poor people of using paid sick leave to go on "hunting trips."[124]

For his support, Manchin demanded that the social spending bill be drastically cut. He also opposed popular and much-needed programs like Medicare expansion to cover dental, hearing, and vision; free community college; paid family and medical leave; the child tax credit; and programs for clean energy. Progressives and the news media called him out for his ties to Big Coal and antagonism toward the EPA, as well as his driving a Maserati while representing one of the poorest states in the nation. A old-time West Virginia politician, Manchin has long been as dirty as the fossil fuels powering his career, including previous membership on ALEC, where he advocated against Medicare and Medicaid and for Big Pharma.

Manchin and Sinema's obstructions and the party's inability to mediate between its centrist and progressive wings created the appearance of chaos around Biden—the kind that erupts when a president tries to serve two masters. Because of the popularity of the progressive agenda, centrist Democrats were forced to balance the desires of their constituents with those of their corporate benefactors. As usual, the latter prevailed. With just six of the most left-leaning members voting nay, the progressive alliance gave in under pressure from Speaker Pelosi and the Congressional Black Caucus. To raise Biden's poll numbers against the threat of another Trump presidency, and hush Republican sneers about rudderless Democrats, Congress passed the infrastructure bill without voting for the social spending legislation. Hours after the vote, austerity hawk Gottheimer promised to vote for the progressive bill only if Congressional Budget Office scoring showed that it was paid for with offsets—that, even though the infrastructure bill he had just voted yes on was expected to increase the federal deficit.

In the end, the social spending bill was cast aside and investigations of Trump and the events of January 6 dominated the Democratic agenda. Amid runaway rates of inflation, neoliberal pundits[125]—led by none other than Obama economic advisors Larry Summers and Steven Rattner[126]—blamed the spiking prices and tight labor market on Biden's COVID-19 stimulus spending,[127] echoing GOP talking points about "wage inflation" and the government "paying people to not work" and putting "too much money in people's pockets."[128] They made these arguments in the face of blatant price gouging by corporate monopolists[129] and clear global supply-chain disruptions associated with the Ukraine war and global resurgence of COVID-19. They also made them knowing full well that workers' wage increases had remained far below price increases and productivity, even for frontline workers whose pay had modestly increased when the pandemic rendered their work life threatening.[130] And they made them knowing that the COVID-19 stimulus was absolutely necessary for preventing starvation and death among the many millions of people languishing in mile-long food pantry lines and intensive care units.

To his credit, when inflation began to rear its ugly head, Biden and the Federal Reserve chairman he reappointed, Jerome Powell, adopted a dovish approach. This was out of character for a Fed that had long proven to be a reliable enforcer of neoliberal discipline. As inflation worsened, however, Powell fell in line with the Summers way. And while Biden pushed back on the anti-worker, pro-business discourse, he allowed the anti-public spending sentiment to undermine his policy agenda, including his promise to pass a trillions-dollar spending bill like Build Back Better. In an attempt to confront soaring gas prices, moreover, Biden expanded permitting of domestic oil and gas drilling on public lands—more than Trump approved during the first three years of his presidency[131]—and Democrats turned to the usual neoliberal tools of deregulation and free trade.[132] Their continued failure and unwillingness to meet the material and emotional needs of working people, and their strategy to go all-in on prosecuting Trump rather than address the root causes of Trumpism—of which they are a part—once again set the stage for the coming of the Far Right to political power.

CHAPTER 4

The Military

On December 10, 2009, almost a year into his presidency, Barack Obama stood before kings, queens, and heads of state in Oslo, Norway, to accept the Nobel Peace Prize. The prize committee said that they selected him for his commitment to nuclear nonproliferation and his "extraordinary efforts to strengthen international diplomacy and cooperation between peoples," including his outreach to the Middle East at a time when the United States was engaged in multiple theaters of war there.[1] During his speech, lauded by the likes of Newt Gingrich and Karl Rove, Obama laid out his "humanitarian" rationale for U.S. imperialism, positioning war as a fact of human civilization and an imperative of the times: "I face the world as it is, and cannot stand idle in the face of threats to the American people. . . . To say that force is sometimes necessary is not a call to cynicism—it is a recognition of history; the imperfections of man and the limits of reason."[2]

C. Wright Mills observed a similar sentiment among state and military leaders of the postwar era, remarking that in America "[t]he only seriously accepted plan for 'peace' is the fully loaded pistol."[3] Since Mills wrote that, the United States has been engaged in five major wars and nonstop conflict.[4] It has overthrown democratically elected leaders and installed despots in their place. Under the aegis of domino theory, it sanctioned the mass murder and poisoning of millions of East Asian and Latin American civilians.[5] After the Cold War, it conducted "interventions" in Eastern Europe and the Horn of Africa. When the World Trade Center was attacked, the United States waged two major, protracted wars in the Middle East and ordered untold numbers of drone strikes. Today, it runs about 750 military bases across the globe,[6] and its special forces are waging secret wars in at least eighty countries.[7]

After the collapse of the Berlin Wall, "globalization" became the mantra for the emergence of a new, supranational layer of authority driven by capital and facilitated by advances in information and communication technologies.[8] Without a rival superpower to check its dominance, the United States and its allied network of state and corporate leaders were given a free hand to impose neoliberal structural adjustment on less powerful nations and wage military interventions to realize their imperial objectives. Akin to the internet, the architecture for this new world order involved complex interrelationships among people, objects, ideas, and information operating across unprecedented spatiotemporal scales. This intensified interplay of states, corporations, and nongovernmental actors yielded new forms of social and financial connectivity, but also increased the potential for multinodal threats and cataclysmic violence.

In 2012, Chairman of the Joint Chiefs of Staff General Martin Dempsey announced that the U.S. Army was moving to a global networked approach to warfare defined by advanced technology, lighter manpower, and robust international partnerships.[9] As part of this new way, the United States and its allies developed intelligence-driven strategies capable of surveilling and comprehending a more totalized grid of security threats and distributed warfare. In the digital age, every object, terrain, and organism on Earth can be reduced to a series of data points to be tracked, and neutralized, in an instant. U.S. heads of state have exploited this limitless and amorphous frontier to validate once taboo policies—such as regime change and preemptive war—by raising the specter of perpetual struggle against fluid and nonlocal enemies. Such was the rationale of the Bush Doctrine, which President Obama criticized on the campaign trail, then adopted as official U.S. policy. Obama's use of soldierless drones and precision bombs created the appearance of bloodless warfare while forming a surveillance bubble around the globe to expand intelligence capacities and clandestinely proliferate signature strikes on military-age men and other demographically determined enemies.

This expansion of executive power is exactly what the founders sought to prevent when they drafted a constitutional framework for declaring war. In his landmark farewell address, President George Washington asserted that the nation must "avoid the necessity of those overgrown Military establishments, which under any form of Government are inauspicious to liberty . . . "[10] Following the experience of the British monarchy, in which the king monopolized military power—raising armies in addition to his role as commander in chief—the founders established a model of a standing army that would expand in times of emergency and recede in peacetime. Once the emergency was over, the country would demilitarize as soldiers returned to civilian life. This model prevailed until the close of World War II, when the United States began maintaining a large military industrial complex in peacetime to combat the perceived threat of communism, succumbing to the grip of militarism that Washington had vigorously warned against.[11]

In addition to a provisional military, the founders instituted clear constraints on the exercise of military power by elected civilian officials and split war powers between the legislative and executive branches. The executive was designated commander in chief, but the responsibility to raise and fund the armed forces lay in the hands of Congress, the branch most accountable to the people. In practice, however, the Constitution's loose wording of Article II has allowed U.S. presidents to deploy creative interpretations of "inherent power"[12]—their power to execute a decision unilaterally—and to use the bureaucratic authority and opacity of the executive branch to conduct military operations without congressional oversight. Following 9/11, this expansion of executive power was abetted by Congress itself with the signing of the 2001 Authorization of Military Force (AUMF) that gave the president unprecedented emergency powers to wage military actions without congressional approval. Since then, the AUMF has become the rule rather than the exception.

The power of the executive branch derives in part from the sheer size, secrecy, and monopoly power of the military industrial complex—including the Pentagon (the largest, most complex bureaucracy on the planet), the eighteen federal agencies that make up the security establishment, and the legion of contracting companies and arms producers working to privatize modern conflict.[13] With the end of the Cold War, the sharp decline in the demand for weapons sparked a spate of mergers and joint ventures in the defense industry that by the late 1990s had fundamentally changed global arms production and trade. Military services were outsourced to help sustain large producers, and the centralization of ownership at the international level produced a handful of extraordinarily large companies with annual profits in the tens of billions. In the wake of 9/11, the bipartisan commitment to permanent war proved a gold rush for what became a trillion-dollar multinational terror industry—and the money has been flowing ever since.

That flow, out of the hands of the American people, through the laundry machine of the Department of Defense (DoD), and into the pockets of defense contractors, remains largely concealed behind a budgetary curtain. The Pentagon and its associated security agencies account for 15 percent of the entire federal budget, but audits are few and far between, and line items on the CIA's multi-billion-dollar black budgets are hidden from congressional appropriators. The result is a growing trend toward the privatization of military operations and rampant fraud, waste, and grift. In the middle of the COVID-19 crisis, for example, the DoD awarded contractors hundreds of millions meant for medical supplies that ended up subsidizing projects that had little or nothing to do with the pandemic.[14] This was not a one-off: nearly every major defense contractor employed by the U.S. government has ended up paying billions of dollars in fines and settlements for misconduct and fraud.[15] This extortionate spending diverts funds that could be used for health care or rebuilding the country's dilapidated bridges and roads, and is reinforced by politicians' overfunding of defense budgets at the expense of domestic programs.

Not only have people in the United States subsidized wars in places previously unknown to them, but they are also funding a war at home. Gun violence and mass shootings—abetted by largely unrestricted access to assault weapons and underwritten with taxpayer-funded contracts—have reached epidemic levels such that parents fear sending their children to school or walking the streets of neighborhoods they have lived in their entire lives. Behind this uniquely American form of domestic terrorism is a gun lobby that churns many billions in profits off the militarization of everyday life—literally making a killing off the sale of tens of millions of guns a year—and a political establishment that churns votes by exploiting the ensuing mass fear with promises of "law and order."

In addition to the misery and chaos brought by gun violence, the American state coerces its subjects to subsidize a war against themselves. The modern state's monopoly on the legitimate use of force was conceived ostensibly to reduce localized violence and foster political equality, based on the dubious assumption that, ultimately, human beings are unable to live in harmony without coercion and social controls. When people stop accepting the capitalist state as an immutable reality and hegemonic forces prove insufficient, repressive state apparatuses—the military, police, and FBI—are there to discipline and repress them.

General Douglas McArthur remarked on these dynamics in his 1957 address to the Sperry Rand Corporation:

> Our government has kept us in a perpetual state of fear, kept us in a continuous stampede of patriotic fervor—with the cry of grave national emergency. Always there has been some terrible evil at home or some monstrous foreign power that was going to gobble us up if we would not blindly rally behind it by furnishing

> the exorbitant funds demanded. Yet, in retrospect, these disasters seem never to have happened, seem never to have been quite real.[16]

Similarly, post-9/11 fearmongering, and the culture of state violence, has frightened citizens into surrendering their constitutional rights and accepting the lack of institutional levers to rein in their government. It has also cooled speech and thwarted journalists' and whistleblowers' ability to check elite power. And, it has fueled superstitions and mass ignorance, enabling power elites to channel the justified outrage of disenfranchised people away from democratic defiance and toward the kind of xenophobic solidarities, citizen policing, and vigilantism that mark world history's darkest hours.

THE COLD WAR

Between the end of World War II and fall of the Berlin Wall, the wartime alliance between the United States and the U.S.S.R. gave way to a major geopolitical and ideological rivalry, with each side forming expansive, militarized blocs. The North Atlantic Treaty Organization (NATO) in the West and Warsaw Pact countries in the East waged proxy wars in Korea, Vietnam, and Afghanistan and lesser-scale conflicts throughout Latin America, Southeast Asia, and the Middle East. In these and other military actions, the United States promoted strategies involving extreme, sometimes genocidal violence, including use of torture, chemical weapons, and saturation airstrikes killing or maiming millions of people and leaving behind a legacy of ruin that would haunt generations to come.

Competition for nuclear dominance begun in the late 1940s had both sides building up their arsenals past the point of mutually assured destruction—a supposed deterrent to apocalyptic war that enriched the defense industry and legitimized the expansion of the U.S. security state and executive branch power. Dwight D. Eisenhower's 1961 warning against the dangers of the military industrial complex foreshadowed the trillion-dollar nuclear arms race that would all but bankrupt the country. As historian Theodore Draper noted, the CIA was becoming "the president's own private army" and intelligence agencies and the National Security Council were "large and varied enough to carry out the president's wishes covertly—even from the rest of the government."[17] The CIA was also functioning as a private army for oil companies, big banks, and the Fortune 500, surveilling and unseating foreign officials on their behalf.

The 1953 U.S.-sponsored coup in Iran that overthrew its democratically elected prime minister Mohammad Mosaddegh was in part a response to Mosaddegh's plans to exile the Anglo-Iranian Oil Company (now British Petroleum) and nationalize Iran's oil industry. With Mohammad Reza Pahlavi, aka "the Shah," in power, opportunities for foreign investment and corporate profit-making increased, as did the billions in the Shah's bank accounts.[18] His palace became a hub for political, banking, and business elites, and Hollywood socialites like Andy Warhol, Farrah Fawcett, and "Million Dollar Man" Lee Majors, known for its caviar and champagne parties hosted by the "beautiful butchers" of the Shah's regime.[19] Outside the palace walls, however, Iranian intelligence officers were arresting and brutalizing communists and leftists and expanding their torture regime throughout the general public, until the Shah was unseated and forced into exile by the revolution.

Among the most powerful brokers of the Cold War era was Henry Kissinger, Nixon's national security advisor and later secretary of state. Kissinger was a leading protagonist of "realism," a theory of foreign policy that reduces all human relations to capitalist competition and maximizing profits. This was the worldview that shaped his maneuvers and policies and that has been estimated to have caused some three to four million deaths.[20] After the joint British-U.S. coup in Iran, Kissinger lent unconditional support to the Shah, overriding State Department and Pentagon objections to allow him broad access to military equipment, and authorizing the CIA to train the Shah's secret police.[21] In the late 1960s, Kissinger was involved in the secret wiretapping of National Security Council staff and urged Nixon to prosecute whistleblower Daniel Ellsberg for releasing the Pentagon Papers. His support for the white majority leadership in South Africa, moreover, helped to buoy Pretoria's apartheid system and attract corporate investment in it.[22]

In the early 1970s, Kissinger helped wage a secret and illegal war in Cambodia that killed some 100,000 civilians and set the stage for the rise of the genocidal Khmer Rouge.[23] He also authorized the secret bombing of Laos, which killed between 50,000 and 70,000 people.[24] In South Asia, he supported Pakistan's military dictatorship and violated U.S. law in allowing secret arms transfers to Pakistan during the India-Pakistan war.[25] In Indonesia, he met with Suharto to authorize the invasion of East Timor in 1975, which led to a genocide against the Timorese people, killing approximately 150,000 of them.[26] That came on the heels of U.S. support for ruthless death squads in Indonesia that killed at least a million people—which a CIA report described as "one of the worst mass murders of the 20th century."[27] As Christopher Hitchens demonstrated in *The Trial of Henry*

Kissinger, Kissinger's war crimes exceeded those of history's most brutal dictators, and then some.

The CIA abetted Kissinger's murderous pursuits and was involved in all aspects of the Vietnam War. That included working with war profiteers like Monsanto, Dow Chemical, and DuPont that price-gouged the U.S. government for the Agent Orange used to poison and disable masses of innocent civilians.[28] Recall from chapter 1 that the CIA-sponsored overthrow of Allende in Chile was the result of a conspiracy led by Kissinger and David Rockefeller (Kissinger was Nelson Rockefeller's advisor when he was New York governor), who stood to lose millions if Allende nationalized copper and other profitable industries. Emblematic of Kissinger's thinking was a remark he made during a meeting of the 40 Committee, a shadowy White House panel in charge of overseeing covert CIA operations:[29] "I don't see why we need to stand by and watch a country go communist due to the irresponsibility of its people. The issues are much too important for the Chilean voters to be left to decide for themselves."[30]

Much of this activity was hidden from public view and, notably, from Congress. Recall that war powers mandated in the U.S. Constitution invest Congress with the authority to declare and fund wars. The Korean and Vietnam Wars, however, did not involve such official sanction. Truman sent U.S. troops to South Korea without petitioning Congress for approval, marking the first time in U.S. history that a president initiated a major war without a congressional declaration. Truman defended the move by claiming that Korea did not constitute a "war," only a "police action," but the Korean War lasted for three years and resulted in about five million dead.[31] Before that, Truman dropped atomic bombs on Hiroshima and Nagasaki without approval from members of Congress, most of whom had no idea that the bomb even existed.

In Vietnam, U.S. forces were initially sent as "military advisors" when the French pulled out of the country in 1954. Their numbers increased under President John F. Kennedy and again under President Lyndon B. Johnson. When the war became widely unpopular and news leaked of Nixon's illegal, clandestine raid on Cambodia, Congress passed the War Powers Act of 1973 to rein in the president. The act did not include a check on the covert wars and paramilitary activities of the CIA, but it did require U.S. presidents to consult with Congress before engaging in armed conflict. Congress would not invoke the War Powers Act until 2018—nearly half a century after it was passed—in a resolution to withdraw military aid for Saudi Arabia's criminal war in Yemen, an offensive that has produced widespread famine and a major humanitarian crisis.[32]

Congressional war powers legislation did not deter Ronald Reagan in his crusade to crush the Cuban-backed Sandinistas in Nicaragua. After Democrats swept the congressional elections in November 1982, they restricted CIA and military operations in Central America, but the Reagan administration continued to assist the Contras covertly. That included selling arms to Iran in exchange for the release of American hostages in Lebanon, then using profits from the sales to support the Contras—funneled through third parties and private funds—until these machinations came to light in the notorious Iran-Contra scandal. The Contras' human rights violations included death squads, assassination, rape, and torture, but for Reagan, the counterrevolutionary force was so near and dear to his heart that he called them "the moral equivalent of the Founding Fathers."[33]

HUMANITARIAN INTERVENTION

As America's first post–Cold War president, Bill Clinton inherited a superpower without rival, which afforded him the opportunity to draw down the military, reduce defense spending, and use the "peace dividend" to invest in the domestic programs on which he had campaigned. His foreign policy agenda emphasized containment and global stability through multilateralism and "engagement," as opposed to isolationism. Those ambitions, outlined in the National Security Strategy for a New Century (1999),[34] prioritized world leadership and protecting U.S. interests through deterrence, multilateral conflict resolution, and open markets. To that end, Clinton brokered nearly 300 free trade agreements, including China's entry into the World Trade Organization, and waged "humanitarian interventions" aimed at strengthening NATO and fostering stability for smooth capital flows and resource extraction. He subsidized defense industry conglomeration and invested in new surveillance technologies, intelligence agencies, and special forces, aka "the dark arts."[35]

During this period, the concept of the "international community" intervening in countries' domestic affairs on the pretense of preventing war crimes or safeguarding "human security" gained legitimacy in the United Nations (UN) and among major countries, despite treaties and norms around state sovereignty and nonintervention. In this new world order, dominant countries used humanitarianism to legitimize the often-violent pursuit of their interests, while undermining the sovereignty of weaker states that international rules and the institution of the UN were meant to protect.

Such was the case with Clinton's "intervention" in the Balkans early in his presidency in response to a three-way civil war among Croats, Serbs, and Bosnian Muslims. Before Clinton took office, George Bush Sr. had airlifted supplies to Sarajevo but stayed out of the deeply nationalist and ethnic conflict. With mass death and displacement mounting, the United States and its NATO allies agreed to forcibly intervene.[36] After launching a series of airstrikes against Bosnian Serb targets, Clinton sent 20,000 U.S. troops as part of a larger NATO contingent to enforce a ceasefire. The war ended with the signing of peace accords in 1995, just in time to enhance Clinton's reelection prospects. Three years later, the Serb province of Kosovo erupted in violence, and by March 1999 over a million refugees had been displaced amid executions, rape, and other war crimes. With Milošević refusing to withdraw, a U.S.-led NATO force initiated a massive bombing campaign targeting military installations but also civilian-run factories, oil refineries, and TV stations. After seventy-nine days of pounding air strikes, Milošević withdrew and NATO declared success.

This "success" emboldened NATO—composed of the world's nineteen wealthiest nations—with a post–Cold War mandate to function as the world's "peacekeeper," opening the door for the future disciplining of countries that might resist integration into the neoliberal world order. Kosovo marked the first time that NATO forces attacked a sovereign nation; and in an effort to avoid Russia's likely veto, it did so without the approval of the UN General Assembly or UN Security Council. It was also the first time that a war was "won" on air power alone, which for Washington and Casteau (NATO's allied command headquarters) fostered a sense that they could conduct other military interventions with minimal risk to their own troops. On the ground, however, the air bombings left the impression that the United States was hiding behind its advanced technology, using drones to sow fear and panic without regard for civilian casualties, and doing more to punish the Serbs than to protect the Kosovars.[37]

Domestic critics of Clinton's Balkans policy argued that it violated the U.S. Constitution on the grounds that since the United States had not been attacked, the decision to go to war required congressional deliberation.[38] They also questioned the wisdom of provoking Russia as well as Clinton's duplicity in using the pretext of humanitarianism while harming and killing so many civilians. There was also the matter of his inconsistency in making a humanitarian intervention in Europe, but not in Africa, where at the time millions of Rwandans were perishing in a genocidal civil war.

Clinton did authorize intervention in Somalia, but unlike in Rwanda, there was an "oil factor." By and large, Republicans tended to oppose humanitarian intervention for fear of overextending the military without a clear benefit to U.S. interests. Yet, in Somalia, Republican oilman George H. W. Bush put boots on the ground to do what he described as "God's work" in a nation devastated by clan warfare. His ostensible mission was to avert mass starvation and prevent airlifted relief supplies from falling into the hands of regional warlords.[39] But as only the *Los Angeles Times* reported, prior to the civil war, four major U.S. oil companies (Conoco, Amoco, Chevron, and Phillips) had acquired access to tens of millions of acres in the Somali countryside—two-thirds of the entire country—for exploration and extraction. Having the U.S. military in place to stabilize the country would enable those companies to confidently proceed with their plans for massive oil speculation.

When Clinton took office, he advanced U.S. objectives in Somalia to include nation building, which then-UN ambassador Madeleine Albright described as an "unprecedented enterprise aimed at nothing less than the restoration of an entire country."[40] But "restoration" is not what actually happened. In a series of missteps with local warlords, U.S. and UN forces exacerbated the conflict by committing a series of war crimes against the Somali people, including an attack on a Mogadishu hospital and bombing of a residential building that killed dozens of people, including clan elders. During one of those attacks, two Black Hawk helicopters were shot down and eighteen U.S. soldiers were killed. One of the pilots was hacked to death by angry crowds and his mangled body was paraded through the town. The gruesome event was memorialized in the blockbuster film *Black Hawk Down*, in which U.S. soldiers are played by an ensemble of Hollywood heartthrobs while Somalis are represented as faceless savages.[41] What the film did not memorialize were the hundreds of Somali civilians who U.S.-UN troops killed that day, nor the sexual assaults, looting of camps for displaced people, and sadistic treatment of Somali children—as evidenced by photographs of Belgian paratroopers forcing a Somali boy over an open fire pit, as if to roast him like a pig.[42]

Under intense criticism, Clinton quickly withdrew U.S. forces and abandoned his relief and nation building ambitions. Warlords remained in control, there was no functional government, and organized crime and religious extremism incubated for years. Emblematic of what humanitarianism really meant to Clinton and the international community, CIA operatives literally dumped their files on Somalia in the Mogadishu airport departure lounge on their way out of the country.[43] (Now, Joint Special Operations Command [JSOC] and the CIA run covert operations in Somalia under the auspices of the War on Terror, as multinationals bill the country as the "new oil and gas frontier."[44])

THE GLOBAL WAR ON TERROR

The attack on the World Trade Center on September 11, 2001—which cost nearly 3,000 lives and injured and traumatized countless more—had a multiplying effect on U.S. militarism that will take generations to overcome. Amid a worldwide outpouring of solidarity and support, the Bush administration exploited the horrors of 9/11 to enlarge the country's power and suspend it in a state of panic and revenge. Various U.S. presidents have used their role as commander in chief to expand presidential power and enhance their political standing. Such was likely the case when Bill Clinton—embroiled in the Monica Lewinsky scandal—ordered the bombing (and cover-up) of a major pharmaceutical factory in Sudan on weak intel that Osama bin Laden was manufacturing chemical weapons there.[45] As manipulative as Clinton was, however, the Bush administration took presidential emergency powers to a new level, overinvoking executive privilege and abusing the institutional independence of the Justice Department's Office of Legal Counsel.[46] Deputy Assistant Attorney General John C. Yoo proved a loyal accomplice in producing a series of memos to legally justify Bush's overreaches, which he couched in dictatorial terms:

> In both the War Powers Resolution and the Joint Resolution, Congress has recognized the President's authority to use force in circumstances such as those created by the September 11 incidents. Neither statute, however, can place any limits on the President's determinations as to any terrorist threat, the amount of military force to be used in response, or the method, timing, and nature of the response. These decisions, under our Constitution, are for the President alone to make.[47]

Bush took a page from the Red Scare playbook by framing the War on Terror as an open-ended, ongoing state of emergency, which enabled his administration to enlarge the U.S. security state and adopt enhanced methods of surveillance and control. In the decade following 9/11, over 1,000 government organizations, and twice as many private companies, were established to perform counterterrorism, homeland security, and intelligence-gathering functions in some 10,000 locations across the country. That involved constructing dozens of building complexes in and around DC—"the equivalent of almost three Pentagons or 22 U.S. Capitol buildings—about 17 million square feet of space," according to the *Washington Post*.[48]

In addition to this massive, authoritarian infrastructure, Bush's USA Patriot Act—"Uniting and Strengthening America by Providing Appropriate Tools Required to Intercept and Obstruct Terrorism"—passed with nearly unanimous bipartisan support, providing the federal government with extraordinary discretion to break in and search people's homes without their knowledge and monitor their phone records, emails, and library activity. Recall that Bush also succeeded in passing the AUMF, with only California representative Barbara Lee dissenting. That authorization effectively signed away Congress's constitutional war powers and allowed the president "to use all necessary and appropriate force against those nations, organizations, or persons he determines planned, authorized, committed, or aided the terrorist attacks that occurred on September 11, 2001, or harbored such organizations or persons."[49]

When the first President Bush "desert-stormed" Iraq, he was explicit that oil was a major driver. Bill Clinton opted for a policy of "containing" Iraq by way of economic sanctions, a massive troop buildup on the Kuwaiti border, and a handful of air strikes. The second President Bush brought a unilateralist approach that positioned the American superpower as the world's protector and policeman, portraying Saddam Hussein and the "Axis of Evil" as existential threats. Congressional hawks, led by Senators John McCain and Lindsey Graham, echoed the crusader rhetoric. A former prisoner of war, McCain blamed his prolonged detention on President Johnson's decision to temporarily halt air strikes in North Vietnam and credited Nixon's pounding bombing campaigns with making his release possible. For Iraq, McCain supported troop surges and intense shows of military force, describing the war as "a fight between a just regard for human dignity and a malevolent force . . . between right and wrong, good and evil. It's no more ambiguous than that."[50]

Bush's ostensible mission to prevent Iraq from manufacturing weapons of mass destruction (WMDs) and "bring democracy" to the world involved similar claims about good vs. evil. It also echoed Clinton's Iraq Liberation Act of 1998, which made "regime change" in Iraq official U.S. policy. With Bush, however, "regime change" meant a Koch-style war: a "free market" imposed by force to facilitate a gold-rush transfer of wealth from ordinary citizens to multinationals and security contractors. In both the Iraq and Afghanistan wars, contractors raked in massive profits by jacking up prices, double-charging for supplies, and billing for services like transportation and construction that they did not perform. What became a Wild West of subcontractors layered upon subcontractors made accountability impossible, and some contractors even hired "the enemy" to provide security, giving illegal payments to combatants who were fighting against U.S. soldiers.[51] According to the Pentagon, 40 percent of the $100+ billion that the DoD paid to contractors in Afghanistan between 2010 and 2012 went to organized crime rings, members of the Taliban, drug traffickers, corrupt Afghan officials, and others.[52]

Amid the chaos, the incompetent Iraq viceroy Paul Bremer burned through some $12 to $14 billion taxpayer dollars—*in cash*—half of which went missing ($1.2 to $1.6 billion in stolen money was later found in a bunker in Lebanon).[53] More than $1 billion in military equipment was unaccounted for as well.[54] Supplying temporary, flexible workforces was billed as a money saver, but in 2013 the Congressional Research Service found that the "waste associated with Iraq relief and reconstruction efforts totaled at least $8 billion . . . and between $31 billion and $60 billion was lost to contract waste and fraud in contingency operations in Iraq and Afghanistan." According to the Special Inspector General for Iraq Reconstruction, those figures were a "conservative estimate."[55]

THE DARK ARTS

In their bestseller *Hubris*, Michael Isikoff and David Corn detail the events leading up to the second Iraq War when suspected al-Qaeda operative Ibn al-Shaykh al-Libi was captured by Pakistani forces in 2001 and handed over to FBI agents in Afghanistan. The agents in charge of al-Libi subscribed to a "good cop" school of interrogation, which, they reasoned, would be defensible in a U.S. court of law. Like every other al-Qaeda operative the FBI questioned, al-Libi denied working with Saddam Hussein. In a power grab, CIA director George Tenet suggested that his agency take over the interrogations. Shortly after, al-Libi was whisked away by CIA agents in the middle of an FBI interrogation session and flown to Egypt, a trusted ally with lax controls on torture. There, he was held in a box only twenty inches high for seventeen hours, then beaten for fifteen minutes straight. Only then did he confess that al-Qaeda members had been training in Iraq on the use of WMDs. Al-Libi later recanted the story, but not before the flimsy intelligence he provided was deployed in testimonies and speeches at the highest levels of U.S. leadership to substantiate their plot to invade Iraq.[56]

Despite abundant evidence of its unreliability, Bush insisted that torture was necessary to combat terrorism, as did his top deputies, including former Stanford University provost Condoleezza Rice and four-star general Colin Powell. Some Democrats were informed of Bush's torture program as well, including House Speaker Nancy Pelosi, who first denied knowledge of it, then admitted to having been briefed on waterboarding, just not the administration's actual use of it, she said.[57]

To avoid legal constraints set forth in the U.S. Constitution and Geneva Conventions, the Bush administration designated terrorism suspects as stateless "enemy combatants" and held them in secret CIA prisons around the world. They also held suspects in the Guantánamo Bay detention camp in Cuba, which was outside U.S. legal jurisdiction. Recall that rendering individuals stateless and removing their citizenship rights was a tactic used by the Nazis to legalize the mass deportation of Jews, as documented by Hannah Arendt in her study of Adolf Eichmann and the "banality of evil."[58] The first cohort of 20 prisoners arrived at Guantánamo in January 2002, and within six months, the number swelled to over 700. Of the 780 total prisoners housed there, 55 percent were found to have committed no hostile act against the United States.[59]

On December 4, 2019, the *New York Times*[60] published a series of drawings by Guantánamo Bay detainee Abu Zubaydah that gut-wrenchingly depict the extreme torture sessions to which he was subjected, including being waterboarded eighty-three times—which the CIA recorded on videotapes that they later destroyed.[61] One of the War on Terror's first "high value" detainees, Zubaydah served as a guinea pig for the CIA and its sadistic team of psychologists who reverse-engineered already-existing soldier training programs on torture to discover creative ways to break suspects—all with the help of the American Psychological Association.[62] As of January 2022, Zubaydah remained in "indefinite law-of-war detention" in Guantánamo, despite the fact that some of the major claims made against him have been invalidated.[63]

Some fifteen years before Zubaydah's sketches were published, the world caught a glimpse of the American torture regime inside the gruesome Abu Ghraib prison in Iraq, where U.S. soldiers abused children, elderly women, and others, many of whom would be found innocent.[64] In his investigation on Abu Ghraib, General Antonio Taguba laid blame for the "systematic regime of torture" he discovered squarely on the commander in chief, stating, "There is no longer any doubt as to whether the current administration has committed war crimes. The only question that remains to be answered is whether those who ordered the use of torture will be held to account." General Taguba further stated that:

> In order for these individuals to suffer the wanton cruelty to which they were subjected, a government policy was promulgated to the field whereby the Geneva Conventions and the Uniform Code of Military Justice were disregarded. The U.N. Convention Against Torture was indiscriminately ignored. And the healing professions, including physicians and psychologists, became complicit in the willful infliction of harm against those the Hippocratic Oath demands they

protect. The former detainees in this report, each of whom is fighting a lonely and difficult battle to rebuild his life, require reparations for what they endured, comprehensive psycho-social and medical assistance, and even an official apology from our government. But most of all, these men deserve justice as required under the tenets of international law and the United States Constitution. And so do the American people.[65]

Following the publication of photos from Abu Ghraib, Senators Kerry and McCain passed an amendment to the defense budget authorization banning the use of torture. Over two dozen generals and admirals sent an open letter in support, including Colin Powell.[66] Rather than veto the bill, Bush assured CIA torturers that he would waive the law for them and issued a signing statement specifying how the executive branch would interpret the measure. This was not an isolated incident: Bush used signing statements over 160 times to skirt various laws and made over 1,000 challenges to distinct provisions of them. All of his predecessors *combined* had used signing statements in less than 600 sections of legislation, but Bush essentially cherry-picked the laws he wanted to execute and recognize as constitutional. This tremendous display of executive power and disregard for the other "coequal" branches of government spurred public debate about signing statements, with the American Bar Association declaring them to be "contrary to the rule of law and our constitutional separation of powers."[67]

In July 2014, CIA officers were caught hacking into the computer network of Senate Intelligence Committee staffers who were preparing a report on the Bush administration's torture program. The investigation was prompted by Republicans' unlawful shredding in 2005 of ninety-plus videotapes documenting the torture experiments performed on Zubaydah at a CIA black site in Thailand.[68] At a Senate Intelligence Committee hearing, chairwoman Senator Dianne Feinstein queried CIA director John Brennan about the break-in and other efforts to obstruct the investigation, but he refused to answer (he later apologized).[69] As deputy director of the CIA at the time, Avril Haines overruled her own inspector general and spared the hackers reprisal for their misdeeds, later awarding them medals.[70] In a last-ditch phone call the night before the report's release, then Secretary of State John Kerry beseeched Feinstein not to publish it—a radical 180-degree turn from his legislative efforts to ban torture, though in keeping with his support for the Iraq war. When Feinstein's committee released the 500-page executive summary of the 6,000-page report, Haines heavily redacted it. In 2021, not even a decade later, the Biden administration rewarded her with a high-level appointment as director of national intelligence.

The Torture Report contained horrific details one has to struggle to stop picturing, including interrogation techniques performed by sadistic wardens and high-paid, inexperienced contractors in what the *New Yorker*[71] called "playgrounds of impunity." Such "playgrounds" included notorious dark sites like the Salt Pit in Afghanistan, described in the report as a veritable dungeon, and Cobalt, where one wrongly accused prisoner was frozen to death, and another innocent, mentally disabled person was tortured just so tapes of his screams could be used to lure intelligence from his family.[72]

As a senator, Obama was an outspoken critic of torture and argued that "nobody is above the law." He vowed to review U.S. torture practices for evidence of criminality and said of the Bush White House, "I think this administration basically viewed any tactic as acceptable, as long as it could spin it and keep it out of the public eye."[73] As president, however, Obama chose John Brennan, a proponent of the torture program, as his CIA director; and according to WikiLeaks cables, his administration secretly worked with Republican operatives to suppress inquiries into U.S. torture by other countries.[74] Chief of Staff Rahm Emanuel and Press Secretary Robert Gibbs publicly pressured their Justice Department to refrain from opening criminal investigations. And when John Yoo's torture memos were made public, Obama declared absolute immunity for the U.S. officials involved in the program and blamed their critics for being divisive, offering U.S. torturers his solidarity: "Nothing will be gained by spending our time and energy laying blame for the past. . . . we must resist the forces that divide us, and instead come together on behalf of our common future."[75] He also invoked secrecy powers and immunity doctrines to block civil cases brought by torture victims.

During his confirmation hearing in January 2009, Eric Holder said that he believed waterboarding was torture and a violation of international law.[76] But as Obama's attorney general, he went with the Nuremburg defense, saying, "It would be unfair to prosecute dedicated men and women working to protect America for conduct that was sanctioned in advance by the Justice Department."[77] In August 2009, with more than 100 detainees having died while in U.S. custody, Holder announced a criminal investigation into CIA detainee abuse, but dropped it less than two years later.[78]

As president, Obama tried to make good on his promise to close Guantánamo Bay, arguing to the public and Congress that torture was immoral and pointing out that each prisoner was costing U.S. taxpayers some $13 million a year.[79] As a matter of national security, he added, Guantánamo was serving as a recruitment tool for terrorists. In response, Republicans cast his plan to release Guantánamo prisoners into U.S. facilities as a threat to American lives. Instead of overriding them with his executive authority, however, Obama chose to release the prisoners to other countries.[80] Before leaving office, he managed to transfer about 80 percent of them, but those sent to the United Arab Emirates were detained even longer, and prisoners of Yemeni descent were released into their home country during a deadly civil war.[81] As of this writing, Guantánamo remains open under severely degraded conditions, including malfunctioning toilets and raw sewage in the cells. The Biden administration vowed to close the camp, but at present, has failed to repatriate those already cleared for release and has left unanswered the important question of whether the United States can continue to hold prisoners indefinitely and without trial.

DIRTY WARS

Obama's image as a liberal Democrat and constitutional lawyer helped him sell his "just war" program and straddle the fence between criticizing Bush's imperial adventurism and not being perceived as a "wimpy Democrat." He campaigned for president on the idea that Iraq was a "dumb war" and that precious taxpayer resources should have been spent going after bin Laden in Afghanistan.[82] Once in office, however, he inscribed many of the same Bush-era policies that he had derided as undemocratic and unconstitutional on the campaign trail. Despite his pledge to be more transparent, he frequently invoked state secrets privilege. Despite promises to safeguard civil liberties, he expanded warrantless wiretapping, cracked down on habeas corpus rights, impinged on press freedoms,[83] and reauthorized the USA Patriot Act. Despite vowing to be less militaristic, he employed mercenaries, more than doubled Bush's record of arms sales to the Middle East,[84] and launched interventions in over half of the world using drones and special operations forces without input from Congress or the American people. As for the so-called smart war in Afghanistan, it lasted two decades and ended with the resumption of Taliban rule and a Saigon-like airlift in which desperate Afghans could be seen climbing on to a U.S. military plane as it took off. Crushed human remains were found inside the wheel well and two men clinging to the plane dropped hundreds of feet to their deaths. Since the withdrawal, conditions have deteriorated to such a degree that Afghans have been forced to sell their kidneys—and their children—to survive.[85]

JSOC—the ultra-elite force that killed Osama bin Laden—became the crown jewel of Obama's new military, grown from a small-scale, rarely used rescue team into a full-on secret army. Obama expanded JSOC's power to run clandestine missions across the globe, and while the CIA was subject to some congressional oversight, JSOC reported directly to him. *The Torture Report* redacted all references to JSOC, and allegedly, its servicemen were instructed to not put into writing any information that could be requested under the Freedom of Information Act. Before the raid on bin Laden, the American public had no idea that JSOC even existed. As one Navy SEAL put it: "We're the dark matter. We're the force that orders the universe but can't be seen."[86]

Unlike Bush, who left the minutiae of his assassination program to his commanders, Obama met with his National Security Council staff weekly on "Terror Tuesdays" to review "kill lists" of suspects whose profiles were printed up as baseball cards.[87] There was no due process. There was no check on the vetting procedures used to determine who the United States would murder next. There was no mandate given by the American people or Congress. While Congress did shift drone operations from the CIA to the Pentagon to "increase accountability," the missions remained highly classified, especially when involving civilian casualties, which were many.

Before the media caught on, drones seemed the perfect tool for Obama's image-obsessed administration. Their supposed precision implied a humanitarianism built into the machines themselves—machines called "Predator" and "Hellfire"—and though some operators reported symptoms of PTSD, they enabled the U.S. military to keep troops largely out of harm's way. Arms developers have sunk billions into trying to reduce the human element of war by developing autonomous weapons with sensory capacity and artificial intelligence nuanced enough to discern friends from enemies. Under Obama, that discernment was based on shockingly imprecise criteria set by the White House. For years, the CIA and U.S. military special forces have performed signature strikes on cities and villages based on digital markings of human identity, life patterns, and objects like weapons and military equipment, without confirming who the targets actually are. Victims are determined by empirically loose demographics, like "military aged males" (aka "MAM"), and are based on "suspicious" behavior patterns thought to be signatures of terrorists. As a senior Obama State Department official described it, when CIA agents observe "three guys doing jumping jacks," they assume it's a terrorist training camp.[88]

By the time Obama accepted the Nobel Peace Prize, he had already ordered more drone strikes than Bush had during his entire presidency.[89] All told, he increased drone "precision bombing" fivefold from the previous administration, killing 3,000 to 5,000 people, 90 percent of whom were not the correct target.[90] In 2011, CIA Director Brennan claimed that "there hasn't been a single collateral death" from the strikes.[91] But a study by the Center for Naval Analyses found that in Afghanistan alone, drone strikes were ten times more likely to kill civilians than those performed by manned fighter jets.[92]

One of the most controversial uses of drones by the Obama administration involved the assassination of American citizens overseas, including Muslim cleric Anwar Al-Awlaki, who had never been charged with—let alone convicted of—any crime. Al-Awlaki was a Yemeni American imam, raised and educated in the United States, whose charisma and increasingly critical rhetoric against the United States earned him a top spot on Obama's kill list. For U.S. citizens, free speech is supposed to be protected under the First Amendment, and individuals are presumed innocent until proven guilty. These rights are designed not only to protect citizens, but also as a check on state power. Nevertheless, Obama unilaterally conducted drone strikes under the sole authority of the executive branch, removing such acts of war from congressional oversight and public scrutiny.

When asked whether the president had authority to target and kill American citizens, the White House Office of Legal Counsel issued two controversial memos. Instead of invoking executive privilege, as Bush had done, they said that the executive had the power to override Awlaki's constitutional rights due to "extraordinary circumstance" and concluded that U.S. citizenship did not impose "constitutional limitations that would preclude the contemplated lethal action under the facts represented to us by the DoD, CIA, and the intelligence community."[93] In other words, the opinions of the DoD, CIA, and other security officials trumped the Constitution and the rights of U.S. citizens delineated in it. Attorney General Eric Holder justified the preemptive killing of Al-Awlaki and other U.S. citizens by asserting that "due process and judicial process are not one and the same. . . . The Constitution guarantees due process, not judicial process."[94] Comedian Stephen Colbert's response was searing: "Trial by jury, trial by fire, rock, paper, scissors, who cares? Due process just means that there is a process that you do. The current process is apparently, first the president meets with his advisors and decides who he can kill. Then he kills them."[95]

Just weeks after his assassination, Al-Awlaki's sixteen-year-old son Abdulrahman—who had left home to search for his father after not seeing him for two years—was enjoying a meal with his seventeen-year-old cousin and some friends when missiles from a U.S. drone killed them all.[96] After a slew of inaccurate explanations for the murder—including false statements about Abdulrahman's age and claims that he was meeting with al-Qaeda—Press Secretary Robert Gibbs revealed the administration's true posture in his response to a press query about the killing: "I would suggest that [the young Abdulrahman] should have a far more responsible father."[97]

Unbelievably, Al-Awlaki's family would lose another child during a botched raid arranged by the Obama administration but carried out under Trump. A week into his presidency, from a dinner table at his Florida golf resort, Trump ordered a commando raid on a suspected terrorist training site in Yemen, but the mission had been compromised and U.S. soldiers were met with resistance. An elite U.S. serviceman was killed, as well as at least sixteen civilians, most of them under the age of thirteen. Most news agencies reported the serviceman's death as the sole U.S. fatality,[98] but the other American killed that night was eight-year-old Nawar Al-Awlaki.[99] Nora, as she was called, was shot in the neck at close range by a U.S. marine, and because it was impossible to get medical attention, she bled to death for over two hours, resiliently comforting her agonizing mother.[100]

Despite Trump's exceptionally brutish and contradictory rhetoric, he did not veer significantly from previous administrations in terms of his deployment of the military. As a candidate, he promised a war-weary public out of one side of his mouth that he was "ending the era of endless wars."[101] But out of the other side, he openly threatened to use torture, not just for interrogation, but like Bush, for revenge.[102] He kept Guantánamo Bay open and pardoned military commanders convicted of heinous war crimes, including revenge killings, indiscriminate shooting of children, and defiling bodies of the dead.[103] Trump railed against the military industrial complex—charging that Pentagon leaders "want to do nothing but fight wars so that all of those wonderful companies that make the bombs and make the planes and make everything else stay happy"[104]—but as president, he oversaw dramatic increases in arms sales and defense spending, including the creation of the Space Force, a sixth branch of the armed forces.[105]

Trump also finessed relations with Israel at a time when U.S. politicians' long-standing, bipartisan consensus to provide "unwavering support" was weakening. As president, Obama maintained a prickly relationship with Netanyahu and, in response to the Israeli prime minister's attempt to sabotage Iran nuclear deal negotiations, he even endeavored to keep him out of office.[106] Trump did the opposite. Against standing U.S. policy, he encouraged Israel to keep building settlements in the West Bank and recognized Israeli sovereignty over the Golan Heights, to which Israel responded by naming one of the settlements "Trump Heights."[107] He also pulled out of the Iran nuclear deal between the United States, Iran, and five other world powers—a delicate compact that the previous administration took pains to achieve. And he moved the U.S. embassy from Tel Aviv to Jerusalem—a slap in the face of Palestinians for whom Jerusalem is their holy city.

During the opening ceremony of the new embassy, with Jared Kushner and Ivanka Trump in attendance, Israeli soldiers killed some sixty unarmed Palestinian protesters at the Gaza border.[108] Kushner, a Zionist with zero foreign policy experience, took it upon himself to draw up a Middle East peace deal—a self-proclaimed "Deal of the Century"—taking the Trumpian game show to the Middle East. His plans were drawn in collaboration with Israelis, but not with Palestinians. When he did acknowledge Palestinian leadership, he infantilized them with juvenile rantings that if they did not accept his deal, "they're going to screw up another opportunity, like they've screwed up every other opportunity that they've ever had in their existence."[109] To defend against criticisms regarding his gross lack of experience, Kushner appeared on Sky News Arabia and boasted, "I've been studying this now for three years. I've read 25 books on it"—to which a *Washington Post* columnist retorted, "I have just read 25 books and am here to perform your open heart surgery."[110]

Kushner's plan to impose corporate governance on Palestine involved convening an investor-driven "Peace to Prosperity" conference, which Palestinian leaders duly boycotted. During his speech at the conference, Kushner spoke about transforming the Gaza Strip into a tourist destination and implored attendees that if they stopped "doing terrorism," it would "allow for much faster flow of goods and people."[111] Michael Koplow of the Israel Policy Forum described the plan as "the Monty Python sketch of Israeli-Palestinian peace initiatives." As additional experts piled on, Kushner explained to reporters that his vision would only be feasible if Palestinian leadership would stop being so "hysterical and stupid."[112]

Trump also courted Saudi Arabia at a time when Congress was reaching a bipartisan consensus regarding the Saudi-driven war in Yemen and the horrific humanitarian crisis that resulted from it. In 2015, when the Obama administration was engaged in tense negotiations over the Iran nuclear deal, Saudi Arabia and its allies began a military campaign in Yemen against Iranian-backed Houthi rebels. With the support of the United States, the Saudi assault in Yemen left tens of thousands dead and caused widespread famine, with 80 percent of the population (twenty-four million) in need of aid. Because Obama initiated U.S. involvement in the war, and had been running a counterterrorism program in Yemen against a local affiliate of al-Qaeda, Democrats were reluctant to change course. However, when it was revealed that the Saudi crown prince (MBS) had ordered the murder and dismemberment of journalist Jamal Khashoggi, Democrats and Republicans joined Representative Ro Khanna and Senator Bernie Sanders to pass a war powers resolution—the first of its kind—directing Trump to withdraw U.S. support for the war. Trump vetoed the resolution, having strengthened U.S. ties with the Saudis through arms sales that had been halted due to the situation in Yemen. In 2019, as the atrocities were becoming difficult to ignore, Trump nevertheless ignored them and authorized the sale of nuclear power technology to Saudi Arabia—which lawmakers warned could trigger a nuclear arms race—and his administration continued to broker arms deals without congressional approval.[113] In March 2022, as Democratic leadership threatened to "isolate" the Saudis while continuing to make arms deals with them, UNICEF described the situation in Yemen as the worst humanitarian crisis in the world and a "living hell" for children.[114]

THE GENERALS

Militarist nations like the United States tend to venerate their soldiers, especially their generals. In the hierarchy of the American power structure, however, generals fall under the civilian command of the president, vice president, defense secretary, and others. That layering is meant to signal a governmental commitment to tempering military power and emphasis on diplomatic solutions to world order and conflict. It is also meant to place generals "above politics" and characterize them as providers of strictly technical and strategic expertise. This perceived independence, as well as their image as dutiful, self-sacrificing heroes driven by love and pride of country, affords them a high degree of status-honor in the society. Yet it also uniquely positions them to perform crucial legitimating functions for war, and to shield the military—and the politicians wielding its power—from public scrutiny and accountability.

Under the first President Bush, General Colin Powell became the face of Desert Storm, his theory of "decisive force" credited with keeping U.S. soldiers out of harm's way and decisively defeating Saddam Hussein. After the war, Powell was feted as a national hero and the embodiment of the American dream—the unlikely conservative who climbed from modest beginnings in the South Bronx and City University ROTC and transcended barriers of race and social class to become a hero and military elite. Powell was asked to throw the first pitch for the Yankees' 1991 season, and when *U.S. News* featured his image on its cover, the caption read "Superstar: From the Pentagon to the White House?"

Powell was riding high on a lucrative wave of book deals, speaking tours, and Fortune 500 boards when the second President Bush tapped him for secretary of state. That a four-star general would serve as the nation's highest diplomat should have forewarned of the blitzkrieg to come. But

Powell was "the most trusted man in America," with public approval ratings as high as 80 percent (up there with Mother Theresa) and a sterling image, etched in the dialect of loyalty, honor codes, and service that shielded military men like him from censure.[115] As secretary, Powell's skepticism alienated him from Bush's neocon inner circle, but his loyalty and above-politics image proved invaluable for selling the Iraq War to the media, to on-the-fence political centrists, and to a reticent public—though not for very long.

On the wall of the entrance to the Security Council room in the UN building in New York City hangs a replica of *Guernica*—Picasso's masterpiece depicting the Nazis' saturation bombing of a Basque village and the suffering of its people, animals, and lands. Nelson Rockefeller commissioned the tapestry in 1955 after Picasso refused to sell him the original, and in the mid-1980s his estate lent it to the UN. On February 5, 2003, UN officials placed a large blue curtain over the tapestry in preparation for Powell's speech to the Security Council, claiming that the curtain was needed to clear the backdrop of *Guernica*'s visual noise. But there was no draping over the irony: Powell's own war doctrine had rendered villagers like those writhing in *Guernica* as collateral damage, whose submission required, in his view, spectacular displays of force and domination. His speech on the second Iraq War aimed to justify more of the same.

In the leadup to his much-anticipated UN appearance, the press buzzed with speculation that this could be Powell's "Adlai Stevenson moment." As UN ambassador under Kennedy, Stevenson appealed to the Security Council on October 25, 1962, with a powerful show of evidence that the Soviet Union, a nuclear superpower, was placing nuclear missiles just ninety miles off U.S. shores in Cuba. The ambassador's momentous address tipped the balance of world public opinion in favor of the United States, helped contain the Soviets, and prevented a nuclear war.

Powell's UN speech had the opposite effect. With each day that Iraq burned, Powell looked more and more like the one who had kicked the hornet's nest and unleashed uncertain fury on the world. Despite media accolades, his address did little to sway the Security Council, and the United States invaded Iraq without its support.[116] When his false claims regarding WMDs were exposed, Powell lost the moral authority he had spent a lifetime cultivating. With elite self-righteousness, he argued that the ends of defeating Saddam justified the means—millions died, trillions spent—and deemed his UN speech a mere "blot" on his otherwise spotless record. Years later, he would deny any culpability and, without a tinge of irony, blame low-level intelligence personnel for not having the courage to speak up.

If Powell's legacy epitomizes the arrogance of power, General David Petraeus's speaks to its excesses. Petraeus served a critical function in helping the Bush administration save face and justify its efforts—including troop surges—at a time when the war was losing legitimacy and descending into chaos. It helped that Petraeus was widely known as a thoughtful, professor-like man with an unrivaled grasp on how to charm reporters, pundits, and elected officials. It also helped that, like Powell, his rise to four-stardom followed an American dream narrative. The son of a librarian and sea captain, Petraeus was said to be obsessed with West Point since he was a boy growing up just a stone's throw from its campus. There, he married the daughter of the academy's superintendent, and through obsessive self-discipline, the story goes, he rose precipitously through the ranks to become an elite general and later director of the CIA. Along the way, he earned a PhD in International Affairs from Princeton (he wanted to someday become the university's president) and made the cover of *Newsweek* three times, including in 2004 when he was (just) a lieutenant general. Selected by President Bush to serve as the front man for the 30,000-troop surge in Iraq in 2007, Petraeus became known in the public eye as the army general who saved U.S. forces from humiliating defeat.[117] That year, the NFL tapped him to do the coin toss at the Super Bowl.

Like Powell, Petraeus had his own war doctrine and developed an army training manual that became a bestseller, the first of its kind to make the *New York Times Book Review*. Petraeus's innovations were lauded as an enlightened form of counterinsurgency that combined aggressive force with cultural sensitivity—a counterbalance to the image of the Bush White House as incompetent warmongers. The media played along. *Time Magazine* named Petraeus a runner-up "Person of the Year" and lionized him as "the man who taught the U.S. military how to transform anarchic war zones into communities again."[118] His ability to jump layers in the chain of command and high status among social and political elites earned him the nickname "King David" by sarcastic peers. There was talk of him becoming chairman of the Joint Chiefs of Staff or initiating a presidential run, but after four-star general Stanley McChrystal made disparaging comments about Obama in an interview with *Rolling Stone*, Petraeus was demoted to replace McChrystal as commander of the coalition forces in Afghanistan.[119]

After thirty-seven years of military service, Petraeus retired and Obama appointed him CIA director. There, he further militarized the agency and worked with JSOC and the Pentagon to expand assassinations and covert wars. He was forced to resign a year and a half in when it was revealed that he shared eight "black books" containing highly classified information with his mistress Paula Broadwell, author of his regrettably titled biography *All In*. Petraeus was spared jail time, but the media published the salacious details of his affair, including a cyberstalking drama involving Beltway socialite Jill Kelley, known for entertaining America's top brass in her Florida mansion. Petraeus was once escorted to a pirate-themed bash at Kelley's palatial home by a twenty-eight-police-motorcycle motorcade. As the dominoes began to fall, Kelley became the center of her own scandal over racy emails she had been trading with General John Allen, the top commanding officer in Afghanistan at the time. Allen would later become president of the Brookings Institution, then fall from grace after the FBI caught him lying about his lucrative, corrupt lobbying on behalf of Qatar, one of Brookings' largest financial backers.[120]

Instead of going from "hero to zero," as the papers claimed, Petraeus took high-profile professorships, and Kohlberg Kravis Roberts (KKR)—the king of 1980s leveraged buyouts and of private equity today—hired him to run their Global Institute.[121] Having acquired defense and intelligence consultant TASC, Inc. (formerly, The Analytic Sciences Corporation) from Northup Grumman just a few years earlier, KKR had much to gain from having a Pentagon notable like Petraeus on its payroll. Of course, Petraeus wasn't the only army general to cash in on his four-star currency by helping redirect the flow of taxpayer dollars from defense budgets to private equity firms. The vast majority (some 80 to 90 percent) of generals and admirals go into the defense industries after they retire, providing valuable public relations and access to defense contracts—while further entrenching America's permanent war economy.[122] In 2021 alone, defense contractors that hired former Pentagon officials received nearly $90 billion in government contracts.[123]

Petraeus was on Trump's short list for a cabinet position, and later, to replace General Flynn as national security advisor, but his probation status prevented it. It seems Petraeus dodged a bullet. The Trump administration was notable for appointing more generals to its cabinet than any other U.S. president, many of them through the revolving door of Boeing, Raytheon, the Spectrum Group, and General Dynamics. But rather than glean political capital from their venerated status, Trump called them "killers" and treated them like muscle for hire. When confronted with their honor codes and restraint, he demeaned them with petty insults, mocking four-star general James "Mad Dog" Mattis as "Moderate Dog" and "Little Baby Kitten," and making fun of national security advisor Lieutenant General H. R. McMaster's civilian attire, saying he dressed "like a beer salesman."[124]

THE TROOPS

In addition to using their status to confer legitimacy, generals command the tremendous and rigid bureaucracy of the American war machine. That bureaucracy employs roughly three million men and women, half of whom serve in uniform, plus about one million reservists, 700,000 civilians, and tens of thousands of CIA agents and contractors.[125] The power that generals exercise, and confer to other elites, derives in part from their personal charisma, but it is also underpinned by the rational, bureaucratic organization of masses of troops—bolstered by a culture of strict discipline and depersonalization, and the military's capacity to transform relatively free individuals into obedient subjects and efficient killing machines.

Military training is scientifically and psychologically designed to break down the individual and rebuild him or her into a skilled, dedicated, and physically fit cog in the machine. Hair is chopped off, uniforms replace personal clothing, every minute of every day is scheduled, and everyone eats the same meals at the same time in the same place. Personal conscience is surrendered to the collective conscience of core and nation, and robotic automatic responses are trained into each recruit to reduce independent judgment and the human tendency for compassion. Indoctrination encourages soldiers to believe that the United States is the superior nation, that killing enemies proves love of country, and that the people they will kill pose a threat to their families and friends, and to decency and freedom in general.

For their global War on Terror, Vice President Cheney and Defense Secretary Rumsfeld exploited the soldiers under their command, most of whom were working-class, and encouraged the dehumanization and terrorizing of local populations in the name of American superiority. While atrocity is intrinsic to war, the War on Terror was awash with abuses and war crimes that were systematically covered up by a military and government leadership hell-bent on projecting the image of a powerful and unified nation—even when their soldiers were engaging in illegal and horrifying behaviors.

At Abu Ghraib, entry-level soldiers like Private Lynndie England became the wanton face of America's torture regime, yet the cruel and perverted methods of intimidation used at the prison had been hatched at the highest levels of government and sanctioned down the chain of command. During the Gardez massacre in Afghanistan, soldiers murdered five innocent Afghan civilians who were celebrating the naming of a newborn in their family, then tried to cover it up by digging the U.S.-manufactured bullets out of the victims' bodies, two of whom were pregnant. After the massacre, survivors of the attack were flown to a dark site where they were interrogated by heavily tattooed, long-bearded men, whom the victims called "the American Taliban."[126] When the cover-up started to fall apart, four-star general William H. McRaven traveled to the village by motorcade and offered the villagers hush money.

The "Black Hearts" tragedy—in which soldiers premediated the gang rape of a fourteen-year-old girl and shot her parents and six-year-old sister in the head as she tried to run away—took place in a crucible of abusive leadership, extreme underdeployment, lack of necessary supplies, and heavy death tolls. Army officials blamed the murders on Iraqis, despite physical evidence to the contrary. One of the soldiers later confessed to the crimes, telling a forensic psychiatrist that he had killed a puppy by throwing it off a roof and saw no difference between that dog and an Iraqi. The psychiatrist concluded that the soldier was a sociopath but classified his danger to others as "low" and authorized his honorable discharge.[127]

The most elite commando force, SEAL Team 6, was known for engaging in similarly horrific war crimes.[128] Having assassinated Osama bin Laden, their elite status and internal code shielded the force from scrutiny, and those who reported wrongdoings, which were plentiful, were ignored or ostracized. In Afghanistan, members of this elite team reportedly taunted dying Afghanis and watched the "bleed out" videos back at the base. They performed "skinnings" of dead enemy fighters, an idea derived from the Nazis. Between 2005 and 2008, when special ops surged in the region, photos of SEAL Team 6's kills captured several instances of "canoeing," whereby soldiers would use a rifle to split open the skulls of their victims and expose their brain matter. Such mutilations and taking of "trophies" were ignored by leadership.

Even less accountable were the private security contractors on the ground, clear pawns in the United States' shadowy, for-profit war. Recall from chapter 2 that in Iraq, the U.S. government paid out some $138 billion to contracting companies, a sizeable share of which ($39.5 billion) went to KBR, a former subsidiary of Dick Cheney's Halliburton.[129] Those companies, numbering in the hundreds, together provided a private security force made up of veterans, retired police officers, security guards, and even cage fighters—mostly white middle-aged men from areas with high unemployment rates who themselves were treated like disposable commodities. These contractors' deaths were not officially reported, which helped U.S. officials create the appearance of low casualties and a waning insurgency. When they were captured, the U.S. government did not try to rescue them or help their families.[130]

Before Paul Bremer left Iraq in June 2004, he granted mercenaries and other contractors immunity from Iraqi law, marking the first time that the Pentagon officially authorized the use of civilians in combat. Like soldiers, "mercs" could use force "when necessary" and assume combat positions on behalf of the American people. While the U.S. military could bring cases against soldiers who broke the law, contractors were considered private citizens subject to the laws of the country in which they were stationed, which in war zones like Iraq and Afghanistan were unenforceable even without immunity. Lacking accountability, some contractors became indistinguishable from roving gangs and insurgents.[131]

Among the most vicious was Blackwater, the security contracting company founded by billionaire Erik Prince, the right-wing religious ideologue (and Betsy DeVos's brother) whose master plan, like Dick Cheney's, included privatizing the U.S. military and exploiting the War on Terror for billions. According to a former employee's sworn testimony, Prince "views himself as a Christian crusader tasked with eliminating Muslims and the Islamic faith from the globe."[132] In Iraq, Blackwater mercs were known to engage in drive-by shootings of innocent pedestrians and run vehicles off the road like the oil-foraging barbarians in George Miller's *The Road Warrior*. The Iraqi government tried to ban Blackwater security forces from the country following their massacre of seventeen Iraqi civilians in Nisoor Square. But the company continued to operate there, deriving its impunity from the U.S. State Department with which it was directly contracted.

THE WAR AT HOME

In addition to its wars abroad, the United States has, for many years, been waging a war at home on its own people. One need not look beyond the events of the 1971 Attica prison uprising to find powerholders like Nixon and New York governor Nelson Rockefeller crushing challenges to their authority by amping up "tough on crime" rhetoric and using indiscriminate violence to discipline and punish. Unsealed in 2015, papers and tapes documenting police retaking the Attica prison reveal how Rockefeller had ordered the blanket execution of prisoners and allowed police to systematically torture those who survived.[133] In one of the recordings, he can be heard describing his hardline stance to Nixon as one that "separated the sheep from the goats," telling the president that he would not be granting amnesty or visiting the prison to help resolve the crisis. After the massacre, Rockefeller's administration was caught lying about prison inmates cutting hostages' throats when in fact they had been shot by his snipers. Nonetheless, he reported to the president that the state troopers and snipers who killed ten hostages and twenty-nine inmates did "a fabulous job."[134] Rockefeller, a billionaire, went on to become the forty-first vice president of the United States.

In the years following Attica, tough-on-crime policies gained political currency and policing in the United States became more militarized. Reagan accelerated Nixon's War on Drugs and Democrat Bill Clinton cracked down on crime through mass incarceration and enlarging police forces. As a result of their and subsequent administrations' policies, the United States now incarcerates approximately two million people a year, by far the highest rate in the world, and spends over $300 million annually on corrections, policing, and judicial and legal functions—more than twice the budget of the Department of Education.[135] Law enforcement agents are known to profile people according to their racial "signatures," treat poor people and those with addictions or mental illness like criminals, and shoot first and ask questions later.

In the 1990s, the Department of Defense began donating military equipment to local police departments and training paramilitary units, turning them into occupying forces and exacerbating the overpolicing of poor and Black and brown communities and nonviolent protestors. Since then, repressive tactics like "no-knock" raids—in which paramilitary units force their way into a person's home without their consent—have increased exponentially. While such specialty units were created to handle high-risk situations, like those involving snipers or terrorists, under the bipartisan War on Drugs the majority of their deployments have been used for preemptive drug raids. Inevitably, such tactics end up harming innocent people and terrorizing communities.[136] In one no-knock raid, in 2014, police tossed a flashbang grenade into the playpen of a nineteen-month-old toddler, disfiguring him for life.[137] In another case in 2020 that helped to bring the issue into a critical spotlight, an innocent medical worker named Breonna Taylor was shot to death in her bed.[138]

Following the 2014 police murder of Michael Brown, a young Black man in Missouri, protests broke out in the city of Ferguson to condemn the killing, and police violence more generally. Local police used tanks and other military equipment to clear the protesters, spurring Rep. Emmanuel Cleaver to remark that "Ferguson resembles Fallujah!"[139] In response to protests in Washington, DC, after the police murder of George Floyd in Minneapolis, President Trump ordered National Guard units to crack down on the peaceful protesters, during which a Black Hawk helicopter dropped to a dangerously low level in performing a "show of force"—the kind that U.S. soldiers use to disperse insurgents in war zones.[140] Ever the opportunists, Democrats sided with the protesters and used the occasion to paint Trump as a hothead dictator, despite their own history of cracking down on protests and racialized police violence.

Recall that Bill Clinton, during his tenure, tried to expand the use of private prisons as a way to balance his budget. Due to horror stories of abuse and fraud, however, subsequent Democratic officials tried to ban the prisons, but were thwarted by Trump exploiting his immigrant crackdowns to help grow that now multi-billion-dollar industry.[141] Like the contractor rings in Afghanistan and Iraq, government oversight of private prisons is basically nonexistent, and with the profit motive as the driving force, the atrocities are many. In some states, the rate of violent assault is two to three times that of state facilities, and juveniles as young as thirteen years old are common targets.[142] In 2008, two Pennsylvania judges were caught in a "kids for cash" scandal in which they were receiving kickbacks for imposing harsh punishments on juveniles to increase the numbers, and thus profits, at for-profit detention centers. Some of those kids spent extended time in jail simply for making fun of their principal on social media or trespassing in an empty building.[143] A handful of private prison conglomerates, some owned by billionaires and private equity giants, make billions a year off the prisons, as well as in-house medical, phone, transportation, clothing, and other services—jacking up prices on a captive population and their already broken families. Though private prisons in the U.S. account for just 8 percent of the country's total prison population (which still is a lot of people), similar to the contractors in U.S. wars, they are emblematic of the avarice and brutality of the neoliberal state, and perhaps are a harbinger of things to come under future right-wing administrations.

The war at home has also involved attacks on civil liberties, usually in the name of preserving them. During the Cold War, political elites used the Red Menace to legitimize their aggressions abroad and foment a war at home in which immigrants, minority groups, trade union members, and political dissidents were surveilled, threatened, and silenced. The FBI's Counter Intelligence Program, or COINTELPRO, was among the U.S. government's most audacious efforts to suppress dissent in the name of national security. Between the mid-1950s and early 1970s, the FBI spied on and disrupted the lives of numerous activists and dissident groups, including the Black Panther and Communist Parties, and civil rights icons like Dr. Martin Luther King Jr. After Watergate and the exposure of Nixon's abuses of power over executive branch agencies, the Church Committee headed by Senator Frank Church of Idaho confirmed that U.S. intelligence agencies had been violating people's constitutional rights, and Congress passed the Foreign Intelligence Surveillance Act (FISA) of 1978 to protect citizens from illegal surveillance. It also established a FISA court to function as a judicial check on such abuses of power. Between 1979 and 2013, however, of the roughly 34,000 requests for surveillance warrants that the court received, it denied only 11 of them.[144]

In the months following 9/11, George W. Bush authorized—secretly and without a FISA warrant—a sweeping National Security Agency (NSA) data-mining program, code-named Stellar Wind, that involved wiretapping the phone and email messages of the domestic population. After a former Justice Department attorney exposed the program, and the press inquired about the lack of a FISA warrant, Attorney General Alberto Gonzales legitimized Bush's abuse of power by pointing to the president's expanded war powers under the AUMF. Soon after, the Office of Legal Counsel issued a white paper citing the president's constitutional authorities, claiming that if FISA had found the NSA program to be unlawful, its decision would have violated the Constitution's Article II delineating the president's "inherent power."[145]

In 2013, the surveillance state's exponential growth under Obama was revealed by whistleblower Edward Snowden, who leaked classified information on NSA programs that he believed to be unconstitutional. At the time, most Americans did not know what a FISA court was or that their government was tapping their phone lines, reading their texts, and monitoring their internet and library searches. Nor did the United States' foreign allies, whose phone conversations were also being monitored. Snowden's revelations of hundreds of thousands of documents, including the NSA's secret "black budget," showed that a FISA court had ordered Google, Yahoo, Microsoft, Apple, and other companies to hand over private user records to the NSA, and that the federal government was using public funds to purchase access to those tech companies' networks. The vast majority of those surveilled were regular, innocent people and not the intended targets.[146] In September 2020, a U.S. federal court ruled that the government's mass surveillance program exposed by Snowden—who is now in exile and wanted for espionage—was illegal and possibly unconstitutional.[147]

Some members of Congress have attempted to rein in the NSA, but have been gagged by national security classification regimes or unable to extract truthful testimony from leadership. During a Senate Intelligence Committee hearing in 2013, for example, Director of National Intelligence James Clapper denied that the NSA had been secretly collecting information on hundreds of millions of Americans. After Snowden's leaks, MSNBC's Andrea Mitchell pressed Clapper to explain his testimony (his lying), to which he replied that Congress's line of inquiry could not be addressed with a simple "yes-or-no" answer, so he answered in what he called the "least untruthful manner."[148]

This chapter examined the militarist aspects of neoliberalism and the deepening collusion among state and corporate elites in war, conflict, and law enforcement. It looked at how elite powerholders have used the coercive arm of the American state to serve their interests, bolster their authority, and secure "market conditions" for transnational capital. Over the last half century, this deployment of military power has involved the expansion of executive authority, the privatization of war, and the enlargement of the military and security industrial complexes. The culmination of this imperial legacy is the War on Terror, a gold rush for the terror industry and a foreshadowing of the future of epic, boundaryless wars. Finally, the chapter examined the U.S. war machine's turning inward against the very people who underwrite it. Today, terrorism by police and the ever-present threat of surveillance and incarceration are traumatizing communities and engendering a culture of fear and hostility that will take generations to overcome.

CHAPTER 5

Wall Street

Today, the top 0.01 percent of the wealthiest people in America hold more of the country's total wealth than that same group did during the Gilded Age, a time of unrestrained financial speculation—but also of grinding poverty, corruption, and racial strife.[1] That extreme concentration of wealth is in large part attributable to the dominance of Wall Street over American life, and bankers and investors' willingness to manufacture and exploit crisis, when the spoils are greatest. The centrality of finance in the United States and across the globe arose through successive waves of neoliberal reform over the last half century involving the privatization of profits and externalization of risk. That process, and its impacts on social inequality and elite power, is the subject of this chapter.

Recalling chapter 1, in the late 1960s and early 1970s, barriers to corporate profit-making and the accumulation of elite wealth were overcome by way of a class program that involved the integration and unfettering of financial institutions and markets worldwide and a shift in the global economy's center of gravity from production to finance—or, "financialization." This restructuring multiplied opportunities for profit-making in a variety of ways, including: technological and financial innovation; structural adjustment; predatory lending; high-risk speculation; and the financial engineering of corporations to extract value by plundering workforces and assets.

Right now, the top 1 percent of wealthiest Americans hold about 38 percent of the value of financial accounts holding stocks; and the top 10 percent control nearly all (84 percent) of it.[2] Economists and politicians applaud economic growth with each uptick of the Dow Jones, but what they are really celebrating is how financial markets create profit-making opportunities for this small slice of the population. For the well-off, teams of financial and asset management experts are there to provide them with high-yield opportunities and returns, and creative ways to skirt taxes on their investments.[3] But for the average person, Wall Street only figures into their lives through the experience of debt, which, for many, is how they compensate for barely rising incomes and the uncertainties associated with declining public services and institutions.

Neoliberalism did not just usher in a new set of financial techniques, it also cultivated a "survival of the fittest" culture and elevated the "free market" as an ultimate authority. While in the aftermath of the financial crisis the word "greed" could hardly be avoided, the fundamental principle driving Wall Street is less about timeless human impulses, like greed, than the historically specific "pursuit of profit and forever *renewed* profit" that sociologist Max Weber identified as intrinsic to capitalism and definitive of its spirit. Neoliberal capitalism marks an intensification of Weber's principle, and finance is the matrix through which it has taken root and metastasized.[4]

THE WASHINGTON CONSENSUS

Following the catastrophic meltdown of the financial system in 1929 and the Great Depression that followed, the Roosevelt administration instituted New Deal regulations to avert future crises by reining in high-risk speculation on Wall Street and regulating the banking industry. A few years later, amid the economic ruin of the Second World War, the Bretton Woods system—including the International Monetary Fund (IMF) and World Bank—was established by the United States and associated countries as a regulatory framework for currency exchange and other cross-border financial transactions and to stabilize the global economy.

As a result of the influx of U.S. dollars into Europe from European exports and the Marshall Plan, a "Eurodollar" market emerged that was not subject to U.S. legal restrictions and reserve requirements, and thus offered investors high returns but with greater risk. During the oil crises of the 1970s, as sharp price increases multiplied OPEC's oil revenues, the IMF, U.S. Treasury, and Federal Reserve encouraged OPEC countries to deposit their surpluses into U.S. banks and the higher-yield Eurodollar market. America's largest banks recycled these petrodollars into highly profitable "jumbo" loans distributed to developing countries that were unable to cover the exorbitant price of oil imports. The majority of the loans were issued with floating interest rates subject to rate fluctuations. This unregulated system allowed corrupt Third World leaders—like Haiti's Jean-Claude "Baby Doc" Duvalier and the Philippines' Ferdinand Marcos—to skim off the loans, then stash the stolen money offshore, where it could be recycled into loans to those same countries. In this circular process, bankers collected more and more fees and corrupt leaders got more and more chances to profit off the loans buoying their ailing economies.

With the growth of petrodollar deposits, U.S. banks expanded their volume of lending and were allowed by regulators to leverage more of their capital, sometimes to the point where more money was being lent out than brought in. According to Citicorp chairman Walter Wriston's biographer, the recycling program was "the biggest peacetime transfer of capital—and biggest lending spree—in world history."[5] Before the early 1970s, bank loans to foreign governments barely existed, but by 1973 international lending accounted for a third of profits among the largest U.S. banks, and by 1976, three-quarters of them.[6] This gold rush ushered in a new subculture of lending in which U.S. and European bankers, some in their twenties, found themselves in the company of heads of state and finance ministers, who courted them with caviar, champagne, fancy cars, and attractive escorts. A former Chase Manhattan banker in Asia recalled of the time: "The world beckoned, and there was a strong feeling that we were laying the foundations of the American century."[7]

When the second oil crisis hit in 1978, the lending spree became even more aggressive and reckless. Loans were being extended to developing countries that were clearly unable to meet their debt obligations and struggling just to pay interest.[8] A neoliberal ideologue and consummate power elite, Wriston viewed this groundswell of Third World lending as a triumph, since "the market" appeared to be solving the liquidity crisis without government intervention.[9] Even when countries' reserve ratios (their ability to absorb loss) dipped to dangerous levels and they were forced to reschedule and re-reschedule their debts, Wriston shrugged it off, collected his obscene profits, and cavalierly remarked, "Countries don't go broke."[10] As it turned out, they actually do. In 1979, the drastic surge in interest rates from the Volcker Shock sent the economies of petrodollar-indebted countries into a tailspin, as their loans had been issued with variable interest rates.[11] In 1974, loans to developing countries through private banks totaled $44 billion; but by the end of 1979, they had ballooned to an astounding $233 billion.[12] In the case of Mexico, its debt climbed from $6 billion in 1970 to $80 billion in 1982, forcing the country to raise some $500 million per week just to service its debt, of which American banks owned a sizable portion.[13]

In the lead-up to Mexico's 1982 debt crisis, Wriston and Treasury Secretary William E. Simon disparaged the IMF as an anti–free market interloper. But when Mexico's economy started to unravel, bankers refused loan forgiveness and welcomed the IMF, and the U.S. Treasury and Federal Reserve, stepping in to stem the crisis. Volcker's concern regarding "systemic risk" impelled him to secretly transfer large sums of money to the U.S. banks holding Mexico's debt. As the crisis persisted into the late 1980s, the U.S. government offered incentives for banks to forgive or restructure the loans. The IMF sweetened the deal by requiring Mexico to open its banking system to foreign investment and encouraging U.S. bankers to purchase its financial institutions at bargain prices.[14] Mexican president Miguel de la Madrid not only helped to usher in the neoliberal reforms, he also was skimming off the petrodollar lending to the tune of $162 million in 1983 alone (equivalent to about $430 million in 2021).[15]

It was around this time that the World Bank and IMF became more intertwined. The IMF's specific mission was to regulate currency rates of exchange, resolve balance-of-payments issues, and provide short-term loans; the World Bank's was to promote long-term growth in developing countries and encourage private investment. In the immediate postwar years, both institutions were founded to resolve economic conflict, foster international cooperation, and manage the world economy. With the free market in Eurodollars generating massive wealth, and neoliberal ideas gaining traction, these twin institutions would become the leading enforcers of neoliberal reform and market discipline around the world.

Treasury Secretary Simon previewed the shape of the new world order in his address at the October 1976 IMF annual meeting, where he defined economic development in terms of removing protectionist controls and barriers to market forces. His remarks echoed an internal Treasury memo dated May 1973 that emphasized the IMF and World Bank's alignment with "a western market-oriented framework" and positioned them as ambassadors of U.S. hegemony: "[T]he strategic significance of the IFIs (international financial institutions) to the U.S. lies in their role as a major instrument for achieving U.S. political, security and economic objectives with particular respect to the developing nations."[16]

Toward the end of Robert S. McNamara's tenure as World Bank president in the early 1980s, he signaled a strategic shift toward direct policy intervention by suggesting that poverty alleviation and economic development be achieved through "structural adjustment."[17] At the time, the World Bank was still making loans for projects involving public ownership; but soon after, it purged its Keynesian elements and welcomed to its helm neoliberals like former Bank of America president and CEO Alden

W. "Tom" Clausen.[18] Ronald Reagan christened the new arrangement in a 1983 speech at the World Bank's annual meeting, where he extolled the "magic of the marketplace" and claimed that "millions of individuals making their own decisions in the marketplace will always allocate resources better than any centralized government planning process."[19] The transition was also canonized by John Williamson—a senior fellow at billionaire Pete Peterson's Institute for International Economics—who in 1989 coined the term "Washington Consensus" to designate the supreme alignment of these institutional arms of empire and to remind the world where its center of power lay.

Under Bill Clinton, the World Bank and IMF adapted its Articles of Agreement to include language on the "orderly liberalization of capital movements" and to emphasize "structural and macroeconomic reforms."[20] This Washington consensus was good for Wall Street, as it opened the door for foreign investment and more extensive "liberalized" lending. Investor-friendly lending terms, or "conditionality," imposed by the World Bank and IMF, helped to cement borrowing states' commitment to privatization, low inflation, and removing regulatory barriers, while opening the doors to free trade, foreign investment, and financial speculation. The often-used term "deregulation" to describe these trends is somewhat of a misnomer as neoliberals sought "orderly liberalization" and replaced Bretton Woods with new rules and institutions aimed at multiplying opportunities for profit-making.

Lending and structural adjustment vis-à-vis the World Bank and IMF lured not just whole countries into the iron cage of debt but also individuals.[21] The World Bank's microcredit program, for example, helped to draw the world's destitute into finance capital by offering small-scale business loans to people in rural communities that were still off the financial grid, billing the program as a pathway out of poverty. It did so through its International Finance Corporation, whose mandate involved "encouraging the growth of the private sector in developing countries" and "creating new markets."[22] The Grameen Bank pioneered microlending in the 1970s, and by the mid-2000s, the United Nations had named 2005 "the Year of Microcredit" and Grameen's founder Muhammad Yunus was awarded a Nobel Peace Prize the following year. Far from a pathway out of poverty, microcredit lenders have been known to charge interest rates around 35 percent, though in many cases, the rates are much higher (70 to 80 percent).[23] Some lenders have reportedly used witch-hunt tactics to collect repayment, including public humiliation, dismantling people's homes, and physical violence—"flogging, pouring pitch over bodies, tonsuring women's hair [and] publicly spitting on a person every time she or he walks by."[24]

From the late 1980s through the end of the '90s, Alan Greenspan—an avowed Ayn Randian—wielded the Federal Reserve's lever on interest rates to navigate the world economy from crisis to crisis. In 1994, after keeping interest rates low, he jerked them upward in response to decreasing unemployment, ostensibly as a means of fighting inflation. Despite Milton Friedman's conviction regarding a "natural rate of unemployment," unemployment continued to drop without raising inflation. The sudden increase in interest rates did, however, trigger another major debt crisis in Mexico, hung over from 1982, to which the United States responded with a mammoth bank bailout ($20 billion), the largest since the Marshall Plan.[25] Congress investigated then–Treasury Secretary Robert Rubin's role in facilitating the bailout, as his bank, Goldman Sachs, was heavily invested in Mexican markets when Rubin was chairman. Within the ten years that followed, Citigroup acquired nearly three-quarters of Mexico's banking system, with Rubin serving on its board of directors.[26] For the people of Mexico, the crisis resulted in major spending cuts in mass transit, trash collection, and health services and education, and a serious crime wave in previously low-crime Mexico City, as broken labor contracts galvanized street protest and, along with it, brutal state repression.

By the late 1990s, "emerging market" economies in East Asia were witnessing astonishing levels of foreign investment and speculative activity, especially in property markets, due to IMF-advised liberalization. Hot money and foreign investment had brought a flood of wealth, infrastructure development, and jobs to the area, but ended up leaving about as fast as it had arrived. The devaluation and floating of the Thai baht crashed the currency, and crisis spread like brush fire across the globe. Investors ran for the hills as banks failed and unemployment spiked, along with rates of poverty. The IMF and World Bank offered bailouts to East Asian countries and others in the developing world with severe terms of structural adjustment, including abolishing food and kerosene subsidies, cutting public spending, privatizing state-owned businesses, and shutting down or selling off dozens of banks.[27] Successive bankruptcies that pummeled the region and forced retrenchment in government spending facilitated new waves of foreign direct investment.

Under the banner of free markets and globalization, world power elites would continue to deploy the immense power of the World Bank, IMF, and World Trade Organization (as well as the Federal Reserve and U.S. Treasury) to realize their class program, effectively forging a global economic system with profitability as its foundational principle. In doing so, they accumulated enormous wealth and political power off the backs of ordinary and often vulnerable people, prying open countries' domestic economies, buying up businesses and banks, pushing governments to cut jobs, public services, and safety nets, and in neocolonial fashion, plundering human and environmental resources.

TOO BIG TO FAIL

The financial crisis in East Asia reverberated throughout the global economy, with Long Term Capital Management (LTCM), one of the largest hedge funds at the time, nearly defaulting until the Federal Reserve bailed it out.[28] LTCM's near-collapse was fundamentally the result of excessive leveraging enabled by weak oversight vis-à-vis Greenspan's free market crusading. According to Greenspan, disclosure requirements and debt ratio limits did not apply to hedge funds since they were already regulated by their lenders—though in reality, hedge funds were not required to disclose their positions.[29] This recurring theme, and glaring contradiction, of bankers and investors being allowed to regulate themselves, while whole countries were forced into structural adjustment, persists to this day, despite proven disastrous consequences.

At the center of the neoliberal regulatory revolution in finance was the New Deal–era Glass-Steagall Act of 1933, which separated low-risk commercial banks from higher-risk investment banks to keep them from speculating with consumers' money. Glass-Steagall also included a "Regulation Q" provision that capped the amount of interest that banks could offer on deposits to prevent them from engaging in risky behaviors while competing for business. An exception was made for "specialized" mortgage lenders or thrifts (Savings & Loans), which were given a quarter-percent advantage to encourage lending in the housing market. In addition, Glass-Steagall mandated the Federal Deposit Insurance Corporation (FDIC) to safeguard consumer deposits and prevent bank failure, and barred commercial banks from nonbanking activities, like selling insurance and trading securities, so they would not use government-backed deposits for high-risk investment and trading.[30]

With runaway inflation afoot in the 1970s, interest rates rose above Regulation Q limits. This drove investors to money markets unencumbered by interest rate caps and reserve requirements, siphoning business away from commercial banks still reeling from Third World lending losses and shut out of securities markets.[31] Banks like Wriston's Citicorp had been lobbying Congress to ease Glass-Steagall restrictions since the 1960s as money markets and other financial instruments were blurring the lines between deposits and securities. They were eager to compete in those markets, and Wriston especially wanted to operate across state lines and form "one-stop shopping" conglomerates. State-driven efforts to remove Regulation Q restrictions dated back to Nixon's Hunt Commission, but it was not until Carter signed the Depository Institutions Deregulation and Monetary Control Act (DIDMCA) that interest rate ceilings were phased out and commercial banks and Savings & Loans were able to compete with money markets.

The removal of interest rate ceilings coincided with changes in usury laws regulating increasingly popular credit cards. The Supreme Court's 1978 *Marquette National Bank v. First of Omaha Service Corp.* allowed national banks to apply the maximum interest rate from their home state to their operations nationwide, incentivizing them to relocate to states with the most bank-friendly regulations.[32] Without federal interest rate ceilings, lenders could charge consumers exorbitant interest rates and fees to compensate for risky loans, setting the stage for predatory subprime lending.

As Carter's DIDMCA negated Savings & Loans' interest rate advantage, Reagan followed up with the Garn-St. Germain Act of 1982, which backed thrifts with federal insurance and allowed them to offer adjustable rate mortgages. By that time, the U.S. government had been encouraging the expansion of private home ownership through the 1977 Community Reinvestment Act (CRA), and mortgage leveraging via home equity lines of credit, which by 1980 had become a $1 billion market. Savings & Loans were meant to serve the expanding housing market as a kind of anti-redlining public service, but with shifts in the regulatory climate and intensified speculation, it was fast becoming a shady business. Garn-St. Germain raised the limit of investment that thrifts could make on commercial real estate (from 20 to 40 percent of their assets) and consumer lending (from 20 to 30 percent of their assets). This allowed, if not encouraged, them to engage in riskier lending practices while holding less capital to back them.[33]

Between the mid-1980s and the early 1990s, thousands of thrifts failed, including Charles Keating's Lincoln Savings. Keating solicited a letter from then-GOP consultant Alan Greenspan urging regulators to exempt Lincoln from a rule limiting nonmortgage investments. He got the waiver, but Lincoln went bust four years later, and Keating, a relentless crusader of anti-porn "decency," was charged with racketeering, fraud, and conspiracy.[34] Five U.S. senators ran to his defense—all of them recipients of campaign donations from Keating—including Senator John McCain, to whom Keating had contributed over $100,000 in campaign funds and private vacations for the McCain family.[35]

Despite Lincoln's bailout having cost taxpayers over $3 billion, Reagan appointed Greenspan to chair the Federal Reserve, where he remained in power for almost two decades. Much of the thrifts' assets were sold in lucrative packages to the well connected, while Wall Street banks collected fees on their sale and distribution.[36] In the end, as a result of shady lending and overleveraging, enabled by bipartisan financial deregulation, U.S. taxpayers footed a $124 billion bailout bill and the banks further consolidated their current "too big to fail" status. Between 1960 and 1979, bank mergers totaled 3,400; from 1980 to 1994, that number increased to 6,345; and from 1995 to 2000, to more than 11,000.[37]

Early in Bill Clinton's new economy, Greenspan's Federal Reserve reinterpreted the Glass-Steagall Act to let banks deal in certain debt and equity securities below 10 percent of their revenues. In 1996, it followed up with a ruling that allowed bank holding companies to engage in investment banking activities with as much as 25 percent of their revenues—essentially negating Glass-Steagall. Before that, Clinton had doubled down on Reagan's market-friendly regulatory program with the Riegle-Neal Interstate Banking and Branching Efficiency Act of 1994, which eased restrictions on cross-state banking and opened the door for mega-mergers.[38]

Following LTCM's collapse and the series of debt crises that preceded it, *Time Magazine*'s Joshua Cooper Ramo wrote a hagiographic essay on "the three marketeers"—Alan Greenspan, Robert Rubin, and Larry Summers—celebrating their "civic devotion" to crisis management, intellectual altruism, and good-humor ribbings over each other's tennis games.

> What holds them together is a passion for thinking and an inextinguishable curiosity about a new economic order that is unfolding before them like an Alice in Wonderland world. The sheer fascination of inventing a 21st century financial system motivates them more than the usual Washington drugs of power and money.[39]

Missing from this fanboy gush is the fact that, on their watch, 40 percent of the economies around the world had fallen into recession or depression over the year and a half leading up to the article's publication. In reference to Francis Fukuyama's influential "end of history" argument[40]—which hastily proclaimed the post–Cold war triumph of capitalism and liberal democracy—Ramo declared that the three marketeers had "outgrown ideology." "Their faith is in the markets and in their own ability to analyze them," he wrote—as if the trio was driven by pure love of technique rather than their unadulterated love of money. In truth, Rubin, Summers, and Greenspan were consummate neoliberal ideologues from elite banking institutions, put in control of the U.S. Treasury and other key levers of the global economy, who were using those levers to enrich themselves and their associates. That enrichment involved deflecting checks on their power by disparaging New Deal regulations as fossils from a previous era, equating rising stock prices with the general welfare, and billing financial deregulation as an inevitable step in economic modernization. As then–under secretary for international affairs Tim Geithner described it, Rubin ran the U.S. Treasury "like an investment bank,"[41] which clearly Wall Street had expected. In 1995, when Rubin was ushered in through the Treasury's revolving door, big bank campaign contributions to the Clinton campaign more than doubled from $11 million in 1992 to $28 million in 1996.

That same corrupt trio played a central role in passing the Financial Services Modernization Act of 1999, aka the Gramm-Leach-Bliley Act, that nullified Glass-Steagall and set the conditions for the 2007 global financial crisis. In February 1998, Citibank planned a merger with Travelers Insurance to become the largest financial services company in the world. The merger was not yet permissible by law and was opposed widely by consumer protection advocates, who were woefully outspent by big bank lobbyists. Citibank itself expended $13 million on political donations between 1990 and 1998, and Bank of America spent $4.6 million in 1998 alone on efforts to repeal Glass-Steagall. Greenspan granted the companies a few years to sort out the merger amid claims that the founding of the euro that year would undermine U.S. global competitiveness. It was the same year, incidentally, that Goldman Sachs assisted the Greek government's entry into the European Union by using derivatives to help shield its shaky debt status.[42]

As treasury secretary, Rubin led the charge for the Gramm-Leach-Bliley Act (along with Greenspan and Summers); then, after the bill passed, he abruptly resigned and took an executive position at Citigroup. *Bloomberg Businessweek* calculated his compensation package as totaling $126 million in the almost ten years he was there, lending credence to the bill's nickname "the Citigroup Authorization Act."[43] More audacious was when Citibank's "imperial chairman" billionaire Sanford "Sandy" Weill—known for ruthlessly cutting jobs and health care benefits from aboard his Gulfstream—accepted the pen that Clinton used to sign the legislation in a gross display of the president's servility, as Citibank's puppet. By 1999, when the law went into effect, the top ten largest banks controlled 45 percent of all banking assets, compared to 26 percent ten years earlier.[44]

In addition to the Gramm-Leach-Bliley Act, struggles over the regulation of derivatives took center stage. By that time, the financial services industry had invented a colorful array of over-the-counter (off-exchange) financial products that, unregulated, enabled traders to overleverage their assets without checks on whether they were taking excessive risks. In the wake of the LTCM failure, in which Nobel Prize–winning economists grossly overleveraged their hedge fund's assets to the extent of systemic-level risk, Brooksley Born, chairwoman of the Commodity Futures Trading Commission (CFTC), waved a red flag about the lack of oversight. At the height of his power, and with deep-pocketed Wall Street lobbyists in his corner, Greenspan waged a major offensive against Born in a chillingly coercive and patronizing way, with the help of Rubin and Summers. When word got out that Born planned to issue a concept paper urging the regulation of derivatives trading, Summers placed a furious call to her: "I have 13 bankers in my office, and they say if you go forward with this you will cause the worst financial crisis since World War II." Politically isolated, Born resigned—and Summers and his thirteen bankers went on to cause the worst financial crisis since World War II.

Through a series of sleights of hand, Senator Phil Gramm (of Gramm-Leach-Bliley) passed the Commodity Futures Modernization Act of 2000 as a rider to an 11,000-page appropriations bill, which passed into law without debate. The act allowed derivatives dealers to self-regulate and included a special exemption for energy derivative trading, known as the "Enron loophole," named after the infamous Texas-based energy company with which Gramm was closely affiliated.[45] Recall from chapter 2 that Wendy Gramm, the senator's wife, lent a strong hand in the lead-up to the legislation. As Ronald Reagan's "favorite economist," she served as the head of his presidential Task Force on Regulatory Relief and chairperson of the CFTC. With two of the five seats on the CFTC vacant, she pushed through a ruling that exempted energy futures contracts from regulation, a major boon for Enron. Weeks after the decision, she resigned and was appointed to Enron's board of directors, for which she was handsomely compensated.[46]

At the time, the litany of crimes that Enron committed was frequently chalked up to the personal depravity of "a few bad apples." However, as journalists and investigators peeled back the layers, it became clear that the "Crooked E" was only possible as a conspiracy, abetted by financial innovations and lack of regulation.[47] Freed from government oversight, Enron extended its domain beyond that of a traditional energy company toward venture capital and derivatives trading. Meant to hedge against losses or preserve profits, derivatives are not directly anchored in tangible commodities, and they rely on speculators to take the other side of a wager. Investors can bet on virtually anything—commodities, as well as interest rates and exchange rates and even "Bowie bonds" (i.e., potential royalties of a popular musician[48]). Enron, with the help of Koch Industries, pioneered the market in weather derivatives, making headlines for its ingenuity in making anything fungible under, and including, the sun.

Beyond Enron, the ability to transform any business pursuit into a stock offering attracted nonfinancial corporations to sell financial services and invest in financial assets and subsidiaries—everything from credit and insurance operations to speculating in volatile currency and futures markets—in many cases to offset losses in production.[49] Much of what Enron touched, however, did not turn to gold. The deregulation of the electricity utility in California created an opening for Enron to create fake shortages and drive up prices (and thus profits), causing serious large-scale blackouts.[50] California's energy crisis was estimated to have cost the state $40 to $45 billion. Like gasoline on a fire, tapes of Enron's traders' arrogant bantering about gaming the people of the state, including its elderly, exposed the industry's degenerate culture.[51]

Enron was able to keep its stock price soaring by pushing losses off the books and offshore through "special purpose vehicles" and accounting fraud. Now those kinds of "vehicles" or shell companies number in the hundreds of thousands; in 2019, the IMF estimated that they were helping to shelter some $15 trillion from taxation.[52] When tech stocks began to fall at the start of the new millennium, an investigative article by *Fortune's* Bethany McLean exposed Enron's malfeasance and its web of colluders.[53] Chief executives Kenneth Lay and Jeffrey Skilling were taken away in handcuffs in spectacular fashion, but it was the employees of the firm, whose retirement savings were locked up in worthless Enron stock, who paid the ultimate price. Meanwhile, derivatives trading continued to expand almost entirely self-regulated, with such a rapid proliferation of trades and creative new instruments that when the financial crisis hit in 2007, it was impossible to accurately sort out values and who owed whom.[54]

THE 2007 GLOBAL FINANCIAL CRISIS

In the wake of Enron and other accounting scandals, the bursting of the dot-com bubble in 2000, and the attack on the World Trade Center, Fed chairman Alan Greenspan turned to housing to divert a coming recession, buoy the economy, and show strength. Through a combination of low mortgage rates and lax lending standards, he and the Bush administration engineered a housing bubble that enabled more and more people to buy homes, even those who had been deemed uncreditworthy. This homebuying spree severely inflated home values and fed illusions of wealth that spurred homeowners to tap into their home equity to finance consumer spending, thereby tweaking the overall economy as Greenspan had intended.[55] According to the Federal Crisis Inquiry Commission, overall mortgage indebtedness in the United States doubled from $5.3 trillion in 2001 to $10.5 trillion in 2007.[56] Home refinancing surged from $460 billion in 2000 to $2.8 trillion in 2003.[57]

Home prices tend to rise apace with inflation, but during the peak of the housing bubble between 1996 and 2006, they increased by more than 70 percent and in some areas more.[58] When prices began to fall sharply in 2007, tens of millions of homeowners were lurched into foreclosure, their homes worth less than what they paid for them. Many of them were saddled with toxic subprime loans with ballooning interest rates and untenable pay schedules. About a quarter of mortgage holders were underwater on their mortgages; in Nevada, the proportion was much greater, over 50 percent.[59]

Middle-class wealth, largely invested in home ownership, was deeply affected by the drop in housing values. Those years, from 2007 to 2010, the median household net worth nearly halved from $108,000 to $57,000.[60] Black communities were especially devastated. Subprime lending was touted as a way to make homeownership available to those who had been denied home mortgages due to the racist policies of bank and insurance redlining. But the majority of subprime loans were refinance loans, and study after study found that African Americans in particular were being targeted for them.[61] A leaked document showed that in Maryland Wells Fargo had been using Black churches to lure people into taking bad loans, with some of the bank's employees referring to members of those communities as "mud people" and the loans as "ghetto loans."[62]

Leo Panitch and Sam Ginden locate the origins of the 2007 housing crisis in the Nixon administration's efforts to end federal housing programs for the needy and redirect government funds to subsiding private homeownership.[63] Over time, this privatization of housing helped to obscure declines in income and social spending by creating the appearance of working- and middle-class wealth. In the bigger picture, moreover, it created umpteen opportunities for profit-making by helping to tighten Wall Street's grip on the culture, with the federal government encouraging inordinately high levels of borrowing by framing homeownership as a marker of success and private finance as an agent of the public interest.

In addition to Greenspan manipulating interest rates and the promise of realizing the American dream through homeownership, the housing crisis can be attributed to shockingly lax government oversight in a context of fast-moving financial innovation. As mortgage brokers sold their loans to Wall Street banks, the banks packaged them into increasingly complex financial instruments ostensibly constructed to avert risk. With money pouring in from around the world in search of greater yields than what U.S. Treasury bonds offered, Wall Street met the demand by packaging more and riskier loans. Rating agencies, paid by the very lenders whose products they rated, abetted the process by deceptively awarding triple-A ratings to all sorts of toxic assets, while the banks followed Enron's lead in using "special purpose vehicles" to unfetter lending from reserve requirements and hide liabilities.

The more complex the financial instruments, the more the federal government left it to Wall Street to self-regulate. This turning a blind eye was especially pronounced in the case of mortgage brokers, a largely unregulated industry that the FBI warned in 2004 was fraught with fraud and malfeasance.[64] Mortgage brokers made a fortune selling subprime mortgages to regular Americans, oftentimes without proper verification and using deceptive methods; they were incentivized to do so, since the riskier the loan, the higher their fees. Subprime lending could be so profitable, in fact, that the loans were peddled to consumers who actually qualified for conventional loans.[65]

As with Hurricane Katrina, the aftermath of the financial crisis was in some ways worse than the storm itself. Phil Gramm had the audacity to call Americans a "nation of whiners" and characterized the crisis as a psychological, rather than a social, problem.[66] Others blamed it on the Community Reinvestment Act's expansion of homeownership to disadvantaged populations, rather than on Wall Street's predatory lending. The massive taxpayer bailout that Bush's treasury secretary, Hank Paulson (a former chairman and CEO of Goldman Sachs), sold to Congress, and that Congress approved, involved restrictions on the banks and assistance for stressed homeowners. But within days, the Federal Reserve and U.S. Treasury decided, without congressional approval, to forego homeowner relief and instead funneled the entire bailout to the banks. Congress felt duped, and when Republican senators David Vitter and James Inhofe fought back with legislation to cancel what was left of the Troubled Asset Relief Program (TARP), Larry Summers penned letters urging legislators to reject it, promising that the funds would go toward lending and employment and not to line the pockets of Wall Street—which simply wasn't true.

TARP's homeowner aid programs were notoriously underfunded and poorly administered, helping to relieve only a small fraction of their targeted recipients.[67] The banks, on the other hand, got their money right away and without much restriction, along with billions in deferred tax credits to write off the losses. The restrictions on bank assistance were so weak that Obama's treasury secretary, Tim Geithner—an acolyte of Henry Kissinger, Robert Rubin, and Larry Summers—became the butt of *Saturday Night Live* skits reflecting Wall Street's blatant disregard for oversight and rules. Despite prohibitions on using TARP funds to pay out bonuses, Fannie

Mae and Freddie Mac spent more than $200 million on bonuses between 2008 and 2010, after taking some $400 billion in bailout funds. American International Group (AIG)—which had been fined in 2005 for fraud and its executives charged with crimes—paid over $1 million *each* to seventy-three employees of AIG Financial Products, the unit said to be responsible for the company's collapse. *Rolling Stone*'s Matt Taibbi reported that among the "retention bonuses" AIG paid out after the bailout, eleven of them went to *ex*-employees, obviously not retained by the company.[68]

Goldman Sachs's near $11 billion 2009 compensation package prompted *Vanity Fair*'s Michael Shnayerson to remark that "what's striking about the figure is that it's exactly as much as U.S. taxpayers just handed over to the firm."[69] Goldman was particularly notable for how it played the crisis, shorting the housing market to the tune of $4 billion, which the *Wall Street Journal* called "one of the biggest windfalls the securities industry has seen in years"—but that also begged the paper to ask, "Why did Goldman continue to peddle CDOs [collateralized debt obligations] to customers early this year while its own traders were betting that CDO values would fall?"[70] Some CEOs—like Jamie Dimon (JPMorgan Chase), Stephen Friedman (Goldman Sachs, and chairman of the New York Fed), and Vikram Pandit (Citigroup CEO)—pushed legal limits on insider trading by buying up stock in their own companies while accepting billions in government loans.[71]

Former Fed chairman Paul Volcker—appointed (at age eighty-two) by Obama as chairman of the President's Economic Recovery Advisory Group—viewed the taxpayer-funded recapitalization of the banking system as a necessary evil but thought the Obama administration should have done more to prevent banking conglomeration and high-risk speculation. He did not go so far as to push for a reinstatement of Glass-Steagall, but he did argue in congressional testimony that while investment banks should be free to risk their own funds, they should not have access to taxpayer-funded bailouts if they fail. Since commercial banks made loans to individuals and businesses that were vital to the financial system, he argued, they deserved federal support, but subject to restrictions.

Volcker's ideas did not see much light until Obama's approval ratings began to sink due to public outrage over Wall Street issuing massive bonuses to its CEOs against the backdrop of the Great Recession. For Democrats, alarms sounded when Republican Scott Brown was elected to the late Edward Kennedy's Senate seat in Massachusetts following Democratic Party gubernatorial defeats in Virginia and New Jersey, where Chris Christie unseated Jon Corzine. Between mid-2007 and early 2009, household wealth declined by almost $17 trillion and over 861,000 families lost their homes.[72] The S&P index fell by 40 percent and the rate of unemployment hovered just below double digits, then hit 10 percent in October 2009. The failures of General Motors and Chrysler cost many more jobs and, unlike the bonus-bearing bank bailouts, forced concessions on wages, pensions, and working conditions—another crisis cum opportunity to discipline labor and starve public programs. States and municipalities across the nation imposed draconian budget cuts in all major areas of public services. At least thirty-one states implemented cuts that reduced low-income children's access to health care; twenty-nine states reduced care for low-income elderly people and those with disabilities; and at least thirty-four cut aid for K-12 public education and forty-three to public colleges and universities.[73]

In January 2010, Obama appeared with Volcker in the White House Diplomatic Reception Room and recommended that Congress pass "the Volcker rule," embedded in the Dodd-Frank Wall Street Reform and Consumer Protection Act. When the bill passed, however, Volcker, along with regulation advocates and financial analysts, lamented the numerous loopholes that defanged his rule and stated openly that it was not likely to prevent another financial meltdown.[74] At the bill's signing, President Obama trumpeted: "Because of this law, the American people will never again be asked to foot the bill for Wall Street's mistakes. There will be no more tax-funded bailouts, period."[75] What amounted to tens of trillions in government outlays, however, involved not just TARP, but a series of additional bailout programs,[76] tax deferrals, and secret loans—some of which only became public after Senator Bernie Sanders forced a rare, one-shot audit of the Federal Reserve.[77] What the auditors found was that the biggest part of the bank rescue came in the form of trillions in cheap emergency lending from the Federal Reserve.[78] Banks parked the money in interest-bearing accounts and used it to subsidize lucrative mergers, some pulling Peter-paying-Paul deals by taking out low-interest federal loans to repay their more costly loans from TARP.[79]

In addition to all of that, after 2008, big banks could borrow much more cheaply than smaller ones, because lenders no longer worried about them going out of business—an "implicit guarantee" subsidy worth billions a year.[80] And, despite gorging themselves at the public trough, they continued to dodge taxes. In 2010, Bank of America, which received more than $1.3 trillion through the bailout and the Federal Reserve, set up more than 200 subsidiaries in the Cayman Islands for a tax refund of $1.9 billion. After getting a bailout of more than $400 billion, JPMorgan Chase made a profit of more than $17 billion in 2013 but received a $1.3 billion tax refund, due to affiliates it incorporated offshore. That same year Citigroup, which received $2.5 trillion in bailout funds from the Federal Reserve, booked profits over $6.3 billion but got a tax refund of $260 million. Goldman Sachs and others did the same.[81]

In 2017, there were thirty-nine banks with more than $50 billion in assets; by the end of the first quarter of 2021, that number jumped to fifty-two.[82] That wave of mergers was in part due to Congress rolling back Dodd-Frank rules that required banks with $50 billion or more in assets to be considered "systemically important financial institutions" (SIFIs) subject to stricter regulations. Congress changed the threshold to $250 billion, which included just a dozen U.S. banks. The rule change—from $50 billion to $250 billion—opened the door for midsized banks to acquire rival banks without fear that they would become subject to more oversight.[83] Due to this increased consolidation, banks that in 2008 were "too big to fail" got even bigger and more powerful. JPMorgan Chase alone is now so massive that if it were a country, it would have the eighth largest economy in the world.[84]

POSTCRISIS FINANCIALIZATION

Amid the widespread distrust of banks and government that the 2007 crisis engendered, new trends in finance emerged that expanded speculators' influence in the global economy and continued to facilitate massive accumulations of wealth. Among such trends was cryptocurrency, a new, digital form of global currency that, according to advocates, would supersede states and conventional financial institutions and "democratize" finance for all. In reality, cryptocurrency has become just another way to privatize and deregulate financial markets and enable speculators to turn anything and everything into a profit-making opportunity.

"Crypto" is digital money that uses cryptography to safeguard transactions. Currently, it is not regulated or backed by any government or institution that would impose restrictions to limit risk and protect consumers and the general public. It is said to be decentralized and open source, meaning no one entity controls it, but in reality, much of crypto's wealth is held by elite investors who can manipulate prices. Nonetheless, the currency's anti-state, anti-regulation image has fostered an outlaw, anarcho-capitalist, hypermasculine culture—hence the often-used term "crypto bros" to describe its adherents.

Beginning with bitcoin in 2009, today there are thousands of cryptocurrencies valued at around $2 trillion, and innumerable other crypto-products, including nonfungible tokens (NFTs) that represent ownership of sometimes worthless things. For example, an NFT of a video meme featuring an animated cat with a Pop-Tart-shaped torso flying through space, leaving a rainbow trail, sold for $580,000 at auction.[85] In January 2019, one bitcoin traded for $3,441; as of summer 2022, it was trading at $23,000, though precipitously down from its peak of over $64,000 in November 2021. Crypto's popularity has come at great public cost, in part because the technology that bitcoin alone runs on consumes huge amounts of energy—as much as the country of Sweden[86]—but also because crypto is highly volatile and susceptible to fraud and theft.

As was the case with predatory subprime lending, lack of regulation has enabled myriad forms of shady and fraudulent activity. Indeed, crypto has become the preferred payment, investment, and lending vehicle of speculators, online bank robbers, terrorists, white-collar criminals, drug cartels and brokers of other barred commodities (child pornography, for example), and criminal organizations looking to operate outside of the established global banking system and dodge taxes. According to the Federal Trade Commission, between October 2020 and March 2021, consumers lost more than $80 million due to fraud, $2 million of which was lost to scams involving Elon Musk impersonators. Meanwhile, as of April 2022, cryptocurrency has made nineteen billionaires, among them Changpeng Zhao, the nineteenth wealthiest person in the world, whose net worth of $65 billion largely derived from his founding of Binance, a leading platform for crypto trading.[87]

Since the 2007 crisis, the financial sector has also witnessed the rise of private equity (PE) as a major-league wealth maker, such that founders of the largest PE firms have become multibillionaires. In a symbolic victory, Bain Capital executive Mitt Romney became the 2012 Republican presidential nominee and is now a U.S. senator. In 2021, twenty-five members of the *Forbes* billionaire list made their money in PE, notably Kohlberg, Kravis, and Roberts (KKR) founder Henry Kravis (net worth $7.4 billion as of this writing) and Stephen Schwarzman (around $30 billion net worth), the cofounder of the PE giant Blackstone, which manages about $1 trillion, a mammoth sum.[88] Schwartzman's reputation for slum-lording, dirty energy investments, shadow banking, and Social Security privatization precedes him, as does his penchant for throwing bacchanal birthday parties—which grabbed headlines in 2007 when people across the country were losing their homes, jobs, and life savings.[89]

PE is a rebranded form of the leveraged buyouts (LBOs) of the Reagan era, memorialized in Oliver Stone's Oscar-winning *Wall Street*—a fictionalized account of how real-life banker-predators like Ivan Boesky speculated on corporate takeovers in the go-go 1980s using illegal insider information, justified with survival-of-the-fittest ideologies and slogans like "greed is good." In that dog-eat-dog world of risk arbitrage, insider information was both money and power. The racket involved buying stock in "target" companies, pushing up bids beyond their actual value, and forcing takeovers. Drexel Burnham's Dennis Levine, on whom Charlie Sheen's character is loosely based, was a prolific insider trader and the ultimate lever in Boesky's downfall. After getting arrested for securities fraud and a host of other crimes, Levine fingered Boesky, who then tipped the dominos further by implicating junk bond king Michael Milken, one of the richest men on Wall Street. Boesky's partners in crime buried money in their mattresses and in dirt piles outside the city, only to be pardoned after short stints in jail (some of them by Bill Clinton). In Milken's case, he paid a $600 million fine in 1990—not much more than his astounding $550 million income in 1987 alone[90]—then did a few years' time, and is now a highly respected philanthropist with a net worth in the billions.[91]

Milken accumulated extraordinary wealth inventing and cornering the market for junk bonds—loans made to noncreditworthy companies that became the preferred tool for corporate raiders—and engaging in unethical business practices like peddling toxic loans and skimming profits without disclosing them to clients.[92] Three billion dollars' worth of junk bonds hit the market in 1976. Because of Milken, that number totaled $50 billion just ten years later.[93] In the 1980s, LBOs and mergers and acquisitions (M&As) were among Wall Street's hottest techniques for making massive amounts of money. Pioneers like KKR's Henry Kravis and George Roberts initiated a veritable LBO movement, as hungry Wharton youth watched them glide up the Forbes 400.

LBOs took public companies private by borrowing against their assets to pay off shareholders (usually at inflated stock prices), with financing from banks and junk bonds. They tended to involve incredibly high debt levels, which were used to justify shop-floor cost cuts at a time when unions were far too weak to prevent them. After pieces of target companies were sold and their workforces "streamlined," the "re-engineered" companies would go public again with new and improved stock prices. LBO players claimed to be purchasing undervalued assets to unlock corporations' value and "rescue" them, but the buyouts were not for innovation and product development—they were for getting rich quickly.

For target companies, LBOs were rarely profitable, but they were big money makers for the bankers and cadres of lawyers and specialists who collected fees on the massively inflated buyout prices. In 1982, for example, former treasury secretary William E. Simon's Wesray Corporation put up a few million dollars to buy Gibson Greeting Cards from RCA in an LBO for $80 million. A year later, Gibson, who personally invested about $330,000, made a public stock offering in which he profited by $70 million. Over a four-year period, he and his associates bought and sold some nineteen companies, banking a total of $8 billion.[94] Volumes of buyouts in the 1980s and 1990s followed similar narratives. In 1977, U.S. companies spent $22 billion on acquisitions, but just four years later, that number rose to $82 billion, and four years after that, $180 billion.[95]

Nowadays, billion-dollar buyout and merger deals total in the trillions and PE has become a powerful engine of financialization, profoundly deepening the reach of wealthy investors in all parts of the economy. As of 2019, assets under PE management totaled more than $6.5 trillion, and in 2020, PE accounted for 6.5 percent of GDP,[96] directly employing nearly 12 million workers and its suppliers employing an additional 7.5 million.[97] By the middle of 2018, PE owned more companies than the number of businesses listed on all of the U.S. stock exchanges combined.[98]

In broad strokes, a PE fund is an unregulated pool of money operating outside of public markets that elite investors buy into. Given the size of the initial outlay, those investors tend to be classified as "high net worth" or are institutional investors, such as universities, insurance companies, or pension funds. Enabled by low interest rates and a politically friendly climate, the pooled funds are used to invest in or buy a target company—toy stores, newspapers, hospitals, pretty much anything under the sun—and then load it up with debt (as much as 90 percent of the sticker price) to finance the purchase. The borrowed money is, theoretically, used as working capital to restructure the company and "unlock" its value, while paying large dividends and funneling profits back to investors. Then, the idea is, they sell the company at a profit.

PE is so lucrative in part because of its generous "2 and 20" fee structure—2 percent in annual fees, plus a 20 percent cut of the profits above a certain level. Under the current tax code, that 20 percent is considered "carried interest" and is thus classified as capital gains, which saves PE firms tens of millions each year in taxes. In June 2007, Congress introduced a bill to close the carried interest loophole, which would have helped the federal government recover an estimated $25 billion in tax revenue (over ten years). The bill did not pass, and the loophole remains in place despite bipartisan fire. When Obama promised to close the loophole during his 2012 campaign against Mitt Romney, Stephen Schwarzman compared his move to "when Hitler invaded Poland in 1939."[99]

PE advertises itself as a benevolent force, as just a group of well-intended entrepreneurs investing in underperforming companies and restructuring them so they become more productive and efficient, and thus good for the economy. Some are. But most of the companies taken over by PE start off healthy and only become distressed after being raided for their value. The purpose is not to make companies productive citizens; it is to maximize the fund's profits and increase a company's appeal to buyers by cutting its operating costs, while shifting the risks associated with their investment onto shell companies and workers.

Companies acquired through leveraged buyouts are more likely to lower wages, cut retirement plans, and have higher rates of bankruptcy. Buyouts of private colleges have led to higher tuition costs and lower graduation rates.[100] Instead of reinvesting profits, as someone trying to build a company would, PE strips them of workers and assets and saddles them with untenable debt repayment schedules to "discipline managers." Such was the case with the dozens of large retailers that PE firms drove into the ground—including the otherwise profitable Toys-R-Us—wiping out millions of jobs and shorting workers of their severance pay. Some PE firms eke out short-term gains by sucking out a company's real estate value—separating out the real estate and then leasing it back to the company and charging it rent. If the company buckles under the weight of the extra costs, the PE fund manager can cycle it through bankruptcy and "restructure" the investment.

The volatility that PE has introduced into the workforce is matched by high-risk lending to companies with poor credit and already high debt loads. PE's incentive structure is such that the more debt one raises against a target company, the less cash that is needed to pay for it, and the higher the returns once the company is sold. PE has also introduced dangerous levels of corporate concentration and monopoly by driving target companies out of business or merging them with other firms in the same industry. After the 2007 financial crisis, for example, Blackstone bought up chunks of "troubled" real estate assets and used them to found a large single-family home rental company, Invitation Homes Inc. After "streamlining" its operations, Invitation Homes went public, then merged with another PE-backed business to create the United States' largest single-family rental company—all off the backs of millions of people forced out of their homes due to a crisis that the banks created. As of 2022, giant PE firms continue to buy up real estate—fostering an epic housing bubble and major affordability crisis, especially for renters—and create increasingly high-risk, shadowy, complex investment vehicles and shell companies to profit off overvalued or worthless assets.

PE's raiding of the U.S. health care system—one of the country's most essential industries, accounting for a fifth of U.S. GDP—has proven disastrous. As a decentralized and fragmented industry composed of small operators, health care was ripe for investors looking to churn profits off mergers and by controlling markets. In 2020, large PE firms invested more than $340 billion to buy health care-related operations around the world, including rural hospitals, nursing homes, ambulance companies, and health care billing and debt collection systems. That year, TeamHealth (owned by Blackstone) and Envision Healthcare (owned by KKR) provided staffing for about a third of the country's emergency rooms. Billionaire Leon Black's Apollo Global Management owned RCCH Healthcare Partners, which operated eighty-eight rural hospital campuses in West Virginia, Tennessee, Kentucky, and twenty-six other states. Steward Health Care, owned by Cerberus Capital Management—a $42 billion investment firm run by billionaire Steve Feinberg—ran thirty-five hospitals and urgent care facilities in eleven states.[101] PE firms have also bought up doctors' practices, such that in 2018 the American Medical Association reported it was the first year that more physicians (over 47 percent) were employees than owners of practices (46 percent). For comparison, in 1988, 72 percent of medical practices were owned by doctors.[102]

This concentration has led to price gouging, hospital closings, predatory billing, cuts in hospital infrastructure and workforces, and declining quality of care. According to a study of PE-owned nursing homes, researchers found "robust evidence of declines in patient health and compliance with care standards" after PE firms took over the facilities.[103] Moreover, despite receiving at least $1.5 billion in interest-free loans from COVID-relief funding streams, PE-backed health care providers cut workers' pay and benefits to make up for lost profits due to the emergency suspension of elective surgeries.[104] They also contributed to shortages of ventilators, masks, and other equipment because their managers did not want to lose potential profits by keeping such equipment on the shelves in their hospitals.[105]

PE managers have been caught grossly overcharging for medical treatment. In 2020, *NBC News* reported that while the median cost for treating a broken arm in an emergency room was about $665, Blackstone's TeamHealth charged almost $3,000. In a typical emergency room, NBC found, a physician group might charge three to four times the Medicare rate, but TeamHealth charged six times the rate.[106] There is also the problem of "surprise billing"—when a patient's hospital is in their insurance network, but not the doctors who are treating them. PE firms found that, especially in emergency rooms, they could squeeze out profits by moving doctors out of network and then extracting higher prices from patients unaware that they are being treated by out-of-network providers.[107] Imagine having a heart attack or some other life-threatening event, being admitted to the emergency room in or near your community, then finding out later that while you were fighting for your life, some already superrich banker was fleecing you for your last dollar.

Naturally, when Congress tried to thwart this criminal behavior, PE lobby groups spent a fortune protecting their interests, including a benevolent-sounding organization called Doctor-Patient Unity, which spent more than $28 million on ads funded by PE-backed companies.[108] The bill did not pass, and to the Biden administration's credit, its Health and Human Services Administration passed a rule in July 2021 banning this egregious practice.[109]

The years since the financial crisis also witnessed the rise of just a handful of asset management firms as a dominant force in the world economy. Asset managers are companies that run investment funds for a variety of retail, institutional, and private investors. While traditionally, ownership of corporate shares has tended to be dispersed across many diverse investors and owners of assets, this vast pool of corporate equity has become increasingly controlled and owned by a small, concentrated group of intermediary financial institutions.

Today, a "big three" of asset management firms—BlackRock, Vanguard, and State Street Global Advisors—together are the largest shareholder in almost 90 percent of the companies in the S&P 500 index, including Apple, Microsoft, ExxonMobil, and GE.[110] As of 2020, they were also the largest shareholder in 40 percent of all publicly listed U.S. companies, employing 23.5 million people, and with combined assets of over $15 trillion—an amount equivalent to more than three-quarters of U.S. GDP.[111] The largest of these firms, BlackRock, not only controls shares in all of these companies but also has been hired by leading governments and central banks to advise them, in some cases making decisions about institutions in which BlackRock is a shareholder.

This infrastructural power and concentration of ownership, largely unknown to the public, allows BlackRock and these other "big three" firms enormous influence over nearly every industry in the world. Among fossil fuel companies alone, in 2020 BlackRock managed more than $87 billion worth of shares, giving it a major hand in decision-making over how to combat the climate crisis, or not combat it at all.[112] Benjamin Braun termed this concentration of ownership "asset manager capitalism" to indicate the systemic effects of this acute consolidation and the novel corporate and financial architecture it has fostered.[113] With a small group of financial companies controlling this architecture and an already large and still growing amount of wealth, they are on course to one day hold voting control of every major corporation and wield an immense, systemic level of power over governments and the global economy.

MONEY IN POLITICS

On the heels of the Obama presidency, the 2016 presidential election became a referendum on Wall Street excess and whether Citibank and Goldman Sachs would continue to run the U.S. Treasury, the Federal Reserve, and the White House. On the Democratic side was Hillary Clinton, whose husband may have done more than any other president to cue the country up for a massive financial crisis, with Hillary standing by his side. During the primary, pundits mused about Hillary's "Goldman Sachs problem," as over the years, she and Bill had collected millions in speaking fees from the big banks, and her 2016 campaign amassed nearly $40 million in donations from the "securities and investment industries."[114] She also supported Obama's historic but failed trade deal, the Trans-Pacific Partnership (TPP), until the political winds drove her to disavow it. The TPP would have further unfettered Wall Street with rules restricting changes in member countries' domestic regimes of financial regulation that "might" negatively impact the industry's future profits, even if they were enacted in response to a crisis.[115]

Clinton's opponent in the 2016 primary, Bernie Sanders, gained unexpected steam running on a platform to reinstate Glass-Steagall, rein in Wall Street, impose a financial transaction tax, and turn credit agencies into nonprofits to avoid the corrupt triple-A rating of toxic financial instruments that helped to precipitate the financial crisis.[116] Sanders also exposed the parasitic behavior of hedge funds amid the apocalyptic economic collapse in Puerto Rico (PR) at their hands. When PR started to default on its debt in the summer of 2016, hedge funds bought up the high-risk (thus high-yield) tax-exempt municipal bonds that the government was selling to keep hospitals and schools open, as well as other essential social services threatened by steep declines in revenue. As the situation worsened, the hedge funds piled on, knowing full well that the commonwealth was hanging on by a thread. When default became imminent, they clamored for their returns—forcing the island to pay them back 100 cents on the dollar—and even sued PR to avoid taking a haircut on their investments.[117] The U.S. Supreme Court responded by putting the territory's fate in the hands of Congress, whose election campaigns are largely funded by hedge fund managers and Wall Street. Instead of a meager stimulus of the kind that Obama issued to stem the 2007 financial crisis, PR's "rescue" involved punishing terms of structural adjustment, even as over half of the island's children were living in poverty. Billionaire hedge fund owners, some of them hiding behind shell companies in Delaware, profited in the hundreds of millions.[118]

During the Democratic primary, both Clinton and Sanders also addressed the growing problem of student debt, which by May 2022 hit a record of more than $1.7 trillion, $1.6 trillion of it federal student debt, spread among 43.4 million borrowers, each owing an average of more than $37,000.[119] Other forms of consumer borrowing were also on the rise, as the "plastic trap" of credit card debt was approaching its July 2008 peak of $1.02 trillion (in the first quarter of 2022, it was around $841 billion, with the average credit card holder owing $6,569 with an interest rate of 17 percent).[120] Sanders proposed canceling student loans and medical and other debt and shifting to U.S. Postal Service banking—a program conceived by the American Postal Workers Union to improve Americans' access to local banks and as an alternative to the big bank predators.

Amid growing anti-Wall Street sentiment across the political spectrum, candidate Donald Trump cast himself as a working man's hero and railed against the "global power structure that is responsible for the economic decisions that have robbed our working class, stripped our country of its wealth and put that money into the pockets of a handful of large corporations and political entities."[121] Despite his own gold-plated lifestyle, his winning strategy involved painting Hillary as "crooked" by pointing to her six-figure Wall Street speaking fees and numerous corruption scandals. Once in office, however, Trump lit a bonfire of financial regulations and passed a massive tax cut for the wealthy, while his Securities and Exchange Commission (SEC) and Justice Department turned a blind eye to ongoing investigations into banking fraud, money laundering, and tax evasion.

Trump also oversaw changes in regulations on the despicable practice of payday and auto lending. In the United States today, alarming numbers of workers, elderly people, and military veterans are ensnared in a Sisyphean struggle against mounting debt, just trying to cover the increasingly steep costs of health care, lifesaving medicines, and other basics, because their wages or Social Security income is not enough for them to get by. Without safety net supports, they resort to short-term, high-interest payday or auto loans issued by big banks, check cashers, and finance companies.

In the case of auto loans, a borrower can take out a loan of around $1,000 in exchange for a lien on the title of their car, which most people rely on for necessities like getting to work or visiting the doctor. Thirty days after they take the loan, they must repay the full balance plus fees and exorbitant interest. If they can't pay, they must roll over the loan and take on more fees or risk losing their car. On average, borrowers roll over a car title loan eight times and end up spending *half* of their monthly income on loan payments. About a tenth of them have their vehicle repossessed. One bank, Santander, was brought up on charges of violating the Servicemembers Civil Relief Act by illegally repossessing vehicles of soldiers stationed overseas.[122]

Researchers estimate that there are more than 20,000 car title and payday lending shops nationwide, heavily concentrated in the South and so-called red states.[123] Big banks like Wells Fargo and Bank of America that can borrow money at exceptionally low interest rates from the Federal Reserve use that credit to issue millions in payday loans to consumers at interest rates as high as 400 to 500 percent.[124] Horror stories abound of lenders threatening and harassing borrowers at their places of work, like loan sharks, and of Americans blowing through their disability or Social Security checks to pay tens of thousands in fees over several years on loans of just a few thousand.

The Obama administration clamped down on payday loans, but recall that Trump's head of the Consumer Financial Protection Bureau, Mick Mulvaney, tried to gut the agency by freezing new investigations, dropping enforcement actions, and mockingly requesting a budget of $0. After Mulvaney left, Kathleen Kraninger stayed the course, pandering to the predatory lending industry's trade group—the Community Financial Services Association of America (CFSA)—whose members poured about $1 million into the Trump Organization's coffers. Indicating the extent to which Democrats learned their lesson in the making of Trump, in July 2021, Ohio Senator Sherrod Brown and other Democrats proposed establishing 36 percent as a federal interest rate cap on payday loans, following the eighteen states that already have such a cap, but begging the question: with progressives like that, who needs conservatives?

In 2020, senators like Bernie Sanders and Elizabeth Warren again tried to use the presidential election to gather support for reining in Wall Street. In response, Wall Street spent a record $2.9 billion on political contributions and 50 percent more on lobbying than it had in 2016. Tellingly, the sector spent around 2.5 times more on electing Democratic Joe Biden than it did on re-electing Republican President Donald Trump. As Sanders and Warren railed against PE "vampires" (Warren's words), thirty-three-year-old Jon Ossoff, a Georgia Democrat, received more money from Wall Street for his first-time senatorial bid than any sitting member of Congress.[125] Biden and his now vice president Kamala Harris (as well as Senator Cory Booker and Mayor Pete Buttigieg) took generous donations from Blackstone and the Carlyle Group, among others.

Blackstone got its money's worth. Founder and chief executive Larry Fink was reportedly on the shortlist of Biden's treasury secretary candidates, and the firm's Brian Deese, former global head of sustainable investing, is, at the time of this writing, leading the Biden White House's National Economic Council. Treasury Secretary Janet Yellen's deputy also hails from BlackRock, as does Mike Pyle, chief economist to the vice president. In light of these appointments, and the Federal Reserve's decision to hire BlackRock to administer its COVID-19 corporate bond purchase program, journalists fittingly nicknamed the company "the fourth branch of government."[126]

This chapter focused on the progression of neoliberal financialization and upward wealth transfer over the last half century and the devastation it has caused and enabled. Between the postwar era, where this story began, and the onslaught of the financial crisis in 2007, financial services' contribution to GDP increased from 2.8 percent in 1950 to 8.3 percent in 2006 (around where it hovers today) and their assets have grown from about a tenth of all corporate profits to a third of them.[127] Today, the big banks are even bigger. PE and asset management firms have stealthily consolidated their control over huge parts of the global economy and U.S. government. And the number of billionaire bankers, hedge fund managers, and financial sector CEOs on billionaires' lists continues to grow. History has shown that this kind of expansion of finance and concentration of ownership is correlated with extreme forms of social and political inequality. And, as our contemporary moment confirms, such extreme social inequality and monopoly power, in turn, are correlated with mass powerlessness, human suffering, and the rise of reactionary forces.

CHAPTER 6
Billionaires

In October 2021, as the coronavirus pandemic continued to rage, a report jointly sponsored by Citizens for Tax Fairness and the Institute for Policy Studies tallied the total number of U.S. billionaires at 745, up from 614 just a year and a half before, when the COVID crisis began. Those 745 individuals reportedly had a combined net worth of $5 trillion—a sum comparable to the GDP of Japan, the third largest economy in the world.[1] On a global scale, Oxfam International estimated in January 2020 that 2,153 billionaires had more wealth than 60 percent of the world's population (4.6 billion people).[2] In a follow-up two years later, the organization reported that over the course of the pandemic "the world's ten richest men more than doubled their fortunes from $700 billion to $1.5 trillion—at a rate of $15,000 per second or $1.3 billion a day." The rest of humanity saw their incomes decline and over 160 million were forced into poverty.[3]

History's first billionaire, John D. Rockefeller Sr., reached "three comma" net worth in 1916, after his flagship company Standard Oil—a monopoly that refined some 90 percent of the country's oil—was broken up in accordance with the Sherman Anti-Trust Act and shares in his splinter companies soared. At the time of his death two decades later, Rockefeller had amassed a fortune worth 1.5 percent of America's total economic output that year—about $340 billion today.[4] No contemporary billionaire has accumulated that kind of wealth, but as Oxfam and other groups have shown, their fortunes—and their political and cultural power and grip on the world economy—are growing at an astonishing rate.

In *The Power Elite*, C. Wright Mills wrote, "If we would understand the very rich we must first understand the economic and political structure of the nation in which they become the very rich."[5] This chapter aims to do just that, first by assessing the technological changes, policy decisions, institutional restructuring, and dynamics of the world economy behind this enlargement of plutocratic power; and second, by teasing out its ideological underpinnings and how neoliberals reproduce their class program through discourses and representations that exalt the very rich as historical protagonists and portray their particular interests as the interests of all.

The chapter also addresses issues specific to the very rich: corporate monopoly, tax evasion, and use of philanthropy to dictate public policy. As with Rockefeller, most of today's billionaires command giant conglomerates with complex arrays of holdings and deep and expansive reach into the global economy. Rather than get broken up, however, their monopoly power has been nurtured and grown amid a withering of antitrust laws and regulations and unfettering of business. This unfettering has also paved the way for billionaires and multimillionaires to infiltrate and undermine the public sector through philanthropic pursuits in education, health care, universities, and a host of other institutions; and to use the appearance of altruism to distract from the underhanded ways in which they accumulate their wealth and abdicate social responsibility.

EXTREME WEALTH AND IDEOLOGY

The explosion of extreme wealth in America since the 1980s has spawned a cottage industry of vindicators, most of which focus on elites' conspicuous consumption—the Swiss boarding schools and Ivy League universities, private clubs and exclusive parties, superyachts and private jets—and how they monetize status markers into cultural capital and what Mills called "the accumulation of advantages." Some, like billionaire financier Jeffrey Epstein, become headline news for committing heinous crimes without consequence until they become cultural spectacles and "ultimate symbol[s] of plutocratic rot," as the *New York Times*'s Michelle Goldberg put it.[6] Others are singled out for their bizarre and grotesque fantasies, like tech billionaire Peter Thiel's investment in sea-steading and alleged interest in anti-aging technologies involving transfusions using the blood of the young.[7] But most simply veil their exploits with philanthropy and sophisticated public relations or curry favor among the public by innovating cool, addictive products and trends. In doing so, they protect their status as celebrities of the corporate world and image as history makers and singular beings. Such was the case with Apple founder Steve Jobs, whom the news media often compared to visionaries like Picasso, Stravinsky, and Edison, despite Jobs's mercurial personality and tendency to demean those around him—and his company's use of sweatshop labor to make its i-products. Similarly, billionaires like Bill Gates and Jeff Bezos have been lionized in public discourse for acting on their God complexes to "revolutionize" public education and space travel (respectively). Never mind that they acquired and maintained their extreme wealth by breaking anti-trust laws, skirting taxes, and mistreating their employees.

One of the most cited, and hagiographic, registers of extreme wealth today is the Forbes 400, *Forbes Magazine's* annual ranking of the 400 wealthiest Americans by net worth. *Forbes* has also released lists of "the most powerful," "the richest in tech," "the Midas list of top investors," and others. The practice of publishing lists of notable rich people dates at least as far back as 1892, with the *New York Tribune*'s list of the 4,000 wealthiest Americans. *Forbes* published its first list of the 30 wealthiest in 1918. Then much later, in 1982, Malcolm Forbes—an heir and ostentatious multimillionaire—created the Forbes 400 based on his "Cost of Living Extremely Well Index," a sick parody of the Cost of Living Index used to determine federal benefits for people in need. The first Forbes 400 had 13 billionaires and inclusion on it required a net worth of more than $75 million. That first year, 23 percent of the Forbes 400's wealth derived from oil, 15 percent from manufacturing, 9 percent from finance, and 3 percent from technology. Fast forward to 2021, and to make *Forbes*'s fortieth annual list, one had to have a net worth of at least $2.9 billion, and the dominant sectors were finance and investments, technology, and the food and drink industry, in that order.[8]

Published in the 1980s, *Forbes*'s *All the Money in the World* characterized America's very rich as "remarkable people, who flourish in the land of opportunity. . . . They bring jobs, energy, ideas, and even joy to their society. They have been responsible . . . for extraordinary advances in technology, the invention of new financial instruments, and the efficient restructuring of American industry." The book paints the decade itself as "a period of extraordinary individual and entrepreneurial energy . . . when American society emphasized the power of corporations."[9] Economists describe 1982 (the Forbes 400's founding year) in starkly different terms, as a time when the economy was in a severe recession with deteriorating labor market conditions and a high unemployment rate that reached nearly 11 percent, the highest since World War II.[10]

The chasm between confetti narratives of the rich and the political-economic realities in which they live and exploit is rooted in the neoliberal tendency to equate revered concepts like freedom and choice with personal, rather than social, responsibility. Nobel Prize–winning economist

Milton Friedman advanced this view, arguing that "the great advances of civilization . . . have never come from centralized government. . . . Their achievements were the product of individual genius, of strongly held minority views, of a social climate permitting variety and diversity. Government can never duplicate the variety and diversity of individual action."[11]

In the 1990s new economy, such "great men" narratives surrounding wealth and political power appeared regularly on bestseller lists and "101" course syllabi. Notable among them was Malcolm Gladwell's *Outliers*, which deployed positivist terminology to sanitize power inequalities as mere deviations from a numerical norm. Instead of unraveling the knot of decisions, policies, and power plays behind the obscene accumulation of wealth and power of the men in his book—which include tax evasion, antitrust violations, insider trading, hostile takeovers, exploitation of workers, and corruption—the intellectual sloths of this "great man" propaganda industry chalk power elitism up to luck, using the same talking points that billionaires themselves use when skirting accountability.[12] For example, when a reporter asked billionaire New York City Mayor Michael Bloomberg how he squared his corrupt housing policies with the story of Desani—a young girl living in his city's decrepit shelter system whose life story was featured in the *New York Times*—he replied: "This kid was dealt a bad hand. I don't know quite why. That's just the way God works. Sometimes some of us are lucky and some of us are not."[13] Whether chalking up extreme wealth to genius or to luck, the outcome is the same: history is told from the perspective of the victors, and the contributions of everyday workers, mothers and fathers, and communities are degraded or erased—and along with them our sense of common purpose and political agency.

CORPORATE POWER

In 2006, billionaire investor Warren Buffett, one of the richest men in the world, remarked, "There's class warfare, all right, but it's my class, the rich class, that's making war, and we're winning."[14] The decade leading up to Buffett's quip witnessed substantial changes in the constitution of elite wealth brought by the increasing porosity of nation-states and rise of a supranational ruling class whose business was (and is) located everywhere yet oftentimes headquartered nowhere. Within this new category of *global* elite are billionaires, chiefs of multinational corporations and financial institutions, and the like, who engage in the making of cross-border mergers and acquisitions, joint ventures, transnational governance structures, and unchecked monopoly power. These corporate titans plan and perform class dominance through events like the World Economic Forum in Davos, along with heads of state, nongovernmental organizations, and "A list" celebrities.

Despite this globalization of the ruling class, states still remain important sites of struggle—over tax policy, public investment, corporate subsidies, regulatory regimes, and the distribution of wealth, income, and environmental and human resources. In the United States, masses of people pay into and rely on government for basic needs like health care, schooling and library access, postal delivery, disaster relief, and transportation. All of these institutions, and more, have been under constant attack by corporate powerholders looking to realize their class interests by pouring large sums of money into controlling the state and its resources.

During the 2016 Democratic Party primary, Senator Bernie Sanders popularized the word "oligarchy" in contesting billionaires' outsized influence on American life.[15] The concept harkens back to Aristotle, who conceived of *oligarchy* as a nexus between wealth and political power in which extreme political inequality and material inequality coincide. In political scientist Jeffrey Winters's extensive writing on the subject, he defines oligarchs as individuals who personally command or control massive wealth that can readily be deployed for political purposes and who are driven primarily by self-interest to defend their dominance from challenges posed by government regulation and fiscal policy. While the power of political mobilization relies on large numbers of people, and the power of coercion relies on control over the means of violence, oligarchic power involves a unique set of political resources that do not require numbers, force, or extensive time investment by wealthy individuals or even class coordination among them.[16]

Because the American state is predicated on property rights, oligarchs can rely on state actors to help secure their wealth, and as such, few of them seek political office. Most prefer manipulating state power from behind the scenes through personal relationships, campaign contributions, revolving-door employment of their associates, and formidable armies of politically connected white-shoe lawyers, consultants, and lobbying firms—what Winters terms the "wealth defense industry."[17] In addition to wealth defense technicians, oligarchs spend millions upon millions on grassroots groups, public advocacy, and corporate activism in defense of their hegemony. Such efforts trace back to Lewis Powell's infamous 1971 memo to the U.S. Chamber of Commerce—a manifesto for reclaiming corporate power in the face of gains by environmental, labor, and consumer protection groups—in which he railed against perceived attacks "on the

American free enterprise system . . . from the college campus, the pulpit, the media, the intellectual and literary journals, the arts and sciences, and from politicians."[18]

Recalling chapter 2, Powell's memo marked the opening salvo of a now-extensive network of individuals and corporations, think tanks, academic institutes, and foundations that exercise significant influence in U.S. politics yet fly under the radar of most people. Today, that network includes think tanks like the Federalist Society, Cato Institute, and Heritage Foundation; trade associations like the National Association of Manufacturers, the National Federation of Independent Business, and the U.S. Chamber of Commerce; and consortia like the American Legislative Exchange Council (ALEC)—a national organization of politicians and Fortune 500 CEOs that drafts and passes pro-business legislation at local and state levels of government. It also has included industry-specific front groups, like the American Pain Foundation and the American Pain Society that the billionaire Sackler family funded to lobby lawmakers and create a "pain movement" to proliferate their highly profitable and addictive prescription drugs.[19]

Billionaires who once invested heavily in party-selected candidates have moved to running "independent" super PACs, and some have gone even further, auditioning and running their own candidates. This evolution in campaign finance can largely be attributed to multibillionaires Charles and David Koch, whose political organizations and donor networks became powerful forces in U.S. politics by pooling oligarchic wealth and creating the appearance of grassroots mobilization. The Koch brothers inherited their vast fortune and namesake conglomerate from their father, Fred, a chemical engineer who invented an efficient process for converting oil into gasoline. In the 1930s, Fred's company helped Stalin's regime set up modern oil refineries and trained its engineers. After the purges, he returned to the United States and joined the John Birch Society, a virulently anticommunist group known for its anti-government fearmongering. Charles and David expanded their father's company into a trillion-dollar empire by refining and processing various commodities and fossil fuels, including dirty Tar Sands oil, and with Enron, gaming energy markets.

Driven by ideology and self-interest, the Kochs have worked for decades to dismantle the tax system and legal structures that protect workers, the poor, and the environment. In 1980, David Koch ran for vice president on the Libertarian Party ticket, promoting a platform that read like an extremist manifesto for taking down the U.S. government. His proposals included abolishing Medicare and Medicaid, Social Security, public schools, and the minimum wage; dismantling federal agencies like the Environmental Protection Agency, the Food and Drug Administration, the IRS, the departments of Energy and Transportation, the Occupational Safety and Health Agency, and the U.S. Postal Service, among others; ending all forms of taxation and campaign finance laws; privatizing railroads and the national highway system; and even eliminating seat belt laws and aid to the poor. After their Libertarian Party bid failed, the Kochs pursued this agenda by pouring energy and money into think tanks and foundations. They were early backers of institutes like Cato and over the years distributed hundreds of grants to college- and university-based scholars and programs, including the Mercatus Center at George Mason University, dedicated to developing "market-oriented ideas."[20]

In addition to underwriting an ideological war, the Koch brothers orchestrated a large donor base to support candidates, directly and through super PACs, and funded advocacy groups engaged in research, lobbying, outreach, and protest. While most large-scale donors have used their money to influence high-profile presidential races, the Kochs also supported races at the state and local levels and, in 2010, funded many of the campaigns that helped win the GOP a majority in the House of Representatives and, four years later, in the Senate. Rather than endorse and fundraise for candidates, as many billionaires do, they formed an expansive, informal political party for vetting, selecting, and funding candidates to serve as mouthpieces for their agenda. And, they created an infrastructure for grassroots organizations to fight the ideological battle on the ground. Remarkably, the Koch network is believed to have mobilized greater human and financial resources than the entire Democratic and Republican Parties put together.[21]

LABOR, TECHNOLOGY, AND MONOPOLY

The enlargement of corporate power that the Powell memo helped set in motion involved struggle over the structuring of the global economy by leading economic powers, and cross-border coordination among state, corporate, and banking elites. As part of this corporate-led globalization, less stable economies were transformed from operating as sites of raw material extraction to export-led manufacturing production, their domestic economies pried open to foreign investment and competition. Dispersed across the globe and stratified into an immense assembly line were suppliers, distributors, bankers, and subsidiaries interconnected as a world system, powered by states and investors as well as millions of human cogs in an unfathomably expansive machine. This machinery was achieved by way of neoliberal monetary and fiscal reforms that effectively altered domestic labor markets and class structures while destroying communities and legal protections.[22] As apparel, tech, and other major companies expanded overseas to take advantage of the sweatshop wages, lack of workplace rights, and other "favorable market conditions," logos like the golden arches and Nike swoosh became universal symbols of U.S. imperialism and capitalist exploitation. Emblematic of these dynamics, in China, Walmart and Apple suppliers hung signs on their factory walls warning: "Work hard on the job today or work hard to find a job tomorrow."[23]

Production processes, labor markets, and class and legal structures in the United States underwent profound restructuring as well. The dispersal of manufacturing away from industrial cities to rural and semirural areas, and overseas, coincided with the spread of lean production methods—the vertical disintegration of production through outsourcing, subcontracting, and offshoring, and increased reliance on nonunion labor—and, into the new millennium, automation. Between 1980 and 1999, the 500 largest U.S. companies cut almost five million jobs, while tripling their assets and profits, and increasing their market value (via stock prices) eightfold. They did this with the help of lower corporate tax rates and weakened regulation, as well as productivity gains associated with investments in new technologies and the diminishment of worker power.[24]

The unmooring of corporations from place through information and communications technologies, financialization, and the availability of low-cost labor abroad enabled the wealthy to redirect investment away from workers and productive activity and toward investors and stock buybacks, though some did reinvest their profits in robotics and surveillance technologies to speed up work. As corporate elites turned their attention to free trade, lax regulatory regimes, and "race to the bottom" labor markets, U.S. workers saw their incomes and workplace protections decline and investment in public institutions and supports significantly wane.

At the center of these trends was Walmart—for many years, the largest retailer and employer in the world with revenues in the trillions—which almost singlehandedly reversed the postwar course toward living wages, pensions, and lifetime employment and replaced it with low-wage and low-benefit jobs that rapidly turned over. Founded in 1962 by Heartland conservative Sam Walton in the foothills of the Ozarks, Walmart rose to retail dominance on a business model based on highly productive labor and tight cost controls. In Walmart's case, that meant cutthroat competition, environmental and labor abuse, flagrant union-busting, and use of part-time and temporary employment to reduce overhead costs associated with health benefits, workers' comp, and overtime.[25]

Walton entered markets untouched by other discounters, mostly in poor, rural communities, and undercut local businesses. Because people in those communities were suffering high levels of unemployment, he was able to exploit their desperation for work, and lure low- and middle-income consumers who could only afford cheap products—all while claiming moral high ground as a job creator. During the Kennedy administration, when Congress extended the minimum wage to retail workers, Walton took advantage of a small business exemption by breaking up his stores into individual entities, allowing him to skirt the minimum wage law and gain a major edge on his competitors.[26] Instead of letting workers bargain collectively, he instituted profit-sharing programs to convince employees that their interests aligned with those of management. He also hired professionals to lecture workers on the negative aspects of unions and even established a "union avoidance program."[27]

Over the years, Walmart has been sued for gender discrimination, forcing employees to work seven days a week without overtime pay, making workers clock out during slack times, adding bogus deductions to paychecks, employing teenagers to work with hazardous materials, and classifying regular employees as contract workers to avoid paying Social Security, unemployment taxes, and workers' comp. Municipalities have fought to prevent the company from colonizing their towns because it eviscerates local economies and mom-and-pop shops and the tax revenue it generates does not compensate for its drag on local resources.

In 2021, Amazon surpassed Walmart as the world's largest retailer, dominating labor markets and using many of the "scientific" data-driven methods that made the Waltons one of the richest families in the world.[28] Amazon extracts value from its workforce by speeding up the pace of work, limiting bathroom breaks, and cutting costs on heating and air conditioning such that workers have to endure extreme cold and heat. It has also experimented with new technologies to boost productivity, such as robotics, tracking devices, and timers to monitor workers. Amazon employees have reported injuries resulting from the grueling pace of work and the pressure of having security cameras and timers clocking their speed.[29] When Amazon set out to build a fleet of delivery trucks to bring in-house what it was outsourcing to UPS and FedEx, it used vans to avoid onerous trucking regulations and contracted untrained drivers. The impossible pace the company set resulted in accidents and even deaths, with Amazon skirting liability because the contractors were considered third parties.

Similar to how Sam Walton fed on the desperation of rural communities, Amazon's low-paid warehouse employees were gleaned from the ranks of the unemployed during the 2007 financial crisis. That crisis also gave birth to a tech-driven "gig" or "sharing economy" that catapulted a handful of boy-geniuses onto billionaire lists, including Uber's Travis Kalanick and Airbnb's millennial cofounders Joe Gebbia and Brian Chesky. In the gig economy, on-demand services are provided by low-wage, insecure labor, whose exploitation is enabled by smartphones and other mobile and internet technologies as well as the availability of venture capital and gentrification of postindustrial cities. A twist on the idea of cost-saving technologies, the gig economy gleans profits off capital investments made by workers themselves so that companies are not saddled with initial capital outlays or burdened with the costs of storing, servicing, or insuring equipment. In some cases, workers will make the initial capital investment, often in rapidly depreciating machinery, like automobiles; others are enticed by the idea of making money off something they already own.

In that context, the online real-estate-subletting giant Airbnb became a posterchild for DIY and grassroots solutions to runaway rents and under- and unemployment. In many places, however, Airbnb has been dominated by commercial operations; and by feeding price-inflated markets, it has exacerbated the country's affordable housing crisis and helped turn cities like New York and San Francisco into destinations rather than places where people can actually live.[30]

Along with the proliferation of capital platforms such as Airbnb are labor platforms like Uber and TaskRabbit. Uber and its rival Lyft are "unfettered" alternatives to government-regulated taxis that offer drivers the freedom to "set their own schedules" and "make as much [money] as they want." TaskRabbit matches online clients with workers willing to do odd jobs, like cleaning out garages or walking dogs, then encourages those workers to outbid each other for work and undercut each other's wages. Gig economy enthusiasts embellish these scams with the usual neoliberal gloss of choice, personal freedom, and flexibility, obscuring the dangers and volatility of unregulated, on-demand work and the undue empowerment of consumers to evaluate workers' job performance. In many cases, gig workers are forced to cobble together a living by working two or more jobs, none of which offer health benefits or pay into Social Security.

The ubiquity of smartphones, and social media, has also enabled tech billionaires to make fortunes off the personal data of regular people—often in flagrant violation of their privacy—and in the process amass substantial economic, political, and cultural power. Shoshana Zuboff coined the term "surveillance capitalism" to describe the logics and techniques of extraction and manipulation built into the business models of these online behemoths.[31] Skirting anti-trust standards, they provide services free of charge to billions of people while monitoring their behavior without their consent. Then they monetize that data through targeted advertising for products, but also for ideas, political campaigns and movements, and even riots. In pairing data extraction with artificial intelligence, moreover, tech companies try to direct and manipulate their users' behaviors, calling it "smart technology."

Pioneering this model is Facebook, the online social networking site that made Mark Zuckerberg the world's youngest billionaire and one of the richest people in the world. Facebook functions as a kind of communications utility, with billions of individuals, businesses, and organizations plugged in and capacitated to interact continuously. Users post personal details about themselves and their families and friends—where they work, their alma maters, pets and vacations—as well as what's on their mind, where they are, and what they're doing, all of which Facebook monetizes into valuable marketing data for advertisers.

Facebook's ad-based business model relies on users staying engaged and online so that it can track their preferences with surgical precision, preying on human beings' need for connection, affirmation, and stimulation—as addictive as any drug. Because Facebook's news feeds are algorithmically curated based on people's preferences, it fosters echo chambers and political polarization and tribalism. And, because its algorithms are set to maximize profits, they tend to favor the sensational, nudging users toward posts that heighten emotion, including material involving violence, hate speech, and conspiracy theories. Living up to Zuckerberg's motto "Move fast and break things," in 2017, posts by Myanmar military personnel turned the social networking site into a tool for ethnic cleansing, inciting murders, rapes, and the forced migration of millions. In the lead-up to January 6, it played a major role in drawing people, some of them socially alienated, into fringe conspiracy and militia groups by affirming their engagement and sensationalist posts, and providing a platform for those looking to cultivate an online public persona.[32] During the coronavirus pandemic, it circulated disinformation and conspiracy at a faster clip than information issued by leading public health agencies.

Like Facebook, Amazon also creates value by surveilling its customers—tracking their behavior online and using the data to sell targeted advertising and cultivate shopping addictions. Its Alexa product, a home device that operates like a personal assistant, listens and learns about users in the context of their homes, enriching Amazon with personal data that no other company could or should have access to. Amazon's cloud infrastructure allows it to monitor other companies and is so massive that most Fortune 500 companies use its platform to manage their data, as does the CIA. Amazon drones gather GPS and other information for delivering customers' orders, and the company sells outdoor motion-detecting cameras and facial recognition tools—using the data to manipulate consumers, but also selling it to police departments and U.S. Immigration and Customs Enforcement.

In addition to controlling vast amounts of information, the size and reach of tech billionaires' enterprises enables them to accumulate wealth by monopolizing entire markets and industries. They can set prices and terms of employment, undermine their competition, and birth new ecosystems of suppliers, producers, customers, financiers, and market players. Mark Zuckerberg, for example, used his wealth and influence to buy up competitors like Instagram and WhatsApp to reinforce his dominance over social media, and as chapter 8 shows, he supplanted large chunks of the newspaper business with Facebook's news feed by usurping vital advertising revenue. Google, one of the wealthiest companies on the planet with a market value of almost $1.5 trillion, came to control more than 90 percent of the online search and advertising market in part through anti-competitive dealmaking that made Google the default search engine on billions of computers and mobile devices and by prohibiting the downloading of other search engines.[33]

Amazon monopolizes the retail space by outpricing and out-advertising competitors, using its market dominance to make deals directly with manufacturers and force them to lower their prices and wages. It gains market share by expanding into new industries and with innovations like subscription services that most retailers cannot offer. As part of Amazon's function as the virtual infrastructure for the online retail market, it charges third-party businesses fees for renting "space" on its site to sell their products. While some of those businesses grow as a result of their affiliation with Amazon, many get swallowed up. By controlling search results on its site, Amazon can bury some sellers' products while elevating its own. Its base of products and services is so wide, in fact, that it can regulate the sale of many, if not most, consumer products in America. This is not just a case of a big fish eating little fish—true to its name, Amazon is the river in which *all* of the fish swim, and it is the largest river in the world.

There was a time in the United States when monopoly and corporate gigantism were eschewed as anti-democratic and uncompetitive. At the turn of the century, when banking, railroad, and steel industries were making millionaires, Supreme Court Justice Louis Brandeis warned of the dangers of corporate power and the curse of bigness: "We may have democracy, or we may have wealth concentrated in the hands of a few, but we can't have both," he said.[34] Early in the twentieth century, Congress passed a series of anti-trust laws to curb corporate power, but by the late 1950s, C. Wright

Mills and others were still warning of the dangers of corporate concentration and sounding alarms about the historical synergy between monopoly and authoritarianism.[35]

Contestations over the role of the state in restraining capitalism and curbing monopoly power were won by Reagan and Chicago School ideologues, backed by Wall Street and multinational corporations pushing the idea that unfettered markets would produce optimal social outcomes. In 1981, Ronald Reagan set a new standard of anti-trust in which the government would only advocate on behalf of weaker competitors if the alleged corporate monopoly raised consumer prices—giving the market the authority to determine government action rather than the other way around.

Since then, nearly every major industry in the United States has become more concentrated, with gigantic companies and conglomerates dominating every aspect of American life—from the food we eat to the airplanes we fly in to our telephone and internet connections, hospitals and pharmaceuticals, energy sources, retail stores, news and entertainment media, and so on. Today's airline industry is dominated by four large carriers, a handful of media conglomerates own most news sources, agribusinesses has eaten up farming, and Walmart, Amazon, Home Depot, and Lowe's have displaced local retail and hardware stores. Now, there are fewer than five major defense contractors, down from over sixty-five a few decades ago. Drugstores have replaced neighborhood pharmacists, and the vast majority of people in the United States, some 80 percent, rely on just three companies for their prescription drugs. As discussed in chapter 5, banking is more consolidated than ever and the "Big Three" asset management firms—BlackRock, Vanguard, and State Street—oversee global assets that total more than three-quarters of U.S. GDP, as of 2020.[36] At this rate, just a handful of large institutional investors will virtually own and control every major corporation in the world.[37]

Under monopoly capitalism, workers and consumers have less choice, less opportunity to work for a living wage, and less power to contest the scientific management of their work processes or forced arbitration. The moral hazard associated with "too big to fail" and its twin "too big to jail" renders the overall economy less stable, not to mention socially unjust. Without competition, gigantic corporations can obtain subsidies by investing in some regions over others; extract wealth by price gouging consumers and extorting suppliers; control markets by cutting off start-ups and small businesses; and drive down wages for workers, especially in underemployed regions.

TAX AVOIDANCE

In 1989, a domestic worker employed by billionaire hotelier Leona Helmsley alleged in her testimony during Helmsley's tax evasion trial that she had overheard her boss say, "Only the little people pay taxes."[38] Helmsley's conviction notwithstanding, it is true that throughout much of the nation's history, America's tax system has favored the interests of the wealthy and many large profitable corporations today do not pay any taxes at all. Through exemptions, deductions, loopholes, and a complex array of tax maneuvers, elites have chipped away at the progressive aspects of the U.S. tax code and found ways to pay much lower effective tax rates, such that between 1980 and 2020, taxes on billionaires decreased by 79 percent.[39] While Republican administrations, especially those of George W. Bush and Donald Trump, reduced taxes mostly for those at the upper end of the income scale, recall from chapter 2 that it was Obama who made the Bush tax cuts permanent. When Bill Clinton was elected president in the early 1990s, the United States' 400 highest-earning taxpayers paid nearly 27 percent of their income in federal taxes; by 2012, when Obama was re-elected, that figure was less than 17 percent.[40]

Tax advantages for the rich were achieved in part through propaganda campaigns against the so-called "evils of big government" and well-funded lobbying efforts to resist progressive taxation and undermine the IRS. Groups like FreedomWorks, Club for Growth, and Americans for Tax Reform, financed by ALEC and billionaires like the Kochs, have gone so far as to call for abolishing the IRS, impeaching its commissioner, running primary candidates against Republicans who vote for higher taxes, and supporting politicians with anti-tax agendas. In 2020, a Congressional Budget Office report found that nearly $400 billion in taxes go unpaid each year and audit rates for the very wealthy are in decline, while those of the poor are on the rise.[41] Under Republican and Democratic administrations, the IRS has been forced to shed thousands of high-level enforcement positions, especially those in charge of auditing charities and nonprofits (dark money). On Obama's watch, the agency's budget was cut by 18 percent, losing about 14 percent of its workforce (roughly 13,000 employees) between 2010 and 2017.[42]

In addition to steering the tax code and undermining the IRS, the wealthy are adept at evading taxes and bending existing laws. It is not unusual for a large profitable corporation, or the billionaire who owns it, to lay out $5 to $10 million to avoid paying $30 to $50 million in taxes by procuring "opinion letters" from Ivy League economists and employing armies of white-shoe law firms, elite investment bankers, estate planners, and tax accountants. This industry of wealth defenders has developed complex instruments for tax dodging, including foundations, convoluted partnerships, opaque family trusts, foreign shell corporations, and new and more gaping loopholes and tax deductions—none of which are available to the average person and all of which far exceed the increasingly anemic IRS's capacity to regulate them.[43]

This corruption of the U.S. tax system was on gross display in the Trump administration's rebranding of Clinton-era "enterprise zones" and Obama-era "promise zones" as "opportunity zones." Trump used declining income and living standards in U.S. cities, and rural and border communities, as an excuse to pass a multi-billion-dollar tax break for real estate developers. The opportunity zone tax incentive was supposedly aimed to spur entrepreneurialism in poor communities, but the real beneficiaries were Trump family members and advisors who poured billions into high-end apartment buildings and hotels designed to exclude the very people who subsidized them.

Among those who exploited the opportunity zone tax cut were billionaire space speculators Elon Musk and Jeff Bezos, the two richest men in the world. Both billionaires had already secured local tax breaks, but Trump's tax break enabled them to avoid capital gains taxes as well. The site of Bezos's space program showed no sign of economic distress and was colonized by hundreds of major companies like Lockheed Martin, Teledyne, and Booz Allen Hamilton. But since it was located near a housing project, the area's per-capita income was below the median and thus qualified for the program.[44]

One of the main ways that corporations and wealthy people avoid taxes is by disguising their income as capital gains, subject to lower tax rates. Currently, there is no tax on unrealized capital gains, and the rate is just 15 percent on long-term realized gains from the sale of stocks and bonds or real estate. Recall from the previous chapter how private equity firms and hedge funds save tens of millions a year in taxes by exploiting the "carried interest loophole" that allows them to register nearly all their income as capital gains. Despite Democratic efforts to close that loophole and force corporations and the wealthy to "pay their fair share," Wall Street and corporate lobbyists have successfully maintained this lucrative tax break.

Some of the most heated political debates over the tax code involve the estate tax, which was instituted in 1916 in response to the grotesque wealth inequalities of the Gilded Age. The estate tax is the United States' only tax on accumulated wealth, levied at the time of a person's death when their assets are handed down to their heirs (excluding 2010, when the tax was briefly eliminated). Former football star turned congressman

Jack Kemp, who also became secretary of the U.S. Department of Housing and Urban Development and was Bob Dole's running mate in 1996, was a protagonist of estate tax repeal. Influenced by neoliberals like Ayn Rand, William F. Buckley Jr., and Arthur Laffer, Kemp used the occasion of his vice presidential bid to become an outspoken proponent for supply-side economics and tax cuts. This was abetted by Proposition 13, a veritable tax revolt in California against the high property taxes of the late 1970s, that lowered property taxes and imposed a two-thirds-majority requirement on future statewide tax increases. At the federal level, with double-digit inflation pushing households into higher income-tax brackets, a newly elected Ronald Reagan passed a three-year, 23 percent tax reduction taken straight from Kemp's legislation, known as the Kemp-Roth tax cut. Just a year later, however, Reagan had to increase taxes due to the significant loss of tax revenue.

During the Dole campaign, Kemp told farmers that a Dole-Kemp administration "wants you to be able to leave your farm to your children without having the Government confiscate it in Washington, D.C."[45] That kind of disinformation and fearmongering is emblematic of the ideological manipulations that conservatives have been tendering for years around the estate tax and their ongoing struggle to legitimize a policy that only benefits the very rich. The estate tax impacts the wealthiest 0.2 percent of Americans—about 5,000 estates a year—and in 2020, just eighty farms and small businesses were subject to it. According to the Farm Bureau, no family farmer has ever lost their farm due to the estate tax.

The most effective tactic for delegitimizing the estate tax, pushed in the mid-1990s by GOP pollster Frank Luntz and others, involved portraying it as a "death tax" to sow confusion that the tax is imposed upon death itself rather than what it really is—a wealth tax.[46] In 1993, U.S. Representative Christopher Cox introduced the first legislation to repeal the estate tax with just 29 cosponsors, but within the year, eliminating the "death tax" became a centerpiece of Republicans' "Contract with America." By 1998, repeal legislation had over 206 House sponsors including the entire Republican leadership.[47] Other key players in the repeal effort included California family office executive Patricia Soldano—working on behalf of Mars, Gallo, Koch, and other wealthy families—who built a formidable and effective consortium of conservative groups devoted to the cause. Those included usual suspects like the Heritage Foundation, the Club for Growth, and Cato, as well as Grover Norquist's Americans for Tax Reform and the National Federation of Independent Businesses (NFIB), an influential business trade association.

Conservative groups also used civil rights as a framework for estate tax repeal, including advertising campaigns that cast the tax as detrimental to disabled people, women, and people of color. In his repeal efforts, George W. Bush joined forces with billionaire Black Entertainment Television (BET) founder Robert L. Johnson, whose estate stood to save millions if the tax was eliminated. Johnson organized a group of Black business leaders to join him in saying that the estate tax drained wealth from the Black community and that repeal would help close the country's racial wealth gap—another verifiably false claim. Johnson would again partner with Bush to weaponize U.S. race politics to privatize Social Security, a program on which large numbers of Black Americans rely.[48]

Tax Havens

In 2016 and 2017, two tranches of leaked documents—the Panama Papers and Paradise Papers—exposed the shady yet often legal means through which wealth management firms help an increasingly entrenched global aristocracy shield their money from taxation. Implicated in these massive tax avoidance schemes were characters of all stripes—baseball players, hedge funders, African diamond dealers, Chinese real estate speculators, Saudi petro-sheiks, Mexican drug lords, and more. In one case, a wealth manager sheltered a client's $100 million-plus in seven banks in six countries through eight shell companies and a foundation.[49] The leaked documents also exposed rampant tax evasion by corporate heads of household brands like Nike, Apple, Uber, and Facebook, in addition to some 120 politicians from 47 countries, and the British queen.

In 2021, an even larger tranche, the Pandora Papers—gleaned from fourteen different financial services entities across the globe covering more than 29,000 offshore accounts—implicated 130 billionaires and 330 public officials in more than 90 countries, as well as British prime minister Tony Blair, pop star Shakira, Russian oligarchs, and Saudi Arabian royals. Importantly, the Pandora Papers revealed how the world's wealthy were moving their vast fortunes out of traditional tax havens and into U.S.-based trusts. An investigation into the papers by the International Consortium of Investigative Journalists cited over 200 U.S. trusts linked to forty-one countries, nearly thirty of them holding assets connected to individuals or corporate entities accused of crimes such as fraud, bribery, and human rights violations. The records also include memos and messages on how to defeat transparency laws and, oops, how to prevent leaks.[50]

Economist Gabriel Zucman estimated in 2015 that roughly 8 percent of the world's wealth is held in tax havens.[51] According to a 2020 Tax Justice Network report, instead of declaring profits where they are generated, each year multinational corporations shift their profits into such shelters, costing governments nearly $247 billion in lost revenue. An additional $182 billion is lost from wealthy individuals hiding undeclared assets offshore, for a total of $427 billion a year lost to tax abuse.[52] As for the United States, 55 percent of foreign profits of U.S. firms are held in tax havens, where they pay an average tax rate of between 3 percent and 6.6 percent on their offshore profits, costing the U.S. government about $126 billion a year in lost revenue.[53] Most Fortune 500 companies have offshore subsidiaries, with tech, pharmaceuticals, and health care alone accounting for half of the untaxed offshore profits.[54]

The first tax havens were operational in Switzerland in the 1920s, when countries with sizeable World War I debts taxed large fortunes to raise revenue; and they grew exponentially in the UK territories in the heyday of the Eurodollar.[55] Today, the United Kingdom and Switzerland remain major players, as the majority (72 percent in 2020) of the world's tax dodging takes place in the "axis of tax avoidance": the United Kingdom, Switzerland, Luxembourg, and the Netherlands.[56] Competition for billionaires' and multinationals' business has resulted in a race to the bottom of corporate tax rates worldwide, and increased specialization and division of labor of international wealth management. The terrain is ever shifting, but at one point Swiss banks were the place to go for securities management, the Caymans were known for hedge funds, and Luxembourg specialized in mutual funds. In some cases, a shell company might be created in Switzerland but domiciled in another country. As a tax haven, the United States will likely surpass Switzerland in the coming years with more and more states adopting lax legal constraints and monitoring.

U.S. policymakers have done little to crack down on tax evasion, and many of them have encouraged it. In 2004, George W. Bush gave corporations a "tax holiday" during which they repatriated some $300 billion in profits at a tax rate of just over 5 percent, instead of the regular 35 percent corporate rate at the time. In 2017, Donald Trump slashed repatriation rates and, under his "territorial" tax system, cut taxes on new foreign profits past a certain threshold to half that of the U.S. effective rate, and in some cases to zero.[57] Despite his "America First" brand, several members of his cabinet modeled tax avoidance behaviors, including Education Secretary Betsy DeVos, whose $40 million 164-foot yacht flies the Cayman Islands flag, allowing her family (which owns nine other yachts) to skirt not only taxes but also labor laws. Taxing that item alone could have brought DeVos's home state of Michigan up to $2.4 million in tax revenue.[58]

Billionaire investors and corporate executives argue, disingenuously, that tax amnesty is good for the U.S. economy because it allows companies to reinvest their foreign earnings domestically. Following the Bush tax holiday, a study by the conservative National Bureau of Economic Research found that an overwhelming majority (92 percent) of the repatriated money was spent on shareholder dividends, stock buybacks, and executive bonuses, rather than on domestic investment, employment, and R&D. For most large profitable corporations, buybacks and CEO and shareholder paydays account for most of their spending, and yet they still blame corporate taxes for supposedly making them less "globally competitive."[59]

With public outrage mounting in the wake of the 2007 global financial crisis, a whistleblower exposed the United Bank of Switzerland (UBS) for sheltering billions of dollars for its wealthy clients. Under pressure, Obama and the U.S. Congress responded by passing the Foreign Account Tax Compliance Act (FATCA) to force foreign financial institutions to disclose the U.S.-owned assets they managed. In a show of confidence, his administration fined UBS, and later Credit Suisse (a whopping $2.6 billion), but the United States still does not reciprocally mandate that its own banks comply with the legislation.[60] In addition, a G-20 agreement called the Common Reporting Standard was established requiring countries to exchange information on the banking assets of each other's citizens, but to date, the United States has refused to sign.

Since FATCA directed a gathering of information from foreign countries—but did not require the United States to share that information with their governments—corporations and the wealthy can still secretly stash their funds in U.S. banks.[61] That loophole enabled states like South Dakota—where there are no taxes on income, inheritance, or capital gains—to operate as world-class tax havens for the ultra-rich by offering favorable laws that shield trusts from various claims. In 2010, South Dakotan trust companies held $57 billion in assets; a decade later, that number grew to $355 billion.[62] It was to South Dakota that Leona Helmsley's trustees moved her $12 million trust for her dog Trouble, whose "care" included surf and turf (Kobe beef and crab cakes) for lunch and dinner, an $8,000 annual grooming budget, and $100,000 for security guards to keep the dog from being kidnapped.[63] Before that, South Dakota was where Walter Wriston moved Citicorp's Mastercard operation in the early 1970s to avoid usury laws, which not only saved his bank but also fueled the rise of the highly profitable credit card industry.[64]

The effects of this lost revenue cannot be overstated. Corporate elites are depriving governments of vital resources and leaving middle- and working-class people to foot the bill for programs and services that subsidize their wealth-making. This includes everything from policing and national security, to bailouts and tax incentives, to education and worker training, and infrastructure development. In this arrangement, small businesses and local industries—lacking armies of white-shoe tax advisors—cannot compete, and rich families are able to entrench their wealth for generations. Furthermore, wealthy people who redomicile themselves in states with favorable tax laws are putting downward pressure on other states to "liberalize" their tax systems as well. In Northern California, where the state income tax is the highest in the nation, Silicon Valley's "millennial millionaires" have avoided taxes by moving to states with lower rates, like Texas and Florida, despite California's generous subsidies for their industry.[65]

Globally, between 1985 and 2018, the average corporate tax rate fell by more than half, from 49 to 24 percent. To reverse this steep decline, President Biden and other world leaders at the October 2021 G20 summit—which included 140 countries representing more than 90 percent of total global economic output—endorsed a new global minimum tax of 15 percent to stem tax evasion. This new tax rate would apply to firms with more than $850 million in annual revenue and is estimated to raise roughly $150 billion in additional global tax revenue each year. The proposal also included tightening rules on partnerships and pass-throughs, and taxes on stock buybacks.

An indicator of where his party's loyalties truly lie, Biden's initial proposal to raise the tax on foreign profits to 21 percent was reduced to 15 percent after negotiations with congressional Democrats.[66] Democratic senators Manchin and Sinema also blocked the president's plan to raise corporate tax rates and rates on wealthy individuals to fund his infrastructure and social spending bills. This was despite the fact that his agenda—to raise capital gains for those earning more than $400,000 and raise the top personal income tax rate back to 39.6 percent from Trump's 37 percent—would have barely restored taxes to pre-Trump levels. Sinema's obstruction in particular prompted Biden to propose a wealth tax on the assets of billionaires to pay for programs like universal pre-K, paid family leave, Medicare expansion, child care, and efforts to combat climate change—an idea long promoted by Senators Bernie Sanders and Elizabeth Warren. As proposed, Biden's wealth tax would have applied to only 700 taxpayers, those with at least $100 million in income for three straight years, or $1 billion in assets, and would have raised hundreds of billions of dollars.

Polls indicate widespread popularity for taxing the wealthy, especially since the rich got so much richer during the pandemic, when most people were barely scraping by.[67]

PHILANTHROPY

In 1967, *Life Magazine*'s "wedding of the year" between Sharon Percy and John D. "Jay" Rockefeller brought a then thirty-two-year-old Pete Peterson into the Rockefeller family's inner orbit. Soon after the wedding, patriarch John D. Rockefeller III summoned Peterson to his Pocantico Hills estate to discuss a matter of "major significance."[68] Like other big philanthropists, Rockefeller had spent many decades, and millions, intervening in public life with grand social engineering projects that displayed his family's influence while distracting from its extensive tax exemptions, as well as the price-fixing, bribery, and general malfeasance that powered his vast fortune.

With the Rockefeller Foundation's budget in 1912 exceeding that of the nation, progressive political forces blocked the mega-philanthropy from acquiring a federal charter (Rockefeller did receive a charter from New York). Senator Robert La Follette called Rockefeller "the greatest criminal of our age," and Theodore Roosevelt, despite his ties to big business, remarked that "no amount of charity in spending such fortunes can compensate in any way for the misconduct in acquiring them."[69] Other large philanthropic groups, like the Russell Sage and Carnegie Foundations, were similarly taken to task for claiming to "improve the human condition" while taking huge tax breaks and intervening in public life with no accountability whatsoever.

By the 1960s, when Rockefeller called Peterson to his estate, working-class struggle against extreme wealth and corporate power was again rearing its head. Congress was considering an array of legislative responses, including heightened regulation, tax increases, and/or capping the size and lifespan of charitable foundations.[70] John D. Rockefeller III—along with John J. McCloy, former World Bank president and chairman of Chase Manhattan Bank (among other top posts[71]), and Doug Dillon, former treasury secretary and chairman of the Brookings Institution—implored Peterson to head an "independent" commission to "study" the problem and essentially steer lawmakers away from increasing taxes and regulation.

Peterson made the rounds on Capitol Hill and consulted with top White House staff from the social networks he had formed as a student at Milton Friedman's Chicago school of economic thought. He then commissioned a nationwide survey and used the findings—that most foundations did not actually engage in charitable giving—to lobby Congress for a minimum payout requirement. The requirement would maintain the generous tax write-off, but only for foundations that made grants each year totaling 5 percent or more of their endowments.[72] The legislation was ostensibly meant to stimulate philanthropic giving but created a way for men like Rockefeller to retain power over their money, rather than allow government and, God forbid, the people to set social priorities and fund them with tax revenue. Of course, lawmakers left open a major loophole by stipulating that the payout requirement could include all "reasonable" administrative expenses—from foundation salaries to trustee fees to travel, receptions, office supplies, equipment, rent, and the construction of new headquarters.[73]

Today, the rich and powerful spend tens of billions a year on philanthropic enterprises and pet projects subsidized by taxpayers. Some of them are driven by delusions of grandeur around space discovery or fountains of youth, while others seek to eradicate diseases that they themselves helped cause, such as oil tycoon David Koch's funding of cancer research. By transferring assets to a foundation, donors reduce their tax burden because the foundation's endowment—often invested in the stock market—is, for the most part, tax free. When billionaires like Bill Gates use their foundation to experiment in public education or Charles Koch gives hundreds of millions to libertarian "advocacy" groups, they do so using tax subsidies that cost the U.S. Treasury hundreds of billions of dollars a year.

In Joyce Purnick's biography of Michael Bloomberg, the multibillionaire is quoted as saying: "Having our names on a plaque, on a scholarship, on a research grant . . . rewards us as long as we live. It puts everyone else—our entire community, our country, and even the whole world—in our debt. What greater satisfaction could we possibly get than watching ourselves do great things for humanity?"[74] In addition to feeding narcissistic impulses like Bloomberg's, and facilitating tax evasion, billionaires use the public relations around philanthropic giving to obscure the nefarious ways they acquired, and defend, their fortunes. In this way, "doing great things for humanity" enabled "junk bond king" Michael Milken to erase his criminal past, Mark Zuckerberg to deflect from Facebook's predatory advertising, and the Sackler family, at least for a time, to dissociate their billions from the opioid crisis that helped make them rich.

It also has enabled the packs of bankers and corporate heads associated with the Robin Hood Foundation to glorify themselves as folkloric heroes, despite their histories of gaming the financial system on the backs of regular people. Whereas Robin Hood redistributed wealth from the rich to the poor, the Robin Hood Foundation uses the *appearance* of helping the needy to sanitize the images of hedge fund and private equity bankers, while further enriching them with tax breaks.[75] Over a dozen billionaires have sat on the foundation's leadership boards and committees, including hedge fund giant Steven Cohen, known for his $700 million art collection and outrageous parties at his Hamptons mansion—but in need of image repair after his company SAC Capital Advisors pled guilty to securities fraud. It has also included Home Depot founder Ken Langone, the anti–Social Security crusader who threatened to rescind his donations to the Catholic Church if Pope Francis continued to criticize capitalism.[76] Also claiming the Robin Hood mantle is Goldman Sachs's Lloyd Blankfein, who advised President Trump to reopen the country for business at the height of the pandemic, when hospital staff were stacking dead bodies in refrigerated trucks parked on the streets of New York City because their morgues had been overrun. Also on the board was billionaire Stanley Druckenmiller, a proponent of the "generational theft" school of entitlement reform (a Pete Peterson favorite) that works to turn young people against their grandparents by making the false claim that Social Security is robbing their future.[77]

Philanthropic giving was not enough, ultimately, to shield the billionaire Sackler family from public scrutiny and disgrace for producing and profiting off the sale of the highly addictive painkiller OxyContin.[78] Once among the twenty wealthiest families in America, the Sacklers branded whole wings of the Louvre, New York's Metropolitan Museum of Art, the Guggenheim, and other iconic institutions in their family name. It was not until their company Purdue Pharma was exposed for intentionally addicting millions of people to opioids that museums began to distance themselves and remove the metal plates bearing their crest.[79] That did not, of course, remove the opioid epidemic's eternal imprint on communities across the country—still claiming tens of thousands of lives each year, draining the country's already-buckling health care system, and bringing infants into the world writhing in drug withdrawal.

To a lesser degree, billionaire David Koch (now deceased) drew similar ire for his company's deadly environmental violations and family's anti-government extremism. Koch deflected by making huge donations to underfunded performing arts institutions and museums in New York City, where he lived in the Fifth Avenue apartment once occupied by Jacqueline Kennedy Onassis (which he sold for $32 million because, apparently, it was too small). The American Museum of Natural History's dinosaur wing bears the Koch name, as does an endowed chair and research center at Memorial Sloan-Kettering Cancer Center, where Koch served on the board and donated more than $40 million.[80] Such generosity doesn't erase the fact that the Koch family single-handedly transformed the country's campaign finance system into a reliable vehicle for billionaires to amass unfathomable wealth and control U.S. elections. Nor does it erase the memory of David Koch's 1980 Libertarian Party platform, which presaged Steve Bannon and the Trump administration's "deconstruction of the administrative state."

A common belief among billionaire philanthropists is that market-based solutions and the private sector are better situated than government and public institutions to solve big social problems. Even when they argue that crises like the coronavirus pandemic require the scale of federal government intervention, they still view wealthy individuals as supreme sources of innovation and discovery. Therefore, instead of allowing government to tax their money and elected officials to reinvest it in society, they seek to control the agenda and set national priorities through philanthropic campaigns. For some of them, such giving is a form of venture capital aimed at the transformation of large-scale public institutions into profit-making enterprises.

These tendencies are especially prevalent in the administration and structuring of the U.S. education system. In higher education, billionaire philanthropists influence knowledge production and ideas by underwriting institutes and endowed chairs, enlarging endowments, and bankrolling infrastructure projects (and securing their children's admission acceptance to boot). Public universities and their faculties are especially vulnerable to manipulation by big-money donors since many of them struggle perpetually with fiscal pressures, budget cuts, and depleted federal research funding. In some disciplines, professors' salaries rely almost entirely on external funding, as is the case with many scientists and medical school faculty. The result, at best, is that billionaires get to influence research priorities and university leaderships' decision-making; at worse, they use university resources to develop and legitimize their political worldviews and serve their class interests.

K-12 education has also attracted significant billionaire interest—from those looking to rescue or "fix" the U.S. education system to entrepreneurs seeking profit-making opportunities through privatization. As both mayor and billionaire philanthropist, Michael Bloomberg has long worked to remake the public school system in the image of a corporation by advocating for privately run, publicly funded charter schools and attacking teacher unions. As New York City mayor, he closed more than 100 schools in low-income communities, and said that he would like to fire half the city's teachers and pay the remaining half more to supervise the larger classes.[81] This was in keeping with his broader offensive against government regulation and spending, including proposals to cut Social Security, and opposition to paid sick leave and increasing the minimum wage. Bloomberg has also suggested that the nation's most vulnerable pay more in Medicaid copays so "they'll think twice before they use services, the services they use will be those that are really needed and not stuff that would be nice to have."[82]

Alongside Bloomberg, and sometimes in partnership with him, other big philanthropists such as Bill and Melinda Gates and the Walton Family have worked to corporatize public education, asserting that if schools were run like businesses, the achievement gap separating poor and minority students from middle-class and affluent students would evaporate. The Waltons put school privatization at the center of their philanthropic activities, advocating for school vouchers and at one point funding one out of every four U.S. charter schools. Gates used some of his billions to discipline teachers and their unions under the banner of "accountability." Though his personal brand projects an image of him as rational and scientific, Gates's interventions in K-12 ignored the consensus among education researchers that poverty, and not teachers or their unions, is the primary source of educational inequality. Students in schools where poverty rates are low tend to excel in nearly all subjects, while those in areas where poverty rates are high are left to struggle. In the United States, over a fifth of public schools have poverty rates over 75 percent, but instead of confronting that poverty head on, Gates developed his own model of education to prove his theories about class sizes and teacher "performance." When his social experiments proved inept and even disastrous, he conveniently blamed elected school board members and teacher unions.

Not surprisingly, many philanthropic adventures similarly end in failure and become someone else's fault or problem. Experimental schools perform poorly and must be shut down; foreign aid projects gentrify Third and Second World cities, open them up to private investors, and drive out indigenous communities; public services and institutions erode due to decreased tax revenues; and democratic decision-making is supplanted by the whims of the ultrawealthy.[83] The billionaires behind these reckless adventures are the embodiment of F. Scott Fitzgerald's rich protagonists in *The Great Gatsby*: "They were careless people, Tom and Daisy—they smashed up things and creatures and then retreated back to their money or their vast carelessness or whatever it was that kept them together, and let other people clean up the mess they had made."

CHAPTER 7

Celebrity

The power of celebrity, and of celebrities, operates on the terrain of hegemony in which class interests are realized through cultural life, consumption, and the manufacturing of consent. It is a form of domination exerted through ideas and meanings, images and language, and appeals to feelings, enjoyment, and transcendence. Through culture, especially popular culture, celebrities naturalize class hierarchies and transmit political propaganda. And as models of the good life, they reinforce capitalism's tendency to tether status and self-worth to commodities and portray the system as the best of what is possible, even when the good life is not accessible to most.

C. Wright Mills located celebrities in the hierarchy of elite power as subordinate to those in command of the military, political, and corporate establishment. Since then, a cadre of celebrities has risen to the highest circles, and with them, a potent sublayer of actors, musicians, athletes, and personalities with varying degrees of hegemonic power. This chapter will show how that rise—to billionaire or near-billionaire status, to governors' mansions, and to the White House—has been due to fundamental changes in communications technologies, branding and advertising, the political economy of entertainment media, and, more generally, cultural life.

As in Mills's time, celebrities today perform important legitimating functions for the capitalist system. By their existence and through the characters they play, they serve as status markers and archetypes of the self-actualized individual in a society that regards success and failure as matters of the will. Celebrities represent, and epitomize, the neoliberal class narrative that history is made by the victors and that individuals can access the good life through self-help and dogged determination—as opposed to recognizing everyday people as history makers and associating the good life with social solidarity and responsibility.

In the current moment, the expansion of communications and entertainment media deeper into everyday life has enabled advertisers and media companies to shape our subjectivity in ways that were not possible in Mills's time. As constituents of this inescapable, high-tech culture industry, celebrities generate profits through the manufacture and circulation of products and images. This power to churn profits is rooted in their ability to offer escape from the boredoms and bureaucracies of everyday life and to capture and monetize attention—widely, to masses of people, and deeply, through pseudo-intimacy and emotion. As a result, some celebrities have accumulated profound levels of wealth, even without having any discernable talent other than their so-called business sense and ability to sell products.

Celebrities' reach into hearts and minds not only offers fertile terrain for the exercise of corporate power but also represents a potent source of political exploitation. In today's climate of mass apathy and distrust in political leaders and institutions, charismatic leadership is trumping bureaucratic-rational forms of authority, and in place of actual agency, emotion and entertainment are occupying a central role in political life. This chapter examines these dynamics and the nature of celebrity more generally.

IMAGE AND IDEOLOGY

Celebrities are vessels of concepts and ideology and transmitters of the prevailing notion that capitalism is the best of what is possible. They perform this legitimating function in a variety of ways, most notably through gross displays of social advantage, conspicuous consumption, and the transmission of ruling-class ideology and political propaganda. In an inspired essay on the rise of Donald Trump, novelist Stephen Marche defined pop culture as "a space for the fulfillment of identity that reduces everyone to a commodity."[1] This commodification defines not only popular culture in America but also the whole of capitalist society in which, as Marx theorized, people fetishize products and possessions, and social relations among them become relations among things.[2]

As idols of privilege and consumption, celebrities are at the center of this commodity fetishism in everyday life and as avatars through the characters they play. Despite the chasm between rich and poor in America, there is still a mass audience for TV shows and tabloids that show off the lifestyles of the rich and famous and dramatize them in soap operas and reality TV. When actor George Clooney staged a $4.6 million wedding in Venice, for example, and rapper Kanye West bought Kim Kardashian a fifteen-carat $4 million engagement ring, audiences gasped at the opulence but nonetheless took pleasure in it. That collective numbness to contradiction is a feature of neoliberal conditioning and its positing of the free market as a great equalizer: in today's capitalist system, so it goes, everyone has an equal opportunity to become like Kim or Kanye if they just mimic what they do and consume their products.

Celebrities also display status, and the spoils of capitalism, through the deference they elicit and their many extravagances and social advantages—from traveling on private jets and being celebrated on red carpets, to direct access to political leaders, to elite privileges in the education and health care systems, and "get out of jail free" cards. When billionaire pop singer Beyoncé gave birth to her twins, it apparently required a large section of the hospital to be put on lockdown to safeguard her security, even though it meant that other maternity patients could not see their families—some of them, not even their newborns.[3] In higher education, celebrities' kids go to top colleges not necessarily because they are top students, but because their parents' money and fame trump merit, as the college admission scandal of 2019 laid bare.[4] During the coronavirus pandemic, some celebrities misguidedly took to social media to complain of their boredom or display maudlin sympathy for the afflicted, posting video messages from the sanctity of their palatial homes, or worse, poolside—as millions of people around the world, without the resources to quarantine or social distance, suffered and died.

In the U.S. legal system, celebrities tend to be treated as if they are above the law. The term "celebrity justice" signifies a widely understood, informal category of impunity reserved for those with money and fame, in stark contrast to the U.S. carceral system's degrading and cruel treatment of poor and working-class people. In 2005, when heiress and reality TV star Paris Hilton and friends crashed their car into a truck, then fled the scene and nearly hit a bystander, police let them go without conducting sobriety tests. As Hilton got back into her Bentley, she blew them a kiss and said, "We love the police!"[5] Two years later, when heiress Nicole Richie, Hilton's reality TV costar, got pulled over for driving in the wrong direction on a busy California highway under the influence of marijuana and Vicodin, she posted $15,000 bail and was released a few hours later.[6] Juxtapose the treatment of these young celebrities and their criminal recklessness with how working-class and poor people, especially Black and Latino, are jailed for the pettiest of offenses, presumed guilty before proven innocent, and denied basic rights for their inability to post bail. Lindsay Lohan, a famous white actress, was given probation, community service, and minimal jail time (she served 14 days) for stealing a $100,000 necklace and multiple probation violations. Meanwhile, George Floyd, an unemployed working-class Black man, was asphyxiated to death by police for unintentionally trying to pass off a fake $20 bill at a convenience store. These are not one-offs; it is how celebrity justice works.

Alarmingly, that same kind of preferential treatment under the law applies in cases of violent crime as well. Most people who commit acts of rape and assault are apprehended, punished, and removed from society as soon as possible. Shielded by their handlers and powerful friends, however, celebrities can avoid such penalties until their crimes become widely known and mass-protested. For example, movie producer Harvey Weinstein and rapper R. Kelly both raped and sexually abused dozens of women for decades with impunity until they were exposed in the context of the "Me Too" movement. In Kelly's case, most of his victims were teenage girls, some as young as thirteen years old. The *Chicago Sun-Times* published the first allegations against Kelly in 2000, reporting that he was using his fame to prey upon high school girls. Two years later, he was brought up on charges of child pornography, then acquitted in 2008.[7] It was not until 2019, when public pressure hit a fever pitch, that Kelly was finally indicted, held without bail, and eventually convicted.

As with the billionaires of the previous chapter, celebrities' social advantages are routinely justified through narratives that attribute the most significant achievements of civilization to the work of exceptional individuals. On the flipside, these narratives claim that anyone can overcome structural inequalities and increase their "value" if they just believe in and invest in themselves.[8] Such narratives hold celebrities up as bastions of self-actualization through hard work and ambition, and therefore, fully deserving of their wealth and privilege. In the bigger picture, this rendering of wealthy and charismatic individuals as protagonists of history warps societal views on vulnerability, aging, and poverty, and obscures the collective achievements of regular people and communities. In doing so, it provides cultural fuel for government policies that reward rich and famous people with economic advantages and an undue say in our political system.

The most prominent evangelist of the neoliberal worldview, and its emphasis on self-help and personal responsibility, is Oprah Winfrey, who exploited her own personal story to prove how in America it is possible to escape from the depths of poverty through sheer strength of will and dogged determination—implying that success is a choice, failure is not an option, and hard work is the pathway to mobility. "I don't think of myself as a poor, deprived ghetto girl who made good," she has said. "I think of myself as somebody who, from an early age, knew I was responsible for myself—and I had to make good."[9]

This narrative was the throughline of Winfrey's long-running TV talk show, which premiered in the throes of Reagan's crusade against the U.S. welfare system and depiction of the poor, especially poor Black women, as lazy and undeserving. Oprah took up that ideological mantle, using her top-rated TV show to explain away the cruelties of Reagan's savage cuts in public spending as consequences of personal failure and individual pathology—and to promote compliance, self-help, and consumption in place of critique, institutional change, and public policy. Her persona as a plainspoken, trustworthy advocate was integral to her appeal, as was her promise of empowerment amid the endemic alienation and political and economic disenfranchisement of the times.

In a 1986 episode of her show titled "Pros and Cons of Welfare," Oprah used her opening monologue to engage the audience in a Thatcher-like attack on poor people: "You know, welfare has become a way of life for millions of people in this country. We want to know how you feel about able-bodied welfare recipients sitting at home with their feet up, as you trudge off to work to support them with the tax dollars that are taken from your paycheck each week. Does it make you angry? A lot of people are." On subsequent shows, she scolded people in economic distress for not "thinking positive" and said that homeless people could get jobs if they really wanted to. She shamed poor mothers for not getting abortions and told female victims of domestic assault not to "smother" their male abusers and just accept them for who they are.[10] She assumed the role of the country's moral and spiritual guide, performing therapeutic "interventions" with guest "experts" and prescribing self-love as a cure for whichever social ill. She advised viewers to replace their negative thoughts with positive ones; to think "out of the box" because creative people are healthier, she said; to decorate their workspace because it will make them feel "less emotionally exhausted and reduce burnout"; and to write down three positive things that happened during their workday in order to "reduce stress and physical pain from work."[11]

In 2006, Oprah dedicated two episodes of her show to Rhonda Byrne's *The Secret*, which argues that one's thoughts have the power to shape reality through magnetic properties that "vibrate" and resonate in the universe. The book includes ludicrous statements like "The only reason any person does not have enough money is because they are blocking money from coming to them with their thoughts" and, with regard to personal illness and empathy for the sick, "You cannot 'catch' anything unless you think you can, and thinking you can is inviting it to you with your thought. You are also inviting illness if you are listening to people talking about their illness."[12] During an interview, Oprah explained to Larry King that Byrne's message was one she herself had been trying to convey her entire career.

Such an open and clear endorsement of neoliberal junk science would be laughable if *The Secret* hadn't been translated into dozens of languages, and grossed $300 million internationally, largely because of Oprah's Midas touch.[13] Because of her wealth, the extent of her reach, and her ability to influence very large numbers of people at the subjective level, Oprah is a power elite of the magnitude that Mills assigned to presidents, generals, and the corporate rich. As a media mogul and celebrity with worldwide name recognition and mass appeal, she can proliferate dangerous ideas to the extent that they become part of the common sense. And as a billionaire power broker with direct access to corporate giants and heads of state, she has the standing to whisper in the ears of the powerful and, importantly, put a friendly, therapeutic face on their brutal executions of class power.

In addition to directly transmitting tenets of neoliberal ideology and representing the interests of power elites, as Oprah has, celebrities sanitize and naturalize ruling-class power through the cultural products they make and the characters they play. This is especially true of actors whose craft involves representing social types outside their lived experience that nonetheless may be glorified by warrant of their association with a star. Despite claims to neutrality, film, TV, and other entertainment media use drama and fantasy to frame representations of social life, naturalize those frames, and associate them with celebrities who large numbers of people trust, admire, and want to emulate. For example, the movie *Working Girl* (1988) cast sex-symbol Melanie Griffith as a business-smart working-class secretary who could only get to the boardroom after striking up a love affair with a male executive. When she "arrives" and gets her own secretary and a private office with a view, the secretaries in her former workplace (none of whom are played by sex symbols) treat her individual success as a win for them all. That kind of glass-ceiling ideology—which argues that women should have a seat at the table of power without questioning the power structure itself—dominates the mainstream of women's rights activism and is reverberated through a diversity of films and TV shows featuring so-called "strong women"—like *Maid in Manhattan* (2002), *Sex and the City* (1998–2004), *Zero Dark Thirty* (2012), the *Bridget Jones's Diary* series (2001–2016), and many others.

More depraved is the catalog of reality TV shows that dramatize poor and working-class people's struggles with poverty, drug addiction, eating disorders, and teenage pregnancy and present their cast members as deviants and failures. The reality show *Repo Games* (2012), for example, depicted people who had fallen behind on their car payments as lazy and/or dim-witted and, by implication, undeserving of basic respect and governmental support. *90-Day Fiancé* (2022) focused on courtships between mostly low-income or working-class Americans and immigrants looking to marry their way into U.S. citizenship. MTV's *16 and Pregnant*, and its spinoffs *Teen Mom* and *Teen Mom OG*, chronicles poor and working-class girls' struggles with motherhood in their teenage years.[14] *Here Comes Honey Boo Boo* (2014), set in McIntyre, Georgia, focused on the daily lives of six-year-old beauty pageant contestant Alana Thompson and her family with the apparent aim of making fun of poor, uneducated southern whites. The show presented family members as culturally incompetent and, in Alana's case, mocked her attempts to emulate standards of ideal white femininity. The show's producers achieved this by sound-enhancing family members' farts and burps, using subtitles to decipher their southern drawls (and not using them for other characters), and exaggerating the sound of the already deafening train that ran through their backyard.[15]

Politics and Propaganda

Celebrities' preferential media access and capacity to influence people at ideological and affective levels affords them outsized influence in U.S. politics and elections, more so than actual policy experts and much more so than regular citizens. Some use their bully pulpit to challenge entrenched power, like when director Michael Moore dedicated his Best Documentary Oscar speech to criticizing George W. Bush for his "fictitious" Iraq War or when actress Susan Sarandon used her Best Actress speech to urge the U.S. government to close an internment camp where 250 HIV-positive Haitians were being held.[16] But more frequently, celebrities co-opt political causes to usurp attention, feed narcissistic impulses, and self-righteously brand themselves with the latest activism.

For elections, especially at the presidential level, political campaigns dedicate whole departments to the handling and scheduling of celebrity surrogates who help to increase candidates' media visibility and pop culture cachet. Those with moneyed social networks tend to be effective fundraisers—actor George Clooney hosted parties for Obama and Hillary Clinton that broke records with $15 million hauls at $40,000 per guest[17]—but they do not deliver much by way of votes. An exception: Oprah Winfrey is estimated to have won Obama over a million votes in a show of political power that liberals believe could have rivaled that of Donald Trump.[18]

Celebrity surrogates go out on the stump for campaigns to create spectacle and, oftentimes in sound bites and rallying cries, promote their candidate's ideas, reflecting a common misconception that J. Lo and Katy Perry actually know something about public policy. Their increasingly central role in politics coincides with the dog-and-pony-show nature of political campaigns in America and the general diminution of the country's political discourse to the intellectual maturity level and aesthetic of the TV commercial, where substance is secondary to image, display, and stimulation.

Movie stars also play an important role in the making and dissemination of political propaganda. In the Reagan-era movie *Red Dawn*—written and produced in consultation with General Alexander Haig—a group of American high school students played by teen idols Patrick Swayze, Charlie Sheen, and C. Thomas Howell use guerilla warfare to defend their home town of Calumet, Colorado, against the invasion of Soviet, Cuban, and Nicaraguan communists. Meant to capitalize on the Cold War sentiment of the day, a consequence of the film's paranoiac red-baiting and glorification of survivalism and militias was to inflame anti-communist anxieties, including that of Oklahoma City bomber Timothy McVeigh, who cited the film as a major inspiration.[19] The 2001 war film *Black Hawk Down* used a similar tactic to justify Bill Clinton's "humanitarian intervention" in oil-rich Somalia, casting an ensemble of Hollywood heartthrobs to play the U.S. soldiers who raided Mogadishu, while the Somalis they attacked were depicted as primitive and savage.

In the Oscar-winning 2014 film *American Sniper*, *People Magazine's* 2011 Sexiest Man Alive,[20] Bradley Cooper, plays Chris Kyle, one of the Iraq War's deadliest marksmen. The movie was released over a decade into one of American history's longest, costliest, and most pointless wars. But when Michael Moore and actor Seth Rogen criticized the film, they were met with a tsunami of backlash. Despite director Clint Eastwood's close ties to the Republican Party—recall his discourse with an empty chair at the 2012 Republican National Convention[21]—he and Cooper defended the work as a neutral, apolitical character study, knowing full well that casting a Hollywood pinup as the sniper would fireman-ize, and sexualize, their subject. Cooper went so far as to marvel at the "incredible charisma" of his real-life subject and the clever framing of the film as a Western, despite the xenophobia that "cowboys and Indians" infers.[22]

As it turns out, the charismatic figure Cooper and Eastwood were celebrating was prone to delusions of grandeur, religious bigotry, and volatile aggression, especially against the "savages" (Kyle's words) he fought in Iraq. In his autobiography, Kyle recalls telling an army colonel, "I don't shoot people with Korans. I'd like to, but I don't," and brags about gunning down two men for trying to steal his truck. He also claims to have sniped "looters" from atop the Superdome amidst the chaos of Hurricane Katrina. One redeeming aspect of the film is its critique of the U.S. government's failure to provide for its military veterans; in real life, Kyle himself not only suffered from PTSD but also died tragically trying to aid a fellow veteran who was similarly traumatized.[23] Nonetheless, the film's mass appeal indicated audiences' willingness, if not desire, to suspend the facts of U.S. imperialism for more palatable narratives that fit within the cultural comfort zone of soldiers as macho action heroes and Americans as exceptional. And, it showed Hollywood's readiness to churn profits from stoking nationalist fears and ethnocentrism.

THE CULTURE INDUSTRY

Historically, the phenomenon of celebrity emerged with the rise of mass media within a capitalist order. That does not mean it is impossible to celebrate exceptional beauty and talent outside the profit motive or have sublime experiences through pseudo-intimacies with one's idols or the social bonds of fandom. Nor does it mean that celebrity can't be deployed in the service of challenging elite power, as was the case with some of the Beatles, R&B greats Marvin Gaye and Sam Cooke, actors like Danny Glover and Harry Belafonte, and many others. But nowadays, in an era of media conglomerates and cross-media marketing, the prevailing tendency among celebrities is to operate as human brands and manufacturers of consent. Within the neoliberal capitalist logic of markets and profit-making, a celebrity's worth is measured in terms of their bankability and advertising value—their capacity to draw and hold attention and monetize it. This is especially true of those without any discernable talent other than the ability to operate as pure marketing schemes.

Today, the wealthiest celebrities, those with billionaire or near-billionaire status, achieved their wealth by parlaying their fame into product endorsements, investments, licensing, and branding, and in the process, accumulated economic power commensurate with that of corporate elites. Starting out first as a news anchor, then as a talk show host, Oprah built a media empire and multiproduct brand by leveraging her show's success and turning it into an advertising machine for large corporations and start-ups. Tyler Perry followed a similar path, using his early acting and filmmaking success to construct a 300-plus-acre studio complex in Atlanta to control every aspect of production of his often-high-grossing films. On the success of their blockbuster movies, directors George Lucas, Steven Spielberg, and Peter Jackson created their own large production and special effects companies and brands and sold them for billions.[24] Rapper Jay-Z made his riches off the sale of his streaming service and high-end spirits and champagne brands.[25] Singer Rhianna made her billion off lingerie and cosmetics. Kanye West became a multibillionaire by partnering with Adidas on the sneaker brand Yeezy and from his stake in his ex-wife (and billionaire) Kim Kardashian's shapewear company and a music catalog valued at around $90 million.[26] All of these celebrities have accumulated over $1 billion in net worth.

West's success with Yeezy followed in a now-decades-old practice of branding sneakers through rap and sports stars. By linking their sneakers to popular basketball players and their athletic prowess, and associating distinct styles with specific players, sporting goods and apparel companies have been able to radically expand their visibility and sales. Paving the way was the classic rap group Run DMC, who pioneered sneaker culture in the mid-1980s with "My Adidas," an ode to the Adidas Superstar. During a tour, one of Run DMC's managers brought Adidas executives to witness audiences holding up their sneakers as the rappers performed the song, after which Run DMC signed an unprecedented $1 million endorsement deal with the company.[27]

Puma and Nike followed suit, with the latter awarding breakout basketball star Michael Jordan the most lucrative celebrity endorsement deal at the time. Nike's marketing of Air Jordans involved a series of ads and an iconic logo linking the shoes to Jordan's remarkable ability to defy gravity when dunking the ball. Early on, Nike went with an outlaw image, building a marketing campaign around an NBA warning to Nike that its Air Jordans violated the league's uniform policy,[28] and including in its branding director Spike Lee, an emerging ambassador of Black cultural power in white-dominated Hollywood. Lee's first feature film, *She's Gotta Have It*, deified Jordan through the character Mars Blackmon, who is so obsessed with his Air Jordans that he won't take them off even for sex. The series of commercials riffing off the Mars Blackmon persona firmly situated Nike between Spike Lee's street cool and Black power politics and Jordan's unparalleled status as the greatest player of all time. Nike punctuated this image with the slogan "Be like Mike" to render Jordan's athletic greatness as accessible to those who wore the shoes bearing his silhouette.

As Jordon grew in popularity, Nike's marketing expanded, notably with the movie *Space Jam*—a one-hundred-minute advertisement for Air Jordans. The film was helmed by a director known for shooting commercials, and as *Forbes* described, "The real point of the movie is to sell, sell, sell"[29]—not just sneakers but also toys, books, sports gear, and after the sequel, even *Space Jam*–branded dog toys. During the 2021 release of *Space Jam 2* featuring Nike basketball star Lebron James, the film's producer is quoted on the company's website as saying, "[The movie] culminates into this epic showdown with real consequences for everyone playing. . . . So when a kid sees the characters wearing Nike gear, their imagination makes the connection that Nike gives you the tools to uncover the best version of yourself."[30]

During his career, Jordan partnered with dozens of other big-name brands selling the same mythical, larger-than-life image. That included Wheaties, which featured a series of celebrity athletes on its boxes—Lou Gehrig, Jesse Owens, Bruce Jenner, Mary Lou Retton, Tiger Woods, and others[31]—to associate their athleticism with eating its cereal. After his retirement, Jordan brought his net worth over the billion-dollar threshold through a shrewd purchase of the Charlotte Hornets franchise at a fraction of its current value.[32]

Jordan's commercial path to wealth and celebrity blazed the fairway for golf champion Tiger Woods, whose initial $40 million, five-year contract with Nike helped make him one of the highest-paid athletes in the world.[33] Like Jordan, Tiger was meticulously branded, a process that his father, Lieutenant Colonel Earl Woods, facilitated long before Nike signed him in 1996. That same year, when Tiger was about to accept the Haskins Collegiate Award for best collegiate golfer, father Earl took the stage:

> My heart fills with so much joy when I realize that this young man is going to be able to help so many people. He will transcend this game and bring to the world a humanitarianism which has never been known before. The world will be a better place to live in by virtue of his existence and his presence. . . . I know that I was personally selected by God Himself to nurture this young man and bring him to the point where he can make his contribution to humanity.

Such totemism might have seemed far afield, but it was par for the course for Earl Woods, who had been marking Tiger for golf greatness since birth. Family photos have Earl giving Tiger a golf club before the boy was even a year old. When Tiger was just two, he booked him on the Mike Douglas show on an episode featuring mega-celebrities Bob Hope and Jimmy Stewart; and at age five, Earl got him on the hit reality TV show *That's Incredible!* That night at the awards banquet, however, Earl took it to another level, branding his son as a universal symbol of triumph and hope and, literally, God's gift to the world. And as Tiger's popularity continued to soar, Earl told him, "Let the legend grow."[34]

Picking up on Earl's effort, Nike launched the provocative "Hello World" ad featuring a montage of Tiger—as a toddler swinging a miniature golf club, as a young man measuring a shot with focus and intensity, and as an adult making winning shots and fist-pumping in a sea of adoring fans—with Tiger's voiceover accompanying the images and script:

> Hello world. I shot in the 70s when I was 8. I shot in the 60s when I was 12. I played in the Nissan Open when I was 16. Hello world. I won the U.S. Amateur when I was 18. I played in the Masters when I was 19. I am the only man to win three consecutive U.S. Amateur titles. Hello world. There are still courses in the U.S. I am not allowed to play because of the color of my skin. Hello world. I've heard I'm not ready for you. Are you ready for me?[35]

In addition to Nike branding him as the Jackie Robinson of golf, Tiger was marketed as a wholesome family man—an image protected by a "Team Tiger" of enablers who shielded him from the press. Behind that shield, however, the golfer had been running amok in Las Vegas playgrounds of excess, where "hosts" supplied him with harems of high-paid prostitutes, in some instances $30,000 to $40,000 worth in a single weekend.[36] When the inevitable fall from grace ensued, a long line of scorned women came forward with juicy details of his exploits, shattering his carefully cultivated image and the tens of millions in corporate endorsements tethered to it. Nike stuck with Tiger, then still golf's biggest draw, and exploited his dramatic 2019 comeback at the Masters as if scripting a Hollywood ending.

When Jordan and Tiger were on the rise, Nike, and the host of corporations that courted them, knew that the best way to sell products was to endow them with aura—to sell feelings rather than just nice things. Coca-Cola pioneered this trend in 1971 with its "Hilltop" ad featuring a diverse ensemble of peace-loving youths incanting about buying the world a home and furnishing it with love, apple trees, and snow-white turtle doves—then linking those idyllic images to "buying the world a Coke."[37] Almost thirty years later, on the cutting edge of advertising, Apple based its "Think Different" campaign on the same principle, hijacking the images of MLK, Picasso, John Lennon, and other historical greats to liken itself and its founder Steve Jobs to their rebellious, creative genius. Had they been asked, few if any of these giants would have endorsed Apple's sweatshop-made i-products or associated themselves with an abusive narcissist like Jobs.

Nike—a child labor mill also run by an abusive narcissist (billionaire Phil Knight)—has made a killing exploiting its athletes' racial identities, and movements for racial justice more generally, while associating its image with Black uplift and street culture. Over the years, the company has come under fire for manufacturing its products in overseas sweatshops and its aggressive marketing to Black youth, promoting "hoop dreams" rather than quality jobs and education. Critics also have admonished Nike for using a "new release" raffle system to create artificial scarcity and sensationalize demand for products that the company could easily mass-produce for pennies on the dollar. During the Air Jordan craze, this criticism intensified with media reports of violence among young people fighting each other over the sneakers, which is exactly what Nike wanted. Corporations will stop at nothing in the pursuit of a surefire hook, and as objects of worship, celebrities are perfectly situated to transform ordinary products into fetish objects, especially products with symbolic and emotional value.

In addition to branded talent, today's multimillionaire and billionaire class of celebrity elites includes a notable subset who are "famous for being famous"—who have bypassed talent altogether and gone straight to branding. These celebrities' wealth and fame depend entirely on their ability to remain visible and hold the public's interest in a saturated yet bottomless attention economy and amid an overflow of aspiring stars. Since most of them rose to stardom through social media, they are especially vulnerable to "cancel culture" in which audiences use online forums to organize boycotts against famous people and ostensibly hold them to account. As part of the "Me Too" movement, audiences "canceled" the careers of an array of sexual predators like movie directors Harvey Weinstein and Woody Allen and NBC news anchor Matt Lauer, despite their wide acclaim and substantial corporate and cultural power.[38]

The expulsion of these giants from the culture industry demonstrated social media's capacity to facilitate virtual protest and mass expressions of consumer power. But it also reinforced neoliberalism's tendency to erase and distort context and treat history as the work of individuals rather than as a product of social and political systems. Under cancel culture, activists get the understandable rush of having nailed a media giant like Lauer and getting him fired. But in firing him, NBC got to claim the progressive mantle while still allowing its news anchors to malign and red-bait left-leaning political candidates.[39] In the framework of cancel culture, Disney can claim the moral high ground in canceling Johnny Depp following ex-wife Amber Heard's accusations of abuse, yet still pay low wages to its masses of workers and foster poor working conditions.[40]

In addition to such contradictions, cancel culture has encouraged a misguided belief among "hashtag movements" that Twitter—which profits off conflict and spectacle—is a righteous conduit of social change and that online mobilization (rallying the troops) is the same as organizing (working to bring new people into a movement). It has also encouraged the idea that using "Twitter hives" to publicly dishonor individuals, some not even public figures, constitutes a form of grassroots democratic power, even though those same tactics are deployed by "MAGA" (Make America Great Again) and other right-wing movements to intimidate people and harass them into silence.

This silencing of individuals has an overall cooling effect on public discourse and, in some instances, treads on important legal and social protections, not to mention general standards of fairness and due process. Objects of cancel culture are subjected to arbitrary applications of unwritten rules and prosecuted in courts of public opinion, often denied the opportunity to prove their innocence or demonstrate the gray areas in which they operated. As a result, innocent people have been harassed and ostracized, and some have lost relationships and livelihoods, over unsubstantiated accusations by self-righteous, yet anonymous, tweeters. One such case of cancel culture gone awry took place after Florida man George Zimmerman was acquitted for his racially motivated murder of Trayvon Martin. In protesting such gross racial injustice under the law, director Spike Lee tweeted to his quarter of a million followers what he thought was Zimmerman's home address. Only it wasn't. It was the address of a couple whose son is named William George Zimmerman, and who, as a result of Lee's post, were forced into hiding as a deluge of hate mail poured in.

Even before personal computers, smartphones, and social media, backlash and shaming were the weapons of choice of right-wing ideologues and hooligans in their efforts to scare and marginalize people based on political and religious beliefs, race, ethnicity, and sexual identity. Such was the case when John Lennon quipped to a reporter that the Beatles were "more popular than Jesus," which set off a firestorm among ultra-conservatives, especially those in the South. A shock jock radio station in Birmingham, Alabama, waged a "Ban the Beatles" campaign that reverberated throughout the Bible Belt and across the country, and DJs smashing Beatles records on air escalated into full-scale record burnings and heavy death threats. Those harassments and threats not only ended the Beatles' touring career at the time, but also inspired the born-again Christian man who murdered Lennon in 1980.[41]

About thirteen years after the Beatles boycotts, a right-wing movement instigated by rock-n-roll radio personalities and record producers targeted and tried to "cancel" the Bee Gees as part of a violent attack against disco and the sexual, racial, and gender barriers it was breaking down. The group's tight pants, gold medallions, falsetto voices—and commercial success—put them literally in the line of fire (they received bomb threats) of reactionary, homophobic, and racist forces. After tens of thousands of rioters at the infamous Disco Demolition Night at the Chicago White Sox's Comiskey Park burned disco and R&B albums in a manner reminiscent of a Nazi book burning, disco was effectively "canceled" from the radio and broader culture.

On the flip side of cancel culture are the various entryways to fame that social media provides for those who would not otherwise have access to it. Unlike the unilateralism of the mainstream press, social media fosters pseudo-intimacies that an aspiring celebrity can exploit to cultivate a fan base and personal brand. Because audience attention is valuable to advertisers, celebrities and "influencers" can build lucrative careers just by being visible, accessible, and provocative (as opposed to being talented). In such a crowded field and fragmented attention economy, being visible requires media saturation and overexposure, including coverage in tabloid and gossip outlets that use tantalizing fodder to absorb fans into celebrities' personal lives. Being accessible means making public appearances and staying plugged in to satisfy fan expectations for greater, seemingly more authentic exchange.

Among the most pioneering and wealthy celebrity influencers are Paris Hilton and Kim Kardashian, who both built billion-dollar brands and accumulated elite cultural and corporate power on their ability to monetize attention—with Hilton accumulating a net worth of around $300 million and Kardashian, over $1 billion. During the Great Depression, gossip columnist Walter Winchell coined the term "celebutante" to mark a new species of celebrity with no apparent talent other than the ability to play to the cameras. Of that genus, Hilton built her brand on the image of a jet-setting heiress and "it girl" with wealthy socialite parents, who in Paris's case actually nicknamed her "Star."[42] When Hilton's family moved to New York City's Waldorf Towers, which they owned, she and her sister Nicky began their ascent to fame by attending charity events with mom and dad, crashing parties at their family's hotel, and being seen on red carpets in South Beach, in the front row at New York Fashion Week, and dancing on tabletops at Los Angeles nightclubs.

The Hilton girls were still teenagers when *Vanity Fair* interviewed them for its "Hip Hop Debs!" cover story that propelled them to stardom. The cover photo, shot by renowned photographer David LaChapelle, featured two rich girls out on the town posing in front of a silver Rolls-Royce in revealing clothes and heavy makeup, with Paris donning a gold choker collar that read "R-I-C-H."[43] After that, Hilton made a hit reality TV show and published a *New York Times* bestseller, but it was her leaked sex tape *One Night in Paris* that brought international fame, which Hilton monetized into a brand empire. From jewelry to hair extensions to a multi-billion-dollar revenue-generating perfume line, she multiplied her inherited wealth into hundreds of millions of dollars, earning as much as $1 million for a single public appearance.[44]

Kim Kardashian's mega-celebrity was also built on spectacle and "sex sells," but more than any other celebrity, she exploited the advertising potential of reality TV and social media to achieve an extraordinary level of wealth. The daughter of O. J. Simpson's lawyer, Kardashian got her start working as Paris Hilton's stylist and appearing with her at nightclubs. Like Hilton, she had a sex tape *Kardashian, Superstar* that brought international fame and was the star of her own reality TV show, which became a long-running hit. *Keeping Up with the Kardashians* spawned spinoff series, launched the careers of Kim's family and friends, and, most importantly, expanded Kim's brand and multiplied her social media following exponentially.

For the show, which debuted a few months after the iPhone was released, TV cameras followed the family, mostly the three girls, in the daily life of the rich and famous—luxury vacations; personal stylists, chefs, and physical trainers; being chauffeured around L.A.; and lounging at home on the couch, barely clothed, poring over their Twitter feeds. In addition to this constant visibility and superficial intimacy with audiences, the show capitalized on socially relevant drama and storylines. When Kim's stepfather, Bruce Jenner, transitioned to Caitlyn, Jenner's *60 Minutes* sit-down interview with Diane Sawyer broke records with a seventeen-million-plus audience,[45] transforming her from decorated Olympian to international symbol of transgender liberation. This, despite her lack of experience with the economic and political struggles that most transgender people face and her identity as a Republican.

Kardashian's massive Twitter and Instagram followings—nearly 73 million on Twitter and over 319 million on Instagram, as of June 2022—allowed her to charge corporate advertisers half a million dollars or more for a single endorsement on her Instagram account.[46] It also enabled her to direct-market her cosmetics and shapewear lines, which proved to be integral to their billion-dollar success. Kardashian's half-sister Kylie Jenner derived her near-billion-dollar net worth using the same formula. With one of the largest Snapchat followings in the social media app's history, Jenner made a fortune direct-marketing her cosmetics line. And when she broadcast in a tweet that she was done with Snapchat, the company's stock price tanked 6 percent, $1.3 billion of its market value.[47]

REALITY TV

In a 2010 interview with *The Guardian* two years before his untimely death, singer-songwriter Robin Gibb observed that the industry of which he had been a part for most of his life was increasingly treating music like "one big karaoke machine."[48] Gibb was no stranger to the big business of music, of course, and it was not uncommon for managers and producers of his and subsequent generations to sell out their clients' creative abilities in the process of making them stars. What he was reacting to, however, is the relatively recent phenomenon of the so-called democratization of fame in which anyone, talented or not, can grab a microphone, take the stage, and become famous—with all the banality and repetition that implies.

Back when the Gibb brothers were dominating the charts, the music industry revolved around DJs and local radio stations, and music videos were still new. Since then, a mix of factors—corporate deregulation and consolidation, major technological breakthroughs, and the enlargement of the media and entertainment industries—has expanded access and quantities of content to the extent that anyone can play any song by any musician at any time. The same trend occurred in visual media with the proliferation of cable TV and twenty-four-hour programming and, more recently, digital cable and streaming services. Audiences that once relied on just a handful of major networks for entertainment, news, and viewing seminal events like the first lunar landing can now access—and contribute to—a limitless catalog of video and film material on myriad radio, TV, and online channels.

The ubiquity of digital media and instantaneous circulation of images have enabled advertisers to saturate the public consciousness with commercial content every waking moment. For viewers, programs like *Good Morning America* and *The Tonight Show* may be staples of news and entertainment, but for advertisers, they are means for extending our waking hours later into the night and earlier into the morning, leaving no second unturned in the pursuit of ever-renewed profit. These trends in mass media, advertising, and consumer demand have multiplied the culture industry's need for content and for new and more faces and, in turn, has intensified competition for audience attention and increased opportunities for both fame and infamy.

Amid these developments, reality TV emerged in the mid-1980s as a solution to the television industry's profitability crisis brought by rising production costs and debt and competition for advertising revenue. In 1988, producers exploited the Writers Guild of America labor strike to bypass unions and labor costs associated with agents, professional actors, and script writers—and avert future strikes—by producing low-cost programming to meet the demands of the new, multichannel environment.[49] Reality TV allowed for greater flexibility and lower risk, as producers could test new shows without making costly investments. In 2019, this relatively new production technique generated some $6 billion a year in profits, in addition to revenue associated with branding, tertiary businesses, and (mostly tabloid) media.[50] The cost savings on actors, writers, and other categories of labor have facilitated huge profit margins. For example, at its peak, *American Idol* was making $96 million in revenue at a profit margin of 77 percent.[51]

Reality TV is an assemblage of melodrama, comedy, and documentary that sensationalizes the dramas of everyday life. Its poor production quality helps to create an aura of authenticity, of regular people in "real life" situations, interspersed with confessional-style interviews. By focusing on everyday people, producers can package their product as a form of "democratizing celebrity" and "discovering" the stars among us. And by focusing on "reality," they can mass-produce content from a seemingly endless stream of subject matter: dating, makeovers, job searches, business innovation and investment, endurance and talent competition, real estate and home renovation, addiction, and many others. As a clear indication of the level of absurdity and exploitation that the genre has engendered, CBS went so far as to produce (and cancel before airing) a reality show featuring A-list singer Usher in which "activists" working on various social causes were set up to compete with each other for the opportunity to appeal to world leaders at a meeting of the G20.

A vital part of producing reality TV is the *caster*, whose job is to construct casts and storylines with commercial value. That means locating "actors" with the ability to deliver ratings and willingness to generate controversy. Like talk shows, the goal is to harvest audiences' attention by exploring the volatile and emotional terrain of the human experience—within thirty-minute segments, including commercial breaks—and use that attention to generate advertising revenue. To glean dramatic performances and draw forth authentic selves, cast members and contestants are often put in high-stress situations and social pressure cookers and pushed to their emotional limits. The more unhinged and unfiltered they are, the better.

Reality TV cast members compete for attention, and against each other, to stay relevant and employed. Oftentimes, this imperative to be spectacular requires them to reveal intimate parts of their lives and endure public ridicule. Moreover, the scarcity of roles and lack of agents and union representation allow production companies to exert total contractual control over cast members' rights—to the use and depiction of their image, to future work and earnings, to appearances in other media, and to the telling of their own life story.[52] Networks that farm celebrities through talent competitions use such contracts to collect on their discovery by usurping legal rights to the burgeoning star's personal management and merchandising and, in the case of music, their publishing, recording, and touring.

Since reality TV productions essentially own their cast members' image, they are free to present it in unflattering and distorting ways. This is not just the case with consenting adults, but with children as well. *Kid Nation* (2008) featured kids ages eight to fifteen in a reality TV version of *Lord of the Flies*. *Toddlers and Tiaras* involved children as young as three years old, some of them dressed up in adult clothes and heavy makeup. The *Toddlers and Tiaras* spinoff series, *Here Comes Honey Boo Boo*, pulled no punches in depicting a six-year-girl living in poverty as ignorant and uncivilized.

Parents and cast members consent to such exploitation because they believe that it is the price of fame and upward mobility, despite the fact that the cultural industry's steep earning disparities and high rates of turnover render celebrity-level success extremely unlikely. A handful of reality TV stars do accumulate enough fame to generate significant, even life-changing, income through spinoff series, hit songs, book deals, and product lines. Donald Trump not only made a major comeback through *The Apprentice*, he translated the show's popularity into political power at the highest level. Bethenny Frankel used *The Real Housewives of New York City* to gain attention for her "Skinny Girl" brand that sold for hundreds of millions of dollars. That kind of jackpot success is the carrot that keeps reality TV casts pursuing fame like hamsters on a wheel while expanding the industry's underpaid, nonunion workforce and undermining worker power.

The Apprentice: White House Edition

As America's celebrity president gathered his cabinet for its first official meeting of 2018, he sat in a leather chair at the center of a long mahogany table and quipped to the press, "Welcome back to the studio. It's nice to have you."[53] It was an obvious reference to the boardroom scene in the president's reality TV show *The Apprentice* in which contestants sat before him to be judged at a similar kind of table, with Trump seated in a leather chair—oversized, to emphasize his authority. As president-elect, Trump told his aides to consider each day of their administration as an episode of a TV show in which he "vanquishes rivals."[54] That debased, throw-down manner marked his long, storied career from Atlantic City casinos, to Miss Universe and WrestleMania, to golf resorts and New York City skyscrapers and the for-profit Trump University—an all-around showman of the P. T. Barnum "a sucker is born every minute" variety.

The Apprentice was crucial to Trump's political success. It was a vehicle for rescuing his brand from a series of business failures; and it was the means through which he presented himself, on a mass scale, as an executive and dealmaker-in-chief. Trump's aim to cast himself as an American success story was apparent in the show's title sequence, which featured a montage of him, steely faced, ascending into a Trump-branded private jet, juxtaposed with a gratuitous shot of a homeless man sleeping on a bench, and a glistening Statue of Liberty: "I fought back and won—big league," he boasted. "I used my brain. I used my negotiating skills."[55] *The Apprentice* brought Trump into people's homes and helped make him electable by rendering him as both familiar and exceptional. He parlayed that primetime celebrity into political power by playing up his Washington outsider status and using the techniques of shock jocks and insult comedy to captivate audiences and lure ratings-hungry media.

In many ways, Trump was a caricature of what the presidency had already become. By the 1970s, it was widely accepted that major political figures would be part of the world of show business, and that mass media and show business would be part of politics. FDR used the fireside chat. Eisenhower went on the *Ed Sullivan Show* with Abbott and Costello. JFK was the first major political candidate to be interviewed on late-night TV.[56] Nixon met with Elvis at the White House and quipped, "Sock it to *me*?" on *Laugh-In*.[57] Ford and Kissinger appeared on *Dynasty*. Reagan was a famous actor and president of the Screen Actors Guild of America. Carter quoted Willie Nelson and Bob Dylan and sat for an interview with *Playboy*. Bill Clinton *was* a playboy who slalomed in and out of tabloid sex scandals and donned shades while playing sax on *The Arsenio Hall Show*. Then there was Obama, poised and photogenic, who crooned Al Green, "slow-jammed the news" with Jimmy Fallon, and inspired audiences with his high school graduation–style speeches. When Obama appeared before over a million people in Berlin as a presidential candidate, his opponent, Senator John McCain released an attack ad called "Celeb" likening him to Britney Spears and Paris Hilton: "He's the biggest celebrity in the world. But is he ready to lead?"[58]

Trump's presidency marked a departure from that of his predecessors, however, who all used pop culture to achieve political ends but nonetheless employed legal-rational means of governing and the tools of law and bureaucracy. In contrast, Trump was a purely charismatic leader who used the tools of celebrity to govern, and who exploited government to expand his celebrity. His was a distinctly anti-institutional form of authority that derived its legitimacy from emotions rather than norms and laws. According to German sociologist Max Weber, charismatic leaders tend to gain traction when rational forms of government and institutions fail, when people lose faith in the establishment, and desire escape from the dehumanizing and alienating effects of bureaucratic life. Unlike kings, who draw power from legacy and tradition, or heads of state, whose authority is vested in their role in a legal-rational order, a charismatic leader's power is rooted in his or her followers' belief and desires for transcendence. When the leader's allure fades or their rebellion is routinized, the basis of their authority breaks down.[59]

Trump exploited every opportunity to play to his supporters' emotions, desire to be entertained, and distrust of the establishment. His many critics tried to discredit him for his lack of expertise, flagrant disrespect for presidential norms, and practice of embellishing wins and distracting from losses. But they consistently failed to undermine his appeal and delegitimize his power, perhaps because his supporters held him to a different set of standards that corresponded with how they had come to know him, through *The Apprentice*. After all, reality TV audiences know that the shows are staged, and that cast members are performing images of their authentic selves, but they tune in and take pleasure in it anyway.

In this regard, Trump's presidency exposed some inconvenient truths about American capitalism and the culture industries that operate on its behalf. Among them is the fact that large swaths of the U.S. electorate preferred their corrupt and undemocratic government in the form of a bombastic showman, rather than shrouded in technocracy and legalism. It also revealed that masses of people are willing to accept affective stimulation as a substitute for actual political power. And it is a grim reminder of the compatibility between neoliberalism, celebrity, and autocracy that was made apparent during the first neoliberal experiments in Pinochet's Chile.

Critical theorists of the postwar era grappled with similar dynamics in studying the role of celebrity, entertainment, and emotion in fascist propaganda. Nazi propagandists used radio and film to forge the Nazis' pathway to power, lacing musical entertainment with political rhetoric, and staging mass rallies starring Hitler, an international celebrity. According to German philosopher Theodor Adorno, fascist propagandists used mechanical rhythms and repetition to displace critical thought and, through film and spectacular public demonstrations, exploited the magnetism of the pack to foster surrender to both dictator and nation (which were one and the same). In the patterning of fascist propaganda, such surrender was of a libidinal nature, involving the excitement of release and a sense of belonging. Followers viewed the dictator as a father figure with total authority over the family (the nation), but also as one of them—relating to his expressions of vulnerability and victimhood, but also venerating him as a symbol of national strength. In him, and him alone, was the resolution of their yearning to escape the repressive routines and civilizing processes of modern life.[60]

The parallels between Trump's celebrity presidency and the patterning of fascist propaganda are plain to see: the relentless repetition and disinformation, the scapegoating of the Other, the strongman identity and victimhood, and the equating of his executive leadership with the greatness of the nation. Those are in addition to his arbitrary application of law, disdain for rules and bureaucracy, and substituting of mass entertainment for political power. Trump was not driven by allegiance to a coherent ideology like some of those in his administration. But his grandiosity, love for chaos, and penchant for tabloid-inspired emotion over fact, recalled history's greatest autocrats—many of whom were also charismatic showmen guided by profits, image, power, and the old P. T. Barnum adage that "The bigger the humbug, the better people will like it."

CHAPTER 8
Publics and Masses

In January 2017, Trump senior advisor and campaign manager Kellyanne Conway appeared on NBC's *Meet the Press* for a postinauguration interview with news anchor Chuck Todd. In response to a question on the White House's verifiably false claim that Trump's inauguration attracted the "largest audience to ever witness an inauguration—period—both in person and around the globe," Conway scolded Todd and told him, "Don't be so overly dramatic about it, Chuck," and then she matter-of-factly argued that the Trump administration was merely offering "alternative facts" to refute existing, evidence-based counts.[1] Within days of the interview, Orwell's *1984* and Huxley's *Brave New World* shot to the top of bestseller lists, joining the flurry in sales of books on authoritarianism and fascist dictatorship that Trump's election, and his administration's penchant for disinformation, inspired.

Set in the year 1984, Orwell's foretelling of a coming authoritarianism advanced through doublethink and other chilling propaganda techniques inspired Neil Postman's now-classic, *Amusing Ourselves to Death,* published in 1985. In it, Postman identified the TV news as an instrument of social control and decay that more resembled Huxleyan amused distraction than Orwellian surveillance and linguistic and intellectual domination. As television became Americans' primary source of consequential information, Postman argued, it degraded public discourse, banalized the news, and chipped away at our ability to discern. In coining the term "infotainment," he pointed to the indistinguishability among news, consumerism, and entertainment as part of TV's innate bias toward superficiality and emotional gratification—at the expense, he said, of critical thought and a democratic public sphere.[2] In 1996, Pierre Bourdieu made similar arguments in his published lectures titled "On Television," where he argued that TV, as a fully commodified medium of information dissemination, encourages homogeneity in our thought and functions as a form of "invisible censorship" with the power to mobilize—or demobilize—the public.[3]

Today, the Huxleyan anesthetization that Postman and Bourdieu lamented appears to have given way to, or been supplemented with, the addictive adrenaline rush of outrage, anger, and fear. News outlets that once played down the middle to capture the broadest possible audience, now, in the era of twenty-four-hour cable TV and deregulated media, gain market share by targeting specific consumer segments and tailoring the news to their consumer tastes. Part of that tailoring involves hooking audiences through spectacle and affirmations meant to stoke social and political division. With just a handful of conglomerates competing to rule the airwaves, journalists and their editors have little incentive to factually report the news when it conflicts with what their audiences, and benefactors, want to hear.

Trump is a consequence of these trends. As "the Fox News President,"[4] he gleaned "alternative facts" from Fox News broadcasts and regularly consulted with Fox personalities like anchor Sean Hannity and founder Roger Ailes. A former TV talk show producer and political operative, Ailes understood the political power of TV and how to effectively deflect attention from inconsistencies and abuses of power. He wrote the book on how to construct compelling visual "realities" that play on audiences' emotions and mobilize them to action. During the 2016 presidential race, Fox and Ailes provided Trump with the necessary airtime and coverage to get him elected and, importantly, the framework of class war. Trump rallies and press conferences invigorated masses of Americans devasted by job loss, stagnant incomes, and declining standards of living. And he used those televised performances to spread distrust by playing off his followers' resentment toward the liberal media establishment, which he called "the enemy of the people"—a phrase that Nazi propagandist Joseph Goebbels used to sow hatred against the Jewish people.[5]

The liberal media did its part by playing the perfect foil, caricaturing Trump supporters as backwards and universally racist, and delivering daily doses of gratuitous snark that played squarely into Trump's underdog narrative. In shameless pursuit of Pulitzers and profits, liberal news outlets donated tens of millions of dollars in unearned media to Trump's campaign with obsessive, around-the-clock coverage.[6] As Les Moonves, chief executive of CBS, explained (before he was ousted over allegations of serial sexual harassment), Trump "may not be good for America, but it's damn good for CBS," adding, "So what can I say? The money's rolling in, this is fun."[7]

The conservative movement that animated Fox and the Trump presidency derived from a lineage of neoliberal zealots—Goldwater, Wallace, Nixon, and Reagan—whose "southern strategy" involved realigning Democratic and GOP conservatives around racial grievance and states' rights, and against the public sphere, especially public education. In her seminal book *Democracy in Chains*, Nancy MacLean exposed in mortifying detail the central role that academics like Nobel Prize economist James M. Buchanan played in the Far Right's relentless, decades-long war of position that it waged from inside universities, corporate media, and think tanks.[8] The propaganda efforts of these early neoliberal ideologues and gathering of corporate power formed the backdrop of Mills's *The Power Elite*, as did the striving of intellectuals worldwide to make sense of the role of media and culture in the rise of European fascism.

In *Behemoth: The Structure and Practice of National Socialism, 1933–1944*, Franz Neumann wrote that "in terms of modern analytical social psychology, one could say that National Socialism is out to create a uniformly sado-masochistic character, a type of man determined by his isolation and insignificance, who is driven by this very fact into a collective body where he shares in the power and glory of the medium of which he has become a part."[9] This framework of mass apathy and alienation undergirded Mills's analysis of elite power, in which he used the theoretical categories of "publics" and "masses" to address the degrading condition of American civic and political life and the ideological forces behind it. Whereas "publics" indicated engaged, knowledgeable, autonomous agents of democratic deliberation and dissent, "masses" were anti-intellectual, privatist, and uninformed, and therefore prone to manipulation. With fascism barely in the rearview mirror, or as he feared, on the horizon, Mills argued that a public sphere of genuine debate, an educated and independent citizenry, and a media conducive to open, two-way communication were fundamental to achieving a truly democratic political life and universal human freedom. This chapter charts the politicization and privatization of today's news media and of U.S. public education—both institutional pillars of democratic engagement and challenging elite power—and the role of that corruption and decline in the production of authoritarian capitalism.

THE CORPORATE MEDIA

In the United States, political extremism and the wholesale commodification of the news media were not always the norm. In the postwar period, a handful of television networks and newspaper chains dominated the news business, but their aim was to reach the widest possible audience and address the country as a whole. This was in part due to the Fairness Doctrine in the Federal Communications Act of 1934 that positioned broadcasters as public trustees in charge of cultivating an informed citizenry and safeguarding the public interest. As a condition of federal licensing to use public airwaves, the Doctrine required broadcasters to cover controversial issues in a fair and nonpartisan way, and as amended in 1959, mandated equal airtime for public office seekers.[10]

Conservatives opposed the Fairness Doctrine, arguing that it favored the liberal media and that the free market, not government, was the optimal means of mediating among disparate viewpoints in the news. They contended that the equal airtime requirement infringed on broadcasters' First Amendment rights, but when they tried to bring it before the U.S. Supreme Court in 1969, the court upheld the Doctrine, asserting that free speech was "the right of the viewers and listeners, not the right of the broadcasters" and that "it is the purpose of the First Amendment to preserve an uninhibited market-place of ideas in which truth will ultimately prevail, rather than to countenance monopolization of that market, whether it be by the Government itself or a private licensee."[11]

If U.S. policymakers were at least in part driven by the value of an informed public, that disappeared in 1987 when Reagan's Federal Communications Commission (FCC) revoked the Fairness Doctrine, citing both First Amendment rights and technological change. Whereas the Doctrine was predicated on a scarcity of news sources available through a handful of major news networks, cable TV enabled access to a diversity of news outlets and opinions that, conservatives argued, should be mediated through market competition and self-regulation.[12]

After Reagan lifted the rule, the number of explicitly conservative, and fascist, media programs skyrocketed, driven by talk radio hosts like Rush Limbaugh and Bob Grant. As Limbaugh grew his audience into the tens of millions with rails against "feminazis" and "environmentalist wackos,"[13] Grant spewed xenophobic rage, calling immigrants "subhumanoids," and African American church-goers "screaming savages."[14] This new generation of deranged radio personalities, hostile to the mainstream news media, provided the foundation for the emergence of conservative news outlets on cable TV like Newsmax and Fox News.

Reagan vetoed Democrats' efforts to save the Doctrine, but when Clinton and the New Democrats took office, corporate-driven deregulation of the media became bipartisan consensus. The same year that he demolished the U.S. welfare system, Clinton signed into law the Telecommunications Act of 1996 with a decisive majority in both the

House (414 in favor, 16 against) and Senate (91 in favor, 5 against), including support from ultra-conservative Republican House Speaker Newt Gingrich.[15] Driving Democrats further away from the idea of the media as a public good, Clinton promoted deregulation as an accelerator of competition that, he assured the country, would bring more consumer options at lower prices. In his pitch for the bill, he gushed about the wonders of the "information superhighway," which, like most great highways, was built by the federal government, and not the private sector as neoliberals would like people to believe.[16] Opponents like then-congressman Bernie Sanders and activist groups like Fairness and Accuracy in Reporting (FAIR) pointed to how media industry lobbyists had "bought and paid for" the legislation and warned that it would increase prices and encourage monopoly, which is exactly what it did.[17]

The Telecommunications Act of 1996 dramatically reduced New Deal–era FCC rules in place to stem conflicts of interest and corporate monopoly on media ownership. It allowed large corporations and wealthy individuals to buy up and dominate media markets, leaving smaller outlets to fail or get "merged" into larger corporations. U.S. telecommunications firms could acquire foreign companies and vice versa, and cross-industry ownership regulations that prohibited firms in one sector from operating in and controlling those in another were relaxed. Notably, the law granted the FCC the authority to review and modify its media ownership rules every four years to ensure that they remained in the public interest. This endowed the FCC with incredible deregulatory power that media giants like News Corp exploited to undermine remaining restrictions on conglomeration.[18] In the name of unfettering the emerging online industry, moreover, the legislation absolved internet companies from liability for user-generated content, which opened the door for the spread of conspiracy theory and disinformation that plagues online media today.[19]

Before Clinton's radical legislation passed into law, approximately fifty companies controlled 90 percent of the media and entertainment industries; as of 2022, only five or six conglomerates control the same market share. With overlapping membership on corporate boards of directors and interconglomerate coordination and joint ventures, just a handful of giant corporations dominate everything from book and magazine publishing, to radio and cable and network TV, to movie studios, music companies, theme parks, and sports teams. In command of these goliaths is a small cadre of billionaires and multimillionaires[20] who exert near-total control over today's global media landscape. In *The New Media Monopoly*, Bob Bagdikian described these dynamics in the starkest of terms, arguing that today's mega-media corporations and their leaders wield "more communications power than was exercised by any despot or dictatorship in history."[21]

In some instances, that despotism has been exercised in broad daylight. When the *Los Angeles Times* reported on Disney's shady business dealings in Anaheim, California, where its theme park is located, the media giant blacklisted the *Times* from its movie screenings and interviews. When billionaire casino mogul Sheldon Adelson secretly purchased the *Las Vegas Review-Journal*, it spurred a mass exodus of journalists and editors citing curtailed editorial freedom and shady business dealings and management.[22] PayPal co-founder, Peter Thiel, a right-wing billionaire, took down Gawker Media by bankrolling a lawsuit against the gossip site in revenge for its reporting on his sexual orientation. When billionaire Michael Bloomberg ran for president, *Bloomberg News* journalists were instructed not to cover it, leading to resignations. For years, billionaire Rupert Murdoch has openly used his vast media empire to advance his political agenda. Many more such manipulations happen behind closed doors, including the inevitable self-censoring of journalists and editors looking to hold on to their sought-after jobs.

Big Tech

In the early years of the new millennium, Big Tech companies like Amazon and Google broke into the news and entertainment industries, and, by warrant of their size and control over large portions of the digital world, quickly became dominant. By 2020, the top three news and information companies in the world—Google (which includes Alphabet and YouTube), Facebook, and Apple—were generating more content than what the traditional, Hollywood entertainment industry produced over its entire history, boasting over a billion viewing hours per day, equivalent to television viewing time.[23]

Big Tech's entry into the news business did not change the fact that most Americans got (and still get) their news from television, especially as TV news has become more entertaining and addictive. But it did fundamentally disable newspapers, especially those operating at the local level. At first, newspaper owners and journalists welcomed the arrival of these gigantic online platforms as tech companies were distributing their news stories to masses of online users. By 2017, Facebook and Google combined accounted for over 70 percent of users directed to the websites of major news publishers.[24] Big Tech companies' ambition was not to aid existing news media, however; it was to use their unique advantages—their extensive consumer data and reach on par with a public utility—to expand their profitability and monopoly power into new markets.

Most Americans think of Facebook and Google as social media and online search platforms, but primarily they are advertising companies that glean enormous profits through targeted advertising. Unlike traditional advertisers that broker between companies selling products and the media through which they are marketed, tech companies operate as both ad brokers and media platforms, in direct competition with TV, radio, and newspapers. Big Tech's edge over traditional news media lay in its ability to collect reliable, granular data on users' friends, tastes, and habits through social networks and internet searches. This window into consumers' souls allows companies that advertise on Google or Facebook to target them with surgical precision and even manipulate their habits.[25] In 2021, U.S. advertisers spent more on digital advertising than they did on the traditional media of TV, radio, and newspapers, with Facebook, Google, and Amazon increasing their market share of the U.S. digital ad market to an estimated 90 percent in 2020.[26]

Aside from subscriptions, meager public funding, and some private funders (usually operating in the red), newspaper journalism has historically been financed through corporate advertising. That changed in the late 1990s when the online classifieds platform Craigslist cut into newspapers' ad dollars and evaporated their classifieds revenue. As Facebook grew its network to nearly a billion users (as of 2022, it was almost three billion), newspapers adopted it and other social media platforms as part of their post-Craigslist growth strategy. Journalists shared their articles on social media and tried to expand their online profiles, and in return, Facebook designed its News Feed algorithms to prioritize content from news organizations. This arrangement was upset after the 2016 presidential election, when Facebook and YouTube were under fire for designing their algorithms to optimize scale without concern for the spread of sensational "clickbait" and conspiracy theory. According to a 2018 *Wall Street Journal* investigation, when YouTube algorithms detected a user's political orientation, it would feed them content that echoed their biases yet "often with more-extreme viewpoints."[27]

Facebook addressed the criticisms by revamping its algorithms to favor individual posts over those from institutions, which effectively demoted newspaper outlets occupying the top spots on its News Feeds. The move allowed Facebook to build on its profiteering off news content—that it did not produce or even fact-check[28]—by charging news agencies a fee for choice placement. Amid outrage from the major outlets, Facebook began paying news organizations for their content, but played favorites in choosing which agencies to partner with, and ultimately maintained control over the news content that its billions of users consumed.[29] The company also responded to the "fake news crisis" by creating a supposedly independent tribunal to determine which posts to take down and which users to ban from the site—further distancing itself from accountability for its users' content. With Clinton's radical telecommunications legislation having relieved internet companies from liability for user-generated content—unlike traditional news organizations, which can be sued for libel or inflicting distress—social media platforms remain hotbeds of disinformation, conspiracy theory, and libel. This has chilled speech and, in some cases, incited fringe groups to political vigilantism.

With tech giants usurping their advertising revenue, leading news outlets like the *New York Times* shifted their business model toward recruiting and retaining subscribers, using demographics and political identity to locate profits in specific consumer segments.[30] Amid the economic downturn associated with COVID-19, thousands of local newspapers folded, went fully online, or were acquired by Wall Street firms and media conglomerates—leaving whole communities to rely on social media for their news, or turn to TV, which nowadays trends conservative. Between 2005 and 2021, an estimated 2,100 local newspapers (1 in 4) closed, several of them during the coronavirus pandemic. Now, hedge funds and private equity firms control half of U.S. daily newspapers, including Tribune, McClatchy, and MediaNews Groups. Recall from chapter 4 that hedge funds and private equity firms make their money by cutting staff, selling off real estate, and defunding workers' pensions. One company, Alden Capital, was found to likely have violated federal law by putting $294 million of newspaper employees' pension savings into its own funds.[31]

In 2000, the daily U.S. circulation of newspapers was around 60 million, but by 2020, that number had been more than halved to just 24.3 million.[32] Over that period, with Trump rolling back protections against monopolies, conglomerate Sinclair Broadcasting binge-bought hundreds of local TV news stations around the country and used them to promote the conservative viewpoints of its owners, the Smith family.[33] When Sinclair's executive chairman and son of its founder, David Smith, met Donald Trump in 2016, he promised, "We are here to deliver your message."[34] In 2018, Sinclair made headlines when a video director at the sports blog *Deadspin* posted an online montage of hundreds of Sinclair news anchors emoting about the dangers of liberal media bias, while all reading from the same politically charged script. In the video, dozens of clips of Sinclair anchors appear all at once, split-screened, their voices combined in dystopian, cultish harmony as they perform the same Trump-inspired lines.[35]

To be fair, in the current climate, news anchors and reporters are under enormous pressure to conform to the political agendas of their news agency's owners and are incentivized to do so with lucrative contracts and the promise of fame. Anchors on national networks and cable TV news can become wealthy celebrities if they are willing to feed the spectacle and deliver the party line. Such was the case with Sean Hannity at Fox News, who, as of 2020, made $40 million annually, and Rachel Maddow, who in 2021 penned a $30 million deal with NBC Universal to move away from anchoring and produce podcasts and documentaries.[36] To augment their network compensation, media celebrities "buckrake" at corporate conferences and think tank seminars, making more in a few hours than what a school teacher or bus driver makes in a single year.[37] For example, each year the billionaire (Pete) Peterson family sponsors a bipartisan "fiscal summit" in Washington, DC featuring panels with military, corporate, and political elites moderated by prominent members of the news media—people like *New York Times* national security correspondent David Sanger or cable TV news anchors like Chuck Todd and Andrea Mitchell (wife of Alan Greenspan). These news figures collect huge fees for appearing at, and thus legitimizing, Peterson's summit, apparently undeterred by his lifelong crusade against Social Security, Medicare, and Medicaid.

This bending of the fourth estate to private interests and profit motives also manifests in the aesthetics and programming of TV news, where success is measured in terms of ratings and ad revenue, rather than whether reporters speak truth to power. Cable TV producers are trained to present the news in ways that affirm the beliefs of their audiences, while amping them up on gripping storylines with potentially long dramatic arcs (a Maddow specialty). When the words "breaking news" flash on screen, it's an indicator that network producers have nailed a story that not only will hook audiences, but also that they can milk for ratings all day and into the night. In an illuminating blog post on how MSNBC makes editorial decisions, a former producer explained how the network chose news topics based on what was trending on Twitter that day and what rated well the day before. She also described how her superiors instructed her to keep news stories bite-sized and visually stimulating, and when she suggested that the network air more substantive news, one "very capable senior producer" told her that "our viewers don't really consider us the news. They come to us for comfort."[38]

In addition to spin—for bosses and target audiences—the media also shape the news by *not* covering certain events and topics or, conversely, by positioning themselves as kingmakers to force a desired outcome. This propagandizing and tipping of scales is especially rampant in the coverage of presidential politics and national security—areas in which an informed public is vitally important. For example, in the year between July 2017 and July 2018, MSNBC chose not to cover the war in Yemen at all, but did manage to produce four hundred and fifty-five segments on Stormy Daniels, the porn star who Trump's lawyer paid hush money to during his 2016 presidential campaign.[39] In failing to cover such important events, and instead prioritizing the banal and sensational, the media undermine electoral processes and leave Americans out of life-and-death decisions being made in their name. Media coverage of the second Iraq War and the 2016 and 2020 Democratic Party primaries are instructive cases in point, as in both instances leading news agencies' gross manipulation of facts and outcomes tipped the scales in consequential and even deadly ways, while severely compromising the legitimacy of the press as an institution.

The Iraq War

Since 2004, major media outlets like the *New York Times*, CNN, and the *Washington Post* have openly admitted that their overzealous reporting on Iraq, and lack of critical analysis, abetted the Bush administration's march to war.[40] Because of their manipulations, a majority of Americans believed that Saddam Hussein had weapons of mass destruction (WMDs) and that this unjustifiable war was justified. On September 17, 2001, when celebrity news anchor Dan Rather appeared on *Late Night with David Letterman*, visibly shaken by the events of 9/11, he told Letterman that "George Bush is the president. He makes the decisions. And you know, as just one American, wherever he wants to line up just tell me where."[41] Years later, Bill Moyers, a former insider in elite politics turned truthteller, asked Rather whether such a statement compromised his credibility as a journalist. Rather walked back his 9/17 comment and revealed to Moyers that in his experience of the U.S. news media, many journalists and news anchors operate in a perpetual state of fear. Always in the back of their minds, he said, is the knowledge that the people they work for have relationships—with government officials, Wall Street bankers, and Fortune 500 CEOs—that they do not want disturbed, or else.

This pressure to stay within the lines accounts in part for the pack mentality that pervades news reporting today, especially in the context of a perfect storm—a national crisis, a popular president, and bipartisan consensus—of the kind surrounding Iraq.[42] While Rupert Murdoch and Roger Ailes did little to conceal the fact that they founded Fox News as a propaganda outfit for pushing the Republican Party rightward, the liberal media establishment has long prided itself as a check on executive power rather than as just an arm of the Democrats. Bush's success in making his case for war depended entirely on achieving consensus between both major parties and their allied media outlets. That consensus involved rejecting the then-prevailing foreign policy paradigm of containment and adopting the neocon worldview that linked American freedom with world dominance, and advanced a "by any means necessary" strategy of unprovoked war, torture, and the suspension of domestic civil liberties.

In March 2003, the United States initiated what became a permanent, privatized war against an abstract enemy and an unending military occupation of the Middle East. The war exacted an unfathomable death toll and fleecing of taxpayers, enabled by widespread fear and the alignment of power elites in media, state, and corporate institutions. Around the one-year anniversary of 9/11, with the country suspended in a state of anxiety and "code oranges,"[43] the Bush administration fanned its top officials out to the major news networks to peddle its case for war. During Dick Cheney's now-infamous appearance on *Meet the Press* (*MTP*), he cited a *New York Times* story authored by Judith Miller and Michael Gordon that claimed Saddam Hussein was acquiring aluminum tubes specifically designed to enrich uranium. "The first sign of a 'smoking gun,'" Miller and Gordon scare-mongered, "may be a mushroom cloud."[44] National Security Advisor Condoleezza Rice repeated the "mushroom cloud" talking point on CNN; Secretary of State Colin Powell made the case on *Fox News Sunday*; and Secretary of Defense Donald Rumsfeld pushed it on CBS's *Face the Nation*. On *MTP*, Cheney assured the country, "We do know, with absolute certainty, that [Saddam] is using his procurement system to acquire the equipment he needs in order to enrich uranium to build a nuclear weapon."[45]

Judith Miller was the *Times*'s hotshot Middle East expert whose experience covering WMDs and unrivaled access to Pentagon officials like Paul Wolfowitz and Richard Perle, rendered her a veritable scoop machine.[46] Cheney's *MTP* interview was especially notable because in his role as vice president, he could not have publicly disclosed national security intelligence. Instead, he tautologically cited Miller and Gordon whose sources were "anonymous administration officials." As Matt Taibbi so aptly described, "The press was used as a laundry machine, tossing dirty information made 'reputable' by attaching it to names of prestigious news agencies."[47] This was especially true of Miller, who relied almost exclusively on government sources and Iraqi opposition leader Ahmed Chalabi, a known conman bent on effecting regime change in Iraq and whom the CIA had dropped as a paid informant.[48] This uncritical dependence on bunk sources was compounded by the fact that Miller and nearly every other journalist covering Iraq were "embedded" in military units that determined what they were allowed to see.

Though Miller was at the center of what turned out to be an epic fail, she was far from the only reporter to shill for the administration. Instead of investigating the veracity of Bush's case for war, most news outlets and journalists repeated despicable phrases like "collateral damage" and direct talking points issued by U.S. and U.K. officials drafted with the intent to deceive. Notable exceptions, Jonathan Landay and Warren Strobel at Knight Ridder's Washington, DC bureau, fact-checked and diffused the complex details that the White House was wittingly distorting and consulted midlevel civil servants and national security officers who disclosed that the administration was fabricating intelligence. Oftentimes, Landay and Strobel's stories were buried on back pages or not published at all.

Unlike Miller, Landay and Strobel were not invited to appear on the Sunday talk shows. Rather, cable news networks featured liberal and neocon "experts" who beat the drum of war with intentionally byzantine storylines and incendiary rhetoric. They compared Saddam to Satan and to Hitler (who at least was a real person), spewed jingoistic rants against France and other countries that denounced the war, and used complex narratives and technical details to distort and distract. With a graphic of an American flag in the corner of the screen, Fox News presented Bush administration talking points around the clock, hiring a composer to create a special dramatic score, and saturating newscasts with talk of American greatness and unity, and revenge. One segment showcased cheesy sensationalist Geraldo Rivera threatening to hunt down Osama bin Laden with a pistol.[49] Under pressure to rival Fox, MSNBC featured its own on-screen American flag and fired its highest-rated host, Phil Donahue, for inviting anti-war guests on his show.[50] MSNBC news anchor Chris Matthews captured the mood when he enthused, "We're all neocons now."[51]

Members of Congress who spoke out were marginalized in the press, including Ted Kennedy, whose historic, impassioned speech against the war was barely covered. Stories that questioned the administration's outlandish claims lined dustbins and those who wrote them were condemned as anti-American. Fox's Bill O'Reilly openly threatened dissenters. At an anti-war "die-in" in Rockefeller Center, a CNN reporter confided in me that she would be fired if she reported positively on the protest. When United Nations (UN) inspectors submitted a highly detailed and lengthy declaration in late November 2002 that Saddam did not have WMDs, the *Washington Post* published it, but the *New York Times* relegated it to page A10.

When Colin Powell delivered his error-ridden speech at the UN in February 2003, the U.S. media gave him rave reviews, even as UN leadership and most foreign governments, including historical allies, expressed deep skepticism. In "A Winning Hand for Powell," *Washington Post* columnist Richard Cohen argued, "The evidence he presented to the United Nations—some of it circumstantial, some of it absolutely bone-chilling in its detail—had to prove to anyone that Iraq not only hasn't accounted for its weapons of mass destruction but without a doubt still retains them. Only a fool—or possibly a Frenchman—could conclude otherwise." Just inches from Cohen's piece, the *Post's* foreign-policy specialist Jim Hoagland wrote: "To continue to say that the Bush administration has not made its case, you must now believe that Colin Powell lied in the most serious statement he will ever make, or was taken in by manufactured evidence. I don't believe that. Today, neither should you." *New York Times* editors asserted in "The Case Against Iraq" that Powell "was all the more convincing because he dispensed with apocalyptic invocations of a struggle of good and evil and focused on shaping a sober, factual case against Mr. Hussein's regime."[52]

During the Obama presidency, manipulation of news and information pertaining to national security intensified in the form of assaults on press freedoms and whistleblowers. Foreshadowing Trump, Obama's White House was known to use social media and sympathetic bloggers to get its message out, which enabled it to basically report on itself and avoid being pressed. Much worse, however, it prosecuted whistleblowers and intimidated government sources by surveilling their phone and email records and forcing them to take polygraphs. In spite of such extreme measures, whistleblowers Edward Snowden and Chelsea Manning exposed Bush and Obama's malfeasance on matters of national security—and in doing so, revealed the chilling magnitude of their manipulation of presidential powers and wanton use of the U.S. military. In 2013, Snowden, a thirty-year-old Booz Allen Hamilton contractor, leaked a mound of top-secret information on National Security Agency (NSA) spying programs, implicating the U.S. and British governments, and telecom and high-tech companies like Verizon and Facebook. Among the NSA's targets were German prime minister Angela Merkel, Mexican president Felipe Calderon, and tens of millions of people in France alone.[53] The drip-drip-drip of leaks revealing this massive, authoritarian surveillance campaign sank Obama's legitimacy both at home and abroad. As a senator, Obama had criticized the war and the USA Patriot Act and vowed to run a transparent administration and restore press freedoms. Snowden's whistleblowing not only exposed the break between Obama's rhetoric and his efforts to ramp up

NSA wiretapping, intimidate the press, and crack down on whistleblowers, but also left many people with the impression, "What else is he lying about?"[54]

Snowden's leaks came on the heels of Chelsea Manning's 2010 disclosure of hundreds of thousands of secret government documents, many of them highly incriminating. An army intelligence information groomer, Manning was deeply troubled by what she described as a U.S. foreign policy bent on "killing and capturing people," including the intentional murder of Iraqi children and civilians.[55] Her mega-leak included a video of a U.S. Apache helicopter crew firing on a group of men and killing several of them, then laughing at the civilian casualties, which included two Reuters journalists. She also leaked the Iraq War Logs, which exposed brutalities committed by U.S. soldiers and their cover-ups of civilian casualties. One of the logs detailed how U.S. troops handcuffed and shot in the head four Iraqi women and five children, then covered it up with an airstrike. All of the children were under five years of age, and one of them was an infant less than five months old.[56] The Iraq War Logs also exposed that the Obama administration knowingly handed over Iraqi prisoners for torture by the Iraqi army and police, despite its self-righteous rhetoric to the contrary.[57]

In explaining his actions, Snowden asserted that he "acted in the public interest" and took strict precautions with his data, reasoning that by sparking a debate, the public would be better able to make informed decisions about which freedoms they would willingly trade off for the sake of national security. He handed his leaked documents over to professional journalists, who vetted, curated, and redacted the material to protect informants and other innocents.[58] Manning's motivation was similar. She viewed herself as a "transparency advocate" fighting for the public's right to know and ability to decide. Unlike Snowden, however, Manning deposited her leaks on WikiLeaks, an online drop box founded by Australian hacker Julian Assange, that published largely unedited material submitted by anonymous sources. For WikiLeaks, anonymity protected whistleblowers, but also signified a rejection of corporate media spin and affirmation of the idea that all people are knowledge producers and news sources. Since the mid-2000s, WikiLeaks has published hundreds of thousands of classified documents, including cables from the Clinton-led State Department and files on Guantánamo Bay detainees. It released a trove of emails from the Democratic National Committee (DNC) and Hillary Clinton campaign manager John Podesta's email accounts, which exposed in embarrassing detail how the Democrats tried to fix the 2016 primary against Bernie Sanders. (Democrats and liberal media are still in denial regarding just how impactful that exposure was in sowing distrust of DNC leadership and playing into Trump's narrative of Clinton as "crooked.")

Tipping the Scales

In covering presidential politics, reporters and pundits tend to deflect discussion on serious policy issues by covering elections as horse races and narrowing political discourse to superficial matters like gaffes, body language, and "beer standards."[59] Their networks air inflammatory and distorting political ads funded by super PACs, giving undue influence to wealthy donors while raking in billions in ad revenue.[60] In some cases, the media intervene directly in political processes, like in 2000, when Fox News allowed George W. Bush's cousin to prematurely call the race in Florida, then had its anchors hammer each day on primetime TV the now-familiar lie that Democrats were trying to steal the election.

Liberal media outlets behaved similarly during the 2016 and 2020 presidential elections, vehemently advocating against Trump but also foreclosing alternatives on the Democratic side. Even in the face of Trump's successful appeals to working-class voters, Democratic Party–allied journalists eschewed class analysis for discourses on identity politics and partisan conflict—anything that directed people away from challenging the fundamentals of the capitalist order. In this context, Bernie Sanders operated outside of the confines of acceptable debate by daring to run against the Party's preferred candidates in 2016 and 2020 and by criticizing the news media for failing to cover substantive issues and check state and corporate power.

Not unlike what Fox did in Florida, during the 2016 Democratic primary in California, Associated Press (AP) reporters called the state's superdelegates and asked them to secretly disclose their votes so that the AP could call the race before all of the ballots were in—which they did, effectively suppressing the vote, especially down-ticket.[61] Prior to that direct intervention in California, the dominant trend in the mainstream media was to delegitimize Sanders's policy agenda through red-baiting and austerity politics, calling it "pie in the sky" and deeming him "unelectable." As part of that onslaught, the *Wall Street Journal* published what the *Left Business Observer*'s Doug Henwood calculated to be a "sensationalized tally" of Bernie's policy agenda, writing, disparagingly, that it would "amount to the largest peacetime expansion of government in modern American history."[62] Paul Krugman used his coveted space on the *New York Times* opinion pages to trash Sanders's single-payer health care plan, "not just because it's politically unrealistic," but also because it intentionally inflated coverage and underestimated costs, he alleged.[63] Two weeks later, a foursome of retired chairs of the Council of Economic Advisers that served under Presidents Obama and Clinton published an open letter to Sanders, likening his budget to the fiscal policy of irresponsible Republicans.[64]

In 2020, the liberal media doubled down on their efforts to disparage Sanders's policies as too costly and politically untenable—providing a level of scrutiny that, if properly directed, might have helped the United States avoid a major war, a global financial crisis, and a P. T. Barnum presidency. During that election cycle, the *New York Times* editorial board televised its candidate endorsement process, and in reporting the results, proffered false equivalencies between Sanders and Trump, dismissing the former's progressive policy agenda as "divisive." This was despite the fact that Sanders's policies were conceived as universal and "for all," meaning they would not be tiered or *divided* along class lines like the policies of the candidates that the *Times* did endorse.[65] Instead of appointing a seasoned political reporter, the kind appropriate to covering a leading presidential candidate, the paper assigned former BlackRock analyst and finance reporter Sydney Ember to cover Sanders, who, in story after story, quoted "experts" without relevant expertise, passed opinions off as straight reporting, and textured them with snide commentary on Sanders's age, demeanor, and base of supporters. Ember cherry-picked polls and avoided calling Sanders "frontrunner" and, despite his worldwide popularity and millions-strong volunteer and donor base, complained that he "grounded his campaign in championing ideas rather than establishing human connections."[66] God forbid.

In an article published a few days before Sanders announced his candidacy, Ember wrote that "his weak track record with black voters—a vital base in the Democratic Party—could be a potential threat to his candidacy," failing to mention a CNN poll published two months earlier in which Sanders registered a higher approval rating among nonwhite voters than any other major candidate.[67] In pressing Sanders on his activism against Reagan's Nicaragua policy, Ember tried to paint him as an extremist for having denounced the U.S. government's illegal funding of the Contras, whose human rights violations included death squads, assassination, rape, and torture. In her writing, she quoted critical comments about Sanders by "expert" Otto J. Reich, who Ember identified as "a former special envoy for Latin America who helped oversee Nicaragua policy for the Reagan administration." What she did not mention is that Reich had been condemned by the U.S. Comptroller General, the General Accounting Office, the Iran-Contra Committee in Congress, and a House Foreign Affairs committee for conducting "prohibited, covert propaganda activities," including psychological operations "beyond the range of acceptable agency public information activities."[68]

In a follow-up, Ember queried Sanders on whether he was aware of anti-American chants at a massive rally he attended in Nicaragua some thirty-five years prior to their interview. When she did not get the answer she was looking for, she defaulted to asking him whether he *would* have stayed at the event if he *had* heard the chants—to which an exasperated Sanders politely replied: "I think, Sydney, with all due respect, you don't understand a word that I'm saying."[69] He then proceeded to give her a history lesson on the United States' record of overthrowing democratically elected governments in Latin America and installing dictators in their place—which today, is common knowledge.

Reporters on cable TV behaved similarly badly, distorting Sanders's policies and political history, misrepresenting his poll numbers, baselessly disputing his frontrunner status, and using Fox News–style scaremongering and redbaiting of him and his supporters. MSNBC news anchor Chuck Todd—exposed by WikiLeaks in 2016 for his collusion with DNC leadership in favoring Clinton—likened Sanders supporters to Nazi brownshirts.[70] Disgraced sexual harasser Chris Matthews compared Sanders's landslide victory in Nevada to the Nazi takeover of France during World War II.[71] During a segment on the role of women's issues in 2020, MSNBC contributor Mimi Rocah—a former assistant U.S. attorney general in the Southern District of New York—remarked that Sanders "makes my skin crawl" and said, "He's anti-woman."[72] NBC anchorman Lester Holt, as moderator of one of the presidential debates, asked Sanders for his view on a poll in which "two-thirds of all voters said they were uncomfortable with a socialist candidate for president." Sanders replied with his own, damning question: "What was the result of that poll? Who is winning?"—referring to the fact that the poll Holt cited had Sanders winning by double digits, 27 percent to Joe Biden's 15 percent.

TRUMP AND FOX NEWS

The crossfire between liberal vs. conservative—and disinforming and radicalization of audiences by news anchors and reporters—is a consequence of America's privatized, deregulated mediascape and conglomerates' despotic, monopoly control over the country's news and communications. Before the Fairness Doctrine was dissolved and news sources proliferated exponentially, most Americans relied on one of just three nightly programs for their news, which enabled them to operate from a shared sense of facts in forming their political views and disagreeing over them. In today's competitive multichannel environment, however, news outlets glean profits and market share by catering to specific demographics and identity groups and tailoring the news to their perspectives. Because news agencies are rewarded for the size and loyalty of their audiences, rather than accuracy, the incentive is to convey information and ideas that viewers want to hear, even if it means distorting the truth.

As in advertising, the quality of the product—in this case, informative news—takes a backseat to the goal of affirming viewers and offering enough drama and suspense to keep them tuned in. The general rule, it seems, is that getting audiences to believe something is akin to making it true. This is especially the case on social media, where lies can spread without accountability, and on cable TV, where each news channel offers its own version of the truth that oftentimes conflicts with the "truths" put forth by their competitors. This politicization of the news media has the effect of fostering social antagonism and distrust and has fundamentally undermined the possibility of a basic, factual order on which people from diverse backgrounds and ideologies can debate and deliberate on vital issues of the day.

While this arrangement is the work of liberals and conservatives alike, Fox News remains singular in having transformed what could have been a passing political trend into a powerful political machine that shifted American politics to the far right. Fox was founded in 1996 by Rupert Murdoch, arguably the most powerful media mogul in the world, whose success can largely be attributed to the suspension of federal ownership laws that his company lobbied for and won. With the relaxing of restrictions on conglomeration, News Corp became a sprawling global media empire composed of hundreds of newspapers and magazines, a major publishing house, and a Hollywood movie studio, as well as dozens of local television stations, and national and regional cable and satellite channels across six continents. Fox News is among News Corp's most profitable holdings. And while it is the nation's most widely watched cable news channel, it also has the dishonor of having the most misinformed consumers.[73]

As Murdoch envisioned, Fox News came to monopolize conservative TV news and became a major force in world politics, helping to power a multicontinent insurgency that has elevated demagogues and mainstreamed nativism. This dominance was achieved in partnership with Roger Ailes, a former media advisor for Nixon, Reagan, and Bush Sr., who, among other things, co-conspired with win-at-any-cost Lee Atwater in concocting the infamous Willie Horton ad and other forms of dog-whistle tactics that he would hone at Fox. Ailes served as a strategist for dozens of major GOP politicians, including former NYC mayor Rudy Giuliani and Senate Majority Leader Mitch McConnell, and using his experience as a former TV producer, helped Big Tobacco in its propaganda efforts to cover up the deadly effects of cigarettes.[74]

An attack dog, paranoiac, and master of the wedge issue, Ailes is said to have embodied Fox's tendency toward conspiracy theory, tribalism, and the culture of bombast, harassment, and machismo that ultimately sank him. Both Murdoch and Ailes shared an interest in the ruthless pursuit of profits and political power, and both resented what they viewed as an elitist and self-righteous liberal media establishment. Against the yuppies at MSNBC who played to the coasts, the Fox brand involved trash talking and incendiary rhetoric in the service of what they deemed an uncompromising conservativism in defense of the American dream. This ethos was fundamental to Ailes's strategy for Fox, which was predicated on his understanding that over half of the country did not trust the news media, according to polls. In appealing to the masses of Americans who felt ignored, and belittled, by the liberal media, Ailes made Fox into a political movement and, with the diabolical use of the motto "Fair and Balanced" (which was retired in 2017), insisted that it was the liberal media, and not Fox, that was guilty of partisan spin.

CNN made its name covering the first Iraq War with "straight reporting" aimed at diverse, international audiences. By contrast, Fox adopted a nationalist posture and exploited politically polarizing domestic issues and events. That included around-the-clock coverage of the Monica Lewinsky scandal that tapped into Ailes's tabloid mentality and knack for treating news as entertainment. Fox's 9/11 and Iraq War coverage propelled the network to number one in the ratings war and set the tone for its competitors in privileging patriotism and revenge over history and facts. Other news channels followed suit, in part out of fear of being baited as anti-American, but more so because that was where the ratings and profits were.

In the making of Fox, Ailes took several pages from the annals of fascist propaganda. As an avowed fan of Leni Riefenstahl, he placed a premium on emotion over substance and adopted historically proven techniques of manipulation—such as catchphrases and repetition—that he likely picked up when he was news director for Television News (TVN), a precursor to Fox funded by the right-wing millionaire Joseph Coors.[75] In Ailes's strategic worldview, entertainment was a potent force of political mobilization, and visual media was essential to the king-making of presidents. Ailes staffed Fox's newsroom with people from the entertainment industry rather than journalists, asserting, "It's not a press conference—it's a television show. Our television show. And the press has no business on the set."[76]

By enabling the Republican Party to circumvent tough questions from establishment reporters and to broadcast its talking points around the clock, Ailes positioned Fox as a commanding force in the GOP. In addition to increasing the party's share of the vote in towns where Fox was broadcast, Ailes and Murdoch turned Fox News into a major source of political fundraising that helped get several conservative governors and members of Congress elected. Recall that Fox intervened directly in the 2000 presidential election by tipping the electoral balance in favor of Bush Jr. Instead of feigning neutrality and allowing the popular vote to take the day, Ailes put Bush's first cousin in charge of the network's decision desk responsible for calling the states on election night. Fox prematurely declared Bush the winner, and for the thirty-three days that followed, it fanatically argued that Al Gore and the Democrats were trying to steal the election. After Bush Jr. left office, the network became a vehicle for twenty-four-hour Obama bashing and Trumpian birtherism, punctuated with daily doses of Bill O'Reilly's signature rants of white male resentment.

Perhaps most significant was Fox's role in providing Donald Trump with the platform he needed to get elected president. The Murdochs were friends with Jared Kushner and Ivanka Trump (they vacationed together on Rupert's yacht), and though he valued Trump as a ratings booster, Murdoch did not consider him a serious candidate for president. After Trump's popularity began to soar on the wings of Fox's loyal base, however, and new right-wing outlets like Breitbart and Sinclair began to eat into Fox's market share by supporting him, Murdoch and Ailes went all in. As president, Trump opened the doors of the White House to Fox personalities and spent much of his day watching cable TV news and tweeting content from Fox broadcasts. In turn, Fox interviewed Trump on the network over 100 times and supported his often-nonsensical claims, including those about the effectiveness of wearing masks to combat the spread of COVID-19 and other deadly ideas.[77]

With Trump in the White House, MSNBC became the yin to Fox's yang. Though they emerged side by side in the mid-1990s, the more culturally polarized the country became, the more Fox and MSNBC operated as two heads of the same hydra—both gleaning profits from the red state/blue state dialectic and remaining unified in their commitment to sensationalism and partisan conflict as a business model. As the self-proclaimed bulwark against "normalizing" Trump, MSNBC fed its audiences daily doses of Trump-inspired outrage, some lazily drawn from "reporting" on his Twitter feed, which had eighty-eight million followers when Twitter shut it down in

January 2021. Trump's Twitter feed was a media phenomenon in itself, but MSNBC and other outfits turned it into an audience-addicting slot machine of gotchas and "breaking news." MSNBC reporters and anchors might have helped to neutralize Trump by using their soap boxes and brain trust to analyze the political and social conditions that made his election possible. They might have evaluated previous administrations' records of untruths and empty promises and their own role in supporting the Democratic Party's tone-deaf strategy of running the wildly unpopular Hillary Clinton against Trump in 2016. Instead, they reduced Trump's win to identity and grievance politics and went far out of their way to undercut the possibility of a progressive alternative.

UNDERMINING PUBLIC EDUCATION

Along with the manipulation of the news media, U.S. power elites since Mills's time have imposed their class program by trying to control the country's primary organs of knowledge production and turn them into profitable industries. At the center of those efforts are public schools, which powerholders have worked to privatize by starving them of material resources as a way to weaken and delegitimize them. They have also used the weapon of "school choice" to equate privatization with individuals' fundamental right to pursue their private interests without interference. By monopolizing the education landscape, they argue, public schools impede the kind of excellence that can only be produced in an unfettered market. Without competition, "state-run" schools have no incentive to improve, students lack motivation, and parents are being denied their right to choose.

This crusade against public education, and for blanket school privatization, began with neoliberal intellectuals' attempts to undermine *Brown v. Board of Education* on the grounds of opposing "federal overreach" in favor of states' rights and school choice. They applied the same precepts in opposing public higher education, and also contended that instead of state-subsidized education, college students should pay full price because those with "skin in the game," they reasoned, would be more likely to focus on their studies and avoid the radicalizing influences of communist faculty. Plus, higher tuition costs would price out the working class, to boot.[78]

A year after *Brown*, Milton Friedman published an academic paper arguing for tax-subsidized vouchers as a way to provide parents with freedom of choice and, by implication, maintain racial segregation in schools.[79] Conservatives have pushed for vouchers ever since, and indicative of Friedman's success, the Obama administration championed "school choice" as part of its agenda to expand charter schools, marketing the move as a matter of racial justice, despite the term's racist history. Democrats have consistently opposed vouchers, but their commitment to corporate reform and willingness to coopt anti-racism to legitimize it, is one of the reasons why they have received generous campaign contributions from pro-reform hedge funds and conservative education activists.[80]

Today, consortia of hedge fund managers and individual billionaires pour millions into the spread of charter schools, using arguments about combatting segregation and racial achievement gaps to justify the creation of an unaccountable parallel education system. The result: democratically elected school boards have been undermined, Black and brown students further isolated, and the fiscal health and reputation of public schools severely compromised. Education reformers claim that charter schools are engines of freedom and choice, but in schools across the country, racial segregation remains at pre-*Brown* levels, which researchers have correlated with the growth of charter schools.[81]

In K-12 education policy, lawmakers on both sides of the aisle have disenfranchised, and downright abused, parents, students, and teachers in their forging of a back door to privatization. From Rahm Emanuel, Democratic mayor of Chicago, to Scott Walker, Republican governor of Wisconsin, elected officials have exploited state-level fiscal crises to justify massive school budget cuts, then scapegoated teachers and their unions for subsequent dips in student performance. Despite the fact that on average charter schools perform no better than public schools, and are more prone to fraud and waste, the neoliberal mantra is to paint public schools and schoolteachers as failing and not competitive with the rest of the world.[82] In 2010, the *Los Angeles Times* went so far as to publish ratings of schoolteachers based on test-score data, publicly shaming and blaming them for social problems far beyond their control, like poverty and crime.[83] Ironically, publishing the scores actually exacerbated educational inequality in California by encouraging wealthy and well-connected parents to get their kids assigned to the top teachers on the *Times's* ratings list the following year.[84]

At both the state and federal levels, bipartisan lawmakers have tied school funding and teacher pay to student performance on standardized tests. Instead of strengthening weaker-performing schools with financial support, they've closed them down and replaced them with (sometimes for-profit) charter schools, exempt from many of the rules governing regular, district schools. They have also undercut teacher unions, compensation, and tenure systems. Today, in schools across the country, teachers are being denied a living wage and must moonlight at Walmart or McDonald's to make ends meet. Some are being replaced by student-workers from Teach for America (TFA), a privatization scheme backed by the Walton family (of Walmart) and other billionaire ideologues that places untrained, non-licensed college students in classrooms.[85] In other countries, TFA has been underwritten by the World Bank, a powerful agent of privatization in the developing world.[86]

In the mix are wealthy education reformers, who sidestep school boards, Congress, and local and state officials to impose their worldviews about how the U.S. education system should work. Such pet projects have wreaked havoc on public schools and reduced children to mere guinea pigs in one failed "philanthropic" social experiment after another.[87] Though they differ on policy solutions (like school vouchers), mega-donors Bill and Melinda Gates, Michael Bloomberg, Mark Zuckerberg, Eli Broad, and the Waltons all share a commitment to the illusion that if schools were run like competitive businesses, achievement gaps would disappear and the United States would have the best education system on earth. In addition to using the sheer force of their money, they've intruded on local ballot and school board races, and in some instances, employed front groups to create the appearance of community support.[88]

Bill Gates used his influence to promote the award-winning documentary *Waiting for Superman*, a veritable advertisement for charter schools that places the blame for systemic problems in the U.S. education system firmly on the shoulders of schoolteachers and their unions. Not surprisingly, the film applauds the work of former Washington, DC schools chancellor, Michelle Rhee, a wanton face of neoliberal school reform. When Rhee was made chancellor, *Time Magazine* celebrated her on its cover as the woman who would "fix American education," picturing her holding a broom with which she would sweep "the bad teachers" out of the schools. Living up to the hype, as chancellor Rhee cultivated a ruthless persona, purging hundreds of teachers and principals from the rolls, ending teacher tenure, and even making a performance out of firing a principal on national TV. She closed dozens of schools without holding public hearings and spent more time in front of media cameras—self-promoting and making reckless, sensational claims about the teachers she fired—than actually visiting schools and trying to understand them.

During her tenure as chancellor, performance among poor and minority students improved only marginally and her standardized testing crusade was discredited due to evidence of fraud in reporting test scores, graduation rates, and student suspensions.[89] After resigning from DC schools, Rhee appeared on *The Oprah Winfrey Show* to promote a new organization that aggressively advocated for abolishing teacher tenure. She served on the transition team of right-wing Republican Rick Scott when he was Florida's governor, and stood with Wisconsin governor Scott Walker to promote school choice at an event hosted by an organization founded by Betsy DeVos. In what may have been the pinnacle of her career, Rhee made Donald Trump's shortlist for education secretary and even auditioned for him at his New Jersey golf club.

In addition to corporate reform of K-12, billionaires have infiltrated higher education, luring resource-starved schools and professors into their fold with deep funding streams for research institutes, endowed chairs, and infrastructure development. Friedman's University of Chicago, Buchanan's University of Virginia, the Koch-funded Mercatus Center at George Mason University, and, frankly, the lion's share of economics departments across the country have trained intellectuals-cum-political operatives to legitimize their benefactors' market fundamentalism and defend corporate interests in pharmaceuticals, fossil fuels, defense, and many other industries.

Such was the case at the University of Chicago in the 1950s, when Friedman prodigy Gary Becker developed his Nobel Prize–winning research on the concept of *human capital*, a term now engrained in the cultural parlance as if its conceptual underpinnings were incontrovertible. In the Becker worldview, education, skills training, and even health care are investments, with calculable ROIs, that individuals can make to increase their value in the labor market. People on the bottom rungs of the socioeconomic ladder can simply opt to be upwardly mobile by making the right calculations and investments in themselves. Such a framework not only treats students as commodities whose value is determined by market forces, but also reduces higher education to jobs training, and denies its vital role as a conduit of intellectual enrichment, citizenship, tolerance, and social solidarity.

The political implications of "human capital" were thrown into broad relief in 2016 when Florida senator Marco Rubio ran for president with a "Student Investment Plan" to address problems of college affordability. Rubio conceived of the plan as a way to help students avoid massive student debt by enabling bankers and other wealthy people to invest in their "human capital"—that is, to pay a student's way through college in return for a share of their future earnings. Due diligence on such a deal, Rubio suggested, might include analysis of the quality and status of the student's school, choice of major, and grades and SAT scores—similar to how Derby bettors evaluate form, official ranking, and gait position to determine which thoroughbred to put their money on. Regardless of such crass implications, the idea of investing in so-called human capital has gained traction on Wall Street and among households hard hit by the coronavirus pandemic.[90] In 2019, a bipartisan group of senators reasserted the idea under the auspices of "Income Share Agreements," already being brokered by private companies.[91]

In addition to turning higher education into a financial product, lawmakers have sought to impose "outcome-based" systems of accreditation and require college admissions officers to provide students with "report card" data correlating majors with postgraduation jobs and salaries. With that information, students are supposed to calculate whether a given course of study is "worth it," and colleges and universities can make investment decisions about which programs will have the biggest payouts. Even without such data, colleges and universities tend to invest more heavily in their finance and business programs than in their supposedly unprofitable liberal arts and humanities departments. As business school budgets expand in universities across the country, the ranks of low-paid contingent faculty continues to grow, and traditional disciplines like sociology, art history, and literature are seeing their tenure lines disappear and professors' purchasing power decline. Many of those contingent faculty earn poverty wages, lack retirement savings and health insurance, and have to work second and third jobs to survive. As colleges and universities take on a Wall Street mentality, and render the college experience purely transactional, they are no longer serving as safe havens for questioning elite power and incubators for contemplating and creating alternatives.

At the heart of neoliberalism is a class program to erase or distort history, present itself as a given, and destroy the social solidarities, intellectual independence, and sense of obligation that constitute egalitarian societies and robust democratic public spheres. To neoliberals, the very idea of a public, a common good, or even a representative state is anathema to human freedom and the unfettered pursuit of property and private interests. With the ascendancy of this worldview, organs of knowledge production and public discourse—schools and universities, political parties, and civic associations—have been coopted or starved of vital resources, and the social solidarities and tolerances they engender greatly diminished.

While some members of the press dedicate their lives to truth-telling and checking power, much of today's media has committed itself to abetting power elites' practice of foreclosing political alternatives and advancing their interests through distortion and manipulation. Day after day, and night after night, the tug of war between liberal and conservative outlets is moving the media further away from its ostensible mission to inform citizens and increasingly toward systemic disinformation and "alternative facts"—with dire consequences for the future. When a society ceases to value intellectual and public life, and when a people are unaware of who controls the information they take as fact, and unsure who to believe, they lose the ability to think and act critically, and to resist authoritarianism in its most violent, and amusing, forms.

Conclusion

Since C. Wright Mills wrote *The Power Elite*, much of the world has undergone major, paradigmatic changes in the structuring of social institutions and political life. These developments are the result of the rise and entrenchment of neoliberal systems and ideas, driven by the inexhaustible pursuit of profits and wealth accumulation by a few. The aim of this book was to assess patterns of elite domination over the past half century and to unmask the people, policies, and power dynamics that animate them. In diffusing the fundamental tenets of neoliberal capitalism and exposing its class program, this text has laid bare the essentially authoritarian character of today's power elites and the human and environmental toll they exact.

In Mills's time, the prevailing view of private property and the state was one in which the latter—through fiscal policy or regulatory measures, for example—tempered capitalism's excesses and mediated a social contract in which workers accepted a degree of exploitation for a degree of relative prosperity. Despite clear political and social inequalities, and the ascendancy of what Mills called "the military metaphysic," leading intellectuals of the postwar era theorized the American system in pluralist terms, positioning the state as a site for the intercourse of myriad political interests on a supposedly level playing field. Mills outed American pluralism as farce and, in doing so, inspired a generation of radicals to contest elite power and fight for more egalitarian forms of life.

On the outskirts of the discourses and power relations that Mills challenged and disrupted was a cadre of self-described "neoliberals" who sought to undermine the state's role in tempering extreme accumulations of wealth and political power and to fully subordinate it—and all aspects of social and political life—to the dictates of capital. From the Cold War until now, their program has hinged on debasing government and exalting the "free market" as an engine of human progress, societal glue, and the equalizing principle of American democracy. As a marker of their success in transforming neoliberalism from a fringe ideology to grand narrative, now, in many parts of the world, the principal measuring stick of the value of any given policy, law, social institution, cultural practice, or idea is how it impacts profitability rather than how it serves societal, individual, and environmental well-being.

From the 1973 military coup in Chile to the presidency of Donald J. Trump and beyond, government elites across Democratic and Republican administrations have exploited one crisis after another to advance the neoliberal program, using the state to secure lines of wealth accumulation and to force into submission powers that might have impeded the march of authoritarianism and the fascist Right. The means by which they have achieved this hegemony range from policy- and rule-making and enforcement, to ideological manipulation, to violence and coercion—all of which reveal increasingly blatant and profound forms of collusion between political and corporate elites and a shrugging off of even the most basic liberal democratic norms and standards of public decency.

These developments are especially pronounced when one considers the recent history of American military power. While the United States was founded with an eye toward preventing dictatorship and what the founders called "military kings," the last half century has witnessed a profound consolidation of executive power and militarist collusion among state and corporate elites in matters of war, conflict, and law enforcement. Following the postwar era, the United States sought to shore up its hegemony by forcibly (and oftentimes covertly) installing political systems around the world to ensure stable market conditions for profit and transnational capital. Today, those efforts have manifested in a global War on Terror that has brought death, humanitarian crisis, and environmental and infrastructural devastation—as well as blowback in the form of terrorism and sectarian violence. Domestically, it has taken the form of an ever-present surveillance and carceral state that continues to terrify communities and engender a culture of fear and hostility. At the hands of today's power elites, trillions of dollars that could have been spent on egalitarian advancements at home and abroad—in education, health, and care for the environment—have instead been spent proliferating disinformation, human suffering, and despoilation.

Among those abetting and profiting from these arrangements are the elites of Wall Street, many of whom have accumulated tremendous wealth and power through exploitive financial techniques. Since the seventies, the accelerated integration of financial markets worldwide, and shift in the global economy's center of gravity to finance, has exponentially increased Wall Street's reach into everyday life, and with it, opened new opportunities for speculatory and usurious profit-making. That restructuring was achieved by way of technological and financial innovation as well as structural adjustment, predatory lending, high-risk speculation, and increased financialization of big business.

At the very top of the corporate power structure are the billionaires, who have demonstrated, decisively, that it is not possible to accumulate "three comma" net worth without disciplining workers, evading taxes, exploiting government resources, and exercising monopoly power. With the help of a well-organized conservative movement and enlarged corporate power, these very rich dominate elections and own government officials. Similar to Gilded Age philanthropists, they bypass legislative bodies and the state in conducting experiments on essential institutions with the intent of turning them into money-spinning industries. And, under the banner of progress and futurism, they glean profits by hyping new technologies that surveil the daily interactions of masses of people and help stoke divisions among them.

To Mills, celebrities' role in the U.S. power hierarchy was one of subordination to political, military, and corporate elites. Since then, a select few have exploited their wealth and popularity to take political power at the highest levels. Most notable among them is Donald Trump, whose authority, like that of most demagogues, was rooted in charismatic appeal—as opposed to a rational basis of authority—and whose presidency threw into broad relief the dominant role that emotion and entertainment play in American politics and capitalist propaganda. Ultra-wealthy celebrities now operate at the highest levels of corporate power as well, some achieving billionaire status by controlling media and retail enterprises with extensive reach and cultural impact. By warrant of their ability to capture and monetize mass attention, celebrities generate enormous profits through branding and the circulation of products and images. And by warrant of their conspicuous beauty, happiness, and wealth, they perform key ideological functions in the reproduction of capitalist hegemony—as images and archetypes of the self-helped, self-made, self-actualized individual.

To neoliberals, the very idea of a public sphere—and representative state—is an anathema to human freedom and the pursuit of private property. Accordingly, their class program has involved destroying or manipulating the social solidarities, intellectual independence, and sense of public obligation that constitute egalitarian societies. To that end, they have shepherded an extreme concentration of ownership and politicization of the news media, and degraded the country's organs of knowledge production, such that now many Americans are willing to accept as truth even the most absurd claims and clownish conspiracies, while a handful of moguls wield more power over the means of communication than any dictator has in world history.[1]

In his "Letter to the New Left," C. Wright Mills dispensed with the notion of what he termed "The Necessary Lever"—pointing to a common belief among leftists that meaningful social change must hinge on the activation of a particular protagonist or social agent.[2] That insight is as important now as it was then. If this book achieved anything in its accumulation of testimony to the ruthlessness and supremacy of today's power elites, it should have proven that (a) no single social or political group or movement, regardless of its salience, can confront these behemoth forces on its own, and (b) no single institution or milieux—from the state to the media to the education system to the environment—should be dismissed as a potential site of contestation, regardless of the degree to which elites have subordinated it to their interests.

Among the greatest strengths of today's (and yesterday's) power elites is their enduring capacity for divide and conquer and their ability to convince masses of people that the current system is the best of what is possible. Diffusing elite power and achieving egalitarian change will therefore require moving past the prevailing tendency of social movements and advocacy campaigns to silo themselves according to particular causes, ideologies, and identities and instead develop extensive and sustained organizing programs aimed at promoting *universal* freedom and genuine social solidarity. Given elites' decades-long attacks on public institutions, it will also entail renewing our sense of a public good—as opposed to the free market—as an equalizing principle and societal glue, and invigorating the institutions that accompany it. And finally, in light of elites' successes in entrenching capitalist ideology and their propensity for distortion, it means reclaiming society's organs of tolerance and knowledge production, and forging new avenues for the development of systemic and institutional alternatives. Without adopting these basic principles and objectives, we risk condemning ourselves and future generations to a world that is fundamentally not of our own making—one that will continue to be dominated by powerful elites with little to no concern for human and planetary life.

NOTES

INTRODUCTION

1. Alison Durkee. "Giuliani Claims His Call for 'Trial by Combat' on Jan. 6 Shouldn't Have Been Taken Literally as Legal Woes Mount." *Forbes*. May 18, 2021. Accessed July 2022. https://www.forbes.com/sites/alisondurkee/2021/05/18/giuliani-claims-his-call-for-trial-by-combat-on-jan-6-shouldnt-have-been-taken-literally-as-legal-woes-mount/. Also see Brian Naylor. "Read Trump's Jan. 6 Speech, a Key Part of Impeachment Trial." *National Public Radio*. Feb. 10, 2021. Accessed July 2022. https://www.npr.org/2021/02/10/966396848/read-trumps-jan-6-speech-a-key-part-of-impeachment-trial.
2. Kevin Phillips. *Wealth and Democracy: A Political History of the American Rich*. New York: Broadway Books, 2002, p. 82. Also see Drew DeSilver. "American Unions Membership Declines as Public Support Fluctuates." Pew Research Center. Feb. 20, 2014. Accessed July 2022. https://www.pewresearch.org/fact-tank/2014/02/20/for-american-unions-membership-trails-far-behind-public-support/.
3. Government Accountability Office. "Federal Social Safety Net Programs: Millions of Full-Time Workers Rely on Federal Health Care and Food Assistance Programs." GAO-21-45. Nov. 18, 2020. Accessed July 2022. https://www.gao.gov/products/gao-21-45. Also see Robert J. Gordon. *The Rise and Fall of American Growth*. Princeton, NJ: Princeton University Press, 2016.
4. "Provisional Drug Overdose Death Counts." Centers for Disease Control and Prevention, National Center for Health Statistics, Office of Communication. May 1, 2022. Accessed July 2022. https://www.cdc.gov/nchs/nvss/vsrr/drug-overdose-data.htm#:~:text=Relative%20to%20final%20data%2C%2012,in%202019%20than%20in%202018.
5. Chuck Collins, Omar Ocampo, and Sophia Paslaski. "Report: Billionaire Bonanza 2020: Wealth Windfalls, Tumbling Taxes, and Pandemic Profiteers." Institute for Policy Studies. April 23, 2020. Accessed July 2022. https://ips-dc.org/billionaire-bonanza-2020/.
6. Chuck Collins and Josh Hoxie. "Report: Billionaire Bonanza: The Forbes 400 and the Rest of Us." Institute for Policy Studies. Washington, DC. Dec. 1, 2015. Accessed July 2022. https://ips-dc.org/billionaire-bonanza/. Also see Marc Fisher, Lizzie Johnson, Christine Spolar, and Nick Aspinwall. "After 1 Million Deaths, COVID Leaves Millions More Forever Changed." *Washington Post*. May 7, 2022. Accessed July 2022. https://www.washingtonpost.com/nation/2022/05/07/one-million-covid-deaths-families/.

7. Oxfam International. "Briefing Paper: Inequality Kills: The Unparalleled Action Needed to Combat Unprecedented Inequality in the Wake of COVID-19." Jan. 17, 2022. Accessed July 2022. https://oxfamilibrary.openrepository.com/bitstream/handle/10546/621341/bp-inequality-kills-170122-en.pdf;jsessionid=A574D9331E9F9BBF81B606E1497A1BC5?sequence=9. Also see Citizens for Tax Fairness and the Institute for Policy Studies. "Press Release: U.S. Billionaire Wealth Surged 70%, or $2.1 Trillion, during the Pandemic; They Are Now Worth a Combined $5 Trillion." Oct. 18, 2021. Accessed July 2022. https://americansfortaxfairness.org/wp-content/uploads/2021-10-18-Billionaires-National-Report-October-2021-1.pdf.
8. Sarah Kate Kramer. "When Nazis Took Manhattan." *National Public Radio*. Feb. 20, 2019. Accessed July 2022. https://www.npr.org/sections/codeswitch/2019/02/20/695941323/when-nazis-took-manhattan. In an address to Congress in 1938 on the dangers of monopoly, Franklin D. Roosevelt laid out the stakes of the moment: "The first truth is that the liberty of a democracy is not safe if the people tolerate the growth of private power to a point where it becomes stronger than their democratic state itself. That, in essence, is Fascism—ownership of Government by an individual, by a group, or by any other controlling private power." Franklin D. Roosevelt. "Message to Congress on Curbing Monopolies." American Presidency Project, UC Santa Barbara. April 29, 1938. Accessed July 2022. https://www.presidency.ucsb.edu/documents/message-congress-curbing-monopolies.
9. Harry S. Truman. "Truman Doctrine: President Harry S. Truman's Address Before a Joint Session of Congress." National Archives. March 12, 1947. Accessed July 2022. https://www.archives.gov/milestone-documents/truman-doctrine.
10. The 1947 National Security Act federated the armed services and consolidated military and intelligence agencies under the executive branch. This included the creation of the National Security Council to coordinate national defense and, as a harbinger of things to come, the CIA, the nation's first peacetime agency of its kind.
11. See National Security Council Paper, NSC-68. "United States Objectives and Programs for National Security." Office of the Historian, U.S. Department of State. April 7, 1950. Accessed July 2022. https://history.state.gov/milestones/1945-1952/NSC68.
12. Judith Stein. *Pivotāl Decade: How the United States Traded Factories for Finance in the Seventies*. New Haven, CT: Yale University Press, 2011, pp. xi, 3–4.
13. The lowest fifth saw their incomes increase by 116 percent, the top fifth grew by 85 percent, and those in the middle gained more than those at the top. See Judith Stein. *Pivotal Decade: How the United States Traded Factories for Finance in the Seventies*. New Haven, CT: Yale University Press, 2011, p. 2.
14. Leo Panitch and Sam Gindin. *The Making of Global Capitalism: The Political Economy of American Empire*. London: Verso, 2012, p. 54. Also see Kevin Phillips. *Wealth and Democracy: A Political History of the American Rich*. New York: Broadway Books, 2002, pp. 74–75; and Bureau of Economic Analysis, U.S. Department of Commerce. "GDP and Other Major NIPA Series, 1929–2012: II." August 2012. Accessed July 2022. https://apps.bea.gov/scb/pdf/2012/08%20August/0812%20gdp-other%20nipa_series.pdf.
15. Chester J. Pack Jr. "Dwight D. Eisenhower: Domestic Affairs." Miller Center, University of Virginia. 2002. Accessed July 2022. https://millercenter.org/president/eisenhower/domestic-affairs. Also see Leo Panitch and Sam Gindin.

The Making of Global Capitalism: The Political Economy of American Empire. London: Verso, 2012, p. 81.

16. Daniel Geary. *Radical Ambition: C. Wright Mills, the Left, and American Social Thought*. Oakland: University of California Press, 2009, pp. 157–62.
17. Robert A. Dahl. *A Preface to Democratic Theory*. Chicago: University of Chicago Press, 1956.
18. See Ralph Miliband's critique of Galbraith's *American Capitalism: The Concept of Countervailing Power*. Boston: Houghton Mifflin, 1952, in "Professor Galbraith and American Capitalism." *The Socialist Register*, March 17, 1968, pp. 215–29.
19. Seymour Martin Lipset. *Political Man: The Social Bases of Politics*. New York: Doubleday, 1960.
20. Daniel Geary. *Radical Ambition: C. Wright Mills, the Left, and American Social Thought*. Oakland: University of California Press, 2009, p. 9.
21. Ralph Miliband. "C. Wright Mills." *New Left Review* 14 (5), September 1962, pp. 263–66.
22. Daniel Geary. *Radical Ambition: C. Wright Mills, the Left, and American Social Thought*. Oakland: University of California Press, 2009, pp. 17–18.
23. Giles Scott-Smith. *The Politics of Apolitical Culture: The Congress for Cultural Freedom and the Political Economy of American Hegemony 1945–1955*. London and New York: Routledge, 2002.
24. The president of the Chicago School even bragged to donors that his school had "the most conservative economics department in the world." See Nancy MacLean. *Democracy in Chains: The Deep History of the Radical Right's Stealth Plan for America*. New York: Viking, 2017, p. 35.
25. C. Wright Mills. *The Power Elite*. New York: Oxford University Press, 1956/2000, p. 274.
26. Michael A. Davis. *Politics as Usual: Thomas Dewey, Franklin Roosevelt, and the Wartime Presidential Campaign of 1944*. Dekalb: Northern Illinois University Press, 2014, p. 38.
27. See Karl Schriftgiesser. *Business Comes of Age: The Impact of the Committee for Economic Development, 1942–1960*. New York: Harper and Brothers, 1960. Also see Leo Panitch and Sam Gindin. *The Making of Global Capitalism: The Political Economy of American Empire*. London and New York: Verso, 2012, pp. 80–82.
28. Leo Panitch and Sam Gindin. *The Making of Global Capitalism: The Political Economy of American Empire*. London and New York: Verso, 2012, pp. 80–82.
29. Friedrich Pollock. "Is National Socialism a New Order?" *Studies in Philosophy and Social Science* 9 (3), 1941, pp. 440–55. Also see Friedrich Pollock. "State Capitalism." *Studies in Philosophy and Social Science* 9 (2), 1941, pp. 200–25.
30. Franz Neumann. *Behemoth: The Structure and Practice of National Socialism, 1933–1944*. Chicago: Ivan R. Dee, 1944/2009, pp. 260–61, 467.
31. See Mills's review of *Behemoth: The Structure and Practice of National Socialism, 1933–1944* in *Power, Politics & People: The Collected Essays of C. Wright Mills*, ed. Irving Louis Horowitz. London, Oxford, New York: Oxford University Press, 1967, pp. 170–78. Originally published in *Partisan Review*, September–October 1942. Copyright 1942, by *Partisan Review*.
32. Mills located the sources of elite power within the institutional structures that pattern the social system and control key resources within it. He did not deny the possibility of a ruling class; rather, he argued that ruling coalitions within institutional orders—like the ones Neumann identified—and the existence of an economic class that rules politically must be demonstrated through

empirical research and historical analysis (see C. Wright Mills. *The Power Elite*. New York: Oxford University Press, 1956/2000, p. 277n). Mills did employ a class lens to demonstrate how the institutional orders that buoy elite power cohere into a singular, yet heterogeneous, "power elite" and how economic class and social status were foundational to their unity. "The higher circles," as he called them, were occupied by men of similar social background, born into families with wealth and occupational prestige, who attended the same exclusive schools, frequented the same social clubs, and married within those circles. By no means did they always agree; after all, it was the elites who uniquely enjoyed the prerogative of debate and disagreement that pluralists attributed to the system as a whole. But like a ruling class, they were prone to advancing their interests as universal and using their power to reinforce their status. Power elites shared a common outlook on the fundamentals of private property and free enterprise, as well as the primacy of the military as the face of American imperialism—thus, they tended to act collectively.

33. C. Wright Mills. *The Power Elite*. New York: Oxford University Press, 1956/2000, p. 229.
34. C. Wright Mills. *The Power Elite*. New York: Oxford University Press, 1956/2000, p. 356.
35. Elizabeth A. Harris and Alexandra Alter. "Book Ban Efforts Spread Across the U.S." *New York Times*. Jan. 30, 2022. Accessed July 2022. https://www.nytimes.com/2022/01/30/books/book-ban-us-schools.html. Also see Quint Forgey and Josh Gerstein. "Justice Thomas: SCOTUS 'Should Reconsider' Contraception, Same-Sex Marriage Rulings." *Politico*. June 24, 2022. Accessed July 2022. https://www.politico.com/news/2022/06/24/thomas-constitutional-rights-00042256; and Aimee Picchi. "Texas Abortion Ban Turns Citizens into 'Bounty Hunters'." *CBS News*, Sept. 3, 2021. Accessed July 2022. https://www.cbsnews.com/news/texas-abortion-law-bounty-hunters-citizens/.
36. For an excellent discussion on Mills and his Marxist critics see Clyde W. Barrow. "Plain Marxists, Sophisticated Marxists, and C. Wright Mills's *The Power Elite*." *Science & Society* 71 (4), October 2007, pp. 400–30.
37. In addition to grounding this analysis in political economy, I follow Paul Sweezy's recommendation to Mills that he center the concept of *exploitation* in his work on elite power (see Paul M. Sweezy. "Power Elite or Ruling Class?" *Modern Capitalism and Other Essays*. New York: Monthly Review Press, 1972/2009. p. 97). For Sweezy, it was not enough to finger elites as irresponsible and immoral, since Americans tend to view the rich and powerful as special and deserving. Rather, he contended, "what is reprehensible about the rich is not that they enjoy the good things of life but that they use their power to maintain a system which needlessly denies the same advantages to others." In his view, understanding elite power through the lens of exploitation and articulating its human costs held greater promise for capturing the fundamental nature of ruling-class power—and providing a basis for its defeat. This book adopts that lens to illustrate the immensurable human suffering that today's power elites have left in their wake and to help motivate due outrage.
38. See Judith Stein. *Pivotal Decade: How the United States Traded Factories for Finance in the Seventies*. New Haven, CT: Yale University Press, 2010. Also see Neil T. Rodgers. *Age of Fracture*. Cambridge, MA: Belknap Press of Harvard University Press, 2011.

CHAPTER 1

1. Quote from Friedman's 1982 preface to *Capitalism and Freedom*, originally published in 1962. Milton Friedman. *Capitalism and Freedom*. Chicago: University of Chicago Press, 2002, p. xiv.
2. Nicholas Shaxson. *The Finance Curse: How Global Finance Is Making Us All Poorer*. New York: Grove Press, 2018, p. 41.
3. Ronald Butt. "Interview with Margaret Thatcher." *Sunday Times*. May 3, 1981. Accessed July 2022. https://www.margaretthatcher.org/document/104475.
4. For more on free trade, see the works of Lori Wallach and Matt Stoller. Also see Physicians for a National Health Program. "TPP and the Dire Threat to Affordable Drug Prices." Aug. 23, 2016. Accessed July 2022. https://pnhp.org/2016/08/23/tpp-and-the-dire-threat-to-affordable-drug-prices/; and "The Trans-Pacific Partnership: What You Need to Know About President Obama's Trade Agreement." Obama White House Archives. Accessed July 2022. https://obamawhitehouse.archives.gov/issues/economy/trade.
5. A. J. Langguth. *Hidden Terrors: The Truth About U.S. Police Actions in Latin America*. New York: Pantheon, 1979, pp. 48–49, 51. Also see William Blum. *Killing Hope: U.S. Military and CIA Interventions Since World War II*. London: Zed Books Ltd., 2014, p. 203.
6. Seymour M. Hirsch. *The Price of Power: Kissinger in the Nixon White House*. New York: Summit Books, 1983, pp. 250–76. Accessed July 2022. http://www.thirdworldtraveler.com/Kissinger/Chile_Hardball_TPOP.html.
7. Florencia San Martín. "Decolonial Temporality in Alfredo Jaar's *The Kissinger Project*." *ASAP/Journal* 4 (2), May 2019, pp. 357, 366–67. Also see "Alliance for Progress." John F. Kennedy Presidential Library and Museum, National Archives. 2022. Accessed July 2022. https://www.jfklibrary.org/learn/about-jfk/jfk-in-history/alliance-for-progress; David Rockefeller. "What Private Enterprise Means to Latin America." *Foreign Affairs*. April 1966. Accessed July 2022. https://www.foreignaffairs.com/articles/south-america/1966-04-01/what-private-enterprise-means-latin-america; and "The Alliance for Progress: A Hemisphere Response to a Global Theat." U.S. Chamber of Commerce. Washington, DC. 1963. Accessed July 2022. https://pdf.usaid.gov/pdf_docs/Pcaaa251.pdf.
8. David Harvey. *A Brief History of Neoliberalism*. London: Oxford University Press, 2005, p. 7. Also see Christopher Hitchens. *The Trial of Henry Kissinger*. New York: Verso, 2001, p. 55; and Greg Grandin. "The Road from Serfdom." *Counterpunch*. Nov. 17, 2006. Accessed July 2022. https://www.counterpunch.org/2006/11/17/the-road-from-serfdom/.
9. Monte Reel and J. Y. Smith. "A Chilean Dictator's Dark Legacy." *Washington Post*. Dec. 11, 2006. Accessed July 2022. https://www.washingtonpost.com/archive/politics/2006/12/11/a-chilean-dictators-dark-legacy/596e14a3-d86c-496f-8568-05f81c199a81/.
10. Nancy MacLean. *Democracy in Chains: The Deep History of the Radical Right's Stealth Plan for America*. New York: Penguin Books, 2017, pp. 155–68.
11. John Prados and Arturo Jimenez-Bacarrdi (eds.). "Gerald Ford White House Altered Rockefeller Commission Report in 1975; Removed Section on CIA Assassination Plots." National Security Archive, George Washington University. Feb. 29, 2016. Accessed July 2022. https://nsarchive.gwu.edu/briefing-book/intelligence/2016-02-29/gerald-ford-white-house-altered-rockefeller-commission-report.

12. Holly Sklar. "Trilateralism: Managing Dependence and Democracy." In *Trilateralism: The Trilateral Commission and Elite Planning for World Management*, ed. Holly Sklar. Boston: South End Press, 1980, p. 2.
13. Judith Stein. *Pivotal Decade: How the United States Traded Factories for Finance in the Seventies*. New Haven, CT: Yale University Press, 2011, p. 159.
14. David D. Kirkpatrick. "How a Chase Bank Chairman Helped the Deposed Shah of Iran Enter the U.S." *New York Times*. Dec. 29, 2019. Accessed July 2022. https://www.nytimes.com/2019/12/29/world/middleeast/shah-iran-chase-papers.html.
15. William K. Tabb. *The Long Default: New York City and the Urban Fiscal Crisis*. New York: Monthly Review Press, 1982, pp. 72, 75, 123.
16. Joshua Freeman. "If You Can Make It Here." *Jacobin*. Oct. 3, 2014. Accessed July 2022. https://www.jacobinmag.com/2014/10/if-you-can-make-it-here/. Also see Phillip L. Zweig. *Wriston: Walter Wriston, Citibank, and the Rise and Fall of American Financial Supremacy*. New York: Crown Business, 1996, pp. 474–75; and William K. Tabb. *The Long Default: New York City and the Urban Fiscal Crisis*. New York: Monthly Review Press, 1982, pp. 21–22.
17. Kim Phillips Fein. *Fear City: New York's Fiscal Crisis and the Rise of Austerity Politics*. New York: Metropolitan Books, 2017, pp. 74–76. Also see William K. Tabb. *The Long Default: New York City and the Urban Fiscal Crisis*. New York: Monthly Review Press, 1982, pp. 22–25.
18. David Harvey. *A Brief History of Neoliberalism*. London: Oxford University Press, 2005, pp. 44–48.
19. Sam Roberts. "Infamous 'Drop Dead' Was Never Said by Ford." *New York Times*. Dec. 28, 2006. Accessed July 2022. https://www.nytimes.com/2006/12/28/nyregion/28veto.html.
20. Patricia Sullivan. "Walter B. Wriston, 85: Chairman of Citicorp." *Washington Post*. Jan. 21, 2005. Accessed July 2022. https://www.washingtonpost.com/wp-dyn/articles/A25323-2005Jan20.html?sub=AR.
21. U.S. Congress Senate Committee on Banking, Housing, and Urban Affairs, Ninety-Fourth Congress. "New York City Financial Crisis." Oct. 9, 10, 18, and 23, 1975. St. Louis Federal Reserve. Accessed July 2022. https://fraser.stlouisfed.org/scribd/?title_id=782&filepath=/docs/historical/senate/senate_nycfincrisis1975.pdf#scribd-open.
22. Phillip L. Zweig. *Wriston: Walter Wriston, Citibank, and the Rise and Fall of American Financial Supremacy*. New York: Crown Business, 1996, p. 475.
23. David Harvey. *A Brief History of Neoliberalism*. London: Oxford University Press, 2005, p. 45.
24. Richard W. Stevenson. "William E. Simon, Ex-Treasury Secretary and High-Profile Investor, Is Dead at 72." *New York Times*. June 5, 2000. Accessed July 2022. https://www.nytimes.com/2000/06/05/us/william-e-simon-ex-treasury-secretary-and-high-profile-investor-is-dead-at-72.html.
25. David Harvey. *A Brief History of Neoliberalism*. London: Oxford University Press, 2005, p. 46.
26. Leo Panitch and Sam Gindin. *The Making of Global Capitalism: The Political Economy of American Empire*. London: Verso, 2012, p. 165.
27. William K. Tabb. *The Long Default: New York City and the Urban Fiscal Crisis*. New York: Monthly Review Press, 1982, pp. 9–10, 21, 42–53.
28. Leo Panitch and Sam Gindin. *The Making of Global Capitalism: The Political Economy of American Empire*. London: Verso, 2012, p. 82.

29. See chapter 6 in Robert M. Collins. *The Business Response to Keynes: 1929–1964*. New York: Columbia University Press, 1981.
30. Anwar Shaikh. "An Introduction to the History of Crisis Theories." *U.S. Capitalism in Crisis*. New York: URPE Monthly Review Press, 2010, pp. 219–41. Also see Anwar Shaikh. "The First Great Depression of the 21st Century." In *Socialist Register 2011: The Crisis This Time*, ed. Leo Panitch, Greg Albo, and Vivek Chibber. London: Merlin Press, vol. 47, 2020, pp. 44–63.
31. "Nation: Carter's Pollster." *Time Magazine* 114 (6), Aug. 6, 1979. Accessed July 2022. https://content.time.com/time/subscriber/article/0,33009,948722,00.html.
32. Jimmy Carter. "Energy and National Goals: Address to the Nation." Jimmy Carter Library, National Archives. July 15, 1979. Accessed July 2022. https://www.jimmycarterlibrary.gov/assets/documents/speeches/energy-crisis.phtml.
33. W. Dale Nelson. *The President Is at Camp David*. New York: Syracuse University Press, 1995, p. 125.
34. Jimmy Carter. "Energy and National Goals: Address to the Nation." Jimmy Carter Library, National Archives. July 15, 1979. Accessed July 2022. https://www.jimmycarterlibrary.gov/assets/documents/speeches/energy-crisis.phtml.
35. William Greider. *Secrets of the Temple: How the Federal Reserve Runs the Country*. New York: Simon and Schuster, 1987, pp. 19–29, 35, and 45–47.
36. Burton A. Abrams and James L. Butkiewicz. "The Political Business Cycle: New Evidence from the Nixon Tapes." *Journal of Money, Credit and Banking* 44 (2/3) March–April 2012, pp. 385–99.
37. Jeff Madrick. *Age of Greed: The Triumph of Finance and the Decline of America, 1970 to the Present*. New York: Vintage Books, 2012, pp. 47–79, 152–53. Also see Robert Pollin. "The Natural Rate of Unemployment: It's All About Class Conflict." *Dollar and Sense Magazine*. Sept./Oct. 1998. Accessed July 2022. http://www.thirdworldtraveler.com/Economics/NaturalUnemployment.html.
38. Samir Sonti. "The World Paul Volcker Made." *Jacobin*. Dec. 20, 2018. Accessed July 2022. https://jacobin.com/2018/12/paul-volcker-federal-reserve-central-bank#:~:text=The%20world%20the%20Volcker%20Shock,had%20been%20eliminated%20with%20it.
39. Jeff Madrick. *Age of Greed: The Triumph of Finance and the Decline of America, 1970 to the Present*. New York: Vintage Books, 2012, pp. 104–9.
40. Tim Barker. "Preferred Shares." *Phenomenal World*. June 24, 2021. Accessed July 2022. https://phenomenalworld.org/analysis/wage-share.
41. James T. Wooten. "Carter's Record as Georgia Governor: Activism and Controversial Programs." *New York Times*. May 17, 1976. Accessed July 2022. https://www.nytimes.com/1976/05/17/archives/new-jersey-pages-carters-record-as-georgia-governor-activism-and.html.
42. Jimmy Carter. "Airline Deregulation Act of 1978 Remarks on Signing S. 2493 into Law." American Presidency Project. Oct. 24, 1978. Accessed July 2022. https://www.presidency.ucsb.edu/documents/airline-deregulation-act-1978-remarks-signing-s-2493-into-law.
43. "Transcript of Carter's Statement Invoking Taft-Hartley in Coal Strike." *New York Times*. March 7, 1978. Accessed July 2022. https://www.nytimes.com/1978/03/07/archives/transcript-of-carters-statement-invoking-tafthartley-in-coal-strike.html.
44. Edward Walsh. "Carter Defends Social Security Cuts, Pentagon Increases." *Washington Post*. Jan. 27, 1979. Accessed July 2022. https://www.washingtonp

ost.com/archive/politics/1979/01/27/carter-defends-social-security-cuts-pentagon-increases/acf79501-230f-4bb8-a7a5-cb7ccccbfa15/. Also see Howard Zinn. *A People's History of the United States*. New York: HarperCollins, 2015, p. 571; and Judith Stein. *Pivotal Decade: How the United States Traded Factories for Finance in the Seventies*. New Haven, CT: Yale University Press, 2011, pp. 192–99.

45. Judith Stein. *Pivotal Decade: How the United States Traded Factories for Finance in the Seventies*. New Haven, CT: Yale University Press, 2011, pp. 190–92.
46. Tim Sablik. "Recession of 1981–82." Federal Reserve History, Federal Reserve Bank of Richmond, July 1981–November 1982. Accessed July 2022. https://www.federalreservehistory.org/essays/recession-of-1981-82. Also see Jeanna Smialek. "Powell Admires Paul Volcker. He May Have to Act Like Him." *New York Times*. March 14, 2022. Accessed July 2022. https://www.nytimes.com/2022/03/14/business/economy/powell-fed-inflation-volcker.html; and Samir Sonti. "The World Paul Volcker Made." *Jacobin*. Dec. 20, 2018. Accessed July 2022. https://jacobin.com/2018/12/paul-volcker-federal-reserve-central-bank#:~:text=The%20world%20the%20Volcker%20Shock,had%20been%20eliminated%20with%20it.
47. Howard Zinn. *A People's History of the United States*. New York: HarperCollins, 2015, p. 571.
48. Robert J. Samuelson. *The Great Inflation and Its Aftermath: The Past and Future of American Affluence*. New York: Random House, 2010, p. 130.
49. Kevin Phillips. *Wealth and Democracy: A Political History of the American Rich*. New York: Broadway Books, 2002, p. 92.
50. Ronald Reagan. "Inaugural Address." Ronald Reagan Presidential Foundation and Institute. Jan. 20, 1981. Accessed July 2022. https://www.reaganfoundation.org/ronald-reagan/reagan-quotes-speeches/inaugural-address-2/.
51. Kevin Phillips. *Wealth and Democracy: A Political History of the American Rich*. New York: Broadway Books, 2002, p. 88, 333.
52. Phillip L. Zweig. *Wriston: Walter Wriston, Citibank, and the Rise and Fall of American Financial Supremacy*. New York: Crown Business, 1996, pp. 449, 708–10.
53. Robert Pear. "The Fairness Issue: Reagan Battles His Image as 'A Rich Man's President.'" *New York Times*. July 25, 1983. Accessed July 2022. https://www.nytimes.com/1983/07/25/us/the-fairness-issue-reagan-battles-his-image-as-a-rich-man-s-president.html.
54. Christopher Ingraham. "The Top Tax Rate Has Been Cut Six Times Since 1980—Usually with Democrats' Help." *Washington Post*. Feb. 27, 2019. Accessed July 2022. https://www.washingtonpost.com/us-policy/2019/02/27/top-tax-rate-has-been-cut-six-times-since-usually-with-democrats-help/. Also see Jeanne Sahadi. "Taxes: What People Forget about Reagan." *CNN Money*. Sept. 12, 2010. Accessed July 2022. https://money.cnn.com/2010/09/08/news/economy/reagan_years_taxes/index.htm; and Edward Cowan. "Reagan's 3-Year, 25% Cut in Tax Rate Voted by Wide Margins in the House and Senate." *New York Times*. July 30, 1981. Accessed July 2022. https://www.nytimes.com/1981/07/30/business/reagan-s-3-year-25-cut-in-tax-rate-voted-by-wide-margins-in-the-house-and-senate.html.
55. Jeff Madrick. *Age of Greed: The Triumph of Finance and the Decline of America, 1970 to the Present*. New York: Vintage Books, 2012, p. 170.
56. Robert J. Gordon. *The Rise and Fall of American Growth: The U.S. Standard of Living Since the Civil War*. Princeton, NJ: Princeton University Press, 2017, p. 587.

57. Harold Meyerson. "Class Warrior." *Washington Post*. June 9, 2004, p. A21. Accessed July 2022. http://www.washingtonpost.com/wp-dyn/articles/A26543-2004Jun8.html. Also see David Harvey. *A Brief History of Neoliberalism*. London: Oxford University Press, 2005, p. 52.
58. "Fact Sheet: Collective Bargaining's Erosion Has Undercut Wage Growth and Fueled Inequality." Economic Policy Institute. March 17, 2015. Accessed July 2022. https://files.epi.org/2015/factsheet_80229.pdf. Also see Matthew Walters and Lawrence Mishel. "How Unions Help All Workers." Economic Policy Institute. Aug. 26, 2003. Accessed July 2022. https://www.epi.org/publication/briefingpapers_bp143/.
59. David Cooper. "The Federal Minimum Wage Has Been Eroded by Decades of Inaction." Economic Policy Institute. July 25, 2016. Accessed July 2021. https://www.epi.org/publication/the-federal-minimum-wage-has-been-eroded-by-decades-of-inaction/.
60. John Schwarz. "Seven Things About Ronald Reagan You Won't Hear at the Reagan Library GOP Debate." *The Intercept*. Sept. 16, 2015. Accessed July 2022. https://theintercept.com/2015/09/16/seven-things-reagan-wont-mentioned-tonight-gops-debate/.
61. Peter Dreier. "Reagan's Legacy: Homelessness in America." *Shelterforce*. May 1, 2004. Accessed July 2022. http://nhi.org/online/issues/135/reagan.html.
62. Jeff Andrews. "Affordable Housing Is in Crisis. Is Public Housing the Solution?" *Curbed.com*. Jan. 13, 2020. Accessed July 2022. https://archive.curbed.com/2020/1/13/21026108/public-housing-faircloth-amendment-election-2020. Also see Yvonne Vissing. *Out of Sight, Out of Mind: Homeless Children and Families in Small-Town America*. Lexington: University of Kentucky Press, 1996.
63. Andre Shashaty. "U.S. Cuts Back and Shifts Course on Housing Aid." *New York Times*. Oct. 18, 1981. Accessed July 2022. https://www.nytimes.com/1981/10/18/realestate/us-cuts-back-and-shifts-course-on-housing-aid.html#:~:text=When%20Congress%20passed%20the%20Housing,annually%20for%20low%2Dincome%20families.
64. David Harvey. *A Brief History of Neoliberalism*. London: Oxford University Press, 2005, pp. 57–62. Also see Tim Dowling. "Coming Soon—(Another) Winter of Discontent?" *The Guardian*. Oct. 4. 2006. Accessed July 2022. https://www.theguardian.com/Columnists/Column/0,,1886951,00.html.
65. David Harvey. *A Brief History of Neoliberalism*. London: Oxford University Press, 2005, pp. 59–61.
66. Ned Resnikoff. "The Other Party of Thatcher: The Democrats and New Labour." *NBC News*. April 9, 2013. Accessed July 2022. https://www.nbcnews.com/id/wbna51480366.
67. Peter T. Kilborn. "Democrats Search for a Winning Issue." *New York Times*. Feb. 26, 1984. Accessed July 2022. https://www.nytimes.com/1984/02/26/business/democrats-search-for-a-winning-issue.html.
68. Jonathan Karl. "Biden Proposed Social Security Freeze in 1984." *ABC News*. Oct. 11, 2021. Accessed July 2022. https://abcnews.go.com/blogs/politics/2012/10/biden-proposed-social-security-freeze-in-1984.
69. Eric Laursen. *The Peoples Pension: The Struggle to Defend Social Security Since Reagan*. Oakland, CA: AK Press, 2012, p. 198.
70. Mickey Kaus. "Telling the Truth About Social Security." *Washington Post*. Nov. 1, 1992. Accessed July 2022. https://www.washingtonpost.com/archive/opinions/

1992/11/01/telling-the-truth-about-social-security/e0c792c0-58ba-466f-8e66-605f12c6f1ab/.

71. William Safire. "Essay: Perot Versus Social Security." *New York Times*. June 15, 1992. Accessed July 2022. https://www.nytimes.com/1992/06/15/opinion/essay-perot-versus-social-security.html.
72. William J. Clinton. "Address Accepting the Presidential Nomination at the Democratic National Convention in New York." American Presidency Project, University of California, Santa Barbara. July 16, 1992. Accessed July 2022. https://www.presidency.ucsb.edu/documents/address-accepting-the-presidential-nomination-the-democratic-national-convention-new-york.
73. David Rieff. "Were Sanctions Right?" *New York Times*. July 27, 2003. Accessed July 2022. https://www.nytimes.com/2003/07/27/magazine/were-sanctions-right.html.
74. Robert Pear. "Attacks Begin on Plan to Cut Social Programs." *New York Times*. Dec. 10, 1994. Accessed July 2022. https://www.nytimes.com/1994/12/10/us/attacks-begin-on-plan-to-cut-social-programs.html.
75. Martin Feldstein. "Social Security Reform and Fiscal Policy in the Clinton Administration." Remarks presented at the Harvard University conference on Economic Policy in the 1990s. Harvard University Economics Department. June 29, 2001. Accessed July 2022. https://scholar.harvard.edu/feldstein/publications/social-security-reform-and-fiscal-policy-clinton-administration. Also see Dean Baker. "Bill Clinton, Who's Known for His Plan to Cut Social Security." *Business Insider*. May 26, 2011. Accessed July 2022. https://www.businessinsider.com/bill-clinton-whos-known-for-his-plan-to-cut-social-security-2011-5.
76. Justice Paul Stevens (opinion). *Atkins v. Virginia*. No. 00-8452. Supreme Court of the United States. June 20, 2002. Cornell Law School. Accessed July 2022. https://www.law.cornell.edu/supct/html/00-8452.ZO.html.
77. Nathan J. Robinson. "The Death of Ricky Ray Rector." *Jacobin*. Nov. 5, 2016. Accessed July 2022. https://www.jacobinmag.com/2016/11/bill-clinton-rickey-rector-death-penalty-execution-crime-racism/.
78. "The Clinton Presidency: Lowest Crime Rates in a Generation." Clinton White House Archives. Accessed July 2022. https://clintonwhitehouse5.archives.gov/WH/Accomplishments/eightyears-06.html.
79. Heidi Gillstrom. "Clinton's 'Superpredators' Comment Most Damaging by Either Candidate." *The Hill*. Sept. 30, 2016. Accessed July 2022. https://thehill.com/blogs/pundits-blog/crime/298693-hillary-clintons-superpredators-still-the-most-damaging-insult-by.
80. Doug Henwood. *My Turn: Hillary Clinton Targets the Presidency*. New York: OR Books, 2015. Also see Michelle Alexander. "Why Hillary Clinton Doesn't Deserve the Black Vote." *The Nation*. Feb. 10, 2016. Accessed July 2022. https://www.thenation.com/article/archive/hillary-clinton-does-not-deserve-black-peoples-votes/.
81. Michelle Alexander. "Why Hillary Clinton Doesn't Deserve the Black Vote." *The Nation*. Feb. 10, 2016. Accessed July 2022. https://www.thenation.com/article/archive/hillary-clinton-does-not-deserve-black-peoples-votes/.
82. Deborah J. Vagins. "Cracks in the System: Twenty Years of Unjust Federal Crack Cocaine Law." American Civil Liberties Union. Oct. 2006. Accessed July 2022. https://www.aclu.org/other/cracks-system-20-years-unjust-federal-crack-cocaine-law.

83. Michelle Alexander. “Why Hillary Clinton Doesn’t Deserve the Black Vote.” *The Nation*. Feb. 10, 2016. Accessed July 2022. https://www.thenation.com/article/archive/hillary-clinton-does-not-deserve-black-peoples-votes/.
84. Bryce Covert. “That Time Newt Gingrich Tried to Take Away Kids from Welfare Recipients and Put Them in Orphanages.” *ThinkProgress*. July 20, 2016. Accessed July 2022. https://archive.thinkprogress.org/that-time-newt-gingrich-tried-to-take-kids-away-from-welfare-recipients-and-put-them-in-orphanages-261e525ea22e/.
85. “Block Grants: Perspectives and Controversies.” Congressional Research Service. Feb. 21, 2020. Accessed July 2022. https://fas.org/sgp/crs/misc/R40486.pdf.
86. Peter Edelman. “The Worst Thing Bill Clinton Has Done.” *The Atlantic*. March 1997. Accessed July 2022. https://www.theatlantic.com/magazine/archive/1997/03/the-worst-thing-bill-clinton-has-done/376797/.
87. Kathryn J. Edin and H. Luke Shaefer. “Twenty Years of Welfare Reform.” *The Atlantic*. Aug. 22, 2016. Accessed July 2021. https://www.theatlantic.com/business/archive/2016/08/20-years-welfare-reform/496730/.
88. Mark Byrnes. “How Jack Kemp Rewrote the Urban Poverty Playbook.” *Bloomberg News*. Jan. 6, 2020. Accessed July 2022. https://www.bloomberg.com/news/articles/2020-01-06/when-jack-kemp-took-on-urban-poverty-and-lost.
89. Sonya Ross. “Clinton: One Strike and Out for Public Housing Criminals.” *Associated Press*. March 28, 1996. Accessed July 2022. https://apnews.com/5a293076655604daadbbe62aa6265174.
90. Ladonna Pavetti. “Report: TANF Studies Show Work Requirement Proposals for Other Programs Would Harm Millions, Do Little to Increase Work.” Center on Budget and Policy Priorities. Nov. 13, 2018. Accessed July 2022. https://www.cbpp.org/research/family-income-support/tanf-studies-show-work-requirement-proposals-for-other-programs.
91. LaDonna Pavetti. “Doubling of Extreme Poverty Belies Welfare Reform Success Claims.” Center on Budget and Policy Priorities. Sept. 22, 2015. Accessed July 2022. https://www.cbpp.org/blog/doubling-of-extreme-poverty-belies-welfare-reform-success-claims.
92. Gigesh Thomas and Johan De Tavernier. “Farmer-Suicide in India: Debating the Role of Biotechnology.” *Life Sciences, Society and Policy* 13 (1), Dec. 2017, p. 8.
93. Robert E. Scott. “The Effects of NAFTA on U.S. Trade, Jobs, and Investment, 1993–2013.” *Review of Keynesian Economics*. Edward Elgar Publishing, 2 (4), Oct. 2014, pp. 429–41.
94. Robert Dreyfuss. “How the DLC Does It.” *American Prospect*. Dec. 19, 2001. Accessed July 2022. https://prospect.org/features/dlc/. Also see Bill Turque. “The Soul and the Steel.” *Newsweek*. Aug. 20, 2000. Accessed July 2022. https://www.newsweek.com/soul-and-steel-158731.
95. David Harvey. *A Brief History of Neoliberalism*. London: Oxford University Press, 2005, pp. 101–3.
96. Nomi Prins. *All the Presidents’ Bankers: The Hidden Alliances That Drive American Power*. New York: Nation Books, 2014, pp. 80, 372.
97. Dylan Matthews. “The Clinton Economy, in Charts.” *Washington Post*. Sept. 5, 2012. Accessed July 2022. https://www.washingtonpost.com/news/wonk/wp/2012/09/05/the-clinton-economy-in-charts/.

CHAPTER 2

1. Jacob Weisberg. "W.'s Greatest Hits." *Slate*. Jan. 12, 2009. Accessed July 2022. https://slate.com/news-and-politics/2009/01/the-top-25-bushisms-of-all-time.html.
2. Christopher Hitchens. *No One Left to Lie to: The Triangulations of Willian Jefferson Clinton*. New York: Twelve, 2012, p. 15.
3. Thomas B. Edsall. "Bush Far Outspent Gore on Recount." *Washington Post*. July 27, 2002. Accessed July 2022. https://www.washingtonpost.com/archive/politics/2002/07/27/bush-far-outspent-gore-on-recount/167301fa-4b5a-468f-b3f4-75d62a2911c5/.
4. Paul Wolfowitz, I. Lewis Libby, and Zalmay M. Khalilizad. "Defense Planning Guidance, FY 1994–1999." National Security Council Archives. April 16, 1992. Accessed July 2022. https://www.archives.gov/files/declassification/iscap/pdf/2008-003-docs1-12.pdf.
5. Project for a New American Century. "Statement of Principles." *Militarist-monitor.org*. June 3, 1992. Accessed July 2022. http://militarist-monitor.org/images/uploads/PNAC_Statement_of_Principles.pdf.
6. Thomas Donnelly, Donald Kagan, and Gary Schmitt. "Rebuilding America's Defenses: Strategy, Forces and Resources for a New Century." Washington, DC: Project for the New American Century. Sept. 2000.
7. Jean Edward Smith. *Bush*. New York: Simon and Schuster, 2016, p. 211.
8. Jean Edward Smith. *Bush*. New York: Simon and Schuster, 2016, p. 225.
9. Andrew Brown. "Bush, Gog and Magog." *The Guardian*. Aug. 10, 2009. Accessed July 2022. https://www.theguardian.com/commentisfree/andrewbrown/2009/aug/10/religion-george-bush.
10. Ron Suskind. "Faith, Certainty and the Presidency of George W. Bush." *New York Times*. Oct. 17, 2004. Accessed July 2022. https://www.nytimes.com/2004/10/17/magazine/faith-certainty-and-the-presidency-of-george-w-bush.html.
11. Michael R. Gordon and Judith Miller. "Threats and Responses: The Iraqis; U.S. Says Hussein Intensifies Quest for A-Bomb Parts." *New York Times*. Sept. 8, 2002. Accessed July 2022. https://www.nytimes.com/2002/09/08/world/threats-responses-iraqis-us-says-hussein-intensifies-quest-for-bomb-parts.html.
12. Don Gonyea. "Radio Broadcast: Terror Alert: Code Orange." *National Public Radio*. Sept. 10, 2002. Accessed July 2022. https://www.npr.org/templates/story/story.php?storyId=1149748.
13. Dan Collins. "Congress Says Yes to Iraq Resolution." *CBS News*. Oct. 3, 2002. Accessed July 2022. https://www.cbsnews.com/news/congress-says-yes-to-iraq-resolution/. Also see "Top Bush Officials Push Case Against Saddam." *CNN*. Sept. 8, 2002. Accessed July 2022. https://www.cnn.com/2002/ALLPOLITICS/09/08/iraq.debate/.
14. Gary Younge and Jon Henley. "Wimps, Weasels and Monkeys—The US Media View of 'Perfidious France.'" *The Guardian*. Feb. 11, 2003. Accessed July 2022. https://www.theguardian.com/world/2003/feb/11/pressandpublishing.usa.
15. Brent Scowcroft. "Don't Attack Saddam." *Wall Street Journal*. Aug. 15, 2002. Accessed July 2022. http://www.wsj.com/articles/SB1029371773228069195.
16. Bootie Cosgrove-Mather. "Poll: Talk First, Fight Later." *CBS News*. Jan. 23, 2003. Accessed July 2022. http:// www.cbsnews.com/news/poll-talk-first-fight-later/.
17. Patrick E. Tyler. "Threats and Responses: New Analysis; A New Power in the Streets." *New York Times*. Feb. 17, 2003. Accessed July 2022. http://www.nyti

mes.com/2003/02/17/world/threats-and-responses-news-analysis-a-new-power-in-the-streets.html.

18. Don Gonyea (reporting) and Melissa Block (host). "Analysis: President Bush Discounts Impact of Anti-War Protest Marches Around the World." *National Public Radio*. Feb. 18, 2003. Accessed July 2022. http://www.npr.org/programs/atc/transcripts/2003/feb/030218.gonyea.html.
19. William A. Galston. "Why a First Strike Will Surely Backfire." *Washington Post*. June 16, 2002, p. B-01. Accessed July 2022. https://www.washingtonpost.com/archive/opinions/2002/06/16/why-a-first-strike-will-surely-backfire/e42529ec-eacb-4f77-8a17-dc5ca59dd20c/.
20. Marc Sandalow. "Rumsfeld Calls Looting 'Untidiness'/Says TV News Overplays Disorder." *SFgate.com*. April 12, 2003. Accessed July 2022. https://www.sfgate.com/news/article/Rumsfeld-calls-looting-an-untidiness-Says-TV-2655658.php.
21. Statistica Research Department. "Number of U.S. Soldiers Killed in Iraq from 2003 to 2020." Statistica. Oct. 25, 2021. Accessed July 2022. https://www.statista.com/statistics/263798/american-soldiers-killed-in-iraq/. Also see Steve Fainaru. *Big Boy Rules: America's Mercenaries Fighting in Iraq*. New York: Da Capo Press, 2009.
22. Medea Benjamin and Nicholas J. S. Davies. "The Staggering Death Toll in Iraq." *Salon*. March 19, 2018. Accessed July 2022. https://www.salon.com/2018/03/19/the-staggering-death-toll-in-iraq_partner/.
23. William Saletan. "Liars' Poker." *Slate*. Jan. 8, 2002. Accessed July 2022. https://slate.com/news-and-politics/2002/01/bush-and-daschle-spin-the-economy.html.
24. Emily Horton. "The Legacy of the 2001 and 2003 'Bush' Tax Cuts." Center on Budget and Policy Priorities. Oct. 23, 2017. Accessed July 2022. https://www.cbpp.org/research/federal-tax/the-legacy-of-the-2001-and-2003-bush-tax-cuts. Also see "President Bush Helped Americans Through Tax Relief." White House Archives: President George W. Bush. Accessed July 2022. https://georgewbush-whitehouse.archives.gov/infocus/bushrecord/factsheets/taxrelief.html.
25. "O'Neill Says Cheney Told Him 'Deficits Don't Matter'." *Chicago Tribune*. Jan. 12, 2004. Accessed July 2022. https://www.chicagotribune.com/news/ct-xpm-2004-01-12-0401120168-story.html. Also see "Bush and the People's Money." *Slate*. March 1, 2001. Accessed July 2022. https://slate.com/news-and-politics/2001/03/bush-and-the-people-s-money.html.
26. Dana Milbank. "Bush Signs $350 Billion Tax Cut Measure." *Washington Post*. May 29, 2003. Accessed July 2022. https://www.washingtonpost.com/archive/politics/2003/05/29/bush-signs-350-billion-tax-cut-measure/6094f654-a6d0-4e3c-8b3c-e0d91a209ebb/.
27. U.S. Senate Permanent Subcommittee on Investigations, Majority Staff Report. "Repatriating Offshore Funds: 2004 Tax Windfall for Select Multinationals." Oct. 11, 2011, p. 9. Accessed July 2022. https://www.hsgac.senate.gov/imo/media/doc/RepatriatingOffshoreFundsReportOct202011wExhibitsFINAL.pdf.
28. Emily Horton. "Report: The Legacy of the 2001 and 2003 'Bush' Tax Cuts." Center on Budget and Policy Priorities. Oct. 23, 2017. Accessed July 2022. https://www.cbpp.org/research/federal-tax/the-legacy-of-the-2001-and-2003-bush-tax-cuts.
29. Jean Edward Smith. *Bush*. New York: Simon and Schuster, 2016, p. 390n.

30. Sandra Vergari. "Federalism and Market-Based Education Policy: The Supplemental Educational Services Mandate." *American Journal of Education* 113 (2), 2007, p. 312.
31. Brian Kisida and Daniel H. Bowen. "Report: New Evidence of the Benefits of Arts Education." Brookings Institution. Feb. 12, 2009. Accessed July 2022. https://www.brookings.edu/blog/brown-center-chalkboard/2019/02/12/new-evidence-of-the-benefits-of-arts-education/.
32. Valerie Strauss. "Arguably the Two Most Appalling Stories About the Standardized Testing Obsession of the 2010s." *Washington Post*. Dec. 31, 2019. Accessed July 2022. https://www.washingtonpost.com/education/2019/12/31/arguably-two-most-appalling-stories-about-standardized-testing-obsession-s/.
33. Claudia Wallis. "No Child Left Behind: Doomed to Fail?" *Time Magazine*. June 8, 2008. Accessed July 2022. http://content.time.com/time/nation/article/0,8599,1812758,00.html.
34. Valerie Strauss and Carol Burris. "Problems with Charter Schools That You Won't Hear Betsy DeVos Talk About." *Washington Post*. June 22, 2017. Accessed July 2022. https://www.washingtonpost.com/news/answer-sheet/wp/2017/06/22/problems-with-charter-schools-that-you-wont-hear-betsy-devos-talk-about/. Also see Joanne Barkan. "Got Dough? How Billionaires Rule Our Schools." *Dissent*. Winter 2011. Accessed July 2022. https://www.dissentmagazine.org/article/got-dough-how-billionaires-rule-our-schools.
35. Donald Rapp. *Bubbles, Booms, and Busts: The Rise and Fall of Financial Assets*, 2nd ed. New York: Springer, 2009, p. 255.
36. Bethany McLean and Peter Elkind. *Smartest Guys in the Room: The Amazing Rise and Scandalous Fall of Enron*. New York: Penguin Group, 2003, p. 272.
37. Richard A. Oppel Jr. "Word for Word/Energy Hogs; Enron Traders on Grandma Millie and Making Out Like Bandits." *New York Times*. June 13, 2004. Accessed July 2022. https://www.nytimes.com/2004/06/13/weekinreview/word-for-word-energy-hogs-enron-traders-grandma-millie-making-like-bandits.html.
38. Christopher Weare. "Report: The California Electricity Crisis: Causes and Policy Options." San Francisco: Public Policy Institute of California. 2003, pp. 2–3. Accessed July 2022. https://www.ppic.org/content/pubs/report/R_103CWR.pdf.
39. U.S. Senate Committee on Governmental Affairs, 117th Congress, 2nd Session. "Hearing: Retirement Insecurity: 401(k) Crisis at Enron." Feb. 5, 2002. Accessed July 2022. https://www.govinfo.gov/content/pkg/CHRG-107shrg78616/html/CHRG-107shrg78616.htm.
40. Sidney Blumenthal. "Hurricane Katrina: No One Can Say They Didn't See It Coming." *Der Spiegel*. Sept. 7, 2005. Accessed July 2022. https://www.globalresearch.ca/hurricane-katrina-no-one-can-say-they-didn-t-see-it-coming/900.
41. Adam Nossiter. "New Orleans Population Is Reduced Nearly 60%." *New York Times*. Oct. 7, 2006. Accessed July 2022. https://www.nytimes.com/2006/10/07/us/07population.html.
42. "Barbara Bush. In Her Own Words, from Political Prognostication to 'Rhymes with Rich.'" *USA Today*. April 17, 2018. Accessed July 2022. https://www.usatoday.com/story/news/2018/04/17/barbara-bush-quotes-memorable-famous/518489002/.
43. Susan Saulny. "5,000 Public Housing Units in New Orleans Are to Be Razed." *New York Times*. June 15, 2006. Accessed July 2022. https://www.nytimes.com/2006/06/15/us/5000-public-housing-units-in-new-orleans-are-to-be-razed.html.

44. George W. Bush. "President's Remarks at Republican Jewish Coalition 20th Anniversary." White House Archives. Sept. 21, 2005. Accessed July 2021. https://georgewbush-whitehouse.archives.gov/news/releases/2005/09/20050921-1.html.
45. Gary Sernovitz. "What New Orleans Tells Us About the Perils of Putting Schools on the Free Market." *New Yorker.* July 30, 2018. Accessed July 2022. https://www.newyorker.com/business/currency/what-new-orleans-tells-us-about-the-perils-of-putting-schools-on-the-free-market.
46. Andrea Gabor. "The Myth of the New Orleans School Makeover." *New York Times.* Aug. 22, 2015. Accessed July 2022. https://www.nytimes.com/2015/08/23/opinion/sunday/the-myth-of-the-new-orleans-school-makeover.html.
47. Amanda Terkel. "Bush Will Not Mention Katrina in State of the Union Speech." *ThinkProgress.* Jan. 23, 2007. Accessed July 2022. https://archive.thinkprogress.org/bush-will-not-mention-katrina-in-state-of-the-union-844f7837b9b7/.
48. Alana Semuels. "Understanding Two Loan Giants; A Primer on Fannie and Freddie and Why Taxpayers Should Care About the Takeover." *Los Angeles Times.* Sept. 8, 2008. Accessed July 2022. https://www.latimes.com/archives/la-xpm-2008-sep-08-fi-qanda8-story.html.
49. Jean Edward Smith. *Bush.* New York: Simon and Schuster, 2016, p. xv.
50. Sue Owen. "Paul Sadler Says National Debt Doubled Under George W. Bush." *PolitiFact.* July 19, 2012. Accessed July 2022. https://www.politifact.com/factchecks/2012/jul/19/paul-sadler/paul-sadler-says-national-debt-doubled-under-georg/.
51. Ronald Brownstein. "Closing the Book on the Bush Legacy." *The Atlantic.* Sept. 11, 2009. Accessed July 2022. https://www.theatlantic.com/politics/archive/2009/09/closing-the-book-on-the-bush-legacy/26402/.
52. Alexandra Tinsley. "Report: Subtracting Students from Communities." Urban Institute. March 23, 2017. Accessed February 2022. https://www.urban.org/features/subtracting-schools-communities.
53. Janell Ross. "Obama Revives His 'Cling to Guns or Religion' Analysis—for Donald Trump Supporters." *Washington Post.* Dec. 21, 2015. Accessed July 2022. https://www.washingtonpost.com/news/the-fix/wp/2015/12/21/obama-dusts-off-his-cling-to-guns-or-religion-idea-for-donald-trump/.
54. Matt Taibbi. "Eric Holder, Wall Street Double Agent, Comes in from the Cold." *Rolling Stone.* July 8, 2015. Accessed July 2022. https://www.rollingstone.com/politics/politics-news/eric-holder-wall-street-double-agent-comes-in-from-the-cold-49262/.
55. Matt Taibbi. "Turns Out That Trillion-Dollar Bailout Was, in Fact, Real." *Rolling Stone.* March 18, 2019. Accessed July 2022. https://www.rollingstone.com/politics/politics-features/2008-financial-bailout-809731/. Also see Matt Taibbi. "Secret and Lies of the Bailout." *Rolling Stone.* Jan. 4, 2013. Accessed July 2022. http://www.rollingstone.com/politics/news/secret-and-lies-of-the-bailout-20130104#ixzz42FZ5zWIS; and Mike Collins. "The Big Banks Bailout." *Forbes.* July 14, 2015. Accessed July 2022. http://www.forbes.com/sites/mikecollins/2015/07/14/the-big-bank-bailout/#52e0fcff3723.
56. Michael Hirsch and *National Journal.* "The Comprehensive Case Against Larry Summers." *The Atlantic.* Sept. 13, 2013. Accessed July 2022. https://www.theatlantic.com/business/archive/2013/09/the-comprehensive-case-against-larry-summers/279651/.

57. Neil M. Barofsky. "Where the Bailout Went Wrong." *New York Times*. March 29, 2011. Accessed July 2022. https://www.nytimes.com/2011/03/30/opinion/30barofsky.html.
58. Jane Mayer. *Dark Money: The Hidden History of the Billionaires Behind the Rise of the Radical Right*. New York: Doubleday, 2016, pp. 203–4.
59. H.R.2356—Bipartisan Campaign Reform Act of 2002, 107th Congress (2001–2002). June 28, 2001. Accessed July 2022. https://www.congress.gov/bill/107th-congress/house-bill/2356.
60. Some presidential candidates whose campaigns predate Sanders's 2016 run, such as that of Dennis Kucinich, refused big money donations but did not run campaigns that were nationally competitive. The Sanders campaign stands apart for having registered a record 8.2 million individual campaign contributions from about 2.5 million donors and raising roughly $228 million, with an average donation of $27.
61. Mike Snider. "Americans Families Finally Got a Big Pay Raise. Why It Might Not Feel Like It." *USA Today*. Sept. 13, 2016. Accessed July 2022. https://www.usatoday.com/story/money/2016/09/13/us-household-income-rises-2015/90302206/. Also see Lawrence Mishel, Josh Bivens, Elise Gould, and Heidi Shierholz. *The State of Working America*, 12th ed. Ithaca, NY: Cornell University Press, 2012. Accessed July 2022. http://www.stateofworkingamerica.org/.
62. Janice Hopkins Tanne. "More Than 26,000 Americans Die Each Year Because of Lack of Health Insurance." *British Medical Journal (Clinical Research Edition)* 336 (7649), April 9, 2008, p. 855. Accessed July 2022. https://www.ncbi.nlm.nih.gov/pmc/articles/PMC2323087/. Also see Steffie Woolhandler and David U. Himmelstein. "The Relationship of Health Insurance and Mortality: Is Lack of Insurance Deadly?" *Annals of Internal Medicine*. Sept. 19, 2017. Accessed July 2022. https://www.acpjournals.org/doi/10.7326/m17-1403.
63. Glenn Greenwood. "Truth About the Public Option Momentarily Emerges, Quickly Scampers Back into Hiding." *Salon*. Oct. 5, 2010. Accessed July 2022. https://www.salon.com/2010/10/05/public_option_24/. Also see David D. Kirkpatrick. "Obama Is Taking an Active Role in Talks on Health Care Plan." *New York Times*. Aug. 12, 2009. Accessed July 2022. https://www.nytimes.com/2009/08/13/health/policy/13health.html.
64. Tom Hamburger. "Obama Gives Powerful Drug Lobby a Seat at the Table." *Los Angeles Times*. Aug. 4, 2009. Accessed July 2022. https://www.latimes.com/health/la-na-healthcare-pharma4-2009aug04-story.html.
65. Emily Willingham. "Why Did Mylan Hike Up Prices 400%? Because They Could." *Forbes*. Aug. 21, 2016. Accessed July 2022. https://www.forbes.com/sites/emilywillingham/2016/08/21/why-did-mylan-hike-epipen-prices-400-because-they-could/?sh=7ff0668f280c.
66. Barack Obama. "Remarks by the President at Signing of Dodd-Frank Wall Street Reform and Consumer Protection Act." White House Office of the Press Secretary. July 21, 2010. Accessed July 2022. https://obamawhitehouse.archives.gov/the-press-office/remarks-president-signing-dodd-frank-wall-street-reform-and-consumer-protection-act.
67. Daniel Roberts. "The Volcker Rule Takes Effect Today After Years of Delays." *Fortune*. July 22, 2015. Accessed July 2022. http://fortune.com/2015/07/22/volcker-rule/.
68. Andrew Ross Sorkin. "What Timothy Geithner Really Thinks." *New York Times Magazine*. May 8, 2014. Accessed July 2022. http://www.nytimes.com/2014/05/

11/magazine/what-timothy-geithner-really-thinks.html. Also see Barack Obama. "Remarks by the President at Signing of Dodd-Frank Wall Street Reform and Consumer Protection Act." White House Office of the Press Secretary. July 21, 2010. Accessed July 2022. https://obamawhitehouse.archives.gov/the-press-office/remarks-president-signing-dodd-frank-wall-street-reform-and-consumer-protection-act.

69. James Felkerson. "$29,000,000,000,000: A Detailed Look at the Fed's Bailout by Funding Facility and Recipient." Economics Working Paper Archive wp_698. Levy Economics Institute, 2011. Accessed July 2022. https://ideas.repec.org/p/lev/wrkpap/wp_698.html. Also see John Carney. "The Size of the Bank Bailout: $29 Trillion." *CNBC*. Dec. 14, 2011. Accessed July 2022. https://www.cnbc.com/id/45674390; and Matt Taibbi. "Secret and Lies of the Bailout." *Rolling Stone*. Jan. 4, 2013. Accessed July 2022. http://www.rollingstone.com/politics/news/secret-and-lies-of-the-bailout-20130104#ixzz42FZ5zWIS.
70. Mike Collins. "The Big Banks Bailout." *Forbes*. July 14, 2015. Accessed July 2022. http://www.forbes.com/sites/mikecollins/2015/07/14/the-big-bank-bailout/#52e0fcff3723. Also see Meredith Shiner. "Sanders Defends Fed Deal." *Politico*. May 7, 2010. Accessed July 2022. https://www.politico.com/story/2010/05/sanders-defends-fed-deal-036940.
71. Liz Halloran. "Obama Humbled by Election 'Shellacking.'" *National Public Radio*. Nov. 3, 2010. Accessed July 2022. https://www.npr.org/templates/story/story.php?storyId=131046118.
72. Lesli A. Maxwell. "Study Points to Drop in Per-Pupil Spending for Pre-K." *Education Week*. April 10, 2012. Accessed July 2022. https://www.edweek.org/teaching-learning/study-points-to-drop-in-per-pupil-spending-for-pre-k/2012/04. Also see Gordon Lafer. *The One Percent Solution: How Corporations Are Remaking America One State at a Time*. Ithaca, NY: Cornell University Press, 2017.
73. Nicholas Confessore and Jeremy W. Peters. "Paterson Says Legislators Put State in Danger." *New York Times*. Jan. 6, 2010. Accessed July 2022. https://www.nytimes.com/2010/01/07/nyregion/07state.html.
74. The Editors. "A Bad News Budget." *The Observer*. Dec. 16, 2008. Accessed July 2022. https://observer.com/2008/12/a-bad-news-budget/.
75. Bryan Lowry. "Gov. Sam Brownback Cuts Funding for Schools and Higher Education." *Wichita Eagle*. Feb. 6, 2015. Accessed July 2022. https://www.kansas.com/news/politics-government/article9351788.html.
76. Nancy MacLean. *Democracy in Chains: The Deep History of the Radical Right's Stealth Plan for America*. New York: Viking, 2017, p. 220.
77. Olivia Nuzzi. "Paul Ryan: Democrats Offer Americans a 'Full Stomach and an Empty Soul'." *The Daily Beast*. July 12, 2017. Accessed July 2022. https://www.thedailybeast.com/paul-ryan-democrats-offer-americans-a-full-stomach-and-an-empty-soul.
78. Marc Caputo and Holly Otterbein. "The Coming Clash Between Bernie and Biden." *Politico*. Jan. 13, 2020. Accessed July 2022. https://www.politico.com/news/2020/01/13/bernie-sanders-joe-biden-clash-2020-098433.
79. Barack Obama. "Remarks on Signing the Tax Relief, Unemployment Insurance Reauthorization, and Job Creation Act of 2010." *Govinfo.gov*. Dec. 17, 2010. Accessed July 2022. https://www.govinfo.gov/content/pkg/DCPD-201001080/html/DCPD-201001080.htm.

80. Howard Gleckman. "The Tax Vox 2010 Lump of Coal Award, Job-Killing Edition." Tax Policy Center. Dec. 23, 2010. Accessed July 2022. https://www.taxpolicycenter.org/taxvox/tax-vox-2010-lump-coal-award-job-killing-edition.
81. David Dayen. "Nancy Pelosi Rams Austerity Provision into House Rules Package over Objections of Progressives." *The Intercept*. Jan. 2, 2019. Accessed July 2022. https://theintercept.com/2019/01/02/nancy-pelosi-pay-go-rule/.
82. National Commission on Fiscal Responsibility and Reform. FiscalCommission.gov. April 6, 2011. Accessed July 2022. https://cybercemetery.unt.edu/archive/fiscal/20110406154234/http://www.fiscalcommission.gov/.
83. "The Sham of Simpson-Bowles." *Reuters*. Oct. 24, 2012. Accessed July 2022. https://www.reuters.com/article/instant-article/idUS91477267320121024.
84. Jeremy Mohler. "The 'Choice' Bait and Switch." *Jacobin*. Jan. 8, 2019. Accessed July 2022. https://www.jacobinmag.com/2019/01/choice-rhetoric-charter-schools-reproductive-rights.
85. Barack Obama. "Text of Obama's D-Day Speech." *CBS News*. June 6, 2009. Accessed July 2022. https://www.cbsnews.com/news/text-of-obamas-d-day-speech/.
86. Paul Krugman. "What Obama Wants." *New York Times*. July 7, 2011. Accessed July 2022. https://www.nytimes.com/2011/07/08/opinion/08krugman.html.
87. Sean Wilentz. "Republican Extremism and the Lessons of History." *Rolling Stone*. Oct. 10, 2013. Accessed July 2022. https://www.rollingstone.com/politics/politics-news/republican-extremism-and-the-lessons-of-history-121865/.
88. "Sanders Files Bill to Strengthen, Expand Social Security." Bernie Sanders homepage. March 12, 2015. Accessed July 2022. https://www.sanders.senate.gov/press-releases/sanders-files-bill-to-strengthen-expand-social-security/.
89. James McBride, Andrew Chatzky, and Anshu Siripurapu. "What's Next for the Trans-Pacific Partnership (TPP)?" Council on Foreign Relations. Sept. 20, 2021. Accessed July 2022. https://www.cfr.org/backgrounder/what-trans-pacific-partnership-tpp#:~:text=Introduction,percent%20of%20the%20global%20economy.
90. Heather Gautney. "Why the Trans-Pacific Partnership Is Bad for Workers, and for Democracy." *Huffington Post*. Feb. 3, 2015. Accessed July 2022. https://www.huffpost.com/entry/why-the-transpacific-part_1_b_6598604.
91. "The TPP & the Environment." Citizens Trade Campaign. March 2012. Accessed July 2022. https://www.citizenstrade.org/ctc/wp-content/uploads/2012/03/TransPacificEnvironment.pdf.
92. Doctors Without Borders. "Report: Trading Away Health: The Trans-Pacific Partnership Agreement (TPP)." March 3, 2013. Accessed July 2022. https://www.doctorswithoutborders.org/what-we-do/news-stories/news/trading-away-health-trans-pacific-partnership-agreement-tpp.
93. "TPP: The 'Trade' Deal That Could Inflate Your Health Care Bill." Public Citizen. Accessed July 2022. https://www.citizen.org/wp-content/uploads/migration/tpp-threats-to-us-healthcare.pdf. Also see "TPP's Investment Rules Harm Public Health." Public Citizens Global Trade Watch. Accessed July 2022. https://www.citizen.org/article/tpps-investment-rules-harm-public-health/.
94. Jordan Fabian. "Obama: More Moderate Republican Than Socialist." *ABC News*. Dec. 14, 2012. Accessed July 2022. https://abcnews.go.com/ABC_Univision/Politics/obama-considered-moderate-republican-1980s/story?id=17973080.
95. Rick Baum. "During Obama's Presidency Wealth Inequality Has Increased and Poverty Levels Are Higher." *CounterPunch*. Feb. 26, 2016. Accessed July 2022.

https://www.counterpunch.org/2016/02/26/during-obamas-presidency-wealth-inequality-has-increased-and-poverty-levels-are-higher/.

96. Matt Egan. "America's Biggest Oil Boom Came Under Obama." *CNN Business*. July 21, 2016. Accessed July 2022. https://money.cnn.com/2016/07/21/investing/trump-energy-plan-obama-oil-boom/index.html.
97. Jennifer Tolbert, Kendal Orgera, and Anthony Damico. "Key Facts About the Uninsured Population." Kaiser Family Foundation. Nov. 6, 2020. Accessed July 2022. https://www.kff.org/uninsured/issue-brief/key-facts-about-the-uninsured-population/.

CHAPTER 3

1. Aaron Couch and Emmet McDermott. "Donald Trump Campaign Offered Actors $50 to Cheer for Him at Presidential Announcement." *Hollywood Reporter.* June 17, 2015. Accessed July 2022. https://www.hollywoodreporter.com/news/donald-trump-campaign-offered-actors-803161.
2. Jake Miller. "Donald Trump Defends Calling Mexican Immigrants 'Rapists.'" *CBS News*. July 2, 2015. Accessed July 2022. https://www.cbsnews.com/news/election-2016-donald-trump-defends-calling-mexican-immigrants-rapists/.
3. Kaiser Family Foundation. "One in Five Americans Can't Afford Prescriptions with Gender Gap Getting Increasingly Worse." *Kaiser Health News*. Nov. 13, 2019. Accessed July 2022. https://khn.org/morning-breakout/one-in-five-americans-cant-afford-prescriptions-with-gender-gap-getting-increasingly-worse/. Also see Adam Edelman. "Fact Check: Trump Vows to 'Protect' Medicare, Social Security. His Budgets Have Sought Cuts." *NBC News*. Nov. 3, 2020. Accessed July 2022. https://www.nbcnews.com/politics/2020-election/blog/2020-08-27-rnc-updates-n1238267/ncrd1238640#blogHeader.
4. Katie Reilly. "Read Hillary Clinton's 'Basket of Deplorables' Remarks About Donald Trump Supporters." *Time Magazine*. Sept. 10, 2016. Accessed July 2022. https://time.com/4486502/hillary-clinton-basket-of-deplorables-transcript/.
5. "Donald Trump Accepts Presidential Nomination: 'I Will Be Your Voice'." *CNN Wire*. July 21, 2016. Accessed July 2022. https://fox59.com/news/national-world/donald-trump-accepts-presidential-nomination-i-will-be-your-voice/.
6. Michael Calderone. "Donald Trump Has Received Nearly $2 Billion in Free Media Attention." *Huffington Post*. March 15, 2016. Accessed July 2022. https://www.huffpost.com/entry/donald-trump-2-billion-free-media_n_56e83410e4b065e2e3d75935.
7. Matt Stieb. "A Brief History of Trump's Feud with John McCain." *New York Magazine*. March 20, 2019. Accessed July 2022. https://nymag.com/intelligencer/2019/03/an-abbreviated-history-of-trumps-feud-with-john-mccain.html.
8. Ryan Struyk and Ali Dukakis. "Donald Trump Gives Out Lindsey Graham's Phone Number." *ABC News*. July 21, 2015. Accessed July 2022. https://abcnews.go.com/Politics/donald-trump-lindsey-grahams-cell-phone-number/story?id=32595139.
9. Lindsay Kimble. "Doubling-Down, Donald Trump Tweets a My-Wife's-Prettier Than Yours Meme Featuring Heidi Cruz—and Ted Fires Back." *People Magazine*. March 24, 2016. Accessed July 2022. https://people.com/celebrity/donald-trump-posts-unflattering-photo-of-heidi-cruz/.
10. Ben Jacobs. "'They Could Be Isis': Trump Warns Against Taking Syrian Refugees." *The Guardian*. Oct. 1, 2015. Accessed July 2022. https://www.theguardian.com/us-news/2015/oct/01/donald-trump-syrian-refugees-could-be-isis.

11. William Saletan. "Trump's New Press Secretary Is an Apologist for Explicit Racism." *Slate*. April 13, 2020. Accessed July 2022. https://slate.com/news-and-politics/2020/04/kayleigh-mcenany-press-secretary-apologist-explicit-racism.html.
12. Olivia Nuzzi. "Five Myths About the Alt-Right." *Washington Post*. Nov. 23, 2016. Accessed July 2022. https://www.washingtonpost.com/opinions/five-myths-about-the-alt-right/2016/11/23/66e58604-b0c2-11e6-be1c-8cec35b1ad25_story.html.
13. Jane Coaston. "Trump's New Defense of His Charlottesville Comments Is Incredibly False." *Vox*. April 26, 2019. Accessed July 2022. https://www.vox.com/2019/4/26/18517980/trump-unite-the-right-racism-defense-charlottesville.
14. Daniel Dale, Marshall Cohen, Tara Subramaniam, and Holmes Lybrand. "Fact-Checking Trump's Attempt to Erase His Previous Coronavirus Response." *CNN*. April 1, 2020. Accessed July 2022. https://www.cnn.com/2020/03/31/politics/fact-check-trump-coronavirus-march-31/index.html. Also see Michael Daly. "Justice Department Is Cracking Down on Coronavirus Bleach 'Cures,' No Matter What Trump Says." *Daily Beast*. April 25, 2020. Accessed July 2022. https://www.thedailybeast.com/justice-department-is-cracking-down-on-coronavirus-bleach-cures-no-matter-what-trump-says; and "Trump: Cruz's Father Helped JFK Assassination." *Daily Beast*. April 13, 2017. Accessed July 2022. https://www.thedailybeast.com/trump-cruzs-father-helped-jfk-assassin.
15. "Report: Federal Workforce Statistics Sources: OPM and OMB." Congressional Research Service. June 28, 2022. Accessed July 2022. https://fas.org/sgp/crs/misc/R43590.pdf.
16. Partnership for Public Service. "Fed Figures 2019: Federal Workforce." January 2019. Accessed July 2022. https://ourpublicservice.org/wp-content/uploads/2019/01/FedFigures_19Shutdown.pdf.
17. Philip Rucker and Robert Costa. "Bannon Vows a Daily Fight for Deconstruction of the Administrative State." *Washington Post*. Feb. 23, 2017. Accessed July 2022. https://www.washingtonpost.com/politics/top-wh-strategist-vows-a-daily-fight-for-deconstruction-of-the-administrative-state/2017/02/23/03f6b8da-f9ea-11e6-bf01-d47f8cf9b643_story.html.
18. Emily Badger, Quoctrung Bui, and Alicia Parlapiano. "The Government Agencies That Became Smaller, and Unhappier, Under Trump." *New York Times*. Oct. 13, 2021. Accessed July 2022. https://www.nytimes.com/2021/02/01/upshot/trump-effect-government-agencies.html.
19. Joanna Partridge. "Boeing 737 Max Back in Skies After Fatal Crash That Killed 346." *The Guardian*. Dec. 9, 2020. Accessed July 2022. https://www.theguardian.com/business/2020/dec/09/boeing-737-max-back-in-the-skies-after-fatal-crashes-that-killed-346.
20. Sinéad Baker. "FAA Boss Says It Let Boeing Partly Self-Regulate the Software Thought to Be Behind Both Fatal 737 Max Crashes." *Business Insider*. March 28, 2019. Accessed July 2022. https://www.businessinsider.com/faa-let-boeing-self-regulate-software-believed-737-max-crashes-2019-3.
21. Benjamin Fearnow. "Countless Deaths Tied to Trump Admin Decimation of Environmental Protections During Pandemic, Experts Say." *Newsweek*. Aug. 24, 2020. Accessed July 2022. https://www.newsweek.com/countless-deaths-tied-trump-admin-decimation-environmental-protections-during-pandemic-experts-1527185.

22. Josh Gerstein. "DOJ Releases Overruled Memos Finding It Illegal for Presidents to Appoint Relatives." *Politico*. Oct. 3, 2017. Accessed July 2022. https://www.politico.com/story/2017/10/03/justice-department-legal-memos-presidents-appoint-relatives-243395.
23. Michelle Goldberg. "Putting Jared Kushner in Charge Is Utter Madness." *New York Times*. April 2, 2020. Accessed July 2022. https://www.nytimes.com/2020/04/02/opinion/jared-kushner-coronavirus.html.
24. Andrea Bernstein. "Who Is Jared Kushner?" *New Yorker*. Jan. 6, 2020. Accessed July 2022. https://www.newyorker.com/news/news-desk/who-is-jared-kushner.
25. Julian E. Barnes. "CIA Concludes That Saudi Crown Prince Ordered Khashoggi Killed." *New York Times*. Nov. 16, 2018. Accessed July 2022. https://www.nytimes.com/2018/11/16/us/politics/cia-saudi-crown-prince-khashoggi.html.
26. Alex Emmons, Ryan Grim, and Clayton Swisher. "Saudi Crown Prince Boasted That Jared Kushner Was 'In His Pocket'." *The Intercept*. March 21, 2018. Accessed July 2022. https://theintercept.com/2018/03/21/jared-kushner-saudi-crown-prince-mohammed-bin-salman/.
27. Ned Parker et al. "Ivanka and the Fugitive from Panama." *Reuters*. Nov. 17, 2017. Accessed July 2022. https://www.reuters.com/investigates/special-report/usa-trump-panama/.
28. Gabrielle Bruney. "Trump Apparently Calls Ivanka 'Baby' During White House Meetings." *Esquire Magazine*. April 12, 2019. Accessed July 2022. https://www.esquire.com/news-politics/a27128853/trump-ivanka-baby-world-bank-un/. Also see Michael D'Antonio. "Ivanka Trump Almost Landed One of the World's Biggest Jobs." *CNN*. Oct. 12, 2021. Accessed July 2022. https://www.cnn.com/2021/10/12/opinions/ivanka-trump-world-bank-dantonio/index.html.
29. Jia Tolentino. "Mike Pence's Marriage and the Beliefs That Keep Women from Power." *New Yorker*. March 31, 2017. Accessed July 2022. https://www.newyorker.com/culture/jia-tolentino/mike-pences-marriage-and-the-beliefs-that-keep-women-from-power.
30. Jane Mayer. "The Danger of President Pence." *New Yorker*. Oct. 16, 2017. Accessed July 2022. https://www.newyorker.com/magazine/2017/10/23/the-danger-of-president-pence.
31. Heather Timmons. "Secretary of State Nominee Mike Pompeo Owes His Political Career to the Koch Brothers." *Quartz*. March 13, 2018. Accessed July 2022. https://qz.com/1227882/secretary-of-state-nominee-mike-pompeo-owes-his-political-career-to-the-koch-brothers/. Also see Nikhel Sus. "Report: Pompeo's Madison Dinners Cost Taxpayers Nearly $65,000." Citizens for Responsibility and Ethics. July 7, 2021. Accessed July 2022. https://www.citizensforethics.org/reports-investigations/crew-investigations/pompeo-madison-dinners-cost-taxpayers-nearly-65000/.
32. Emily Stewart. "Mick Mulvaney Once Called the CFPB a 'Sick, Sad' Joke. Now He Might Be in Charge of It." *Vox*. Nov. 16, 2017. Accessed July 2022. https://www.vox.com/policy-and-politics/2017/11/16/16667266/mick-mulvaney-cfpb-cordray-omb-joke.
33. Nicholas Confessore. "Mick Mulvaney's Master Class in Destroying a Bureaucracy from Within." *New York Times Magazine*. April 16, 2019. Accessed July 2022. https://www.nytimes.com/2019/04/16/magazine/consumer-financial-protection-bureau-trump.html.
34. Brad Plumer. "Trump's EPA Pick Is an Ardent Foe of Virtually Everything Obama's EPA Has Done." *Vox*. Dec. 7, 2016. Accessed July 2022. https://

www.vox.com/energy-and-environment/2016/12/7/13873894/scott-pru itt-trump-epa.

35. Oliver Milman. "EPA Head Scott Pruitt Says Global Warming May Help 'Humans Flourish'." *The Guardian*. Feb. 7, 2018. Accessed July 2022. https://www.theguard ian.com/environment/2018/feb/07/epa-head-scott-pruitt-says-global-warming-may-help-humans-flourish.
36. David A. Graham. "What Finally Did In Scott Pruitt?" *The Atlantic*. July 7, 2018. Accessed July 2022. https://portside.org/2018-07-07/what-finally-did-scott-pru itt. Also see Steve Eder and Hiroko Tabuchi. "Scott Pruitt Before the EPA: Fancy Homes, a Shell Company, and Friends with Money." *New York Times*. April 21, 2018. Accessed July 2022. https://www.nytimes.com/2018/04/21/us/politics/scott-pruitt-oklahoma-epa.html.
37. Scott Brontstein, Curt Divine, and Drew Griffin. "Whistleblower: EPA's Pruitt Kept Secret Calendar to Hide Meetings." *CNN*. July 3, 2018. Accessed July 2022. https://www.cnn.com/2018/07/02/politics/scott-pruitt-whistleblower-secret-calendar/index.html.
38. Jason Le Miere. "Scott Pruitt Told Donald Trump He Is President Because of 'God's Providence' in Resignation Letter." *Newsweek*. July 5, 2018. Accessed July 2022. https://www.newsweek.com/scott-pruitt-donald-trump-god-1010529.
39. Bess Levin. "Tom Price Used Taxpayer-Funded Luxury Jets for a Weekend Getaway and Lunch with His Son." *Vanity Fair*. Sept. 27, 2017. Accessed July 2022. https://www.vanityfair.com/news/2017/09/tom-price-used-taxpayer-fun ded-luxury-jets-for-a-weekend-getaway-and-lunch-with-his-son.
40. Hilary McQuie. "Alex Azar Is Bad Medicine for HHS." *The Hill*. Jan. 6, 2018. Accessed July 2022. https://thehill.com/opinion/healthcare/367740-alex-azar-is-bad-medicine-for-hhs.
41. Sarah Karlin-Smith. "Trump's HHS Secretary Nominee Boosted Drug Prices While at Eli Lilly." *Politico*. Nov. 14, 2017. Accessed July 2022. https://www.polit ico.com/story/2017/11/14/alex-azar-eli-lilly-drug-prices-244888.
42. Nadia Prupis. "Trump Expected to Name Anti-worker Billionaire Wilbur Ross as Commerce Secretary." *Commondreams*. Nov. 24, 2016. Accessed July 2022. https://www.commondreams.org/news/2016/11/24/trump-expected-name-anti-worker-billionaire-wilbur-ross-commerce-secretary. Also see Josh Israel. "Who Is Wilbur Ross?" *ThinkProgress*. Dec. 5, 2016. Accessed July 2022. https://archive.thinkprogress.org/who-is-wilbur-ross-5e22fab68f47/.
43. Aaron Ament and Randi Weingarten. "Betsy DeVos Is Letting For-Profit Colleges Trap Students in Debt They Can Never Repay." *Fortune Magazine*. Feb. 6, 2020. Accessed July 2022. https://fortune.com/2020/02/06/betsy-devos-gainful-emp loyment-rule/.
44. Jeremy Scahill. "Blackwater Founder Erik Prince Implicated in Murder." *The Nation*. Aug. 4, 2009. Accessed July 2022. https://www.thenation.com/article/archive/blackwater-founder-implicated-murder/.
45. Max Fisher. "The Real Blackwater Scandal Is That the State Department Kept Hiring Them." *Vox*. June 30, 2014. Accessed July 2022. https://www.vox.com/2014/6/30/5858556/the-real-blackwater-scandal-is-that-the-state-department-kept-hiring.
46. John Ydstie. "Trump's Potential Treasury Secretary Headed a 'Foreclosure Machine.'" *National Public Radio*. Nov. 29, 2016. Accessed July 2022. https://www.npr.org/2016/11/29/503755613/trumps-potential-treasury-secretary-hea ded-a-foreclosure-machine.

47. Bob Moser. "Mitch McConnell: The Man Who Sold America." *Rolling Stone*. Sept. 17, 2019. Accessed July 2022. https://www.rollingstone.com/politics/politics-features/mitch-mcconnell-man-who-sold-america-880799/. Also see Jane Mayer. "How Mitch McConnell Became Trump's Enabler-in-Chief." *New Yorker*. April 12, 2020. Accessed July 2022. https://www.newyorker.com/magazine/2020/04/20/how-mitch-mcconnell-became-trumps-enabler-in-chief.
48. "Trump Has Appointed More Generals in His Cabinet Than Any President Since World War II." *Democracy Now*. Dec. 16, 2017. Accessed July 2022. https://www.democracynow.org/2016/12/16/trump_has_appointed_more_generals_in.
49. Amanda Macias and Dan Mangan. "How Veteran Affairs Department Secretary David Shulkin Fell from Grace." *CNBC*. March 28, 2018. Accessed July 2022. https://www.cnbc.com/2018/03/28/how-veteran-affairs-department-secretary-david-shulkin-fell-from-grace.html.
50. Noah Lanard and Dan Friedman. "This Is the Very Expensive Yacht Steve Bannon Got Arrested On." *Mother Jones*. Aug. 20, 2020. Accessed July 2022. https://www.motherjones.com/politics/2020/08/this-is-the-very-expensive-yacht-steve-bannon-got-arrested-on/.
51. Benjamin Weiser. "After Pardon for Bannon, 2 Admit Bilking Donors for Border Wall." *New York Times*. April 21, 2022. Accessed July 2022. https://www.nytimes.com/2022/04/21/nyregion/trump-bannon-border-wall.html.
52. Jason Le Miere. "Ronny Jackson Known as 'Candy Man,' Would Allegedly Go Through Plane Giving Drugs to Passengers, Democrat Says." *Newsweek*. April 24, 2018. Accessed July 2022. https://www.newsweek.com/ronny-jackson-candy-man-drugs-899985.
53. Tim Mak and Amelia Warshaw. "Trump's Labor Secretary Pick, Andrew Puzder, Is Swamped in His Own Workplace Lawsuits." *Daily Beast*. April 13, 2017. Accessed July 2022. https://www.thedailybeast.com/trumps-labor-secretary-pick-andrew-puzder-is-swamped-in-his-own-workplace-lawsuits.
54. Jennifer Jacobs and Josh Eidelson. "Trump to Name New Labor Nominee, Appears to Rule Out Templeton." *Bloomberg News*. Feb. 15, 2017. Accessed July 2022. https://www.bloomberg.com/news/articles/2017-02-15/puzder-said-to-be-ready-to-withdraw-as-trump-s-labor-nominee.
55. Josh Gerstein. "Unsealed Documents Detail Alleged Epstein Victim's Recruitment at Mar-a-Lago." *Politico*. Aug. 9, 2019. Accessed July 2022. https://www.politico.com/story/2019/08/09/epstein-mar-a-lago-trump-1456221.
56. Dahlia Lithwick. "How Alex Acosta Got Away with It for So Long." *Slate*. July 11, 2019. Accessed July 2022. https://slate.com/news-and-politics/2019/07/acosta-epstein-plea-deal-2008-ignored-victims.html. Also see Pilar Melendez. "New Jeffrey Epstein Victims, Including 11-Year-Old Girl, Come Forward in Lawsuit." *Daily Beast*. Aug. 14, 2020. Accessed July 2022. https://www.thedailybeast.com/new-jeffrey-epstein-victims-including-11-year-old-girl-come-forward-in-lawsuit.
57. See Richard Nixon. "Transcript of David Frost's Interview with Richard Nixon." Teaching American History. 1977. Accessed July 2022. https://teachingamericanhistory.org/library/document/transcript-of-david-frosts-interview-with-richard-nixon/. Also see Mike Allen. "Exclusive: Trump Lawyer Claims the 'President Cannot Obstruct Justice.'" *Axios*. Dec. 4, 2017. Accessed July 2022. https://www.axios.com/exclusive-trump-lawyer-claims-the-president-cannot-obstruct-justice-2514742663.html.
58. Colin Dwyer. "Sessions Tells Prosecutors to Seek 'Most Serious' Charges, Stricter Sentences." *National Public Radio*. May 12, 2017. Accessed July 2022. https://

www.npr.org/sections/thetwo-way/2017/05/12/528086525/sessions-tells-prosecutors-to-seek-most-serious-charges-stricter-sentences.

59. Sarah Stillman. "Jeff Sessions and the Resurgence of Civil Asset Forfeiture." *New Yorker*. Aug. 15, 2017. Accessed July 2022. https://www.newyorker.com/news/news-desk/jeff-sessions-and-the-resurgence-of-civil-asset-forfeiture.
60. Ankush Khardori. "There's Never Been a Better Time to Be a White-Collar Criminal." *New Republic*. July 23, 2020. Accessed July 2022. https://newrepublic.com/article/158582/theres-never-better-time-white-collar-criminal.
61. Ben Protess, Robert Gebeloff, and Danielle Ivory. "Trump Administration Spares Corporate Wrongdoers Billions in Penalties." *New York Times*. Nov. 3, 2018. Accessed July 2022. https://www.nytimes.com/2018/11/03/us/trump-sec-doj-corporate-penalties.html.
62. Dara Lind. "Jeff Sessions Gave Trump the Immigration Crackdown He Wanted." *Vox*. Nov. 7, 2018. Accessed July 2022. https://www.vox.com/2018/5/23/17229464/jeff-sessions-resign-trump-immigration.
63. Jeff Gerth and Stephen Labaton. "Prisons for Profit: A Special Report; Jail Business Shows Its Weakness." *New York Times*. Nov. 24, 1995. Accessed July 2022. https://www.nytimes.com/1995/11/24/us/prisons-for-profit-a-special-report-jail-business-shows-its-weaknesses.html.
64. Ginger Thompson. "Children Cry and Plead for Their Parents at the Border in Audio Released by ProPublica." *PBS News Hour*. June 18, 2018. Accessed July 2022. https://www.pbs.org/newshour/politics/children-cry-and-plead-for-their-parents-at-the-border-in-audio-released-by-propublica.
65. Miriam Valverde. "Fact-Checking Biden on Use of Cages for Immigrants During Obama Administration." *PolitiFact*. Sept. 13, 2019. Accessed July 2022. https://www.politifact.com/factchecks/2019/sep/13/joe-biden/fact-checking-biden-use-cages-during-obama-adminis/.
66. Chantal Da Silva. "Obama Held More Than Double the Number of Children in Shelters Compared to Trump White House." *Newsweek*. May 30, 2018. Accessed July 2022. https://www.newsweek.com/trump-administration-holding-more-immigrant-children-shelters-ever-949099.
67. Jonathan Blitzer. "How Stephen Miller Manipulates Trump to Further His Immigration Obsession." *New Yorker*. March 2, 2020. Accessed July 2021. https://www.newyorker.com/magazine/2020/03/02/how-stephen-miller-manipulates-donald-trump-to-further-his-immigration-obsession.
68. Ginger Thompson. "Children Cry and Plead for Their Parents at the Border in Audio Released by ProPublica." *PBS News Hour*. June 18, 2018. Accessed July 2022. https://www.pbs.org/newshour/politics/children-cry-and-plead-for-their-parents-at-the-border-in-audio-released-by-propublica.
69. Justine Coleman. "White House Officials Voted by Show of Hands on 2018 Family Separations: Report." *The Hill*. Aug. 20, 2020. Accessed July 2022. https://thehill.com/homenews/administration/513025-white-house-officials-voted-by-show-of-hands-on-family-separations-in.
70. Charles Bethea. "Trump Reportedly Called Sessions a 'Dumb Southerner.' What Do Alabama Republicans Think of That?" *New Yorker*. Sept. 5, 2018. Accessed July 2022. https://www.newyorker.com/news/news-desk/trump-reportedly-called-sessions-a-dumb-southerner-what-do-alabama-republicans-think-of-that.
71. Kevin Johnson and Christal Hayes. "Attorney General Jeff Sessions Defends Himself—Again—in Face of Attacks from President Trump." *USA Today*. Aug.

23, 2018. Accessed July 2022. https://www.usatoday.com/story/news/politics/2018/08/23/jeff-sessions-donald-trump-criticism/1074761002/.

72. David Rohde. “William Barr, Trump’s Sword and Shield.” *New Yorker*. Jan. 13, 2020. Accessed July 2022. https://www.newyorker.com/magazine/2020/01/20/william-barr-trumps-sword-and-shield.
73. Charlie Savage. “Barr Bridges the Reagan Revolution and Trump on Executive Power.” *New York Times*. Nov. 18, 2019. Accessed July 2022. https://www.nytimes.com/2019/11/18/us/politics/barr-executive-power-trump.html.
74. Evan Osnos. “Trump vs. the ‘Deep State.’” *New Yorker*. May 14, 2018. Accessed July 2022. https://www.newyorker.com/magazine/2018/05/21/trump-vs-the-deep-state.
75. Debra Cassens Weiss. “Transformation of the Judiciary Is Trump’s ‘Most Consequential Accomplishment,’ Says Non-profit Founder.” *American Bar Association Journal*. Jan. 19, 2021. Accessed July 2022. https://www.abajournal.com/news/article/transformation-of-judiciary-is-trumps-most-consequential-accomplishment-says-nonprofit-founder. Also see Mark Sherman, Kevin Freking, and Matthew Daly. “Trump’s Impact on Courts Likely to Last Long Beyond His Term.” *Associated Press*. Dec. 26, 2020. Accessed July 2022. https://apnews.com/article/joe-biden-donald-trump-mitch-mcconnell-elections-judiciary-d5807340e86d05fbc78ed50fb43c1c46; and Ian Millhiser. “What Trump Has Done to the Courts, Explained.” *Vox*. Sept. 29, 2020. Accessed July 2022. https://www.vox.com/policy-and-politics/2019/12/9/20962980/trump-supreme-court-federal-judges.
76. Jacqueline Thomsen. “Supreme Court Rules in Favor of Businesses Seeking to Block Class Action Lawsuits.” *The Hill*. April 24, 2019. Accessed July 2022. https://thehill.com/regulation/court-battles/440395-supreme-court-rules-in-favor-of-businesses-seeking-to-block-class. Also see Adam Liptak. “Corporations Find a Friend in the Supreme Court.” *New York Times*. May 4, 2013. Accessed July 2022. https://www.nytimes.com/2013/05/05/business/pro-business-decisions-are-defining-this-supreme-court.html.
77. Jason Silverstein. “New Brett Kavanaugh Sexual Misconduct Accusation Sets Off Calls for Supreme Court Impeachment.” *CBS News*. Sept. 16, 2019. Accessed July 2022. https://www.cbsnews.com/news/brett-kavanaugh-sexual-misconduct-accusation-sets-off-calls-for-supreme-court-impeachment/.
78. Dianne Feinstein et al. “Press Release: Judiciary Democrats to Trump: All Release of Kavanaugh Documents.” Senator Dianne Feinstein homepage. Sept. 4, 2018. Accessed July 2022. https://www.feinstein.senate.gov/public/index.cfm/press-releases?ID=A8ADE494-4F7C-427B-936D-20BC10E7A033. Also see Cheyenne Haslett. “Democrats Raise Alarm After 42,000 Kavanaugh Documents Released Last Night Before Hearing.” *ABC News*. Sept. 3, 2018. Accessed July 2022. https://abcnews.go.com/Politics/democrats-raise-alarm-white-house-decision-withhold-kavanaugh/story?id=57563344.
79. Stephanie Mencimer. “Amy Coney Barrett Is the Least Experienced Supreme Court Nominee in Thirty Years.” *Mother Jones*. Oct. 23, 2020. Accessed July 2022. https://www.motherjones.com/politics/2020/10/amy-coney-barrett-is-the-least-experienced-supreme-court-nominee-in-30-years/.
80. Ian Millhiser. “The Sinister History Underlying Neil Gorsuch’s Decision Lashing Out at American Workers.” *ThinkProgress*. May 23, 2018. Accessed July 2021. https://thinkprogress.org/neil-gorsuch-lashes-out-at-american-workers-cfaf9930ddf1/. Also see Charlie Savage. “E.P.A. Ruling Is Milestone in Long Pushback

to Regulation of Business." *New York Times*. June 30, 2022. Accessed July 2022. https://www.nytimes.com/2022/06/30/us/supreme-court-epa-administrative-state.html.

81. David Lawder and Lindsay Dunsmuir. "Trump Changes Tune on Tax Hikes for Wealthy Americans." *Reuters*. May 8, 2016. Accessed July 2022. https://www.reuters.com/article/us-usa-election-trump-idUSKCN0XZ0I3.
82. Allegra Kirkland. "Trump Ditches Press Pool to Eat Steak, Tell NYC Elite He'll Cut Their Taxes." *Talking Points Memo*. Nov. 16, 2016. Accessed July 2022. https://talkingpointsmemo.com/livewire/trump-ditches-press-pool-eat-steak-offer-tax-breaks.
83. Dylan Matthews. "The Republican Tax Bill Got Worse: Now the Top 1% Gets 83% of the Gains." *Vox*. Dec. 18, 2017. Accessed July 2022. https://www.vox.com/policy-and-politics/2017/12/18/16791174/republican-tax-bill-congress-conference-tax-policy-center.
84. Matthew Gardner and Steve Wamhoff. "Report: 55 Corporations Paid $0 in Federal Taxes on 2020 Profits." Institute on Taxation and Economic Policy." April 2, 2021. Accessed July 2022. https://itep.org/55-profitable-corporations-zero-corporate-tax/.
85. Alan Cobham, Javier Garcia-Bernardo, Miroslav Palansky, and Mark Bou Mansour. "The State of Tax Justice 2020: Tax Justice in the Time of COVID-19." Global Alliance for Tax Justice. Nov. 2020. Accessed July 2022. https://taxjustice.net/wp-content/uploads/2020/11/The_State_of_Tax_Justice_2020_ENGLISH.pdf.
86. "Key Statistics and Graphs." U.S. Department of Agriculture Economic Research Service. 2020. Accessed July 2022. https://www.ers.usda.gov/topics/food-nutrition-assistance/food-security-in-the-us/key-statistics-graphics.aspx#insecure.
87. Maggie Haberman and Alan Rappeport. "Trump Tries to Walk Back Entitlement Comments as Democrats Pounce." *New York Times*. Jan. 23, 2020. Accessed July 2022. https://www.nytimes.com/2020/01/23/us/politics/trump-social-security.html. Also see Adam Edelman. "Fact Check: Trump Vows to 'Protect' Medicare, Social Security. His Budgets Have Sought Cuts." *NBC News*. Nov. 3, 2020. Accessed July 2022. https://www.nbcnews.com/politics/2020-election/blog/2020-08-27-rnc-updates-n1238267/ncrd1238640#blogHeader.
88. Patricia Kime. "'Any Way You Cut It, This Is Going to Be Bad': VA Official Sounded Early COVID-19 Warning." *Military.com*. April 13, 2020. Accessed July 2022. https://www.military.com/daily-news/2020/04/13/any-way-you-cut-it-going-be-bad-va-official-sounded-early-covid-19-warning.html.
89. Oliver Milman. "Trump Administration Cut Pandemic Early Warning Program in September." *The Guardian*. April 3, 2020. Accessed July 2022. https://www.theguardian.com/world/2020/apr/03/trump-scrapped-pandemic-early-warning-program-system-before-coronavirus.
90. Lauren Egan. "Trump Calls Coronavirus Democrats' 'New Hoax.'" *NBC News*. Feb. 28, 2020. Accessed July 2022. https://www.nbcnews.com/politics/donald-trump/trump-calls-coronavirus-democrats-new-hoax-n1145721.
91. Mitch McConnell. "McConnell Discusses Supplemental Funding to Combat Coronavirus." Senator Mitch McConnell Senate homepage. Feb. 27, 2020. Accessed July 2022. https://www.republicanleader.senate.gov/newsroom/remarks/mcconnell-discusses-supplemental-funding-to-combat-coronavirus.
92. Gregg Gonsalves and Forrest Crawford. "How Mike Pence Made Indiana's HIV Outbreak Worse." *Politico*. March 2, 2020. Accessed July 2022. https://www.polit

ico.com/news/magazine/2020/03/02/how-mike-pence-made-indianas-hiv-outbreak-worse-118648.
93. "Tracking Coronavirus in New York: Latest Map and Case Count." *New York Times*. July 12, 2022. Accessed July 2022. https://www.nytimes.com/interactive/2021/us/new-york-covid-cases.html. For 2022 figures, see New York City Department of Health. "COVID-19 Trends and Totals: Long Term Trends: Cases, Hospitalizations, and Deaths." Accessed Feb. 1, 2022. https://www1.nyc.gov/site/doh/covid/covid-19-data-totals.page.
94. Deena Zaru. "New England Patriots Plane Transports 1.7 Million N95 Masks from China amid Coronavirus Pandemic." *ABC News*. April 2, 2020. Accessed July 2021. https://abcnews.go.com/Health/england-patriots-plane-transports-17-million-n95-masks/story?id=69935611.
95. Ben Gittleson. "After Kushner Says 'It's Our Stockpile,' HHS Website Changed to Echo His Comments on Federal Crisis Role." *ABC News*. April 3, 2020. Accessed July 2022. https://abcnews.go.com/Politics/kushner-stockpile-hhs-website-changed-echo-comments-federal/story?id=69936411.
96. Ryan Gabrielson et al. "A Closer Look at Federal COVID Contractors Reveals Inexperience, Fraud Accusations, and a Weapons Dealer Operating Out of Someone's House." *ProPublica*. May 27, 2020. Accessed July 2022. https://www.propublica.org/article/a-closer-look-at-federal-covid-contractors-reveals-inexperience-fraud-accusations-and-a-weapons-dealer-operating-out-of-someones-house.
97. Katherine Eban. "'That's Their Problem': How Jared Kushner Let the Markets Decide America's COVID-19 Fate." *Vanity Fair*. Sept. 17, 2020. Accessed July 2022. https://www.vanityfair.com/news/2020/09/jared-kushner-let-the-markets-decide-covid-19-fate.
98. "Hydroxychloroquine Does Not Benefit Adults Hospitalized with COVID-19." National Institutes of Health. Nov. 9, 2020. Accessed July 2022. https://www.nih.gov/news-events/news-releases/hydroxychloroquine-does-not-benefit-adults-hospitalized-covid-19.
99. "Video: What Do You Have to Lose? How Trump Has Promoted Malaria Drug." *New York Times*. April 22, 2020. Accessed July 2022. https://www.nytimes.com/video/us/politics/100000007101599/trump-coronavirus-hydroxychloroquine.html.
100. Matt Flegenheimer. "Trump's Disinfectant Remark Raises a Question About the 'Very Stable Genius.'" *New York Times*. April 26, 2020. Accessed July 2022. https://www.nytimes.com/2020/04/26/us/politics/trump-disinfectant-coronavirus.html.
101. "Coronavirus: Disinfectant Firm Warns After Trump Comments." *BBC News*. April 24, 2020. Accessed July 2022. https://www.bbc.com/news/world-us-canada-52411706.
102. Tim Mak. "Sen. Richard Burr's Pre-Pandemic Stock Sell-Offs Highly Unusual, Analysis Shows." *National Public Radio*. April 16, 2020. Accessed July 2022. https://www.npr.org/2020/04/16/836126532/senator-burrs-pre-pandemic-stock-sell-offs-highly-unusual-analysis-shows.
103. Allan Sloan. "The CARES Act Sent You a $1200 Check but Gave Millionaires and Billionaires Far More." *ProPublica*. June 8, 2020. Accessed July 2022. https://www.propublica.org/article/the-cares-act-sent-you-a-1-200-check-but-gave-millionaires-and-billionaires-far-more.

104. Carl Gibson. "Workers Are Getting the Short End of the Stick from the Cares Act." *Barron's*. April 15, 2020. Accessed July 2022. https://www.barrons.com/articles/cares-act-workers-companies-unfair-coronavirus-aid-51586983332.
105. Chris Strohm. "Barr Threatens Legal Action Against Governors over Lockdowns." *Bloomberg News*. April 21, 2020. Accessed July 2022. https://www.bloomberg.com/news/articles/2020-04-21/barr-says-doj-may-act-against-governors-with-strict-virus-limits.
106. Thomas L. Friedman. "A Plan to Get America Back to Work." *New York Times*. March 22, 2020. Accessed July 2022. https://www.nytimes.com/2020/03/22/opinion/coronavirus-economy.html.
107. Philip Bump. "Trump Is Right That with Lower Testing, We Record Fewer Cases. That's Already Happening." *Washington Post*. July 23, 2020. Accessed July 2021. https://www.washingtonpost.com/politics/2020/07/23/trumps-right-that-with-less-testing-we-record-fewer-cases-fact-thats-already-happening/.
108. Miles Parks. "Trump, While Attacking Mail Voting, Casts Mail Ballot Again." *National Public Radio*. Aug. 19, 2020. Accessed July 2022. https://www.npr.org/2020/08/19/903886567/trump-while-attacking-mail-voting-casts-mail-bal lot-again.
109. Chelsey Cox. "Fact Check: New Postmaster General Invested in Post Service Competitors." *USA Today*. Aug. 13, 2020. Accessed July 2022. https://www.usato day.com/story/news/factcheck/2020/08/13/fact-check-postmaster-general-louis-dejoy-invested-competitors/5550480002/.
110. Dan Alexander. "Trump's Businesses Hauled in $2.4 Billion During Four Years He Served as President." *Forbes Magazine*. July 19, 2021. Accessed July 2022. https://www.forbes.com/sites/danalexander/2021/07/19/trumps-business-hau led-in-24-billion-during-four-years-he-served-as-president/.
111. Tim Dickinson. "How Trump Took the Middle Class to the Cleaners." *Rolling Stone*. Oct. 26, 2020. Accessed July 2020. https://www.rollingstone.com/polit ics/politics-features/trump-covid-response-economy-jobs-taxes-inequality-1080 345/. Also see Betsy Klein. "Trump Spent 1 of Every 5 Days in 2019 at a Golf Club." *CNN*. Dec. 31, 2019. Accessed July 2020. https://www.cnn.com/2019/12/31/politics/trump-golfing-vacation/index.html.
112. Maegan Vazquez, Christopher Hickey, Priya Krishnakumar, and Janie Boschma. "Donald Trump's Presidency by the Numbers." *CNN*. Dec. 18, 2020. Accessed July 2022. https://www.cnn.com/2020/12/18/politics/trump-presidency-by-the-numbers/index.html.
113. Daniel Villarreal. "Hate Crimes Under Trump Surged Nearly 20 Percent Says FBI Report." *Newsweek*. Nov. 16, 2020. Accessed July 2022. https://www.newsweek.com/hate-crimes-under-trump-surged-nearly-20-percent-says-fbi-report-1547 870. Also see Stephanie Nebehay. "America's Poor Becoming More Destitute Under Trump: U.N. Expert." *Reuters*. June 2, 2018. Accessed July 2022. https://www.reuters.com/article/us-usa-rights-un/americas-poor-becoming-more-destit ute-under-trump-u-n-expert-idUSKCN1IY0C3; and Julia Ainsley. "Thousands More Migrant Kids Separated from Parents Under Trump Than Previously Reported." *NBC News*. Jan. 17, 2019. Accessed July 2022. https://www.nbcnews.com/politics/immigration/thousands-more-migrant-kids-separated-parents-under-trump-previously-reported-n959791.
114. John Haltiwanger and Aylin Woodward. "Damning Analysis of Trump's Pandemic Response Suggested 40% of US COVID-19 Deaths Could Have Been Avoided." *Business Insider*. Feb. 11, 2012. Accessed July 2022. https://www.busi

nessinsider.com/analysis-trump-covid-19-response-40-percent-us-deaths-avoidable-2021-2. Also see Alvin Powell. "What Might COVID Cost the U.S.? Try $16 Trillion." *Harvard Gazette*. Nov. 10, 2020. Accessed July 2022. https://news.harvard.edu/gazette/story/2020/11/what-might-covid-cost-the-u-s-experts-eye-16-trillion/.

115. Michael D. Shear and Stephanie Saul. "Trump, in Taped Call, Pressured Georgia Official to 'Find' Votes to Overturn Election." *New York Times*. Jan. 3, 2021. Accessed July 2022. https://www.nytimes.com/2021/01/03/us/politics/trump-raffensperger-call-georgia.html.
116. Linda So. "Trump-Inspired Death Threats Are Terrorizing Election Workers." *Reuters*. June 11, 2021. Accessed July 2022. https://www.reuters.com/investigates/special-report/usa-trump-georgia-threats/.
117. Alison Durkee. "Giuliani Claims His Call for 'Trial by Combat' on Jan. 6 Shouldn't Have Been Taken Literally as Legal Woes Mount." *Forbes*. May 18, 2021. Accessed July 2022. https://www.forbes.com/sites/alisondurkee/2021/05/18/giuliani-claims-his-call-for-trial-by-combat-on-jan-6-shouldnt-have-been-taken-literally-as-legal-woes-mount/. Also see Brian Naylor. "Read Trump's Jan. 6 Speech, a Key Part of Impeachment Trial." *National Public Radio*. Feb. 10, 2021. Accessed July 2022. https://www.npr.org/2021/02/10/966396848/read-trumps-jan-6-speech-a-key-part-of-impeachment-trial.
118. "More Than 1 in 3 Americans Believe a 'Deep State' Is Working to Undermine Trump." *IPSOS*. Dec. 30, 2020. Accessed July 2022. https://www.ipsos.com/en-us/news-polls/npr-misinformation-123020.
119. Mychael Schnell. "35 Percent of Voters in New Poll Say 2020 Election Should Be Overturned." *The Hill*. Oct. 27, 2021. Accessed July 2022. https://thehill.com/homenews/administration/578645-35-percent-of-voters-in-new-poll-say-2020-election-should-be.
120. Jonathan Weissman and Reid J. Epstein. "GOP Declares Jan. 6 Attack 'Legitimate Political Discourse.'" *New York Times*. Feb. 4, 2022. Accessed July 2022. https://www.nytimes.com/2022/02/04/us/politics/republicans-jan-6-cheney-censure.html.
121. Alleen Brown. "Bipartisan Infrastructure Bill Includes $25 Billion in Potential New Subsidies for Fossil Fuels." *The Intercept*. Aug. 3, 2021. Accessed July 2022. https://theintercept.com/2021/08/03/bipartisan-infrastructure-bill-climate-subsidies-fossil-fuel/.
122. Sara Sirota. "Josh Gottheimer's Obstructionist Crew Raised Millions During Showdown with Nancy Pelosi." *The Intercept*. Oct. 25, 2021. Accessed July 2022. https://theintercept.com/2021/10/25/josh-gottheimer-donors-build-back-better/.
123. Jamelle Bouie. "Joe Manchin Should Stop Talking About 'Entitlement'." *New York Times*. Oct. 8, 2021. Accessed June 2022. https://www.nytimes.com/2021/10/08/opinion/joe-manchin-biden.html.
124. Elizabeth Spiers. "No, Joe Manchin, Parents Won't Use Paid Leave to Go on 'Hunting Trips'." *Washington Post*. Dec. 21, 2021. Accessed June 2022. https://www.washingtonpost.com/outlook/2021/12/21/joe-manchin-hunting-trip/.
125. Jeanna Smialek. "A Regional Fed Analysis Suggests Biden's Stimulus Is Temporarily Stoking Inflation." *New York Times*. Oct. 18, 2021. Accessed July 2022. https://www.nytimes.com/2021/10/18/business/economy/fed-inflation-stimulus-biden.html. Also see Andrew Prokop. "Biden's American Rescue Plan Worsened Inflation. The Question is How Much?" *Vox*. May 12, 2022. Accessed

July 2022. https://www.vox.com/23036340/biden-american-rescue-plan-inflation; and James Surowiecki. "How Did They Get Inflation So Wrong?" *The Atlantic*. June 10, 2022. Accessed July 2022. https://www.theatlantic.com/ideas/archive/2022/06/what-is-causing-inflation-janet-yellen-jerome-powell/661237/.

126. Washington Post Live. "Transcript: The Path Forward: The U.S. Economy with Lawrence H. Summers." *Washington Post*. May 31, 2022. Accessed July 2022. https://www.washingtonpost.com/washington-post-live/2022/05/31/transcript-path-forward-us-economy-with-lawrence-h-summers/.
127. Marc A. Thiessen. "It's Almost As if Democrats Are Trying to Make Sure Trump Wins in 2024." *Washington Post*. June 14, 2022. Accessed July 2022. https://www.washingtonpost.com/opinions/2022/06/14/it-almost-if-democrats-are-trying-ensure-trump-wins-2024/. Also see Robert Kuttner. "Deflating Larry Summers." *American Prospect*. June 1, 2022. Accessed July 2022. https://prospect.org/blogs-and-newsletters/tap/deflating-larry-summers/.
128. U.S. Small Business Administration Inspector General. "Report: SBA's Handling of Potentially Fraudulent Paycheck Protection Program Loans." Report Number 22-13. May 26, 2022. Accessed July 2022. https://www.oversight.gov/sites/default/files/oig-reports/SBA/SBA-OIG-Report-22-13.pdf.
129. The Groundwork Collaborative. "Report: The Real Inflation Problem: Corporate Profiteering." March 2022. Accessed July 2022. https://groundworkcollaborative.org/wp-content/uploads/2022/03/Corporate-Profiteering-22.03.23-1.pdf.
130. Robert Kuttner. "Deflating Larry Summers." *American Prospect*. June 1, 2022. Accessed June 2022. https://prospect.org/blogs-and-newsletters/tap/deflating-larry-summers/. Also see Samir Sonti. "What You Need to Know About Inflation." *Jacobin*. June 6, 2022. Accessed July 2022. https://jacobin.com/2022/06/what-you-need-to-know-about-inflation.
131. Maxine Joselow and Alexandra Ellberbeck. "Biden Is Approving More Oil and Gas Drilling on Public Lands Than Trump, Analysis Finds." *Washington Post*. Dec. 6, 2021. Accessed July 2022. https://www.washingtonpost.com/politics/2021/12/06/biden-is-approving-more-oil-gas-drilling-permits-public-lands-than-trump-analysis-finds/.
132. Ben Ritz. "Congressional Democrats Just Offered Their Best Inflation Plan Yet." *Forbes*. June 8, 2022. Accessed July 2022. https://www.forbes.com/sites/benritz/2022/06/08/congressional-democrats-just-offered-their-best-inflation-plan-yet/.

CHAPTER 4

1. "Barack H. Obama: Facts." NobelPrize.org. Nobel Prize Outreach AB 2022. June 30, 2022. Accessed July 2022. https://www.nobelprize.org/prizes/peace/2009/obama/facts/.
2. Barack Obama. "Remarks by the President at the Acceptance of the Nobel Peace Prize." White House Office of the Press Secretary. Dec. 20, 2009. Accessed July 2021. https://www.nobelprize.org/prizes/peace/2009/obama/26183-nobel-lecture-2009/.
3. C. Wright Mills. *The Power Elite*. New York: Oxford University Press, 1956/2000, p. 184.
4. "America's Wars." Department of Veteran's Affairs. Accessed July 2022. https://www.va.gov/opa/publications/factsheets/fs_americas_wars.pdf.

5. Henry Giroux. “Neoliberal Fascism and the Echoes of History.” *Truthdig*. Aug. 2, 2018. Accessed July 2022. https://www.truthdig.com/articles/neoliberal-fascism-and-the-echoes-of-history/.
6. Mohammed Hussein and Mohammed Haddad. “Infographic: U.S. Military Presence Around the World.” *Al Jazeera*. Sept. 10, 2021. Accessed July 2022. https://www.aljazeera.com/news/2021/9/10/infographic-us-military-presence-around-the-world-interactive.
7. Mark Bowden. “American Special Ops Forces Are Everywhere.” *The Atlantic*. April 2021. Accessed July 2022. https://www.theatlantic.com/magazine/archive/2021/04/how-special-ops-became-the-solution-to-everything/618080/.
8. See Michael Hardt and Antonio Negri. *Empire*. Boston: Harvard University Press, 2001.
9. “A Conversion with General Martin Dempsey.” Carnegie Endowment for International Peace. May 1, 2012. Accessed July 2022. https://carnegieendowment.org/2012/05/01/conversation-with-general-martin-dempsey-event-3648.
10. George Washington. “George Washington, September 17, 1796, Farewell Address.” George Washington Papers, Series 2, Letterbooks 1754–1799: Letterbook 24. April 3, 1793–March 3, 1797. Accessed July 12, 2022. https://www.loc.gov/resource/mgw2.024/?sp=235&st=text.
11. See Chalmers Johnson. *The Sorrows of Empire: Militarism, Secrecy, and the End of the Republic*. New York: Henry Holt and Company, 2004, pp. 23–40, 58–62.
12. Louis Fisher. “Invoking Inherent Powers: A Primer.” *Presidential Studies Quarterly* 37 (1), Feb. 6, March 2007, pp. 1–22. .
13. “Members of the IC.” Office of the Director of National Intelligence. Accessed July 2022. https://www.dni.gov/index.php/what-we-do/members-of-the-ic.
14. Chandelis Duster. “Washington Post: Pentagon Used Funds for Coronavirus Response Supplies for Jet Engine Parts, Body Armor.” *CNN*. Sept. 22, 2020. Accessed July 2022. https://www.cnn.com/2020/09/22/politics/pentagon-coronavirus-relief-defense-contractors-washington-post/index.html.
15. “Sanders to Hold Budget Committee Hearing on Wasteful Pentagon Spending.” *Vermontbiz*. May 10, 2021. Accessed July 2022. https://vermontbiz.com/news/2021/may/10/sanders-hold-budget-committee-hearing-wasteful-pentagon-spending-0.
16. William J. Astore. “Our Enemy, Ourselves.” *Salon*. Feb. 9, 2018. Accessed July 2022. https://www.salon.com/2018/02/09/our-enemy-ourselves_partner/.
17. Theodore Draper. *A Very Thin Line: The Iran-Contra Affairs*. New York: Hill and Wang, 1991, pp. 4–6. Also see Chalmers Johnson. *The Sorrows of Empire: Militarism, Secrecy, and the End of the Republic*. New York: Henry Holt and Company, 2004, p. 56.
18. William Branigin. “Pahlavi Fortune: A Staggering Sum.” *Washington Post*. Jan. 17, 1979. Accessed July 2022. https://www.washingtonpost.com/archive/politics/1979/01/17/pahlavi-fortune-a-staggering-sum/ef54b268-15c5-4ee5-b0a1-194f90d87bba/.
19. Alexander Cockburn, James Ridgeway, and Jan Albert. “Beautiful Butchers: The Shah Serves Up Caviar and Torture.” *Village Voice*. Nov. 4, 1977. Accessed July 2022. https://www.villagevoice.com/2020/08/04/beautiful-butchers-the-shah-serves-up-caviar-and-torture/.
20. Greg Grandin. *Kissinger’s Shadow: The Long Reach of America’s Most Controversial Statesman*. New York: Metropolitan Books, 2015.

21. Greg Grandin. "Kissinger Poisoned the Middle East: America Is Living in a Quagmire of His Making." *Salon*. Sept. 30, 2015. Accessed July 2022. https://www.salon.com/2015/09/30/kissinger_poisoned_the_middle_east_america_is_living_in_a_quagmire_of_his_making_partner/.
22. "Henry Kissinger, Hillary Clinton's Tutor in War and Peace." *The Nation*. Feb. 5, 2016. Accessed July 2022. https://www.thenation.com/article/archive/henry-kissinger-hillary-clintons-tutor-in-war-and-peace/. Also see Floyd Abrams. "The Pentagon Papers a Decade Later." *New York Times*. June 7, 1981. Accessed July 2022. https://www.nytimes.com/1981/06/07/magazine/the-pentagon-papers-a-decade-later.html.
23. "Henry Kissinger: Good or Evil?" *Politico*. Oct. 10, 2015. Accessed July 2022 https://www.politico.com/magazine/story/2015/10/henry-kissinger-history-legacy-213237.
24. Karen Coates and Jerry Redfern. "Henry Kissinger Is Not Telling the Truth About His Past Again." *Washington Post*. Sept. 18, 2014. Accessed July 2022. https://www.washingtonpost.com/posteverything/wp/2014/09/18/henry-kissinger-is-not-telling-the-truth-about-his-past-again/.
25. "Henry Kissinger: Good or Evil?" *Politico*. Oct. 10, 2015. Accessed July 2022. https://www.politico.com/magazine/story/2015/10/henry-kissinger-history-legacy-213237 Also see Gary Bass. "Looking Away from Genocide." *New Yorker*. Nov. 19, 2013. Accessed July 2022. https://www.newyorker.com/news/news-desk/looking-away-from-genocide.
26. Ben Kiernan. "War, Genocide, and Resistance in East Timor, 1975–99: Comparative Reflections on Cambodia." In *War and State Terrorism: The United States, Japan, and the Asia Pacific in the Long Twentieth Century*, ed. Mark Selden and Alvin Y. So. Lanham, MD: Rowman and Littlefield, 2003, p. 200.
27. John Pilger. "'Saving' East Timor: How One of the 20th Century's Worst Mass Murders Was Covered Up." *Truthout*. March 4, 2016. Accessed July 2022. https://truthout.org/articles/saving-east-timor-how-one-of-the-20th-century-s-worst-mass-murders-was-covered-up/.
28. Gary G. Kohls. "War Crimes: Agent Orange, Monsanto, Dow Chemical, and Other Ugly Legacies of the Vietnam War." Centre for Research on Globalization. Nov. 13, 2005. Accessed July 2022. https://www.globalresearch.ca/war-crimes-agent-orange-monsanto-dow-chemical-and-other-ugly-legacies-of-the-vietnam-war/5488004.
29. The 40 Committee was a semi-clandestine oversight body in Nixon's executive branch that Kissinger chaired in the 1970s. See David Wise. "The Secret Committee Called '40.'" *New York Times*. Jan. 19, 1975. Accessed July 2022. https://www.nytimes.com/1975/01/19/archives/the-secret-committee-called-40-at-least-in-theory-it-controls-the.html.
30. Henry Kissinger, quoted in Lars Schoultz. *Beneath the United States: A History of U.S. Policy Toward Latin America*. Cambridge, MA: Harvard University Press, p. 349. Kissinger's comment was made during a 40 Committee meeting on June 27, 1970.
31. Louis Fisher. "Invoking Inherent Powers: A Primer." *Presidential Studies Quarterly* 37 (1), March 2007, pp. 1–22. . Also see Louis Fisher. *Presidential War Power*, 2nd ed. Lawrence: University Press of Kansas, 2013, pp. 99–100.
32. "U.S. Senate Blames Saudi Prince Salman for Khashoggi's Death and Votes to Stop Military Aid in Yemen." *MercoPress*. Dec. 14, 2018. Accessed July 2022.

https://en.mercopress.com/2018/12/14/us-senate-blames-saudi-prince-salman-for-khashoggi-s-death-and-votes-to-stop-military-aid-in-yemen.
33. Norman A. Graebner, Richard Dean Burns, and Joseph M. Siracusa. *Reagan, Bush, Gorbachev: Revisiting the End of the Cold War*. Westport, VT: ABC-CLIO, 2008, p. 78.
34. "National Security Strategy for a New Century [December 1999]." Homeland Security Digital Library. Center for Homeland Defense and Security. December 1999. Accessed July 2022. https://www.hsdl.org/?abstract&did=487539.
35. Harvey M. Sapolsky, Eugene Gholz, and Caitlin Talmadge. *U.S. Defense Politics: The Origins of Security Policy,* 3rd ed. New York: Routledge, 2017.
36. Robert M. Gates. *Exercise of Power: American Failures, Successes, and a New Path Forward in a Post-Cold War World*. New York: Knopf, 2020, pp. 132–35.
37. Hugh Gusterson. *Drone: Remote Control Warfare*. Boston: MIT Press, 2016.
38. "Press Release: ACLU Says Military in Kosovo Violates Constitution and War Powers Act." American Civil Liberties Union (ACLU). April 28, 1999. Accessed July 2022. https://www.aclu.org/press-releases/aclu-says-military-action-kosovo-violates-constitution-and-war-powers-act.
39. Martin Walker. "U.S. Troops in Somalia Will Do God's Work, Says Bush." *The Guardian*. Dec. 5, 1992. Accessed July 2022. https://www.theguardian.com/theguardian/2012/dec/05/somalia-george-bush-senior-mogadishu-1992.
40. Julia Preston. "U.N. Establishes Force for Somalia." *New York Times*. March 27, 1993. Accessed July 2022. https://www.washingtonpost.com/archive/politics/1993/03/27/un-establishes-force-for-somalia/3b67b84c-5b3d-4042-8599-bf1af97e5388/.
41. George Monbiot. "Both Saviour and Victim: Black Hawk Down Creates a New and Dangerous Myth of American Nationhood." *The Guardian*. Jan. 28, 2002. Accessed July 2022. https://www.theguardian.com/film/2002/jan/29/2002inreview.features.
42. Raf Casert. "In Italy, Belgium and Italy [*sic*], Somalia Peacekeeping Scandals Growing." *Associated Press*. June 23, 1997. Accessed July 2022. https://apnews.com/article/deea729ccf6dfe142799ed245261b675.
43. Aiden Hartley. "Why Somalia Matters." *Vanity Fair*. Dec. 12, 2008. Accessed July 2022. https://www.vanityfair.com/magazine/2008/12/somalia200812.
44. "Somalia: The New Oil and Gas Frontier." *The Africa Report*. Nov. 9, 2020. Accessed July 2022. https://www.theafricareport.com/49364/somalia-the-new-oil-and-gas-frontier/. Also see Reuters Staff. "Somalia Says Shell, Exxon Agree to Pay $1.7 Million for Oil Blocks Lease." *Reuters*. Oct. 28, 2019. Accessed July 2022. https://www.reuters.com/article/us-somalia-oil/somalia-says-shell-exxon-agree-to-pay-1-7-million-for-oil-blocks-lease-idUSKBN1X70V9.
45. Nathan J. Robinson. "Bill Clinton's Act of Terrorism." *Jacobin*. Oct. 12, 2016. Accessed July 2022. http://www.jacobinmag.com/2016/10/bill-clinton-al-shifa-sudan-bombing-khartoum.
46. Louis Fisher. "Invoking Inherent Powers: A Primer." *Presidential Studies Quarterly* 37 (1), Feb. 6, 2007, pp. 1–22.
47. Memorandum from John C. Yoo, Deputy Assistant Attorney Gen., U.S. Department of Justice, to the Deputy Counsel to the President. "The President's Constitutional Authority to Conduct Military Operations Against Terrorists and Nations Supporting Them." Sept. 25, 2001. Accessed July 2022. https://fas.org/irp/agency/doj/olc092501.html.

48. Dana Priest and William M. Arkin. "Top Secret America: A Hidden World, Growing Beyond Control." *Washington Post*. July 19, 2010. Accessed July 2022. http://projects.washingtonpost.com/top-secret-america/articles/a-hidden-world-growing-beyond-control/.
49. 107th Congress Public Law 40. "Joint Resolution to Authorize the Use of United States Armed Forces Against Those Responsible for the Recent Attacks Launched Against the United States." SS.J. Res. 23. Sept. 18, 2001. Accessed July 2022. http://www.gpo.gov/fdsys/pkg/PLAW-107publ40/html/PLAW-107publ40.htm.
50. David D. Kirkpatrick. "Response to 9/11 Offers Outline of McCain Doctrine." *New York Times*. Aug. 16, 2008. Accessed July 2022. https://www.nytimes.com/2008/08/17/us/politics/17mccain.html. McCain quoted in Elisabeth Bumiller. "The Struggle for Iraq: The President; Bush and McCain, Together, Call Iraq War a Conflict Between Good and Evil." *New York Times*. June 19, 2004. Accessed July 2022. https://www.nytimes.com/2004/06/19/world/struggle-for-iraq-president-bush-mccain-together-call-iraq-war-conflict-between.html.
51. Edwin Mora. "Taliban Extorting 'Protection Payments' from Taxpayer-Funded Private Security Contract." *CNS News*. June 24, 2010. Accessed July 2022. https://www.cnsnews.com/news/article/taliban-extorting-protection-payments-taxpayer-funded-private-security-contract.
52. Christina Wilkie. "'9/11 Millionaires' and Mass Corruption: How American Money Helped Break Afghanistan." *CNBC*. Sept. 10, 2021. Accessed July 2022. https://www.cnbc.com/2021/09/10/9/11-millionaires-and-corruption-how-us-money-helped-break-afghanistan.html.
53. James Risen. "Investigation into Missing Iraqi Cash Ended in Lebanon Bunker." *New York Times*. Oct. 12, 2014. Accessed July 2022. https://www.nytimes.com/2014/10/12/world/investigation-into-missing-iraqi-cash-ended-in-lebanon-bunker.html.
54. Laura Strickler. "$1B in Military Equipment Missing in Iraq." *CBS News*. Dec. 6, 2007. Accessed July 2022. https://www.cbsnews.com/news/1b-in-military-equipment-missing-in-iraq/.
55. Moshe Schwartz and Jennifer Church. "Department of Defense's Use of Contractors to Support Military Operations: Background, Analysis, and Issues for Congress." Congressional Research Service Report. May 17, 2013. Accessed July 2022. https://fas.org/sgp/crs/natsec/R43074.pdf. Also see Spencer Ackerman. "Over $8Bn of the Money You Spent Rebuilding Iraq Was Wasted Outright." *Wired Magazine*. March 6, 2013. Accessed July 2022. https://www.wired.com/2013/03/iraq-waste/.
56. Michael Isikoff and David Corn. *Hubris: The Inside Story of Spin, Scandal and the Selling of the Iraq War.* New York: Crown Publishers, 2006, pp. 119–23.
57. Jeremy Scahill. *Dirty Wars: The World Is a Battlefield*. New York: Nation Books, 2013, pp. 87–89. Also see Carl Hulse. "Pelosi Said She Knew of Waterboarding by 2003." *New York Times*. May 14, 2009. Accessed July 2022. https://www.nytimes.com/2009/05/15/us/politics/15cong.html.
58. Hannah Arendt. *Eichmann in Jerusalem: A Report on the Banality of Evil.* New York: Penguin Classics, 2006.
59. Rosa Brooks. *How Everything Became War and the Military Became Everything: Tales from the Pentagon*. New York: Simon and Schuster, 2017, pp. 52–54, 60.

60. Carol Rosenberg. "What the C.I.A.'s Torture Program Looked Like to the Tortured." *New York Times*. Dec. 4, 2019. Accessed July 2022. https://www.nytimes.com/2019/12/04/us/politics/cia-torture-drawings.html.
61. Jason Leopold. "Senate Intelligence Committee Takes Up 'the Pentagon Papers of the CIA Torture Program' Behind Closed Doors: Report Remains Under Wraps." *Truthout*. Dec. 13, 2012. Accessed July 2022. http://truth-out.org/news/item/13333-senate-intelligence-committee-takes-up-pentagon-papers-of-cia-torture-program-behind-closed-doors-report-remains-under-wraps. Also see Jason Leopold. "Government Recants Major Terror Claims Against High-Value Detainee Abu Zubaydah." *Truthout*. March 30, 2010. Accessed July 2022. https://truthout.org/articles/government-recants-major-terror-claims-against-highvalue-detainee-abu-zubaydah/.
62. Memorandum for John Rizzo, Acting General Counsel of the Central Intelligence Agency. "Interrogation of al Qaeda Operative." U.S. Department of Justice. Office of Legal Counsel. Aug. 1, 2002. Accessed July 2022. https://www.justice.gov/sites/default/files/olc/legacy/2010/08/05/memo-bybee2002.pdf. Also see James Risen. "American Psychological Association Bolstered C.I.A. Torture Program, Report Says." *New York Times*. April 30, 2015. Accessed July 2022. https://www.nytimes.com/2015/05/01/us/report-says-american-psychological-association-collaborated-on-torture-justification.html.
63. Rebecca Gordon. "The CIA Waterboarded the Wrong Man 83 Times in 1 Month." *The Nation*. April 25, 2016. Accessed July 2022. https://www.thenation.com/article/archive/the-cia-waterboarded-the-wrong-man-83-times-in-1-month/. Also see Charles L. Church. "What Politics and the Media Still Get Wrong about Abu Zubaydah." *Lawfare*. Aug. 1, 2018. Accessed July 2022. https://www.lawfareblog.com/what-politics-and-media-still-get-wrong-about-abu-zubaydah.
64. Raymond A. Schroth, SJ. "Facing Up to Torture: Uncovering a Shameful, Secret History." *America Magazine*. Nov. 11, 2013. Accessed July 2022. https://www.americamagazine.org/issue/facing-torture.
65. Physicians for Human Rights. "Broken Laws, Broken Lives: Medical Evidence of Torture by U.S. Personnel and Its Impact." June 2008. Accessed July 2022. https://phr.org/wp-content/uploads/2008/06/BrokenLaws_ExecSummary14.pdf.
66. Jean Edward Smith. *Bush*. New York: Simon and Schuster, 2016, p. 458.
67. [Author name redacted]. "Presidential Signing Statements: Constitutional and Institutional Implications." Congressional Research Service. Jan. 4, 2012. Accessed July 2022. https://www.everycrsreport.com/files/20120104_RL33667_8e67dd21b7737fb5a72093f92955fd92ad2bb91b.pdf. Also see Charlie Savage. "Specter Takes Steps to Halt Bush Signing Statements." *Boston Globe*. July 26, 2006. Accessed July 2022. http://archive.boston.com/news/nation/washington/articles/2006/07/27/specter_takes_step_to_halt_bush_signing_statements/.
68. The Senate Select Committee on Intelligence decided to initiate the study in March 2009, based on the desire to investigate the CIA's destruction of some ninety videotapes of its interrogations of Al-Qaeda suspects Abu Zubaydah and Abd al-Rahim al-Nashiri in 2002 at a black site in Thailand. The Department of Justice special prosecutor, John Durham, who conducted a criminal investigation in 2010, decided not to file criminal charges. See U.S. Senate Select Committee on Intelligence. "Committee Study of the Central Intelligence Agency's Detention and Interrogation Program." Dec. 9, 2014. Accessed July 2022. https://www.intelligence.senate.gov/sites/default/files/publications/

CRPT-113srpt288.pdf. Also see Mark Mazzetti and Charlie Savage. "No Criminal Charges Sought over CIA Tapes." *New York Times*. Nov. 9, 2010. Accessed July 2022. http://www.nytimes.com/2010/11/10/world/10tapes.html?_r=0.

69. Ali Watkins. "New Sparks Fly Between CIA, Senate Intelligence Committee." *McClatchy News*. Sept. 12, 2014. Accessed July 2022. https://www.mcclatchydc.com/news/nation-world/national/national-security/article24773098.html.
70. Medea Benjamin and Marcy Winograd. "Biden's Pick for Intelligence Chief, Avril Haines, Is Tainted by Drones and Torture." *Salon*. Dec. 30, 2020. Accessed July 2022. https://www.salon.com/2020/12/30/bidens-pick-for-intelligence-chief-avril-haines-is-tainted-by-drones-and-torture/.
71. Amy Davidson Sorkin. "The Torture Report: Inhumane Scenes from the CIA Prisons." *New Yorker*. Dec. 9, 2014. Accessed July 2022. http://www.newyorker.com/news/amy-davidson/inhumane-scenes-cia-prisons.
72. The Open Society's "Globalizing Torture" Report suggests that fifty-four countries were implicated in CIA dark sites and rendition centers in varying degrees. See Open Society Justice Initiative. "Globalizing Torture: CIA Secret Detention and Extraordinary Rendition." Open Society Foundations. 2013. Accessed July 2022. http://www.opensocietyfoundati.ns.org/sites/default/files/globalizing-torture-20120205.pdf.
73. Jeremy Scahill. *Dirty Wars: The World Is a Battlefield*. New York: Nation Books, 2013, p. 245.
74. David Corn. "Obama and GOPers Worked Together to Kill Bush Torture Probe." *Mother Jones*. Dec. 1, 2010. Accessed July 2022. https://www.motherjones.com/politics/2010/12/wikileaks-cable-obama-quashed-torture-investigation/. Also see Glenn Greenwald. "Obama's Justice Department Grants Final Immunity to Bush's CIA Torturers." *The Guardian*. Aug. 31, 2012. Accessed July 2022. https://www.theguardian.com/commentisfree/2012/aug/31/obama-justice-department-immunity-bush-cia-torturer.
75. Barack Obama. "Statement by the President: Report of the Senate Select Committee on Intelligence." White House Office of the Press Secretary. Dec. 9, 2014. Accessed July 2022. http://www.whitehouse.gov/the-press-office/2014/12/09/statement-president-report-senate-select-committee-intelligence.
76. Satyam Khanna. "Holder Breaks with Mukasey, Says 'Waterboarding Is Torture.'" *ThinkProgress*. Jan. 15, 2009. Accessed July 2022. https://thinkprogress.org/holder-breaks-with-mukasey-says-waterboarding-is-torture-4385fd222ab6/. Also see Brett Lang. "Torture Memos Released." *CBS News*. April 16, 2009. Accessed July 2022. https://www.cbsnews.com/news/torture-memos-released/.
77. "Press Release: Department of Justice Releases Four Office of Legal Counsel Opinions." U.S. Department of Justice Office of Public Affairs. April 16, 2009. Accessed July 2022. https://www.justice.gov/opa/pr/department-justice-releases-four-office-legal-counsel-opinions.
78. Chris Strohm. "Justice to Drop Investigations into CIA Officials Involved in Torture." *Government Executive*. June 30, 2011. Accessed July 2022, https://www.govexec.com/defense/2011/06/justice-to-drop-investigations-into-cia-officials-involved-in-torture/34275/.
79. Carol Rosenberg. "The Cost of Running Guantánamo Bay: $13 Million per Prisoner." *New York Times*. Sept. 16, 2019. Accessed July 2022. https://www.nytimes.com/2019/09/16/us/politics/guantanamo-bay-cost-prison.html.
80. Gregory B. Craig and Cliff Sloan. "The President Doesn't Need Congress's Permission to Close Guantánamo." *Washington Post*. Nov. 6, 2015. Accessed July

2022. https://www.washingtonpost.com/opinions/the-president-doesnt-need-congresss-permission-to-close-guantanamo/2015/11/06/4cc9d2ac-83f5-11e5-a7ca-6ab6ec20f839_story.html.

81. "15 Guantánamo Detainees Sent to UAE in Major Transfer." *NBC News*. Aug. 16, 2016. Accessed July 2022. https://www.nbcwashington.com/local/dc-wtop-15-guantanamo-detainees-sent-to-uae-in-major-transfer/58380/.
82. Barack Obama. Transcript: Obama's Speech Against the Iraq War. *National Public Radio*. Jan. 20, 2009. Accessed July 2022. https://www.npr.org/templates/story/story.php?storyId=99591469.
83. Leonard Downie Jr., with reporting by Sarah Rafksy. "The Obama Administration and the Press: Leak Investigations and Surveillance in Post-9/11 America." Special Report of the Committee to Protect Journalists. Oct. 10, 2013. Accessed July 2022. https://cpj.org/reports/2013/10/obama-and-the-press-us-leaks-surveillance-post-911/.
84. Marcus Weisgerber and Caroline Houck. "Obama's Final Arms-Export Tally More Than Doubles Bush's." *Defense One*. Nov. 8. 2016. Accessed July 2022. https://www.defenseone.com/business/2016/11/obamas-final-arms-export-tally-more-doubles-bushs/133014/.
85. M. Mursal and Zahra Nader. "'I've Already Sold My Daughters; Now My Kidney': Winter in Afghanistan's Slums." *The Guardian*. Jan. 23, 2022. Accessed January 2022. https://www.theguardian.com/global-development/2022/jan/23/ive-already-sold-my-daughters-now-my-kidney-winter-in-afghanistans-slums.
86. Dana Priest and William M. Arkin. "'Top Secret America': A Look at the Military's Joint Special Operations Command." *Washington Post*. Sept. 2, 2011. Accessed July 2022. http://www.washingtonpost.com/world/national-security/top-secret-america-a-look-at-the-militarys-joint-special-operations-command/2011/08/30/gIQAvYuAxJ_story.html.
87. Jo Becker and Scott Shane. "Secret 'Kill List' Proves a Test of Obama's Principles and Will." *New York Times*. May 29, 2012. Accessed July 2022. https://www.nytimes.com/2012/05/29/world/obamas-leadership-in-war-on-al-qaeda.html?pagewanted=all.
88. Jo Becker and Scott Shane. "Secret 'Kill List' Proves a Test of Obama's Principles and Will." *New York Times*. May 29, 2012. Accessed July 2022. https://www.nytimes.com/2012/05/29/world/obamas-leadership-in-war-on-al-qaeda.html.
89. Alice Ross, Chris Woods, and Sarah Leo. "The Reaper Presidency: Obama's 300th Drone Strike in Pakistan." Bureau of Investigative Journalism. Dec. 3, 2012. Accessed July 2022. https://www.thebureauinvestigates.com/stories/2012-12-03/the-reaper-presidency-obamas-300th-drone-strike-in-pakistan.
90. Rosa Brooks. *How Everything Became War and the Military Became Everything: Tales from the Pentagon*. New York: Simon and Schuster, 2017, p. 107.
91. Scott Shane. "C.I.A. Is Disputed on Civilian Toll in Drone Strikes." *New York Times*. Aug. 11, 2011. Accessed July 2022. https://www.nytimes.com/2011/08/12/world/asia/12drones.html.
92. Spencer Ackerman. "U.S. Drone Strikes More Deadly to Afghan Civilians Than Manned Aircraft—Adviser." *The Guardian*. July 2, 2013. Accessed July 2022. https://www.theguardian.com/world/2013/jul/02/us-drone-strikes-afghan-civilians.
93. Christopher J. Coyne and Abigail R. Hall. *Tyranny Comes Home: The Domestic Fate of U.S. Militarism*. Palo Alto, CA: Stanford University Press, 2018, p. 133.

94. Eyder Peralta. “Attorney General Holder Defends Targeted Killings of Americans.” *National Public Radio*. March 5, 2012. Accessed July 2022. https://www.npr.org/sections/thetwo-way/2012/03/05/147992097/attorney-general-holder-defends-targeted-killings-of-americans.
95. Adam Serwer. “Colbert on Targeted Killing: ‘Due Process Just Means There’s a Process That You Do.’” *Mother Jones*. March 7, 2012. Accessed July 2022. https://www.motherjones.com/politics/2012/03/colbert-targeted-killing-due-process-just-means-theres-process-you-do/.
96. Tom Junod. “Obama’s Administration Killed a 16-Year-Old American and Didn’t Say Anything About It. This Is Justice?” *Esquire Magazine*. July 9, 2012. Accessed July 2022. https://www.esquire.com/news-politics/news/a14796/abdulrahman-al-awlaki-death-10470891/.
97. Jeremy Scahill. “Inside America’s Dirty Wars.” *The Nation*, April 24, 2013. Accessed July 2022. https://www.thenation.com/article/archive/inside-americas-dirty-wars/.
98. Cynthia McFadden, William M. Arkin, and Tim Uehlinger. “How the Trump Team’s First Military Raid in Yemen Went Wrong.” *NBC News*. Oct. 2, 2017. Accessed July 2022. https://www.nbcnews.com/news/us-news/how-trump-team-s-first-military-raid-went-wrong-n806246. Also see Bing Xiao. “Father of Fallen SEAL Condemns President Trump in Political Ad.” *Military.com*. Aug. 29, 2020. Accessed July 2022. https://www.military.com/daily-news/2020/08/29/father-of-fallen-seal-condemns-president-trump-political-ad.html.
99. Glenn Greenwald. “Obama Killed a 16-Year-Old American in Yemen. Trump Just Killed his 8-Year-Old Sister.” *The Intercept*. Jan. 30, 2017. Accessed July 2022. https://theintercept.com/2017/01/30/obama-killed-a-16-year-old-american-in-yemen-trump-just-killed-his-8-year-old-sister/. Also see Spencer Ackerman, Jason Burke, and Julian Borger. “Eight-Year-Old American Girl ‘Killed in Yemen Raid Approved by Trump.’” *The Guardian*. Feb. 1, 2017. Accessed July 2022. https://www.theguardian.com/world/2017/feb/01/yemen-strike-eight-year-old-american-girl-killed-al-awlaki.
100. “U.S. Soldiers Shoot and Kill 8-Year-Old Girl in Yemen.” *MEMO: Middle East Monitor*. Jan. 30, 2017. Accessed July 2022. https://www.middleeastmonitor.com/20170130-us-soldiers-shoot-and-kill-8-year-old-girl-in-yemen/.
101. Peter Baker and Zach Montague. “Trump Speaks at West Point Graduation amid Tensions with Military Leaders.” *New York Times*. Dec. 23, 2020. Accessed July 2022. https://www.nytimes.com/2020/06/13/us/politics/trump-west-point-graduation.html.
102. Associated Press. “Sent from Gitmo to UAE, Detainees Fear Final Stop: Yemen.” *U.S. News*. Oct. 22, 2020. Accessed July 2022. https://www.usnews.com/news/politics/articles/2020-10-22/sent-from-gitmo-to-uae-detainees-fear-final-stop-yemen. Also see Clyde Haberman. “No, Mr. Trump, Torture Doesn’t Work.” *New York Times*. Dec. 13, 2017. Accessed July 2022. https://www.nytimes.com/2017/12/13/opinion/trump-torture-guantanamo.html.
103. Richard Luscombe. “Navy Seal Pardoned of War Crimes by Trump Described by Colleagues as ‘Freaking Evil.’” *The Guardian*. Dec. 27, 2019. Accessed July 2022. https://www.theguardian.com/us-news/2019/dec/27/eddie-gallagher-trump-navy-seal-iraq.
104. Associated Press. “Trump: Pentagon Leaders Want War to Keep Contractors ‘Happy.’” *ABC News*. Sept. 8, 2020. Accessed July 2022. https://abcnews.go.com/Politics/wireStory/trump-pentagon-leaders-war-contractors-happy-72870085.

105. Merrit Kennedy. "Trump Created the Space Force. Here's What It Will Actually Do." *National Public Radio*. Dec. 21, 2019. Accessed July 2022. https://www.npr.org/2019/12/21/790492010/trump-created-the-space-force-heres-what-it-will-do.
106. Henry Olsen. "Opinion: Why the Reported Israeli-Saudi Meeting Is Such a Big Deal." *Washington Post*. Nov. 23, 2020. Accessed July 2022. https://www.washingtonpost.com/opinions/2020/11/23/why-reported-israeli-saudi-meeting-is-such-big-deal/.
107. "Israel Names Golan Heights Town 'Trump Heights' in Honor of U.S. President." *CBS News*. June 16, 2019. Accessed July 2022. https://www.cbsnews.com/news/israel-golan-heights-renames-town-trump-heights-in-honor-of-donald-trump-today-2019-06-16/.
108. Alexia Underwood. "The Controversial U.S. Jerusalem Embassy Opening, Explained." *Vox*. May 16, 2018. Accessed July 2022. https://www.vox.com/2018/5/14/17340798/jerusalem-embassy-israel-palestinians-us-trump.
109. Justine Coleman. "Kushner Says Palestinians Will 'Screw Up' if They Reject Peace Deal." *The Hill*. Jan. 28, 2020. Accessed July 2022. https://thehill.com/policy/international/middle-east-north-africa/480358-jared-kushner-palestinians-have-blown-every.
110. Alexandra Petri. "I Have Just Read 25 Books and Am Here to Perform Your Open-Heart Surgery." *Washington Post*. Jan. 29, 2020. Accessed June 2022. https://www.washingtonpost.com/opinions/2020/01/29/i-have-just-read-25-books-am-here-perform-your-open-heart-surgery/.
111. Bess Levin. "Jared Kushner: Palestinians Have Never Done Anything Right in Their Sad, Pathetic Lives." *Vanity Fair*. Jan. 29 2020. Accessed July 2022. https://www.vanityfair.com/news/2020/01/jared-kushner-peace-plan-palestinians. Also see Ibrahim Fraihat. "The 'Deal of the Century' as a Deliberate Deception." *Al Jazeera*. June 29, 2019. Accessed July 2022. https://www.aljazeera.com/opinions/2019/6/29/the-deal-of-the-century-as-a-deliberate-deception.
112. Bess Levin. "In Charm Offensive, Kushner Calls Palestinians 'Hysterical and Stupid.'" *Vanity Fair*. July 3, 2019. Accessed July 2022. https://www.vanityfair.com/news/2019/07/jared-kushner-hysterical-and-stupid.
113. Reuters. "Trump Administration Approves Secret Nuclear Power Work for Saudi Arabia." *CNBC*. March 28, 2019. Accessed July 2022. https://www.cnbc.com/2019/03/27/us-approved-secret-nuclear-power-work-for-saudi-arabia-reuters.html.
114. Catherine Russell. "Remarks by UNICEF Executive Director Catherine Russell at the High-Level Pledging Event on the Humanitarian Crisis in Yemen." UNICEF. March 16, 2022. Accessed July 2022. https://www.unicef.org/press-releases/remarks-unicef-executive-director-catherine-russell-high-level-pledging-event. Also see Tara Golshan. "Bernie Sanders's Political Revolution on Foreign Policy, Explained." *Vox*. May 8, 2019. Accessed July 2022. https://www.vox.com/2019/5/8/18525486/bernie-sanders-foreign-policy-2020-yemen-war-powers; and Alex Ward. "The Pentagon Won't Check if US Bombs Killed Kids in Yemen. CNN Did It for Them." *Vox*. Aug. 20, 2018. Accessed July 2022. https://www.vox.com/2018/8/20/17760322/yemen-children-bomb-bus-pentagon.
115. Clarence Page. "Did Loyalty Finally Trip Up Colin Powell?" *Chicago Tribune*. April 21, 2004. Accessed July 2022. https://www.chicagotribune.com/news/ct-xpm-2004-04-21-0404210129-story.html. Also see Bootie Cosgrove-Mather. "The

Most Trusted Man in America." *CBS News*. Feb. 4, 2003. Accessed July 2022. http://www.cbsnews.com/news/the-most-trusted-man-in-america/.

116. Richard Cohen. "A Willing Hand for Powell." *Washington Post*. Feb. 6, 2003. Accessed July 2022. https://www.washingtonpost.com/archive/opinions/2003/02/06/a-winning-hand-for-powell/aa1e6dd9-dbf9-4b71-bb86-9c42a4a5a427/. Also see The Editors. "The Case Against Iraq." *New York Times*. Feb. 6, 2003. Accessed July 2021. http://www.nytimes.com/2003/02/06/opinion/the-case-against-iraq.html.
117. See *Newsweek* cover: "Can This Man Save Iraq?" July 5, 2004.
118. Joe Klein. "Person of the Year. Runners Up: David Petraeus." *Time Magazine*. Dec. 19, 2007. Accessed July 2022. http://content.time.com/time/specials/2007/personoftheyear/article/0,28804,1690753_1695388_1695379,00.html.
119. Michael Hastings. "The Runaway General: The Profile that Brought Down McChrystal." *Rolling Stone*. June 22, 2010. Accessed July 2022. https://www.rollingstone.com/politics/politics-news/the-runaway-general-the-profile-that-brought-down-mcchrystal-192609/.
120. Mark Mazzetti and David D. Kirkpatrick. "Retired General Investigated over Undisclosed Lobbying for Qatar." *New York Times*. June 7, 2022. Accessed July 2022. https://www.nytimes.com/2022/06/07/us/politics/general-john-allen-lobbying-qatar.html.
121. Petraeus's appointment at the City University of New York caused a scandal of its own. Faculty and students criticized the general and the university for his $200,000-plus salary offer, which was well above that of the average faculty member and far above that of part-time, contingent faculty members. Petraeus tried to placate his critics by reducing his pay to $1 per year, but they still protested him as a war criminal.
122. Bryan Bender. "From the Pentagon to the Private Sector." *Boston Globe*. Dec. 26, 2010. Accessed July 2022. http://archive.boston.com/news/nation/articles/2010/12/26/defense_firms_lure_retired_generals/.
123. Ryan Summers. "The Pentagon's Revolving Door Keeps Spinning." Project on Government Oversight. Jan. 20, 2022. Accessed July 2022. https://www.pogo.org/analysis/2022/01/the-pentagons-revolving-door-keeps-spinning-2021-in-review/. Also see Austin Wright. "DoD's Revolving Door in Full Swing." *Politico*. Oct. 24, 2013. Accessed July 2022. https://www.politico.com/story/2013/10/department-of-defenses-revolving-door-in-full-swing-098813.
124. Derrick Chollet. "An Inside Look at Trump's Foreign Policy: 'This Is Literally Insane.'" *Washington Post*. Dec. 10, 2019. Accessed July 2022. https://www.washingtonpost.com/outlook/an-inside-look-at-trumps-foreign-policy-this-is-literally-insane/2019/12/10/5405fb26-07f0-11ea-924a-28d87132c7ec_story.html.
125. Rosa Brooks. *How Everything Became War and the Military Became Everything: Tales from the Pentagon*. New York: Simon and Schuster, 2017, p. 162.
126. Jeremy Scahill. *Dirty Wars: The World Is a Battlefield*. New York: Nation Books, 2013, p. 346.
127. Jim Frederick. *Black Hearts: One Platoon's Descent into Madness in the Iraq War's Triangle of Death*. London: Pan Macmillan, p. 279.
128. Dave Philipps. "Navy SEALs Were Warned Against Reporting Their Chief for War Crimes." *New York Times*. April 23, 2019. Accessed July 2022. https://www.nytimes.com/2019/04/23/us/navy-seals-crimes-of-war.html.

129. Anna Fifield. "Contractors Reap $138B from Iraq War." *CNN International*. March 19, 2013. Accessed July 2022. http://edition.cnn.com/2013/03/19/business/iraq-war-contractors/.
130. Steve Fainaru. *Big Boy Rules: America's Mercenaries Fighting in Iraq*. New York: Da Capo Press, 2009, p. 70.
131. Steve Fainaru. *Big Boy Rules: America's Mercenaries Fighting in Iraq*. New York: Da Capo Press, 2009, p. 62.
132. Jeremy Scahill. "Blackwater Founder Erik Prince Implicated in Murder." *The Nation*. Aug. 4, 2009. Accessed July 2022. https://www.thenation.com/article/archive/blackwater-founder-implicated-murder/.
133. Alan Yuhas. "New Attica Documents Reveal Inmate Accounts of Torture After 1971 Prison Riot." *The Guardian*. May 22, 2015. Accessed July 2022. https://www.theguardian.com/us-news/2015/may/22/new-attica-documents-reveal-inmate-torture.
134. Sam Roberts. "Rockefeller on the Attica Raid, From Boastful to Subdued." *New York Times*. Sept. 12, 2011. Accessed July 2022. https://www.nytimes.com/2011/09/13/nyregion/rockefeller-initially-boasted-to-nixon-about-attica-raid.html.
135. "Frequently Asked Questions." Bureau of Justice Statistics. July 1, 2022. Accessed July 2022. https://bjs.ojp.gov/frequently-asked-questions#faq-how-much-do-federal-state-and-local-governments.
136. Peter B. Kraska. "Militarization and Policing—Its Relevance to 21st Century Police." *Policing: A Journal of Policy and Practice* 1 (4), 2007, pp. 1–13.
137. Christopher J. Coyne. *Tyranny Comes Home: The Domestic Fate of U.S. Militarism*. Palo Alto, CA: Stanford University Press, 2018, p. 96.
138. Darcy Costello and Tessa Duvall. "Why Were Police at Breonna Taylor's Home? Here's What an Investigative Summary Says." *USA Today*. Sept. 4, 2020. Accessed July 2022. https://www.usatoday.com/story/news/nation/2020/09/04/report-details-why-louisville-police-wanted-search-breanna-taylors-home/5706161002/.
139. Jonathan Topaz. "Cleaver: Ferguson Looks Like Fallujah." *Politico*. Aug. 19, 2014. Accessed July 2022. https://www.politico.com/story/2014/08/emanuel-cleaver-ferguson-reaction-110139.
140. Thomas Gibbons-Neff, Helene Cooper, Eric Schmitt, and Jennifer Steinhauer. "Former Commanders Fault Trump's Use of Troops Against Protesters." *New York Times*. June 2, 2020. Accessed July 2022. https://www.nytimes.com/2020/06/02/us/politics/military-national-guard-trump-protests.html.
141. Tim Requarth. "How Private Equity Is Turning Public Prisons into Big Profits." *The Nation*. April 30, 2019. Accessed July 2022. https://www.thenation.com/article/archive/prison-privatization-private-equity-hig/. Also see Ciara O'Neill. "Private Prisons Pour Millions into Lobbying State Lawmakers." *Followthemoney.com*. July 2, 2018. Accessed July 2022. https://www.followthemoney.org/research/blog/private-prisons-pour-millions-into-lobbying-state-lawmakers.
142. James Ridgeway and Jean Casella. "America's 10 Worst Prisons: Walnut Grove." *Mother Jones*. May 13, 2013. Accessed July 2022. https://www.motherjones.com/politics/2013/05/america-10-worst-prisons-walnut-grove-youth-correctional-facility-mississippi/.
143. Ed Pilkington. "Jailed for a MySpace Parody, the Student Who Exposed America's Cash for Kids Scandal." *The Guardian*. March 6, 2009. Accessed July 2022.

https://www.theguardian.com/world/2009/mar/07/juvenille-judges-cash-detention-centre.

144. Erika Eichelberger. "FISA Court Has Rejected .03 Percent of All Government Surveillance Requests." *Mother Jones*. June 10, 2013. Accessed July 2022. https://www.motherjones.com/crime-justice/2013/06/fisa-court-nsa-spying-opinion-reject-request/. Also see Christopher J. Coyne. *Tyranny Comes Home: The Domestic Fate of U.S. Militarism*. Palo Alto, CA: Stanford University Press, 2018, p. 89.
145. Memorandum from John C. Yoo, Deputy Assistant Attorney Gen., U.S. Department of Justice, to the Deputy Counsel to the President. "The President's Constitutional Authority to Conduct Military Operations Against Terrorists and Nations Supporting Them." Sept. 25, 2001. Accessed July 2022. https://fas.org/irp/agency/doj/olc092501.html.
146. Barton Gellman, Julie Tate, and Ashkan Soltani. "In NSA-Intercepted Data Those Not Targeted Far Outnumber the Foreigners Who Are." *Washington Post*. July 5, 2014. Accessed July 2022. https://www.washingtonpost.com/world/national-security/in-nsa-intercepted-data-those-not-targeted-far-outnumber-the-foreigners-who-are/2014/07/05/8139adf8-045a-11e4-8572-4b1b969b6322_story.html.
147. Chris Walker. "NSA Surveillance Program Exposed by Snowden Was Illegal, Rules Appeals Court." *Truthout*. Sept. 3, 2020. Accessed July 2022. https://truthout.org/articles/nsa-surveillance-program-exposed-by-snowden-was-illegal-rules-appeals-court/.
148. Glenn Kessler. "James Clapper's 'Least Untruthful' Statement to the Senate." *Washington Post*. June 12, 2013. Accessed July 2022. http://www.washingtonpost.com/blogs/fact-checker/post/james-clappers-least-untruthful-statement-to-the-senate/2013/06/11/e50677a8-d2d8-11e2-a73e-826d299ff459_blog.html.

CHAPTER 5

1. Ethan Wolff-Mann. "Super Rich's Wealth Concentration Surpasses Gilded Age Level." *Yahoo Finance*. July 7, 2021. Accessed July 2022. https://finance.yahoo.com/news/super-richs-wealth-concentration-surpasses-gilded-age-levels-210802327.html.
2. Robert Gebeloff. "Who Owns Stocks? Explaining the Rise of Inequality During the Pandemic." *New York Times*. Jan. 26, 2021. Accessed July 2022. https://www.nytimes.com/2021/01/26/upshot/stocks-pandemic-inequality.html.
3. Jesse Eisinger, Jeff Ernsthausen, and Paul Kiel. "The Secret IRS Files: Trove of Never-Before-Seen Records Reveal How the Wealthiest Avoid Income Tax." *ProPublica*. June 8, 2021. Accessed July 2022. https://www.propublica.org/article/the-secret-irs-files-trove-of-never-before-seen-records-reveal-how-the-wealthiest-avoid-income-tax.
4. Max Weber. *The Protestant Ethic and the Spirit of Capitalism*. New York: Merchant Books, 2013.
5. Phillip L. Zweig. *Wriston: Walter Wriston, Citibank, and the Rise and Fall of American Financial Supremacy*. New York: Crown Business, 1996, p. 385.
6. Jeff Madrick. *Age of Greed: The Triumph of Finance and the Decline of America 1970 to the Present*. New York: Vintage Books, 2012, p. 103.
7. According to *Time Magazine,* "It became an everyday event for one or two lead banks in the U.S. or Western Europe to round up dozens of partners by telephone to put together so-called jumbo syndicates for loans to developing countries. Some bankers were so afraid of missing out that during lunch hours

they even empowered their secretaries to promise $5 million or $10 million as part of any billion-dollar loan package for Brazil or Mexico. To seal and celebrate big deals, bankers staged signing ceremonies, complete with champagne and caviar, in opulent settings, sometimes a British castle or a mansion in Newport, R.I." Charles P. Alexander. "Jumbo Loans, Jumbo Risks." *Time Magazine*. Dec. 3, 1984. Accessed July 2022. http://content.time.com/time/subscriber/article/0,33009,923771,00.html.

8. Jeff Madrick. *Age of Greed: The Triumph of Finance and the Decline of America 1970 to the Present*. New York: Vintage Books, 2012, p. 104.
9. Ronald Reagan's assistant secretary of state, Robert Hormats, described Wriston this way: "In many ways, Walter Wriston had more influence on foreign policy, over America's role in the world, than many secretaries of state. . . . He probably played as large a role as anyone in extending America's financial presence around the world." See Phillip L. Zweig, *Wriston: Walter Wriston, Citibank, and the Rise and Fall of American Financial Supremacy*. New York: Crown Business, 1996, pp. 324–411, 438–49.
10. Phillip L. Zweig. *Wriston: Walter Wriston, Citibank, and the Rise and Fall of American Financial Supremacy*. New York: Crown Business, 1996, p. 397. Also see Nomi Prins. *All the Presidents' Bankers: The Hidden Alliances That Drive American Power*. New York: Nation Books, 2014, p. 294; and Youssef Cassis. *Crisis and Opportunities: The Shaping of Modern Finance*. London: Oxford University Press, 2013, p. 40.
11. David Harvey. *A Brief History of Neoliberalism*. London: Oxford University Press, 2005, pp. 98–104.
12. Jeff Madrick. *Age of Greed: The Triumph of Finance and the Decline of America 1970 to the Present*. New York: Vintage Books, 2012, p. 104. Also see Nomi Prins. *All the Presidents' Bankers: The Hidden Alliances That Drive American Power*. New York: Nation Books, 2014, p. 276.
13. Youssef Cassis. *Crisis and Opportunities: The Shaping of Modern Finance*. London: Oxford University Press, 2013, pp. 39–40.
14. David Harvey, *A Brief History of Neoliberalism*. London: Oxford University Press, 2005, p. 98–104.
15. Nicholas Shaxson. *The Finance Curse: How Global Finance Is Making Us All Poorer.* New York: Grove Press, 2018, p. 70.
16. Leo Panitch and Sam Gindin. *The Making of Global Capitalism: The Political Economy of American Empire*. London: Verso, 2012, pp. 155–57.
17. Joseph E. Stiglitz. *Globalization and Its Discontents*. New York: W.W. Norton & Company, 2002, pp. 13–14.
18. Isaac A. Kamola. "'Realities of the Global Economy': A. W. Clausen and the Banker's Global Imaginary." *Making the World Global: U.S. Universities and the Production of the Global Imaginary*. Durham, NC: Duke University Press, 2019, pp. 118–38. Also see Leo Panitch and Sam Gindin. *The Making of Global Capitalism: The Political Economy of American Empire*. London: Verso, 2012, pp. 239–40.
19. Catherine Gwin. *U.S. Relations with the World Bank: 1945–1992.* Washington, DC: Brookings Institution Press, 1994, p. 40.
20. "Press Conference by Interim Committee Chairman and IMF Managing Director." IMF Headquarters, Washington, DC. April 28, 1997. Accessed July 2022. http://www.imf.org/external/np/tr/1997/tr970428.htm.

21. Leo Panitch and Sam Gindin. *The Making of Global Capitalism: The Political Economy of American Empire*. London: Verso, 2012, pp. 155–59.
22. "About IFC." International Finance Corporation, World Bank Group. Accessed July 2022. https://www.ifc.org/wps/wcm/connect/corp_ext_content/ifc_external_corporate_site/about+ifc_new.
23. Christoph Kneiding and Richard Rosenberg. "Variations in Microcredit Interest Rates." CGAP Brief. World Bank. Washington, DC. July 2008. Accessed July 2022. https://openknowledge.worldbank.org/handle/10986/9510. Also see Amy Yee. "Why Microfinance Loans Have Such High Rates." *Wall Street Journal*. Aug. 11, 2015. Accessed July 2022. https://www.wsj.com/articles/why-microfinance-loans-have-such-high-rates-1439321404.
24. Silvia Federici. "From Commoning to Debt: Financialization, Microcredit, and the Changing Architecture of Accumulation." *South Atlantic Quarterly* 113 (2), Spring 2014, p. 237.
25. Nora Lustig. "Mexico in Crisis, the U.S. to the Rescue. The Financial Assistance Package of 1982 and 1995." Brookings Institution. Jan. 1, 1997. Accessed July 2022. https://www.brookings.edu/articles/mexico-in-crisis-the-u-s-to-the-rescue-the-financial-assistance-packages-of-1982-and-1995/. Also see Mary Beth Sheridan. "Mexico Plans to Repay Much of U.S. Bailout 2 Years Early." *Los Angeles Times*. June 19, 1996. Accessed July 2022. https://www.latimes.com/archives/la-xpm-1996-06-19-fi-16468-story.html.
26. Nomi Prins. *All the Presidents' Bankers: The Hidden Alliances That Drive American Power*. New York: Nation Books, 2014, p. 374. Also see Rex Nutting. "Rubin Accused of Conflict of Interest." United Press International. Feb. 28. 1995. Accessed July 2022. https://www.upi.com/Archives/1995/02/28/Rubin-accused-of-conflict-of-interest/5601793947600/.
27. David Harvey. *A Brief History of Neoliberalism*. London: Oxford University Press, 2005, pp. 96–97.
28. Leo Panitch and Sam Gindin. *The Making of Global Capitalism: The Political Economy of American Empire*. London: Verso, 2012, pp. 263–7, 313.
29. Jeff Madrick. *Age of Greed: The Triumph of Finance and the Decline of America, 1970 to the Present*. New York: Vintage Books, 2012, pp. 225, 239–40.
30. Matthew Sherman. "A Short History of Financial Deregulation in the United States." Center for Economic and Policy Research. July 2009. Accessed July 2022. http://cepr.net/documents/publications/dereg-timeline-2009-07.pdf. Also see Youssef Cassis. *Crisis and Opportunities: The Shaping of Modern Finance*. London: Oxford University Press, 2013, p. 111.
31. Leo Panitch and Sam Gindin. *The Making of Global Capitalism: The Political Economy of American Empire*. London: Verso, 2012, pp. 128–30. Also see Saskia Sassen. *The Global City: New York, London, Tokyo*. Princeton, NJ: Princeton University Press, 2001, pp. 66–72.
32. Matthew Sherman. "A Short History of Financial Deregulation in the United States." Center for Economic and Policy Research. July 2009. Accessed July 2022. http://cepr.net/documents/publications/dereg-timeline-2009-07.pdf. Also see Leo Panitch and Sam Gindin. *The Making of American Capitalism: The Political Economy of American Empire*. London: Verso, 2012, p. 139.
33. Nomi Prins. *All the Presidents' Bankers: The Hidden Alliances That Drive American Power*. New York: Nation Books, 2014, pp. 333–34, 352. Also see Matthew Sherman. "A Short History of Financial Deregulation in the United States."

Center for Economic and Policy Research. July 2009. Accessed July 2022, pp. 6–7. http://cepr.net/documents/publications/dereg-timeline-2009-07.pdf.
34. "Obituary—Charles Keating: Crusader and Fraud." *The Economist*. April 15, 2014. Accessed July 2021. http://www.economist.com/news/obituary/21600648-charles-keating-moral-crusader-and-financial-snake-oil-sales man-died-march-31st-aged.
35. Tom Fitzpatrick. "McCain: The Most Reprehensible of the Keating Five." *Phoenix News Times*. Nov. 29, 1989. Accessed July 2021. https://www.phoenixnewtimes.com/news/mccain-the-most-reprehensible-of-the-keating-five-6431838.
36. Patricia Sullivan. "S&L Industry Leader William B. O'Connell, 82." *Washington Post*. Jan. 15, 2006. Accessed July 2022. https://www.washingtonpost.com/archive/local/2006/01/15/s38/ddf0bee8-fdd2-4aab-bfaf-1b30b4faa8dc/. Also see Nomi Prins. *All the Presidents' Bankers: The Hidden Alliances That Drive American Power*. New York: Nation Books, 2014, p. 354; and Kevin Phillips. *Wealth and Democracy: A Political History of the American Rich*. New York: Broadway Books, 2002, pp. 95–96.
37. Nomi Prins. *All the Presidents' Bankers: The Hidden Alliances That Drive American Power*. New York: Nation Books, 2014, p. 382.
38. Matthew Sherman. "A Short History of Financial Deregulation in the United States." Center for Economic and Policy Research. July 2009. Accessed July 2022. http://cepr.net/documents/publications/dereg-timeline-2009-07.pdf.
39. Joshua Cooper Ramo. "The Three Marketeers." *Time Magazine*. Feb. 15, 1999. Accessed July 2022. http://content.time.com/time/world/article/0,8599,2054093,00.html.
40. Francis Fukuyama. "The End of History." *The National Interest*, (16), Summer 1989, pp. 3–18.
41. Joshua Cooper Ramo. "The Three Marketeers." *Time Magazine*. Feb. 15, 1999. Accessed July 2022. http://content.time.com/time/world/article/0,8599,2054093,00.html.
42. Nomi Prins. *All the Presidents' Bankers: The Hidden Alliances That Drive American Power*. New York: Nation Books, 2014, pp. 381–87.
43. Nomi Prins. *All the Presidents' Bankers: The Hidden Alliances That Drive American Power*. New York: Nation Books. 2014, pp. 389–90.
44. Jeff Madrick. *Age of Greed: The Triumph of Finance and the Decline of America, 1970 to the Present*. New York: Vintage Books, 2012, pp. 286–317.
45. Bob Herbert. "Enron and the Gramms." *New York Times*. Jan. 17, 2002. Accessed July 2021. http://www.nytimes.com/2002/01/17/opinion/enron-and-the-gramms.html. Also see Eric Lipton. "Gramm and the 'Enron Loophole'." *New York Times*. Nov. 14, 2008. Accessed July 2022. https://www.nytimes.com/2008/11/17/business/17grammside.html.
46. Nomi Prins. *All the Presidents' Bankers: The Hidden Alliances That Drive American Power*. New York: Nation Books, 2014, pp. 364–68.
47. "Panel: Banks Were in Bed with Enron." *CBS News*. July 18, 2002. Accessed July 2022. http://www.cbsnews.com/news/panel-banks-were-in-bed-with-enron/.
48. Paul Kix. "The Man Who Would Save the Economy." *Boston Magazine*. Jan. 28, 2008. Accessed July 2022. https://www.bostonmagazine.com/2008/01/28/the-man-who-would-save-the-economy/.
49. Kevin Phillips. *Wealth and Democracy: A Political History of the American Rich*. New York: Broadway Books, 2002, p. 143.

50. Richard A. Oppel Jr. and Jeff Gerth. “Enron Forced Up Energy Prices, Documents Show.” *New York Times*. May 7, 2022. Accessed July 2022. Also see Jeff Madrick. *Age of Greed: The Triumph of Finance and the Decline of America 1970 to Present*. New York: Vintage Books, 2012, pp. 336–37.
51. Richard A. Oppel Jr. “Word for Word/Energy Hogs; Enron Traders on Grandma Millie and Making Out Like Bandits.” *New York Times*. June 13, 2004. Accessed July 2022.
52. Jannick Damgaard, Thomas Elkjaer, and Niels Johannesen. “The Rise of Phantom Investments.” International Monetary Fund. *Finance & Development*. 56 (3), September 2019. Accessed July 2021. https://www.imf.org/external/pubs/ft/fandd/2019/09/the-rise-of-phantom-FDI-in-tax-havens-damgaard.htm.
53. Bethany McLean. “Is Enron Overpriced? (Fortune 2001).” *Fortune Magazine*. Dec. 13, 2015. Accessed July 2022. https://fortune.com/2015/12/30/is-enron-overpriced-fortune-2001/.
54. Matthew Sherman. “A Short History of Financial Deregulation.” Center for Economic and Policy Research. July 2009. Accessed July 2022. http://cepr.net/documents/publications/dereg-timeline-2009-07.pdf.
55. Jeff Madrick. *Age of Greed: The Triumph of Finance and the Decline of America, 1970 to the Present*. New York: Vintage Books, 2012, p. 351.
56. Edward J. Schoen. “The 2007–2009 Financial Crisis: An Erosion of Ethics: A Case Study.” *Journal of Business Ethics* 146, 2017, pp. 805–30. Accessed July 2022. https://doi.org/10.1007/s10551-016-3052-7.
57. “The Financial Crisis Inquiry Report.” Final Report of the National Commission on the Causes of the Financial and Economic Crisis in the United States. Pursuant to Public Law 111-21. Jan. 25, 2011, pp. 5–7. Accessed July 2022. https://www.gpo.gov/fdsys/pkg/GPO-FCIC/pdf/GPO-FCIC.pdf.
58. Matthew Sherman. “A Short History of Financial Deregulation in the United States.” Center for Economic and Policy Research. July 2009. Accessed July 2022. http://cepr.net/documents/publications/dereg-timeline-2009-07.pdf.
59. “Clark County, NV: Ground Zero of the Housing and Financial Crisis.” Field Hearing Before the Congressional Oversight Panel. 110th Congress, 2nd Session, Las Vegas, NV. Dec. 16, 2008. Accessed July 2022. https://www.govinfo.gov/content/pkg/CHRG-110shrg51705/html/CHRG-110shrg51705.htm.
60. Nicholas Shaxson. *The Finance Curse: How Global Finance Is Making Us All Poorer.* New York: Grove Press, 2018, p. 195.
61. Nathalie Baptiste. “Staggering Loss of Black Wealth Due to Subprime Scandal Continues Unabated.” *American Prospect*. Oct. 13, 2004. Accessed July 2022. https://prospect.org/justice/staggering-loss-black-wealth-due-subprime-scandal-continues-unabated/. For more on subprime lending, see Christy Rogers and John A. Powell’s collection *Where Credit Is Due: Bringing Equity to Credit and Housing After the Housing Market Meltdown*. Lanham, MD: University Press of America, 2013.
62. Michael Powell. “Bank Accused of Pushing Mortgage Deals on Blacks.” *New York Times*. June 6, 2009. Accessed July 2022. https://www.nytimes.com/2009/06/07/us/07baltimore.html.
63. Leo Panitch and Sam Gindin. *The Making of Global Capitalism: The Political Economy of American Empire*. London: Verso, 2012, pp. 140, 148–52. Also see Joseph P. Fried. “Nixon’s Housing Policy.” *New York Times*. Sept. 29, 1973. Accessed July 2022. https://www.nytimes.com/1973/09/29/archives/nixons-housing-policy-opponents-say-proposal-for-cash-payments-wont.html.

64. Terry Frieden. "FBI Warns of Mortgage Fraud 'Epidemic'." *CNN*. Sept. 17, 2004. Accessed July 2022. https://www.cnn.com/2004/LAW/09/17/mortgage.fraud/.
65. Matthew Sherman. "A Short History of Financial Deregulation." Center for Economic and Policy Research. July 2009. Accessed July 2022. http://cepr.net/documents/publications/dereg-timeline-2009-07.pdf.
66. Sunlen Miller, Bret Hovell, and Jennifer Parker. "Obama Blasts McCain over Advisor's 'Mental Recession' Comments." *ABC News*. July 10, 2008. Accessed July 2022. https://abcnews.go.com/Politics/Vote2008/story?id=5350099&page=1.
67. Reid Wilson. "States Slow to Spend Billions in TARP Funds for Underwater Homeowners." *Washington Post*. Oct. 30, 2013. Accessed July 2022. https://www.washingtonpost.com/blogs/govbeat/wp/2013/10/30/states-slow-to-spend-billions-in-tarp-funds-for-underwater-homeowners/. Also see Annie Lowrey. "Treasury Faulted in Effort to Relieve Homeowners." *New York Times*. April 12, 2012. Accessed July 2022. https://www.nytimes.com/2012/04/12/business/economy/treasury-department-faulted-in-effort-to-relieve-homeowners.html; and Matt Taibbi. "Secrets and Lies of the Bailout." *Rolling Stone*. Jan. 4, 2013. Accessed July 2022. http://www.rollingstone.com/politics/news/secret-and-lies-of-the-bailout-20130104.
68. Matt Taibbi. "Secrets and Lies of the Bailout." *Rolling Stone*. Jan. 4, 2013. Accessed July 2022. http://www.rollingstone.com/politics/news/secret-and-lies-of-the-bailout-20130104. Also see Edmund L. Andrews and Peter Baker. "A.I.G. Planning Huge Bonuses After $170 Billion Bailout." *New York Times*. March 14, 2009. Accessed July 2022. http://www.nytimes.com/2009/03/15/business/15AIG.html?_r=0.
69. Michael Shnayerson. "Wall Street's $18.4 Billion Bonus." *Vanity Fair*. March 2009. Accessed July 2022. http://www.vanityfair.com/news/2009/03/wall-street-bonuses200903.
70. Kate Kelly. "How Goldman Won Big on Mortgage Meltdown." *Wall Street Journal*. Dec. 14, 2007. Accessed July 2022. http://www.wsj.com/articles/SB119759714037228585.
71. Matt Taibbi. "Secrets and Lies of the Bailout." *Rolling Stone*. Jan. 4, 2013. Accessed July 2022. http://www.rollingstone.com/politics/news/secret-and-lies-of-the-bailout-20130104.
72. William R. Emmons and Bryan J. Noeth. "Household Financial Stability: Who Suffered the Most from the Crisis?" Federal Reserve Bank of St. Louis. July 1, 2012. Accessed July 2022. Also see Les Christie. "Foreclosures Up a Record 81% in 2008." *CNN*. Jan. 15, 2009. Accessed July 2022. https://money.cnn.com/2009/01/15/real_estate/millions_in_foreclosure/.
73. Nicholas Johnson, Phil Oliff, and Erica Williams. "An Update on State Budget Cuts: At Least 46 States Have Imposed Cuts That Hurt Vulnerable Residents and the Economy." Center on Budget and Policy Priorities. Feb. 9, 2011. Accessed July 2022. http://www.cbpp.org/cms/index.cfm?fa=view&id=1214.
74. Stephen Gandel. "Volcker Loopholes: Here Are All the Crazy Trades Big Banks Can Still Make." *Fortune Magazine*. Dec. 10, 2013. Accessed July 2022. http://fortune.com/2013/12/10/volcker-loopholes-here-are-all-the-crazy-trades-big-banks-can-still-make/.
75. Andrew Ross Sorkin. "What Timothy Geithner Really Thinks." *New York Times*. May 8, 2014. Accessed July 2022. http://www.nytimes.com/2014/05/11/magazine/what-timothy-geithner-really-thinks. Also see Barack Obama. "Remarks by

the President at the Signing of the Dodd-Frank Wall Street Reform Consumer Protection Act." White House Office of the Press Secretary. July 21, 2010. Accessed July 2022. https://obamawhitehouse.archives.gov/the-press-office/remarks-president-signing-dodd-frank-wall-street-reform-and-consumer-protection-act.

76. Matt Taibbi. "Secrets and Lies of the Bailout." *Rolling Stone*. Jan. 4, 2013. Accessed July 2022. http://www.rollingstone.com/politics/news/secret-and-lies-of-the-bailout-20130104.
77. Mike Collins. "The Big Bank Bailout." *Forbes*. July 14, 2010. Accessed July 2021. http://www.forbes.com/sites/mikecollins/2015/07/14/the-big-bank-bailout/#52e0fcff3723. Also see Senator Bernie Sanders. "The Fed Audit." Bernie Sanders Senate homepage. July 21, 2011. Accessed July 2022. https://www.sanders.senate.gov/press-releases/the-fed-audit/.
78. Chris Isadore. "Fed Made $9 Trillion in Emergency Overnight Loans." *CNN*. Dec. 1, 2010. Accessed July 2022. https://money.cnn.com/2010/12/01/news/economy/fed_reserve_data_release/index.htm.
79. Matt Taibbi. "Secrets and Lies of the Bailout." *Rolling Stone*. Jan. 4, 2013. Accessed July 2022. http://www.rollingstone.com/politics/news/secret-and-lies-of-the-bailout-20130104.
80. Matt Taibbi. "Secrets and Lies of the Bailout." *Rolling Stone*. Jan. 4, 2013. Accessed July 2022. http://www.rollingstone.com/politics/news/secret-and-lies-of-the-bailout-20130104.
81. Bernie Sanders. *Our Revolution: A Future to Believe In*. New York: Thomas Dunne Books, 2016, pp. 269–76.
82. Nathaniel Melican and Fatima Aitizaz. "With the Sting Taken Out of Crossing $50B in Assets, Banks Pursue M&A." S&P Global Market Intelligence. July 6, 2021. Accessed July 2022. https://www.spglobal.com/marketintelligence/en/news-insights/latest-news-headlines/with-the-sting-taken-out-of-crossing-50b-in-assets-banks-pursue-m-a-65182869.
83. Donna Borak and Ted Barrett. "Senate Votes to Roll Back Parts of Dodd-Frank Banking Law." *CNN*. March 14, 2018. Accessed July 2022. https://www.cnn.com/2018/03/14/politics/banking-bill-vote-mike-crapo/index.html.
84. As of July 2022, JPMorgan Chase's assets totaled $2.6 trillion. See "Our Business." JPMorgan Chase homepage. Accessed July 2022. https://www.jpmorganchase.com/about/our-business#:~:text=Our%20company%20is%20a%20leading,transactions%20processing%20and%20asset%20management. For the World Bank's Country Rankings by GDP see: "Gross Domestic Product 2021." World Development Indicators database, World Bank. July 1, 2022. Accessed July 2022. https://databank.worldbank.org/data/download/GDP.pdf.
85. Eric Griffith. "Why an Animated Flying Cat with a Pop-Tart Body Sold for Almost $600,000." *New York Times*. Feb. 22, 2021. Accessed July 2022. https://www.nytimes.com/2021/02/22/business/nft-nba-top-shot-crypto.html.
86. See Sheelah Kolatkar. "The Challenges of Regulating Cryptocurrency." *New Yorker*. Oct. 6, 2021. Accessed July 2022. https://www.newyorker.com/business/currency/the-challenges-of-regulating-cryptocurrency. Also see Doug Henwood. "Bitcoin, a Commentary." *Left Business Observer*. Dec. 22, 2017. Accessed July 2022. https://lbo-news.com/2017/12/22/bitcoin-a-commentary/; Edward Ongweso Jr. and Jacob Silverman. "Crypto Is Making Everything Worse." *Jacobin*. March 2022. Accessed July 2022. https://www.jacobinmag.com/2022/03/cryptocurrency-bitcoin-speculative-asset-digitization-metaverse; and

Sohale Andrus Mortazavi. "Cryptocurrency Is a Giant Ponzi Scheme." *Jacobin*. January 2022. Accessed April 2022. https://jacobinmag.com/2022/01/cryptocurrency-scam-blockchain-bitcoin-economy-decentralization.

87. John Hyatt. "The Richest Crypto and Blockchain Billionaires in the World 2022." *Forbes*. April 5, 2022. Accessed July 2022. https://www.forbes.com/sites/johnhyatt/2022/04/05/the-richest-crypto-and-blockchain-billionaires-in-the-world-2022/?sh=6c58d8ad580d.
88. Kevin Dowd. "Blackstone Might Reach Its $1 Trillion Goal Four Years Ahead of Schedule." *Forbes*. Jan. 30, 2022. Accessed July 2022. https://www.forbes.com/sites/kevindowd/2022/01/30/blackstone-might-reach-its-1-trillion-goal-four-years-ahead-of-schedule/?sh=145229fb15c1. Also see Miriam Gottfried. "As Blackstone Barrels Toward Trillion Dollar Asset Goal Growth Is In, Value Out." *Wall Street Journal*. March 21, 2021. Accessed July 2022. https://www.wsj.com/articles/as-blackstone-barrels-toward-trillion-dollar-asset-goal-growth-is-in-value-out-11616319002; Stephen Feinberg. "The 25 Richest People in Private Equity." *Business Insider*. July 26, 2021. Accessed July 2022. https://www.businessinsider.in/finance/the-25-richest-people-in-private-equity/slidelist/51231689.cms; and Tony Owusu. "Blackstone Posts Record $684 Billion in Assets Under Management." *The Street*. July 22, 2021. Accessed July 2022. https://www.thestreet.com/investing/blackstone-bx-stock-earnings-record-growth-assets.
89. Dealbook. "Inside Steve Schwarzman's Birthday Bash." *New York Times*. Feb. 14, 2007. Accessed July 2022. https://dealbook.nytimes.com/2007/02/14/inside-stephen-schwarzmans-birthday-bash/?_r=0. Also see Branko Marcetic. "3 Reasons to be Worried about the Blackstone Group—and Their Friend Hillary Clinton." *In These Times*. Oct. 19, 2016. Accessed July 2022. https://inthesetimes.com/article/3-reasons-to-be-worried-about-the-blackstone-groupand-their-friend-hillary.
90. Kurt Eichenwald. "Wages Even Wall Street Can't Stomach." *New York Times*. April 3, 1989. Accessed July 2022. https://www.nytimes.com/1989/04/03/business/wages-even-wall-st-can-t-stomach.html.
91. "#807 Michael Milken." *Forbes*. June 30, 2022. Accessed July 2022. https://www.forbes.com/profile/michael-milken/?sh=1e198243b390.
92. "Highlights of the Wall Street Scandal: From Levine Arrest to Drexel Settlement." *New York Times*. Dec. 22, 1988. Accessed July 2022. http://www.nytimes.com/1988/12/22/business/highlights-of-the-wall-street-scandal-from-levine-arrest-to-drexel-settlement.html. Also see Jeff Madrick. *Age of Greed: The Triumph of Finance and the Decline of America, 1970 to the Present*. New York: Vintage Books, 2012, pp. 202–21.
93. Nomi Prins. *All the Presidents' Bankers: The Hidden Alliances That Drive American Power*. New York: Nation Books, 2014, pp. 341–42.
94. Ken Auletta. *Greed and Glory on Wall Street: The Rise and Fall of the House of Lehman*. New York: Open Road Integrated Media, 2015, p. 8. Also see Ann Crittenden. "Reaping the Big Profits from a Fat Cat." *New York Times*. August 7, 1983. Accessed July 2022. https://www.nytimes.com/1983/08/07/business/reaping-the-big-profits-from-a-fat-cat.html.
95. "An Industrial Policy for America: Is It Needed?" Subcommittee on Economic Stabilization of the Committee on Banking, Finance and Urban Affairs. House of Representatives, 98th Congress, First Session. April 1983, p. 15. Also see Michael C. Jensen. "The Free Cash Flow Theory of Takeovers: A Financial Perspective on

Mergers and Acquisitions and the Economy," in "The Merger Boom," Proceedings of a Conference sponsored by the Federal Reserve Bank of Boston. October 1987. pp. 102–43.

96. "Report: A New Decade for Private Markets." McKinsey & Company. February 2020. Accessed July 2022. https://www.mckinsey.com/~/media/mckinsey/industries/private%20equity%20and%20principal%20investors/our%20insights/mckinseys%20private%20markets%20annual%20review/2020/mckinsey-global-private-markets-review-2020-v4.pdf.
97. Ernst & Young. "2020 Economic Impact: Private Equity & the Economic Recovery." Report Prepared for the American Investment Council. May 2021. Accessed July 2022. https://www.investmentcouncil.org/economicimpact/.
98. Jakob Wilhelmus and William Lee. "Report: Companies Rush to Go Private." Milken Institute. August 2018, p. 2. Accessed August 9, 2022. https://milkeninstitute.org/sites/default/files/reports-pdf/WP-083018-Companies-Rush-to-Go-Private-FINAL2.pdf. Also see Bethany McLean. "Too Big to Fail, COVID-19 Edition: How Private Equity Is Winning the Coronavirus Crisis." *Vanity Fair.* April 9, 2020. Accessed July 2022. https://www.vanityfair.com/news/2020/04/how-private-equity-is-winning-the-coronavirus-crisis.
99. Michael J. De La Merced. "Schwarzman's Unfortunate War Analogy." *New York Times*. Aug. 16, 2010. Accessed July 2022. https://dealbook.nytimes.com/2010/08/16/schwarzmans-unfortunate-war-analogy/.
100. "Everything Is Private Equity Now." *Bloomberg News*. Oct. 8, 2019. Accessed July 2022. https://www.bloomberg.com/news/features/2019-10-03/how-private-equity-works-and-took-over-everything.
101. Gretchen Morgenson and Emmanuelle Saliba. "Private Equity Firms Now Control Many Hospitals, ERs, and Nursing Homes. Is It Good For Health Care?" *NBC News*. May 13, 2020. Accessed July 2022. https://www.nbcnews.com/health/health-care/private-equity-firms-now-control-many-hospitals-ers-nursing-homes-n1203161.
102. Carol K. Kane. "Updated Data on Physician Practice Arrangements: For the First Time, Fewer Physicians Are Owners Than Employees." American Medical Association. 2019. Accessed July 2022. https://www.ama-assn.org/system/files/2019-07/prp-fewer-owners-benchmark-survey-2018.pdf.
103. Gretchen Morgenson and Emmanuelle Saliba. "Private Equity Firms Now Control Many Hospitals, ERs, and Nursing Homes. Is it Good for Health Care?" *NBC News*. May 13, 2020. Accessed July 2022. https://www.nbcnews.com/health/health-care/private-equity-firms-now-control-many-hospitals-ers-nursing-homes-n1203161.
104. Frank J. Lexa, MD, MBA. "Private Equity-Backed Hospitals Investments and the Impact of the Coronavirus Disease (COVID-19) Epidemic." *Journal of the American College of Radiology*, 17 (8), August 2020, pp. 1049–52..
105. Gretchen Morgenson and Emmanuelle Saliba. "Private Equity Firms Now Control Many Hospitals, ERs, and Nursing Homes. Is It Good For Health Care?" *NBC News*. May 13, 2020. Accessed July 2022. https://www.nbcnews.com/health/health-care/private-equity-firms-now-control-many-hospitals-ers-nursing-homes-n1203161.
106. Gretchen Morgenson and Emmanuelle Saliba. "Private Equity Firms Now Control Many Hospitals, ERs, and Nursing Homes. Is It Good For Health Care?" *NBC News*. May 13, 2020. Accessed July 2022. https://www.nbcnews.com/hea

lth/health-care/private-equity-firms-now-control-many-hospitals-ers-nursing-homes-n1203161.

107. Zack Cooper, Fiona Scott Morton, and Nathan Shekita. "Working Paper: Surprise! Out of Network Billing for Emergency Care in the United States." National Bureau of Economic Research. Issued July 2017. Accessed July 2022. https://www.nber.org/papers/w23623.
108. Margot Sanger-Katz, Julie Creswell, and Reed Abelson. "Mystery Solved: Private-Equity-Backed Firms Are Behind Ad Blitz on 'Surprise Billing.'" *New York Times*. Sept. 30, 2019. Accessed July 2022. https://www.nytimes.com/2019/09/13/upshot/surprise-billing-laws-ad-spending-doctor-patient-unity.html.
109. "HHS Announces Rule to Protect Consumers from Surprise Medical Bills." Department of Health and Human Services. July 1, 2022. Accessed July 2021. https://www.hhs.gov/about/news/2021/07/01/hhs-announces-rule-to-protect-consumers-from-surprise-medical-bills.html.
110. Jan Fichtner, Eelke Heemskerk, and Javier Garcia-Bernardo. "These Three Firms Own Corporate America." *The Conversation*. May 10, 2017. Accessed July 2022. https://theconversation.com/these-three-firms-own-corporate-america-77072.
111. Graham Steele. "The New Money Trust: How Large Money Managers Control Our Economy and What We Can Do About it." American Economic Liberties Project. Nov. 23, 2020. Accessed July 2022. https://www.economicliberties.us/our-work/new-money-trust/. Also see Jan Fichtner, Eelke Heemskerk, and Javier Garcia-Bernardo. "These Three Firms Own Corporate America." *The Conversation*. May 10, 2017. Accessed July 2022. https://theconversation.com/these-three-firms-own-corporate-america-77072.
112. Graham Steele. "The New Money Trust: How Large Money Managers Control Our Economy and What We Can Do About it." American Economic Liberties Project. Nov. 23, 2020. Accessed July 2022. https://www.economicliberties.us/our-work/new-money-trust/.
113. Benjamin Braun. "Asset Manager Capitalism as a Corporate Governance Regime." *SocArXiv*. June 18, 2020. Accessed July 2022. https://osf.io/preprints/socarxiv/v6gue.
114. Jim Zarroli. "Emails Reveal Clinton's Mixed Relationship with Wall Street." *National Public Radio*. Oct. 8, 2016. Accessed July 2022. https://www.npr.org/sections/thetwo-way/2016/10/08/497204286/emails-reveal-clintons-mixed-relationship-with-wall-street.
115. David Dayen. "TPP Trade Pact Would Give Wall Street a Trump Card to Block Regulations." *The Intercept*. Nov. 6, 2015. Accessed July 2022. https://theintercept.com/2015/11/06/ttp-trade-pact-would-give-wall-street-a-trump-card-to-block-regulations/. Also see "TPP Final Text: Chapter 11 Financial Services." U.S. Trade Representative. Accessed July 2022. https://ustr.gov/sites/default/files/TPP-Final-Text-Financial-Services.pdf.
116. Bourree Lam. "What Bernie Sanders Thinks Is Wrong with the Fed." *The Atlantic*. Jan. 6, 2016. Accessed July 2022. http://www.theatlantic.com/business/archive/2016/01/bernie-sanders-reform-revolving-door/422772/.
117. Mary Williams Walsh. "Hedge Funds Sue Puerto Rico's Governor, Claiming Money Grab." *New York Times*. July 20, 2016. Accessed July 2022. http://www.nytimes.com/2016/07/21/business/hedge-funds-sue-puerto-ricos-governor-claiming-money-grab.html. Also see David Dayen. "We Can Finally Identify One of the Largest Holders of Puerto Rican Debt." *The Intercept*. Oct. 3, 2017.

Accessed July 2022. https://theintercept.com/2017/10/03/we-can-finally-identify-one-of-the-largest-holders-of-puerto-rican-debt/.

118. Heriberto Martínez-Otero and Ian J. Seda-Irizarry. "The Origins of the Puerto Rican Debt Crisis." *Jacobin*. August 10, 2015. Accessed July 2022. https://jacobin.com/2015/08/puerto-rico-debt-crisis-imf/. Also see David Dayen. "We Can Finally Identify One of the Largest Holders of Puerto Rican Debt." *The Intercept*. Accessed July 2021. https://theintercept.com/2017/10/03/we-can-finally-identify-one-of-the-largest-holders-of-puerto-rican-debt/.
119. Melanie Hanson. "Student Loan Debt Statistics." *EducationData.org*. May 30, 2022. Accessed July 2022. https://educationdata.org/student-loan-debt-statistics.
120. AnnaMaria Andriotis and Robin Sidel. "Balance Due: Credit-Card Debt Nears $1 Trillion as Banks Push Plastic." *Wall Street Journal*. May 20, 2016. Accessed July 2022. https://www.wsj.com/articles/balance-due-credit-card-debt-nears-1-trillion-as-banks-push-plastic-1463736600. Also see Ethan Wolff-Mann. "The Average American Is in Credit Card Debt, No Matter the Economy." *Money*. Feb. 9, 2016. Accessed July 2022. https://money.com/average-american-credit-card-debt/; and Megan Cerullo. "Credit Card Debt Is Getting Pricier. Here's How to Pay It Off." *CBS News*. June 24, 2022. Accessed July 2022. https://www.cbsnews.com/news/credit-card-debt-rising-interest-rates-how-to-pay-if-off/.
121. Donald Trump. "TRANSCRIPT: Donald Trump's Speech Responding to Assault Accusations." *Colorado Public Radio*. Oct. 13, 2016. Accessed July 2022. https://www.cpr.org/2016/10/13/transcript-donald-trumps-speech-responding-to-assault-accusations/.
122. Jennifer Silver-Greenberg. "Santander Consumer Reaches $9.35 Million Settlement over Military Repossessions." *New York Times*. Feb. 25, 2015. Accessed July 2022. https://www.nytimes.com/2015/02/26/business/dealbook/santander-consumer-reaches-9-35-million-settlement-over-car-repossessions.html.
123. Napp Nazworth. "Payday Lending 'Grinds the Faces of the Poor into the Ground,' Russell Moore Says; New Left-Right Christian Coalition Seeks to End Practice." *Christian Post*. May 19, 2015. Accessed July 2022. https://www.christianpost.com/news/payday-lending-grinds-the-faces-of-the-poor-into-the-ground-russell-moore-says-new-left-right-christian-coalition-seeks-to-end-practice-139258/.
124. "Report: Fraud and Abuse Online: Harmful Practices in Internet Payday Lending." Pew Charitable Trusts. Oct. 2, 2014. Accessed July 2022. https://www.pewtrusts.org/-/media/assets/2014/10/payday-lending-report/fraud_and_abuse_online_harmful_practices_in_internet_payday_lending.pdf. Also see "CFPB Sues Online Payday Lender for Cash-Grab Scam." Consumer Finance Protection Bureau. Sept. 17, 2014. Accessed July 2022. http://www.consumerfinance.gov/newsroom/cfpb-sues-online-payday-lender-for-cash-grab-scam/; "Payday Lending Abuses and Predatory Practices." Center for Responsible Lending. September 2013. Accessed July 2021. http://www.responsiblelending.org/state-of-lending/reports/10-Payday-Loans.pdf; and Susanna Montezemolo. "Payday Lending Abuses and Predatory Practices." The State of Lending in America and Its Impact on U.S. Households. Center For Responsible Lending. Sept. 2013. Accessed July 2022 http://www.responsiblelending.org/state-of-lending/reports/10-Payday-Loans.pdf.
125. "Wall Street Money in Washington 2019–2020 Campaign and Lobby Spending by the Financial Sector." Americans for Financial Reform. March 2021. Accessed

July 2022. https://ourfinancialsecurity.org/wp-content/uploads/2021/04/FINAL-4.15-AFR-Wall-Street-Money-in-Politics-2021.pdf.

126. Samir Sonti. "The Crisis of U.S. Labor, Past and Present." *Socialist Register* 58, October 2021, pp. 135–58. Also see Anna Massa and Caleb Melby. "In Fink We Trust: BlackRock Is Now the 'Fourth Branch of Government.'" *Bloomberg Business*. May 21, 2020. Accessed July 2022. https://www.bloomberg.com/news/articles/2020-05-21/how-larry-fink-s-blackrock-is-helping-the-fed-with-bond-buying.
127. Nicholas Shaxson. *The Finance Curse: How Global Finance Is Making Us All Poorer.* New York: Grove Press, 2018, p. 6. Also see Robin Greenwood and David Sharfstein. "The Growth of Finance." *Journal of Economic Perspectives* 27 (2), Spring 2013, pp. 3–28. Accessed July 2022. https://www.hbs.edu/ris/Publication%20Files/Growth%20of%20Finance_6ec86a21-8e68-4abc-bb09-45abaacd7be5.pdf.

CHAPTER 6

1. Citizens for Tax Fairness and the Institute for Policy Studies. "Press Release: U.S. Billionaire Wealth Surged 70%, or $2.1 Trillion, During the Pandemic; They Are Now Worth a Combined $5 Trillion." Oct. 18, 2021. Accessed July 2022. https://americansfortaxfairness.org/wp-content/uploads/2021-10-18-Billionaires-National-Report-October-2021-1.pdf.
2. "World's Billionaires Have More Wealth Than 4.6 Billion People." *Oxfam*. Jan. 20, 2020. Accessed July 2021. https://www.oxfam.org/en/press-releases/worlds-billionaires-have-more-wealth-46-billion-people. Also see Claire Coffey et al. "Report: Time to Care: Unpaid and Underpaid Care Work and the Global Inequality Crisis." Oxfam International. Jan. 2020. Accessed July 2022. https://oxfamilibrary.openrepository.com/bitstream/handle/10546/620928/bp-time-to-care-inequality-200120-en.pdf.
3. Oxfam International. Press Release: "Ten Richest Men Double Their Fortunes in Pandemic While Incomes of 99 Percent of Humanity Fall." Jan. 17, 2022. Accessed July 2022. https://www.oxfam.org/en/press-releases/ten-richest-men-double-their-fortunes-pandemic-while-incomes-99-percent-humanity.
4. Carl O'Donnell. "The Rockefellers: The Legacy of History's Richest Man." *Forbes*. July 11, 2014. Accessed July 2022. http://www.forbes.com/sites/carlodonnell/2014/07/11/the-rockefellers-the-legacy-of-historys-richest-man/#7c6d166760e7.
5. C. Wright Mills. *The Power Elite*. New York: Oxford University Press, 1956/2000, p. 98.
6. Michelle Goldberg. "Jeffrey Epstein Is the Ultimate Symbol of Plutocratic Rot." *New York Times*. July 8, 2019. Accessed July 2022. https://www.nytimes.com/2019/07/08/opinion/jeffrey-epstein-trump.html.
7. Oliver Wainright. "Seasteading—A Vanity Project for the Rich or Future of Humanity?" *The Guardian*. June 24, 2020. Accessed August 2022. https://www.theguardian.com/environment/2020/jun/24/seasteading-a-vanity-project-for-the-rich-or-the-future-of-humanity.. Also see Maya Kosoff. "Peter Thiel Wants to Inject Himself with Young People's Blood." *Vanity Fair*. Aug. 1, 2016. Accessed August 2022. https://www.vanityfair.com/news/2016/08/peter-thiel-wants-to-inject-himself-with-young-peoples-blood.
8. Kerry A. Dolan, Chase Peterson-Withorn, and Jennifer Yang. "Forbes 400: The Definitive Ranking of the Wealthiest Americans in 2021." *Forbes*. Oct. 5, 2021.

Accessed July 2021. https://www.forbes.com/forbes-400/. Also see Rachel Sandler. "Nearly Half of America's Richest Billionaires Have Fortunes in These Two Industries." *Forbes*. Oct. 26, 2021. Accessed July 2022. https://www.forbes.com/sites/rachelsandler/2021/10/26/nearly-half-of-americas-richest-billionaires-have-fortunes-in-these-two-industries/?sh=3fcb027b5d74.

9. Peter W. Bernstein and Annalyn Swan. *All the Money in the World: How the Forbes 400 Make—and Spend—Their Fortunes*. New York: Knopf Doubleday Publishing Group, 2008, p. 4.
10. Michael A. Urquhart and Marilyn A. Hewson. "Unemployment Continued to Rise in 1982 as Recession Deepened." *Monthly Labor Review*. Bureau of Labor and Statistics. Feb. 1983. Accessed July 2022. http://www.bls.gov/opub/mlr/1983/02/art1full.pdf.
11. Milton Friedman. *Capitalism and Freedom*, 40th ed. Chicago: University of Chicago Press, 2003, p. 4.
12. Also in this category is David Rothkopf's *Superclass: The Global Elite and the World They Are Making*. New York: Farrar, Straus and Giroux, 2009, pp. 290–92.
13. Aviva Shen. "Mayor Bloomberg on Homeless Girl Featured in *New York Times*: 'That's Just the Way God Works'." *ThinkProgress*. Dec. 18, 2013. Accessed July 2022. https://archive.thinkprogress.org/mayor-bloomberg-on-homeless-girl-featured-in-the-new-york-times-thats-just-the-way-god-works-c2d2e6f76b95/.
14. Ben Stein. "In Class Warfare, Guess Which Class Is Winning." *New York Times*. Nov. 26, 2006. Accessed July 2022. https://www.nytimes.com/2006/11/26/business/yourmoney/26every.html.
15. Fred Dews. "Sen. Bernie Sanders: We Have a Government of, by, and for Billionaires." Brookings Institution. Feb. 9, 2015. Accessed July 2022. https://www.brookings.edu/blog/brookings-now/2015/02/09/sen-bernie-sanders-we-have-a-government-of-by-and-for-billionaires/..
16. Jeffrey A. Winters. *Oligarchy*. New York: Cambridge University Press, 2011, pp. 14–20.
17. Jeffrey A. Winters. *Oligarchy*. New York: Cambridge University Press, 2011, pp. 20–25.
18. Lewis F. Powell Jr. "Powell Memorandum: Attack on American Free Enterprise System." 1971. Accessed July 2022. https://scholarlycommons.law.wlu.edu/powellmemo/1.
19. Julia Lurie. "Unsealed Documents Show How Purdue Pharma Created a 'Pain Movement.'" *Mother Jones*. Aug. 29, 2019. Accessed July 2022. https://www.motherjones.com/crime-justice/2019/08/unsealed-documents-show-how-purdue-pharma-created-a-pain-movement/.
20. Dave Levinthal. "Spreading the Free Market Gospel." *The Atlantic*. Oct. 30, 2015. Accessed July 2022. https://www.theatlantic.com/education/archive/2015/10/spreading-the-free-market-gospel/413239/.
21. Kenneth P. Vogel. "Koch Brothers Plan $125M Spree." *Politico*. May 2014. Accessed July 2022. https://www.politico.com/story/2014/05/koch-brothers-americans-for-prosperity-2014-elections-106520. Also see Philip Bump. "Americans for Prosperity May Be America's Third-Biggest Political Party." *Washington Post*. June 19, 2014. Accessed July 2022. https://www.washingtonpost.com/news/the-fix/wp/2014/06/19/americans-for-prosperity-is-americas-third-biggest-political-party/.

22. Leo Panitch and Sam Gindin. *The Making of Global Capitalism: The Political Economy of American Empire*. London: Verso, 2012, pp. 224–26.
23. Peter S. Goodman and Phillip P. Pan. "Chinese Workers Pay for Walmart's Low Prices." *Washington Post*. Feb. 8, 2008. Accessed July 2022. https://www.washingtonpost.com/archive/politics/2004/02/08/chinese-workers-pay-for-wal-marts-low-prices/54d72114-6919-4eca-a950-d6f2032efda6/. Also see Charles Duhigg and David Barboza. "In China, Human Costs Are Built into an iPad." *New York Times*. Jan. 25, 2012. Accessed July 2022. http://www.nytimes.com/2012/01/26/business/ieconomy-apples-ipad-and-the-human-costs-for-workers-in-china.html?_r=0.
24. Kevin Phillips. *Wealth and Democracy: A Political History of the American Rich*. New York: Broadway Books, 2002, p. 113.
25. For a comprehensive historical analysis of these trends, see Nelson Lichtenstein. *Walmart: The Face of Twenty-First-Century Capitalism*. New York: New Press, 2006.
26. Harold Meyerson. "In Walmart's Image." *American Prospect*. Aug. 14, 2009. Accessed July 2022. https://prospect.org/culture/wal-mart-s-image/.
27. Karen Olsson. "Up Against Walmart." *Mother Jones*. March/April 2003. Accessed July 2022. http://www.motherjones.com/politics/2003/03/against-wal-mart. Also see Sam Walton. *Sam Walton: Made in America*. New York: Bantam, June 2013, pp. 162–69.
28. "2020 American's Richest Families Net Worth: #1 Walton Family." *Forbes*. Dec. 16, 2020. Accessed July 2022. https://www.forbes.com/profile/walton-1/.
29. Zephyr Teachout. *Break 'Em Up: Recovering Our Freedom from Big Ag, Big Tech, and Big Money*. Stuttgart: All Points Books, 2020, p. 45.
30. Sonali Kohli. "Developers Have Figured Out the Secret Sauce for Gentrifying Neighborhoods." *Quartz*. June 21, 2015. Accessed July 2022. https://qz.com/408986/developers-have-figured-out-the-secret-sauce-to-gentrification/.
31. Shoshana Zuboff. *The Age of Surveillance Capitalism: The Fight for a Human Future at the New Frontier of Power*. New York: Public Affairs, 2019.
32. Stuart A. Thompson and Charlie Warzel. "They Used to Post Selfies, Now They're Trying to Reverse the Election." *New York Times*. Jan. 14, 2021. Accessed July 2022. https://www.nytimes.com/2021/01/14/opinion/facebook-far-right.html. Also see Jonathan Berr. "Google, Facebook Reportedly Facing Multiple Lawsuits." *Forbes*. Nov. 30, 2020. Accessed July 2022. https://www.forbes.com/sites/jonathanberr/2020/11/30/google-facebook-reportedly-facing-multiple-antitrust-lawsuits/?sh=c9c23af7ad20/; and Cecilia Kang and Mike Isaac. "U.S. and States Say Facebook Illegally Crushed Competition." *New York Times*. Dec. 9, 2020. Accessed July 2022. https://www.nytimes.com/2020/12/09/technology/facebook-antitrust-monopoly.html.
33. *The United States v. Google, LLC*. Case 1:20-cv-03010, Filed 10/20/20. United States District Court for the District of Columbia. Accessed July 2022. https://s3.documentcloud.org/documents/7273448/DOC.pdf.
34. Joseph McAuley. "The Legacy of Louis Brandeis, 100 Years After His Historic Nomination." *America Magazine*. Jan. 27, 2016. Accessed July 2022. https://www.americamagazine.org/content/all-things/justice-brandeis-and-right-be.
35. John Bellamy Foster, Robert W. McChesney, and R. Jamil Jonna. "The Internationalization of Monopoly Capitalism." *Monthly Review* 63 (2), June 2011. Accessed July 2022. https://monthlyreview.org/2011/06/01/the-internationalization-of-monopoly-capital/.

36. Graham Steele. "The New Money Trust: How Large Money Managers Control Our Economic and What We Can Do About It." American Economic Liberties Project. Nov. 23, 2020. Accessed July 2022. https://www.economicliberties.us/our-work/new-money-trust/#.
37. John C. Bogle. "Bogle Sounds a Warning on Index Funds." *Wall Street Journal*. Nov. 29, 2018. Accessed July 2022. https://www.wsj.com/articles/bogle-sounds-a-warning-on-index-funds-1543504551.
38. "Top Ten Tax Dodgers." *Time Magazine*. Accessed July 2021. http://content.time.com/time/specials/packages/article/0,28804,1891335_1891333_1891317,00.html.
39. Hiatt Woods. "How Billionaires Saw Their Net Worth Increase by Half a Trillion Dollars During the Pandemic." *Business Insider*. Oct. 30, 2020. Accessed July 2022. https://www.businessinsider.com/billionaires-net-worth-increases-coronavirus-pandemic-2020-7.
40. Noam Scheiber and Patricia Cohen. "For the Wealthiest, a Private Tax System That Saves Them Billions." *New York Times*. Dec. 29, 2015. Accessed July 2022. https://www.nytimes.com/2015/12/30/business/economy/for-the-wealthiest-private-tax-system-saves-them-billions.html?_r=0.
41. Paul Kiel. "It's Getting Worse: The IRS Now Audits Poor Americans at About the Same Rate as the Top 1%." *ProPublica*. May 30, 2019. Accessed July 2022. https://www.propublica.org/article/irs-now-audits-poor-americans-at-about-the-same-rate-as-the-top-1-percent. Also see Brandon Debot, Emily Horton, and Chuck Marr. "Trump Budget Continues Multi-year Assault on IRS Funding Despite Mnuchin's Call for More Resources." Center on Budget and Policy Priorities. March 16, 2017. Accessed July 2022. https://www.cbpp.org/research/federal-budget/trump-budget-continues-multi-year-assault-on-irs-funding-despite-mnuchins; and "Report: Trends in the Internal Revenue Service's Funding and Enforcement." Congressional Budget Office. July 8, 2020. Accessed July 2022. https://www.cbo.gov/publication/56422.
42. Brandon Debot, Emily Horton, and Chuck Marr. "Trump Budget Continues Multi-year Assault on IRS Funding Despite Mnuchin Calls for More Resources." Center on Budget and Policy Priorities. March 16, 2017. Accessed July 2022. https://www.cbpp.org/research/federal-budget/trump-budget-continues-multi-year-assault-on-irs-funding-despite-mnuchins.
43. Noam Scheiber and Patricia Cohen. "For the Wealthiest, a Private Tax System That Saves Them Billions." *New York Times*. Dec. 29, 2015. Accessed July 2022. https://www.nytimes.com/2015/12/30/business/economy/for-the-wealthiest-private-tax-system-saves-them-billions.html?_r=0.
44. Jesse Drucker and Eric Lipton. "How a Trump Tax Break to Help Poor Communities Became a Windfall for the Rich." *New York Times*. Sept. 27, 2020. Accessed July 2022. https://www.nytimes.com/2019/08/31/business/tax-opportunity-zones.html.
45. Frank Bruni. "Kemp, in Montana, Urges End to Estate Taxes." *New York Times*. Sept. 2, 1993. Accessed July 2022. https://www.nytimes.com/1996/09/02/us/kemp-in-montana-urges-end-to-estate-taxes.html. Also see Timothy Noah. "Jack Kemp: The Bleeding-Heart Conservative Who Changed America." *New York Times*. Nov. 4, 2015. Accessed July 2022. https://www.nytimes.com/2015/11/08/books/review/jack-kemp-the-bleeding-heart-conservative-who-changed-america.html.

46. Joshua Green. "Meet Mr. Death." *American Prospect*. Dec. 19, 2001. Accessed July 2022. https://prospect.org/features/meet-mr.-death/.
47. Rosie Hunter and Chuck Collins. "'Death Tax' Deception." *Dollars and Sense*. Jan. 3, 2003. Accessed July 2022. http://www.dollarsandsense.org/archives/2003/0103hunter.html.
48. Jonathan Chait. "Paint It Black." *New Republic*. Sept. 3, 2001. Accessed July 2022. https://newrepublic.com/article/64228/paint-it-black.
49. Eric Lipton and Julie Creswell. "Panama Papers Show How Rich United States Clients Hid Millions Abroad." *New York Times*. June 5, 2016. Accessed July 2022. https://www.nytimes.com/2016/06/06/us/panama-papers.html.
50. Greg Miller, Debbie Cenziper, and Peter Whoriskey. "Billions Hidden Beyond Reach." *Washington Post*. Oct. 3, 2021. Accessed July 2022. https://www.washingtonpost.com/business/interactive/2021/pandora-papers-offshore-finance/?itid=lk_inline_manual_2.
51. Gabriel Zucman. *The Hidden Wealth of Nations: The Scourge of Tax Havens*. Chicago: University of Chicago Press, 2015, pp. ix, 3.
52. Alan Cobham, Javier Garcia-Bernardo, Miroslav Palansky, and Mark Bou Mansour. "The State of Tax Justice 2020: Tax Justice in the Time of COVID-19." Global Alliance for Tax Justice. Nov. 2020. Accessed July 2022. https://taxjustice.net/wp-content/uploads/2020/11/The_State_of_Tax_Justice_2020_ENGLISH.pdf.
53. Frank Clemente, Hunter Blair, and Nick Trokel. "Corporate Tax Chartbook." Economic Policy Institute. June 1, 2017. Accessed July 2022. https://www.epi.org/publication/corporate-tax-chartbook-how-corporations-rig-the-rules-to-dodge-the-taxes-they-owe/.
54. Tim Dickinson. "The Biggest Tax Scam Ever." *Rolling Stone*. Aug. 27, 2014. Accessed July 2022. https://www.rollingstone.com/politics/politics-news/the-biggest-tax-scam-ever-67528/.
55. Nicholas Shaxson. *The Finance Curse: How Global Finance Is Making Us All Poorer*. New York: Grove Press, 2018. Also see Noam Scheiber and Patricia Cohen. "For the Wealthiest, a Private Tax System That Saves Them Billions." *New York Times*. Dec. 29, 2015. Accessed July 2022. https://www.nytimes.com/2015/12/30/business/economy/for-the-wealthiest-private-tax-system-saves-them-billions.html?_r=0.
56. "Watershed Data Indicates More Than a Trillion Dollars of Corporate Profit Smuggled Into Tax Havens." Tax Justice Network. July 8, 2020. Accessed July 2022. https://www.taxjustice.net/press/watershed-data-indicates-more-than-a-trillion-dollars-of-corporate-profit-smuggled-into-tax-havens/.
57. Matthew Gardner and Steve Wamhoff. "Trump-GOP tax Law Encourages Companies to Move Jobs Offshore—and New Tax Cuts Won't Change That." Institute on Taxation and Economy Policy. June 2, 2020. Accessed July 2022. https://itep.org/trump-gop-tax-law-encourages-companies-to-move-jobs-offshore-and-new-tax-cuts-wont-change-that/. Also see Tim Tankersley "Trump Administration Scaling Back Rules Meant to Stop Corporate Inversions." *New York Times*. Oct. 31, 2019. Accessed July 2022. https://www.nytimes.com/2019/10/31/business/trump-treasury-corporate-inversions.html.
58. Dan Desai Martin. "Tax-Dodging Trump Flunky Won't Fly the U.S. Flag on Her $40 Million Yacht." *American Independent*. Aug. 9, 2018. Accessed July 2021. https://americanindependent.com/betsy-devos-yacht-american-flag/.

59. David Kocieniewski. "Companies Push for Tax Break on Foreign Cash." *New York Times*. June 19, 2011. Accessed July 2022. https://www.nytimes.com/2011/06/20/business/20tax.html. Also see William Lazonick. "U.S. Corporations Don't Need Tax Breaks on Foreign Profits." Institute for New Economic Thinking. Dec. 21, 2015. Accessed July 2021. https://www.ineteconomics.org/perspectives/blog/u-s-corporations-dont-need-tax-breaks-on-foreign-profits.
60. Katie Benner. "Justice Dept. Asked to Examine Whether Swiss Bank Kept Helping Tax Dodgers." *New York Times*. April 27, 2021. Accessed July 2022. https://www.nytimes.com/2021/04/27/us/politics/justice-department-credit-suisse.html.
61. Reuven Avi-Yonah. "The Shame of Tax Havens." *American Prospect*. Dec. 1, 2015. Accessed July 2022. https://prospect.org/economy/shame-tax-havens/.
62. Oliver Bullough. "The Great American Tax Haven: Why the Super-Rich Love South Dakota." *The Guardian*. Nov. 14, 2019. Accessed July 2022. https://www.theguardian.com/world/2019/nov/14/the-great-american-tax-haven-why-the-super-rich-love-south-dakota-trust-laws.
63. Oliver Bullough. "The Great American Tax Haven: Why the Super-Rich Love South Dakota." *The Guardian*. Nov. 14, 2019. Accessed July 2022. https://www.theguardian.com/world/2019/nov/14/the-great-american-tax-haven-why-the-super-rich-love-south-dakota-trust-laws.
64. Robin Stein. "The Ascendancy of the Credit Card Industry." *PBS Frontline*. Nov. 23, 2004. Accessed July 2022. https://www.pbs.org/wgbh/pages/frontline/shows/credit/more/rise.html.
65. Dominic Rushe. "U.S. Cities and States Give Big Tech $9.3bn in Subsidies in Five Years." *The Guardian*. July 2, 2018. Accessed July 2022. https://www.theguardian.com/cities/2018/jul/02/us-cities-and-states-give-big-tech-93bn-in-subsidies-in-five-years-tax-breaks.
66. Jeff Stein and Seung Min Kim. "Biden, Other G-20 World Leaders Formally Endorse Groundbreaking Global Corporate Minimum Tax." *Washington Post*. Oct. 30, 2021. Accessed July 2022. https://www.washingtonpost.com/us-policy/2021/10/30/biden-g20-global-minimum-tax/. Also see Alan Rappeport and Liz Alderman. "Global Deal to End Tax Havens Moves Ahead as Nations Back 15% Rate." *New York Times*. Oct. 8, 2021. Accessed July 2022. https://www.nytimes.com/2021/10/08/business/oecd-global-minimum-tax.html.
67. Josh Boak. "Explainer: What's a 'Wealth Tax' and How Would It Work?" *Associated Press*. Oct. 27, 2021. Accessed July 2022. https://apnews.com/article/coronavirus-pandemic-joe-biden-business-health-personal-taxes-bb51ab8b987c32e00c743a05d428079c. Also see Jonathan Weisman. "Sinema's Blockade on Tax Rates Prods Democrats Toward Billionaires' Tax." *New York Times*. Oct. 27, 2021. Accessed July 2022. https://www.nytimes.com/2021/10/22/us/politics/sinema-wealth-taxes.html.
68. Peter G. Peterson. *The Education of an American Dreamer: A Memoir*. New York: Twelve, 2010, pp. 123–25.
69. On Roosevelt's relationship to big business, see Leroy G. Dorsey. "Theodore Roosevelt and Corporate America, 1901–1909: A Reexamination." *Presidential Studies Quarterly* 25, 1995, pp. 725–39. Also see Linsey McGoey. *No Such Thing as a Free Gift: The Gates Foundation and the Price of Philanthropy*. New York: Verso, 2015; and Paul Vallely. "How Philanthropy Benefits the Superrich." *The Guardian*.

Sept. 8, 2020. Accessed July 2022. https://www.theguardian.com/society/2020/sep/08/how-philanthropy-benefits-the-super-rich.

70. Peter G. Peterson. *The Education of an American Dreamer: A Memoir*. New York: Twelve, 2010, pp. 124–25.
71. "John J. McCloy, Lawyer and Diplomat, Is Dead at 93." *New York Times*. March 12, 1989. Accessed July 2022. http://www.nytimes.com/1989/03/12/obituaries/john-j-mccloy-lawyer-and-diplomat-is-dead-at-93.html?pagewanted=all.
72. Peter G. Peterson. *The Education of an American Dreamer: A Memoir.* New York: Twelve, 2010, pp. 126–29.
73. Chris Stadler. "Charitable Giving Is Broken—Here's an Easy Way to Fix It." *Forbes*. March 29, 2021. Accessed July 2022. https://www.forbes.com/sites/globalcitizen/2021/03/29/charitable-giving-is-broken--heres-an-easy-way-to-fix-it/?sh=4d7ecd4a3dfe.
74. Joyce Purnick. *Mike Bloomberg: Money, Power, Politics*. New York: Public Affairs, 2010, p. 194.
75. "About Robinhood." *Robinhood.org.* Accessed July 2021. https://www.robinhood.org/. Also see Lynn Parramore. "Meet the Hedge Funders and Billionaires Who Pillage Under the Shield of Philanthropy." *Truthout*. Aug. 5, 2015. Accessed July 2022. http://www.truth-out.org/news/item/32227-meet-the-hedge-funders-and-billionaires-who-pillage-under-the-shield-of-philanthropy.
76. Michelle Caruso-Cabrera. "Pope's Sharp Words Make a Wealthy Donor Hesitate." *CNBC*. Dec. 30, 2013. Accessed July 2022. https://www.cnbc.com/2013/12/30/pope-francis-wealthy-catholic-donors-upset-at-popes-rhetoric-about-rich.html.
77. Julia LaRoche. "Hedge Funder Stan Druckenmiller Wants Every Young Person in America to See These Charts About How They're Getting Screwed." *Business Insider*. Sept. 20, 2013. Accessed July 2020. https://www.businessinsider.com/stan-druckenmiller-on-generational-theft-2013-9.
78. Patrick Radden Keefe. "The Family That Built an Empire of Pain." *New Yorker*. Oct. 23, 2017. Accessed July 2022. https://www.newyorker.com/magazine/2017/10/30/the-family-that-built-an-empire-of-pain.
79. Kerry A. Dolan. "Billion-Dollar Dynasties: These Are the Richest Families in America." *Forbes*. Dec. 17, 2017. Accessed July 2022. https://www.forbes.com/sites/kerryadolan/2020/12/17/billion-dollar-dynasties-these-are-the-richest-families-in-america/?sh=7f91cbce772c.
80. Jane Mayer. "Covert Operations." *New Yorker*. Aug. 30, 2010. Accessed July 2022. https://www.newyorker.com/magazine/2010/08/30/covert-operations.
81. Al Baker. "Teachers Irate as Bloomberg Likens Union to N.R.A." *New York Times*. Jan. 7, 2013. Accessed July 2022. https://www.nytimes.com/2013/01/07/education/michael-bloomberg-compares-teachers-union-to-the-nra.html. Also see Philissa Cramer. "Bloomberg's Class Size Comments More Strident but in Character." *Chalkbeat*. Dec. 2, 2011. Accessed July 2022. https://ny.chalkbeat.org/2011/12/2/21109805/bloomberg-s-class-size-comments-more-strident-but-in-character.
82. "Resurfaced Video Shows Bloomberg Calling for Cuts to Medicare and Social Security." *DemocracyNow*. Feb. 19, 2020. Accessed July 2022. https://www.democracynow.org/2020/2/19/headlines/resurfaced_video_shows_bloomberg_calling_for_cuts_to_medicare_and_social_security. Also see Dana Rubenstein. "Today Is Simpson-Bowles Day for Bloomberg." *Politico*. March 29, 2012. Accessed July 2021. https://www.politico.com/states/new-york/albany/story/2012/03/today-is-simpson-bowles-day-for-michael-bloomberg-003164; and Zaid Jilani. "Mayor

Bloomberg Claims 'Occupy Wall Street' Protesters Are Targeting Bankers Who 'Are Struggling to Make Ends Meet.'" *ThinkProgress*. Sept. 30, 2011. Accessed July 2022. https://thinkprogress.org/mayor-bloomberg-claims-occupy-wall-street-protesters-are-targeting-bankers-who-are-struggling-to-5c78ef0ee216/.

83. Robert Reich. "What Are Foundations For?" *Boston Review*. May 28, 2013. Accessed July 2022. http://bostonreview.net/forum/foundations-philanthropy-democracy. Also see William J. Broad. "Billionaires with Big Ideas Are Privatizing American Science." *New York Times*. March 15, 2014. Accessed July 2022. https://www.nytimes.com/2014/03/16/science/billionaires-with-big-ideas-are-privatizing-american-science.html; and Michael E. Porter and Mark R. Kramer. "Philanthropy's New Agenda: Creating Value." *Harvard Business Review*. Nov./Dec. 1999. Accessed July 2022. https://www.hbs.edu/faculty/Pages/item.aspx?num=9617.

CHAPTER 7

1. Stephen Marche. "Celebrity Warfare: Image and Politics in the Age of Trump." *Los Angeles Review of Books*. May 23, 2017. Accessed July 2022. https://lareviewofbooks.org/article/celebrity-warfare-image-politics-age-trump/.
2. Karl Marx. "The Fetishism of Commodities and the Secret Thereof." *Capital, Volume I*. London: Penguin, 2004, Part 1, Section 4.
3. Nina Bernstein. "After Beyoncé Gives Birth, Patients Protest Celebrity Security at Lenox Hill Hospital." *New York Times*. Jan. 9, 2012. Accessed July 2022. https://www.nytimes.com/2012/01/10/nyregion/after-birth-by-beyonce-patients-protest-celebrity-security-at-lenox-hill-hospital.html.
4. Jennifer Medina, Katie Benner, and Kate Taylor. "Actresses, Business Leaders and Other Wealthy Parents Charged in U.S. College Entry Fraud." *New York Times*. March 12, 2019. Accessed July 2022. https://www.nytimes.com/2019/03/12/us/college-admissions-cheating-scandal.html.
5. Reuters. "L.A. Police Investigate Paris Hilton Car Crash." *Today.com*. Nov. 9, 2005. Accessed July 2022. https://www.today.com/news/l-police-investigate-paris-hilton-car-crash-wbna9984497.
6. "Nicole Richie Charged with Driving Under Influence." *Reuters*. Jan. 20, 2007. Accessed July 2022. https://www.reuters.com/article/us-richie/nicole-richie-charged-with-driving-under-influence-idUSN1121641220061211.
7. Anastasia Tsioulcas. "The Allegations Against R. Kelly: An Abridged History." *National Public Radio*. June 28, 2019. Accessed July 2022. https://www.npr.org/2019/01/11/683936629/r-kelly-allegations-an-abridged-history#dero.
8. Milton Friedman. *Capitalism and Freedom*, 40th ed. Chicago: University of Chicago Press, 2003, p. 4.
9. Charles R. Geisst. *Encyclopedia of American Business History*. New York: Fact on File Inc./Infobase Publishing, 2006, p. 476.
10. Janice Peck. *The Age of Oprah: Cultural Icon for the Neoliberal Era*. Boulder, CO: Paradigm Publishers, 2008, pp. 70–72, 93–95. The show's earlier episodes focused on tabloid topics like devil worshippers, the KKK, "battered wives," "deadbeat fathers," "men who pay for sex," and "men who wear women's clothes," in addition to how-to episodes like "How to get a guy to marry you" and "How fat affects marriages." During one show, Oprah wheeled out a red wagon containing sixty-seven pounds of animal fat to show off how much weight she had lost.
11. Peter Birkenhead. "Oprah's Ugly Secret." *Salon*. March 5, 2007. Accessed July 2022. https://www.salon.com/2007/03/05/the_secret/. Also see Nicole Aschoff.

"Oprah Winfrey: One of the World's Best Neoliberal Capitalist Thinkers." *The Guardian*. May 9, 2015. Accessed July 2022. https://www.theguardian.com/tv-and-radio/2015/may/09/oprah-winfrey-neoliberal-capitalist-thinkers.

12. Rhonda Bryne. *The Secret*. New York: Simon and Schuster, 2006, pp. 99, 132.
13. Sam Thielman. "Author of The Secret Hasn't 'the Time and Energy' to Sell House for Asking Price." *The Guardian*. May 27, 2015. Accessed July 2022. https://www.theguardian.com/books/2015/may/27/rhonda-byrne-the-secret-estate-montecito-sale.
14. Josh Katz. "'Duck Dynasty' vs. 'Modern Family:' 50 Maps of the U.S. Cultural Divide." *New York Times*. Dec. 27, 2016. Accessed July 2022. https://www.nytimes.com/interactive/2016/12/26/upshot/duck-dynasty-vs-modern-family-television-maps.html#teen_mom.
15. Tasha R. Rennels. "Here Comes Honey Boo Boo: A Cautionary Tale Starring White Working Class People." *Communication and Critical/Cultural Studies* 12 (3), Sept. 2015, pp. 271–88.
16. Michael Moore (Erik Hayden). "Michael Moore: Why I Gave That Infamous Anti-Bush Oscars Speech." *Hollywood Reporter*. Feb. 23, 2017. Accessed July 2022. https://www.hollywoodreporter.com/news/michael-moores-2003-oscars-speech-filmmaker-reveals-full-story-977566.
17. Dominic Patten. "Hillary Clinton Snags $15M+ from George Clooney-Hosted SF & LA Fundraisers." *Deadline.com*. April 15, 2016. Accessed July 2022. https://deadline.com/2016/04/george-clooney-hillary-clinton-fundraisers-jeffrey-katzenberg-steven-spielberg-bernie-sanders-1201738559/.
18. Brian Stelter. "Oprah Worth a Million Votes to Obama?" *New York Times*. Aug. 11, 2008. Accessed July 2022. https://www.nytimes.com/2008/08/11/business/worldbusiness/11iht-11oprah.15161325.html.
19. Peter Bart. "'Red Dawn': Shooting It the McVeigh Way." *Variety*. June 16, 1997. Accessed July 2022. https://variety.com/1997/voices/columns/red-dawn-shooting-it-the-mcveigh-way-1117859589/.
20. Alex Chiu and Charlotte Triggs. "Bradley Cooper Is PEOPLE's Sexiest Man Alive!" *People Magazine*. Nov. 16, 2011. Accessed July 2022. https://people.com/celebrity/bradley-cooper-sexiest-man-alive-2011-on-people-3/.
21. Maryl Gottlieb. "Clint Eastwood Finally Explains His Infamous Empty-Chair Speech and Calls It 'Silly.'" *Business Insider*. August 3, 2016. Accessed July 2022. https://www.businessinsider.com/clint-eastwood-explains-empty-chair-speech-at-2012-rnc-2016-8.
22. "Bradley Cooper: 'Sniper' Controversy Distracts from the Film's Message About Vets." *National Public Radio*. Feb. 2, 2015. Accessed July 2022. https://www.npr.org/transcripts/383062401?storyId=383062401.
23. Nicholas Schmidle. "In the Crosshairs." *New Yorker*. May 17, 2013. Accessed July 2022. https://www.newyorker.com/magazine/2013/06/03/in-the-crosshairs.
24. Taylor Nicole Rogers and Debanjali Bose. "7 Celebrities Who Reached Billionaire Status." *Business Insider*. April 6, 2021. Accessed July 2022. https://www.insider.com/hollywood-celebrity-billionaires-oprah-jay-z-kylie-jenner-2019-6.
25. Mark Sweney. "Jay-Z Sells Majority Stake in Tidal Music Streaming Service to Jack Dorsey's Square." *The Guardian*. March 4, 2021. Accessed July 2022. https://www.theguardian.com/business/2021/mar/04/jay-z-sells-majority-stake-in-tidal-music-streaming-service-to-jack-dorseys-square.
26. Nicholas Rice. "Kanye West Is Worth $6.6 Billion—and More Than Half of It Is Thanks to His Yeezy Brand." *People Magazine*. March 17, 2021. Accessed July

2022. https://www.yahoo.com/entertainment/kanye-west-worth-6-6-190004160.html.

27. Gary Warnett. "How Run-DMC Earned Their Adidas Stripes." *MR Porter*. May 27, 2016. Accessed July 2022. https://www.mrporter.com/en-us/journal/lifestyle/how-run-dmc-earned-their-adidas-stripes-826882.
28. Nick DePaula. "The True Story of the 'Banned' Air Jordans." *Yahoo Finance*. July 21, 2016. Accessed July 2022. https://finance.yahoo.com/news/nike-celebrating-banned-air-jordans-with-new-release-174631314.html.
29. Robert W. McChesney. *Corporate Media and the Threat to Democracy*. New York: Seven Stories Press, 1997, p. 28.
30. "Space Jam: A New Legacy Focuses on the Fun." Nike homepage. June 8, 2021. Accessed July 2022. https://news.nike.com/news/nike-and-converse-space-jam-a-new-legacy-collection-official-images-release-date.
31. Kurt Badenhausen. "The 25 Highest-Paid Athletes of All Time." *Forbes*. Dec. 13, 2017. Accessed July 2022. https://www.forbes.com/sites/kurtbadenhausen/2017/12/13/the-25-highest-paid-athletes-of-all-time/?sh=7195e4544b64.
32. Yashima Bhatia. "Why Did Michael Jordan Buy the Charlotte Hornets? Price, Estimated Worth and More." *Essentially Sports*. Oct. 25, 2020. Accessed July 2022. https://www.essentiallysports.com/nba-news-why-did-michael-jordan-buy-the-charlotte-hornets-price-estimated-worth-and-more/.
33. Kurt Badenhausen. "Tiger Woods Is Back on Top of the World's Highest-Paid Athletes." *Forbes*. June 5, 2013. Accessed July 2022. https://www.forbes.com/sites/kurtbadenhausen/2013/06/05/tiger-woods-is-back-on-top-of-the-worlds-highest-paid-athletes/?sh=66b7580f2559.
34. Jaimie Diaz. "Twenty-Five Years Later, Tiger Woods' First Start in a Professional Tournament Remains a Memorable Opening Act." *Golf Digest*. Feb. 13, 2017. Accessed July 2022. https://www.golfdigest.com/story/twenty-five-years-later-tiger-woods-first-start-in-a-professional-tournament-remains-a-memorable-opening-act.
35. Jeff Benedict and Armen Keteyian. *Tiger Woods*. Simon and Schuster, 2018, p. 119–20.
36. "Tiger Woods Paid Up to $40,000 for a Weekend with Women." *International Business Times*. Dec. 11, 2009. Accessed July 2022. https://www.ibtimes.com/tiger-woods-paid-40000-weekend-women-352882.
37. "Creating 'I'd Like to Buy the World a Coke.'" Coca-Cola Company homepage. Accessed July 2022. https://www.coca-colacompany.com/company/history/creating-id-like-to-buy-the-world-a-coke.
38. Aja Romano. "Why We Can't Stop Fighting About Cancel Culture." *Vox*. Aug. 25, 2020. Accessed July 2022. https://www.vox.com/culture/2019/12/30/20879720/what-is-cancel-culture-explained-history-debate.
39. Ben Smith. "Record Ratings and Record Chaos on Cable News." *New York Times*. May 31, 2020. Accessed July 2022. https://www.nytimes.com/2020/05/31/business/media/cable-news-fox-msnbc-cnn.html. Also see Lesley Goldberg and Kim Masters. "NBC Insiders Say Entertainment Boss Fostered Toxic Culture, Under Investigation." *The Hollywood Reporter*. July 31, 2020. Accessed July 2022. https://www.hollywoodreporter.com/tv/tv-features/nbc-insiders-say-entertainment-boss-fostered-toxic-culture-under-investigation-1305307/.
40. Peter Dreier. "Disney Is Not the Greatest Place on Earth to Work." *The Nation*. March 12, 2020. Accessed July 2022. https://www.thenation.com/article/economy/disney-iger-labor/.

41. Jordan Runtagh. "When John Lennon's 'More Popular Than Jesus' Controversy Turned Ugly." *Rolling Stone*. July 29, 2016. Accessed July 2022. https://www.rollingstone.com/feature/when-john-lennons-more-popular-than-jesus-controversy-turned-ugly-106430/.
42. Krista Smith. "The Inescapable Paris." *Vanity Fair*. Oct. 2005. Accessed July 2022. https://archive.vanityfair.com/article/share/a70bab08-9be7-4752-aaf6-850addcc8e90?inline.
43. Nancy Jo Sales. "Hip Hop Debs." *Vanity Fair*. Sept. 1, 2000. Accessed July 2021. https://www.vanityfair.com/culture/2000/09/hiltons200009.
44. Sean Michaels. "Paris Hilton Earns Up to $1m for a Single DJ Set." *The Guardian*. Oct. 23, 2014. Accessed July 2022. https://www.theguardian.com/music/2014/oct/23/paris-hilton-earns-up-to-1m-single-dj-set.
45. Dominic Patten. "Bruce Jenner Interview Ratings Hits Newsmag Demo Record in Live+3." *Deadline.com*. April 29, 2015. Accessed July 2021. https://deadline.com/2015/04/bruce-jenner-interview-ratings-diane-sawyer-20-20-1201416149/.
46. Kate Taylor. "Kim Kardashian Revealed in a Lawsuit That She Demands Up to Half a Million Dollars for a Single Instagram Post and Other Details About How Much She Charges for Endorsement Deals." *Business Insider*. May 9, 2019. Accessed July 2022. https://www.businessinsider.com/how-much-kim-kardashian-charges-for-instagram-endorsement-deals-2019-5.
47. Kaya Turieff. "Snapchat Stock Loses $1.3 Billion After Kylie Jenner Tweet." *CNN*. Feb. 23, 2018. Accessed July 2022. https://money.cnn.com/2018/02/22/technology/snapchat-update-kylie-jenner/index.html.
48. Rosanna Greenstreet. "Q&A: Robin Gibb." *The Guardian*. July 30, 2010. Accessed July 2022. https://www.theguardian.com/lifeandstyle/2010/jul/31/robin-gibb-interview.
49. Sue Collins. "Making the Most Out of 15 Minutes: Reality TV's Dispensable Celebrity." *Television & New Media* 9 (2), Jan. 16, 2008, p. 96. Also see Jackie Raphael and Celia Lam (eds). *Becoming Brands: Celebrity, Activism, and Politics*. New York: WaterHill Publishing, 2017; and David Grazian. "Neoliberalism and the Realities of Reality Television." *Contexts* 9 (2), May 1, 2010, p. 69.
50. Troy Devolld. "Five Myths About Reality Television." *Washington Post*. April 19, 2019. Accessed July 2022. https://www.washingtonpost.com/outlook/five-myths/five-myths-about-reality-television/2019/04/19/fdab858c-6125-11e9-9ff2-abc984dc9eec_story.html. Also see David Dayen. "The Real World of Reality TV: Worker Exploitation." *In These Times*. Oct. 14, 2014. Accessed July 2021. https://inthesetimes.com/article/reality-tv-production-workers-win-collective-bargaining.
51. Kate Allan. "Reality TV Changed the Economics of Television, and Now, It's Paying for It." *Business Insider*. April 4, 2018. Accessed July 2022. https://www.thechainsaw.com/reality-tv-changed-the-economics-of-television-and-now-its-paying-for-it-2018-4. Also see Edward Wyatt. "Despite Lower Ratings, Cash Flow Rises for 'Idol'." *New York Times*. May 10, 2009. Accessed July 2022. https://www.nytimes.com/2009/05/11/business/media/11idol.html.
52. Breeanna Hare. "The 'Real World' of Reality Show Contracts." *CNN*. Dec. 30, 2009. Accessed July 2021. http://www.cnn.com/2009/SHOWBIZ/TV/12/30/legal.reality.contracts/index.html. Also see Sue Collins. "Making the Most Out of 15 Minutes: Reality TV's Dispensable Celebrity." *Television & New Media* 9 (2), Jan. 16, 2008, pp. 87–110.

53. Brett Samuels. "Trump Tells Media at a Cabinet Meeting: 'Welcome Back to the Studio'." *The Hill*. Jan. 10, 2018. Accessed July 2022. https://thehill.com/homenews/administration/368311-trump-welcomes-media-to-cabinet-meeting-welcome-back-to-the-studio/.
54. Maggie Haberman, Glenn Thrush, and Peter Baker. "Inside Trump's Hour-by-Hour Battle for Self-Preservation." *New York Times*. Dec. 9, 2017. Accessed July 2022. https://www.nytimes.com/2017/12/09/us/politics/donald-trump-president.html?utm_source=newsletter&utm_medium=email&utm_campaign=newsletter_axiosam&stream=top-stories.
55. Mike McIntire, Russ Buettner, and Susanne Craig. "How Reality-TV Fame Handed Trump a $427 Million Lifeline." *New York Times*. Sept. 28, 2020. Accessed July 2022. https://www.nytimes.com/interactive/2020/09/28/us/donald-trump-taxes-apprentice.html.
56. Ron Simon. "See How JFK Created a Presidency for the Television Age." *Time Magazine*. May 30, 2017. Accessed July 2021. https://time.com/4795637/jfk-television/. Also see Jack Martinez. "A History of Politicians on Late Night." *Newsweek*. Sept. 13, 2015. Accessed July 2022. https://www.newsweek.com/late-night-politicians-presidential-candidates-371394.
57. Greg Daugherty. "Did Nixon's 'Laugh-In' Cameo Help Him Win the 1968 Election?" *History.com*. Oct. 9, 2018. Accessed July 2022. https://www.history.com/news/richard-nixon-laugh-in-cameo-1968.
58. Gil Kaufman. "John McCain Ad Compares Barack Obama to Britney Spears, Paris Hilton." *MTV*. July 30, 2008. Accessed July 2022. http://www.mtv.com/news/1591820/john-mccain-ad-compares-barack-obama-to-britney-spears-paris-hilton/.
59. Max Weber. *Economy and Society: An Outline of Interpretive Sociology*. Berkeley: University of California Press, 1978, pp. 1111–56.
60. Theodor Adorno. "Freudian Theory and the Pattern of Fascist Propaganda." In *The Essential Frankfurt School Reader*, ed. Andrew Arato and Eike Gephardt. New York: Continuum, 1982, pp. 118–37.

CHAPTER 8

1. Rebecca Sinderbrand. "How Kellyanne Conway Ushered in the Era of 'Alternative Facts'." *Washington Post*. Jan. 2, 2017. Accessed July 2022. https://www.washingtonpost.com/news/the-fix/wp/2017/01/22/how-kellyanne-conway-ushered-in-the-era-of-alternative-facts/.
2. Neil Postman. *Amusing Ourselves to Death: Public Discourse in the Age of Show Business*. New York: Penguin Books, 1985, p. 87.
3. Pierre Bourdieu. *On Television*, transl. Priscilla Parkhurst Ferguson. New York: New Press, 1999.
4. Philip Bump. "The Fox News President." *Washington Post*. Oct. 16, 2017. Accessed July 2022. https://www.washingtonpost.com/news/politics/wp/2017/10/16/the-fox-news-president/. Also see Jane Mayer. "The Making of the Fox News White House." *New Yorker*. March 4, 2019. Accessed July 2022. https://www.newyorker.com/magazine/2019/03/11/the-making-of-the-fox-news-white-house.
5. Brett Samuels. "Trump Ramps Up Rhetoric on Media, Calls Press 'the Enemy of the People.'" *The Hill*. April 5, 2019. Accessed July 2022. https://thehill.com/homenews/administration/437610-trump-calls-press-the-enemy-of-the-people.

6. Nicholas Confessore and Karen Yourish. "$2 Billion Worth of Free Media for Donald Trump." *New York Times.* March 15, 2016. Accessed July 2022. https://www.nytimes.com/2016/03/16/upshot/measuring-donald-trumps-mammoth-advantage-in-free-media.html.
7. Lee Fang. "CBS CEO: 'For Us, Economically, Donald's Place in This Election Is a Good Thing.'" *The Intercept*. Feb. 29, 2016. Accessed July 2022. https://theintercept.com/2016/02/29/cbs-donald-trump/.
8. On Antonio Gramsci's concept of a "war of position" see Antonio Gramsci. "Selections from the prison notebooks." *The Applied Theatre Reader*. Oxfordshire: Routledge. 2020, p. 141–142.
9. Franz Neumann. *Behemoth: The Structure and Practice of National Socialism, 1933–1944*. Chicago: Ivan R. Dee. 1944/2009, p. 402.
10. Dylan Matthews. "Everything You Need to Know About the Fairness Doctrine in One Post." *Washington Post.* Aug. 23, 2011. Accessed July 2022. https://www.washingtonpost.com/blogs/ezra-klein/post/everything-you-need-to-know-about-the-fairness-doctrine-in-one-post/2011/08/23/gIQAN8CXZJ_blog.html.
11. *Red Lion Broadcasting Co., Inc. et al. v. Federal Communications Commission et al.* Supreme Court of the United States. 395 U.S. 367. Decided June 9, 1969. Accessed July 2022. http://law2.umkc.edu/faculty/projects/ftrials/conlaw/redlion.html.
12. Tom A. Collins. "The Future of Cable Communications and the Fairness Doctrine." College of William & Mary Law School. Faculty Publications 506, 1975. Accessed July 2022. https://scholarship.law.wm.edu/facpubs/506.
13. Bob Baker. "What's the Rush? Radio Loudmouth Rush Limbaugh Harangues Feminazis, Environmental Wackos, and Commie Libs, While His Ratings Soar." *Los Angeles Times*. Jan. 20, 1991. Accessed July 2022. https://www.latimes.com/archives/la-xpm-1991-01-20-tm-836-story.html.
14. Tom Hays. "Bob Grant, Conservative Radio Host, Dies at 84." *Washington Post*. Jan. 3, 2014. Accessed July 2022. https://www.washingtonpost.com/national/bob-grant-conservative-radio-host-dies-at-84/2014/01/03/3efbcb20-748a-11e3-8b3f-b1666705ca3b_story.html. Also see Paul Vitello. "Bob Grant, a Combative Personality on New York Talk Radio, Dies at 84." *New York Times*. Jan. 2, 2014. Accessed July 2022. https://www.nytimes.com/2014/01/03/nyregion/bob-grant-a-pioneer-of-right-wing-talk-radio-dies-at-84.html. Despite the dangerous media environment that suspending the Fairness Doctrine unleashed, in 2011 Obama's FCC dissolved the Doctrine entirely—or as *Rolling Stone*'s Tim Dickinson put it, shot it "in the head and then danc[ed] on its grave . . . with all the enthusiasm of News Corp lobbyist." Tim Dickinson. "So Long, Fairness Doctrine." *Rolling Stone*. Aug. 24, 2011. Accessed July 2022. https://www.rollingstone.com/politics/politics-news/so-long-fairness-doctrine-75444/.
15. Eric Boehlert. "One Big Happy Channel?" *Salon*. June 28, 2001. Accessed July 2022. https://www.salon.com/2001/06/28/telecom_dereg/.
16. "Telecommunications Bill Signing." C-SPAN. Feb. 8, 1996. Accessed July 2022. https://www.c-span.org/video/?69814-1/telecommunications-bill-signing%20Feb%208.
17. Michael Corcoran. "Democracy in Peril: Twenty Years of Media Consolidation Under the Telecommunications Act." *Truthout*. Feb. 11, 2016. Accessed July 2022. https://truthout.org/articles/democracy-in-peril-twenty-years-of-media-consolidation-under-the-telecommunications-act/.

18. James Fallows. "The Age of Murdoch." *The Atlantic*. Sept. 2003. Accessed July 2022. https://www.theatlantic.com/magazine/archive/2003/09/the-age-of-murdoch/302777/.
19. 47 U.S. Code § 230—Protection for Private Blocking and Screening of Offensive Material. Legal Information Institute. Cornell University Law School. Accessed July 2022. https://www.law.cornell.edu/uscode/text/47/230.
20. Jim Rutenberg. "Behind the Scenes, Billionaires' Growing Control of News." *New York Times*. May 27, 2016. Accessed July 2022. https://www.nytimes.com/2016/05/28/business/media/behind-the-scenes-billionaires-growing-control-of-news.html. Also see Rupert Neate. "'Extra Level of Power': Billionaires Who Have Bought up the Media." *The Guardian*. May 3, 2022. Accessed July 2022. https://www.theguardian.com/news/2022/may/03/billionaires-extra-power-media-ownership-elon-musk.
21. Ben H. Bagdikian. *The New Media Monopoly*. Boston: Beacon Press, 2004, p. 3.
22. Laura Wagner. "More Journalists Leaving 'Las Vegas Review-Journal' After Sale to Billionaire." *National Public Radio*. May 9, 2016. Accessed July 2022. https://www.npr.org/sections/thetwo-way/2016/05/09/477423367/more-journalists-leaving-las-vegas-review-journal-after-sale-to-billionaire.
23. Jack Nicas. "YouTube Tops 1 Billion Hours of Video a Day, on Pace to Eclipse TV." *Wall Street Journal*. Feb. 27, 2017. Accessed July 2022. https://www.wsj.com/articles/youtube-tops-1-billion-hours-of-video-a-day-on-pace-to-eclipse-tv-1488220851?mod=article_inline.
24. Justin Schlosberg. "The Media–Technology–Military Industrial Complex." *OpenDemocracy*. Jan. 27, 2017. Accessed July 2022. https://www.opendemocracy.net/en/media-technology-military-industrial-complex/.
25. Tim Wu. *The Attention Merchants: The Epic Scramble to Get Inside Our Heads*. New York: Vintage Books, 2017.
26. Keach Hagey and Suzanne Vranica. "How Covid-19 Supercharged the Advertising 'Triopoly' of Google, Facebook and Amazon." *Wall Street Journal*. March 19, 2021. Accessed July 2022. https://www.wsj.com/articles/how-covid-19-supercharged-the-advertising-triopoly-of-google-facebook-and-amazon-11616163738.
27. Jack Nicas. "How YouTube Drives People to the Internet's Darkest Corners." *Wall Street Journal*. Feb. 7, 2018. Accessed July 2022. https://www.wsj.com/articles/how-youtube-drives-viewers-to-the-internets-darkest-corners-1518020478.
28. Betsy Klein. "White House Reviewing Section 230 Amid Efforts to Push Social Media Giants to Crack Down on Misinformation." *CNN*. July 20, 2021. Accessed July 2022. https://www.cnn.com/2021/07/20/politics/white-house-section-230-facebook/index.html. Also see Joanne Lipman. "Tech Overlords Google and Facebook Have Used Monopoly to Rob Journalism of Its Revenue." *USA Today*. June 11, 2019. Accessed July 2022. https://www.usatoday.com/story/opinion/2019/06/11/google-facebook-antitrust-monopoly-advertising-journalism-revenue-streams-column/1414562001/.
29. Paris Martineau. "Facebook Tries Again with News, This Time Paying Publishers." *Wired*. Oct. 25, 2019. Accessed July 2022. https://www.wired.com/story/facebook-tries-again-news-paying-publishers/.
30. "Report: Section 4: Demographics and Political Views of News Audiences." Pew Research Center. Sept. 27, 2012. Accessed July 2022. https://www.pewresearch.org/politics/2012/09/27/section-4-demographics-and-political-views-of-news-audiences/.

31. Edward Helmore. "Fears for Future of American Journalism as Hedge Funds Flex Power." *The Guardian*. June 21, 2021. Accessed July 2022. https://www.theguardian.com/media/2021/jun/21/us-newspapers-journalism-industry-hedge-funds.
32. "Newspapers Fact Sheet." Pew Research Center. June 29, 2021. Accessed July 2022. https://www.pewresearch.org/journalism/fact-sheet/newspapers/.
33. Edmund L. Andrews. "Media Consolidation Means Less Local News, More Right Wing Slant." Stanford Graduate School of Business. June 30, 2019. Accessed July 2022. https://www.gsb.stanford.edu/insights/media-consolidation-means-less-local-news-more-right-wing-slant. Also see Ryan Bort. "This Is What a Pro-Trump Local News Monopoly Would Look Like." *Rolling Stone*. June 25, 2018. Accessed July 2022. https://www.rollingstone.com/politics/politics-news/this-is-what-a-pro-trump-local-news-monopoly-would-look-like-666068/.
34. Jon Swaine. "Sinclair TV Chairman to Trump: 'We Are Here to Deliver Your Message.'" *The Guardian*. April 10, 2018. Accessed July 2022. https://www.theguardian.com/media/2018/apr/10/donald-trump-sinclair-david-smith-white-house-meeting.
35. Timothy Burke. "How America's Largest Local TV Owner Turned Its News Anchors into Soldiers in Trump's War on the Media." *Deadspin*. March 31, 2018. Accessed July 2022. https://deadspin.com/how-americas-largest-local-tv-owner-turned-its-news-anc-1824233490.
36. Brian O'Connell. "Who Are the Highest-Paid TV Anchors?" *The Street*. Aug. 25, 2019. Accessed July 2022. https://www.thestreet.com/lifestyle/highest-paid-news-anchors-15062420. Also see Lachlan Cartwright and Maxwell Tani. "Inside the Massive MSNBC Deal Paying Rachel Maddow to Work Less." *Daily Beast*. Aug. 25, 2021. Accessed Oct. 2022. https://www.thedailybeast.com/inside-the-massive-msnbc-deal-paying-rachel-maddow-to-work-less.
37. Andrew Perez, David Sirota, Walker Bragman, and Julia Rock. "Tucker Carlson Calls Himself a Populist. He Has No Problem Taking Private Equity Money." *Jacobin*. Nov. 11, 2020. Accessed July 2022. https://www.jacobinmag.com/2020/11/tucker-carlson-speaking-fees-private-equity.
38. Ariana Neol Pekary. "Personal News: Why I'm Now Leaving MSNBC." Ariana Noel Pekary website. Aug. 3, 2020. Accessed July 2022. https://www.arianapekary.net/post/personal-news-why-i-m-now-leaving-msnbc.
39. Adam Johnson. "MSNBC Has Done 455 Stormy Daniels Segments in the Last Year—But None on U.S. War in Yemen." *Salon*. July 25, 2018. Accessed July 2022. https://www.salon.com/2018/07/25/msnbc-has-done-455-stormy-daniels-segments-in-the-last-year-but-none-on-the-war-in-yemen/.
40. Howard Kurtz. "Media's Failure on Iraq Still Stings." *CNN*. March 11, 2013. Accessed July 2022. https://www.cnn.com/2013/03/11/opinion/kurtz-iraq-media-failure/index.html. Also see New York Times Editorial Board. "From the Editors: The Times and Iraq." *New York Times*. May 26, 2004. Accessed July 2022. https://www.nytimes.com/2004/05/26/world/from-the-editors-the-times-and-iraq.html; and Gary Younge. "Washington Post Apologizes for Underplaying WMD Skepticism." *The Guardian*. Aug. 12, 2004. Accessed July 2022. https://www.theguardian.com/world/2004/aug/13/pressandpublishing.usa.
41. James P. Winter. *Lies the Media Tells Us*. Montreal: Black Rose Books, 2007, p. 17.
42. See Howard Friel and Richard Falk. *The Record of the Paper: How the New York Times Misreports U.S. Foreign Policy*. New York: Verso, 2004. Also see Alan MacLeod. "Manufacturing Consent in Venezuela: Media Misreporting of a Country, 1998–2014." *Critical Sociology* 46 (2), Dec. 31, 2018, pp. 273–79.

43. Jonathan Stein and Tim Dickinson. "Lie by Lie: A Timeline of How We Got into Iraq." *Mother Jones*. Sept./Oct. 2006. Accessed July 2022. https://www.motherjones.com/politics/2011/12/leadup-iraq-war-timeline/.
44. Michael R. Gordon and Judith Miller. "Threats and Responses: The Iraqis; U.S. Says Hussein Intensifies Quest for A-Bomb Parts." *New York Times*. Sept. 8, 2002. Accessed July 2022. https://www.nytimes.com/2002/09/08/world/threats-responses-iraqis-us-says-hussein-intensifies-quest-for-bomb-parts.html.
45. Andrew Glass. "Bush Makes Case for War with Iraq, Sept. 4, 2002." *Politico*. Sept. 4, 2018. Accessed July 2022. https://www.politico.com/story/2018/09/04/this-day-in-politics-sept-4-2002-805725.
46. Jack Shafer. "Miller Time (Again)." *Slate*. Feb. 12, 2004. Accessed July 2022. https://slate.com/news-and-politics/2004/02/miller-time-again.html. Also see Neil Lewis. "What We Can Learn from Judith Miller's Rehab Tour." *Columbia Journalism Review*. April 23, 2016. Accessed July 2022. https://www.cjr.org/first_person/what_we_can_learn_from_judith_miller.php; and Jack Shafer. "The Real Problem with Judith Miller." *Politico*. April 10, 2015. Accessed July 2022. https://www.politico.com/magazine/story/2015/04/judy-miller-book-nytimes-116869.
47. Matt Taibbi. *Hate, Inc: Why Today's Media Makes Us Despise One Another*. New York: OR Books, Oct. 8, 2019, p. 230.
48. Douglas Jehl. "Pentagon Pays Iraq Group, Supplier of Incorrect Spy Data." *New York Times*. March 11, 2004. Accessed July 2022. https://www.nytimes.com/2004/03/11/world/pentagon-pays-iraq-group-supplier-of-incorrect-spy-data.html.
49. Tom Dickinson. "How Roger Ailes Built the Fox News Fear Factory." *Rolling Stone*. May 25, 2011. Accessed July 2022. https://www.rollingstone.com/politics/politics-news/how-roger-ailes-built-the-fox-news-fear-factory-244652/.
50. "Phil Donahue on His 2003 Firing from MSNBC, When Liberal Network Couldn't Tolerate Antiwar Voices." *Democracy Now*. March 21, 2013. Accessed July 2022. https://www.democracynow.org/2013/3/21/phil_donahue_on_his_2003_firing.
51. Bill Moyers. "Video: Buying the War." *PBS*. 2007. Accessed July 2022. https://www.pbs.org/moyers/journal/btw/watch.html.
52. Richard Cohen. "A Winning Hand for Powell." *Washington Post*. Feb. 6, 2003. Accessed July 2022. https://www.washingtonpost.com/archive/opinions/2003/02/06/a-winning-hand-for-powell/aa1e6dd9-dbf9-4b71-bb86-9c42a4a5a427/. Also see The Editors. "The Case Against Iraq." *New York Times*. Feb. 6, 2003. Accessed July, 2022. http://www.nytimes.com/2003/02/06/opinion/the-case-against-iraq.html; and Norman Soloman. "War Loving Pundits." Fairness & Accuracy in Reporting (FAIR). March 16, 2006. Accessed July 2022. https://fair.org/media-beat-column/war-loving-pundits/.
53. Angelique Chrisafis and Sam Jones. "Snowden Leaks: France Summons U.S. Envoy over NSA Surveillance Claims." *The Guardian*. Oct. 21, 2013. Accessed July 2022. https://www.theguardian.com/world/2013/oct/21/snowden-leaks-france-us-envoy-nsa-surveillance. Also see Richard Fausset. "U.S. Spied on Mexico's Felipe Calderon, Leak Reportedly Shows." *Los Angeles Times*. Oct. 20, 2013. Accessed July 2022. https://www.latimes.com/world/la-fg-mexico-spying-20131021-story.html#axzz2iPerF5bh; and Reuters in Berlin. "NSA Tapped German Chancellery for Decades, WikiLeaks Claims." *The Guardian*. July 8, 2015. Accessed July 2022. https://www.theguardian.com/us-news/2015/jul/08/nsa-tapped-german-chancellery-decades-wikileaks-claims-merkel.

54. Sara Rafsky. "The Obama Administration and the Press." Committee to Protect Journalists Report. Oct. 2013. Accessed July 2022. https://cpj.org/reports/2013/10/obama-and-the-press-us-leaks-surveillance-post-911/.
55. Richard A. Serrano. "Bradley Manning Says USA 'Obsessed' with Killing Opponents." *Los Angeles Times*. Feb. 28, 2013. Accessed July 2022. https://www.latimes.com/politics/la-xpm-2013-feb-28-la-pn-manning-us-obsessed-killing-opponents-20130228-story.html.
56. Matthew Schoefield. "WikiLeaks: Iraqi Children in U.S. Raid Shot in Head, U.N. Says." *McClatchy News*. Aug. 31, 2011. Accessed July 2022. https://www.mcclatchydc.com/news/special-reports/article24696685.html.
57. "Obama Administration Handed Over Detainees Despite Reports of Torture." Bureau of Investigative Journalism. Oct. 3, 2010. Accessed July 2022. https://www.thebureauinvestigates.com/stories/2010-03-10/obama-administration-handed-over-detainees-despite-reports-of-torture.
58. James Risen. "Snowden Says He Took No Secret Files to Russia." *New York Times*. Oct. 17, 2013. Accessed July 2022. https://www.nytimes.com/2013/10/18/world/snowden-says-he-took-no-secret-files-to-russia.html.
59. Joey Redner. "Change You Can Believe In: Presidential Brews." *Tampa Bay Times*. Oct. 24, 2008. Accessed July 2022. https://www.tampabay.com/archive/2008/10/24/change-you-can-believe-in-presidential-brews/.
60. Georg Szalai. "TV Station Giants to Benefit from Record Political Ads in 2020, Analyst Says." *Hollywood Reporter*. Sept. 9, 2020. Accessed July 2022. https://www.hollywoodreporter.com/news/general-news/tv-station-giants-to-benefit-from-record-political-ads-in-2020-analyst-says-4057114/. Also see "Fox Revenue Rises, Boosted by Political Advertising." *Fox Business*. Feb. 9, 2020. Accessed July 2022. https://www.foxbusiness.com/markets/fox-revenue-rises-boosted-political-advertising.
61. Melissa Batchelor Warnke. "Opinion: The AP's Call for Hillary Clinton Ruined California's Election Party—and Here's Why That Matters." *Los Angeles Times*. June 7, 2016. Accessed July 2022. https://www.latimes.com/opinion/opinion-la/la-ol-sanders-clinton-california-associated-press-20160607-snap-story.html. Also see Glenn Greenwald. "Perfect End to Democratic Primary: Anonymous Superdelegates Declare Winner through Media." *The Intercept*. June 7, 2016. Accessed July 2022. https://theintercept.com/2016/06/07/perfect-end-to-democratic-primary-anonymous-super-delegates-declare-winner-through-media/.
62. Laura Meckler. "Price Tag of Bernie Sanders's Proposals: $18 Trillion." *Wall Street Journal*. Sept. 14, 2015. Accessed July 2022. http://www.wsj.com/articles/price-tag-of-bernie-sanders-proposals-18-trillion-1442271511. Also see Doug Henwood. "Bernie's New Deal." *Jacobin*. Sept. 17, 2015. Accessed July 2022. https://www.jacobinmag.com/2015/09/sanders-medicare-social-security-higher-education/.
63. Paul Krugman. "Weakened at Bernie's." *New York Times*. Jan. 19, 2016. Accessed July 2022. http://krugman.blogs.nytimes.com/2016/01/19/weakened-at-bernies/. Also see Paul Krugman. "Single Payer Trouble." *New York Times*. Jan. 28, 2016. Accessed July 2022. http://krugman.blogs.nytimes.com/2016/01/28/single-payer-trouble/?_r=0.
64. "An Open Letter from Past CEA Chairs to Senator Sanders and Professor Gerald Friedman." *Letter to Sanders* (blog). Feb. 17, 2016. Accessed July 2022. https://lettertosanders.wordpress.com/2016/02/17/open-letter-to-senator-sanders-and-professor-gerald-friedman-from-past-cea-chairs/.

65. New York Times Editorial Board. "Bernie Sanders: Senator from Vermont." *New York Times*. Jan. 13, 2020. Accessed July 2022. https://www.nytimes.com/interactive/2020/01/13/opinion/bernie-sanders-nytimes-interview.html. Also see New York Times Editorial Board. "When Bernie Sanders Came to Visit." *New York Times*. Jan. 20, 2020. Accessed July 2022. https://www.nytimes.com/2020/01/20/opinion/editorials/choice-podcast-sanders-endorsement.html.
66. Glenn Thrush and Sydney Ember. "The Bernie Sanders Personality Test." *New York Times*. March 6, 2020. Accessed July 2022. https://www.nytimes.com/2020/03/06/us/politics/bernie-sanders-image.html. Also see Sydney Ember. "Why Bernie Sanders Stood Out at the Iowa State Fair." *New York Times*. Aug. 12, 2019. Accessed July 2022. https://www.nytimes.com/2019/08/12/us/politics/bernie-sanders-iowa.html.
67. For a thorough assessment of *New York Times* bias against Sanders, see Katie Halper. "Meet Sydney Ember, the New York Times' Senior Anti-Bernie Correspondent." *Jacobin*. July 2, 2019. Accessed July 2022. https://jacobin.com/2019/07/bernie-sanders-sydney-ember-new-york-times.
68. See Halper's July 2, 2019, essay mentioned above, and Thomas Blanton, ed. "Public Diplomacy and Covert Propaganda. The Declassified Record of Ambassador Otto Juan Reich." National Security Archive Electronic Briefing Book No. 40. National Security Archive, George Washington University. March 2, 2001. Accessed July 2022. https://nsarchive2.gwu.edu/NSAEBB/NSAEBB40/.
69. Sydney Ember. "'I Did My Best to Stop American Foreign Policy': Bernie Sanders on the 1980s." *New York Times*. May 18, 2019. Accessed July 2022. https://www.nytimes.com/2019/05/18/us/bernie-sanders.html. Also see Alexander Burns and Sydney Ember. "Mayor and 'Foreign Minister:' How Bernie Sanders Brought the Cold War to Burlington." *New York Times*. May 17, 2019. Accessed July 2022. https://www.nytimes.com/2019/05/17/us/bernie-sanders-burlington-mayor.html?module=inline.
70. Jake Johnson. "MSNBC's Chuck Todd Under Fire for Reciting Quote Comparing Sanders Supporters to Nazis." *Salon*. Feb. 12, 2020. Accessed July 2022. https://www.salon.com/2020/02/12/msnbcs-chuck-todd-under-fire-for-reciting-quote-comparing-sanders-supporters-to-nazis_partner/.
71. Michael M. Grynbaum. "Chris Matthews Apologizes to Bernie Sanders for Remarks on Nevada Win." *New York Times*. March 2, 2020. Accessed July 2022. https://www.nytimes.com/2020/02/24/business/media/chris-matthews-bernie-sanders-apology.html.
72. Katie Halper. "MSNBC's Ridiculous War on Bernie Sanders." *Jacobin*. Aug. 5, 2019. Accessed July 2022. https://jacobinmag.com/2019/08/msnbc-poll-bernie-sanders-presidential-campaign.
73. Clay Ramsay, Steven Kull Evan Lewis, and Stefan Subias. "Report: Misinformation and the 2010 Election: A Study of the U.S. Electorate." World Public Opinion and Knowledge Networks. Dec. 10, 2010. Accessed July 2022. https://drum.lib.umd.edu/bitstream/handle/1903/11375/Misinformation_Dec10_rpt.pdf?sequence=4&isAllowed=y.
74. Gabriel Sherman. *The Loudest Voice in the Room: How the Brilliant, Bombastic Roger Ailes Built Fox News—and Divided a Country*. New York: Random House, 2014, pp. 133–52.
75. Gabriel Sherman. *The Loudest Voice in the Room: How the Brilliant, Bombastic Roger Ailes Built Fox News—and Divided a Country*. New York: Random House, 2014, pp. 104–9.

76. Tim Dickinson. "How Roger Ailes Built the Fox News Fear Factory." *Rolling Stone*. May 25, 2011. Accessed July 2022. https://www.rollingstone.com/politics/politics-news/how-roger-ailes-built-the-fox-news-fear-factory-244652/.
77. Bill McCarthy. "Tucker Carlson Distorts New CDC Report, Makes False Mask Claim." *PolitiFact*. Oct. 15, 2020. Accessed July 2022. https://www.politifact.com/factchecks/2020/oct/15/tucker-carlson/tucker-carlson-distorts-new-cdc-report-makes-false/.
78. Nancy MacLean. *Democracy in Chains: The Deep History of the Radical Right's Stealth Plan for America*. New York: Penguin Books, 2017, pp. 65–73.
79. Milton Friedman. "The Role of Government in Education." Austin: The University of Texas at Austin, 1955. Accessed July 2022. http://la.utexas.edu/users/hcleaver/330T/350kPEEFriedmanRoleOfGovttable.pdf.
80. Justin Miller. "Hedging Education." *American Prospect*. May 6, 2016. Accessed July 2022. https://prospect.org/power/hedging-education/.
81. Erica Frankenberg, Jongyeon Ee, Jennifer B. Ayscue, and Gary Orfield. "Harming Our Common Future: America's Segregated Schools 65 Years After *Brown*." Center for Education and Civil Rights, UCLA. May 10, 2019. Accessed July 2022. https://www.civilrightsproject.ucla.edu/research/k-12-education/integration-and-diversity/harming-our-common-future-americas-segregated-schools-65-years-after-brown/Brown-65-050919v4-final.pdf. Also see Tomás Monarrez, Brian Kisida, and Matthew M. Chingos. "Report: Charter School Effects on School Segregation." Urban Institute. July 24, 2019. Accessed November 2022. https://www.urban.org/research/publication/charter-school-effects-school-segregation.
82. "Report: Still Asleep at the Wheel: How the Federal Charter Schools Program Results in a Pile-Up of Fraud and Waste." Network for Public Education. February 2020. Accessed July 2022. https://networkforpubliceducation.org/wp-content/uploads/2020/02/Still-Asleep-at-the-Wheel.pdf.
83. Jason Felch, Jason Song, and Doug Smith. "Who's Teaching L.A.'s Kids?" *Los Angeles Times*. Aug. 14, 2020. Accessed July 2022. https://www.latimes.com/local/la-me-teachers-value-20100815-story.html.
84. Larry Abramson. "'L.A. Times' Teacher Ratings Database Stirs Debate." *National Public Radio*. Aug. 27, 2010. Accessed July 2022. https://www.npr.org/templates/story/story.php?storyId=129456212.
85. Annie Waldman. "How Teach for America Evolved into an Arm of the Charter School Movement." *ProPublica*. June 18, 2019. Accessed July 2022. https://www.propublica.org/article/how-teach-for-america-evolved-into-an-arm-of-the-charter-school-movement.
86. George Joseph. "This Is What Happens When You Criticize Teach for America." *The Nation*. Oct. 29, 2014. Accessed July 2022. https://www.thenation.com/article/archive/what-happens-when-you-criticize-teach-america/.
87. Jeremy Berke. "A $1 Billion Gates Foundation-Backed Education Initiative Failed to Help Students, According to a New Report—Here's What Happened." *Business Insider*. June 27, 2018. Accessed July 2022. https://www.businessinsider.com/bill-melinda-gates-foundation-education-initiative-failure-2018-6.
88. Joanne Barkan. "Hired Guns on Astroturf: How to Buy and Sell School Reform." *Dissent Magazine*. Spring 2012. Accessed July 2022. https://www.dissentmagazine.org/article/hired-guns-on-astroturfhow-to-buy-and-sell-school-reform.
89. Emma Brown, Valerie Strauss, and Perry Stein. "It Was Hailed as the National Model for School Reform. Then the Scandals Hit." *Washington Post*. March 10,

2018. Accessed July 2022. https://www.washingtonpost.com/local/education/dc-school-scandals-tell-me-that-its-not-great-and-that-youre-dealing-with-it/2018/03/10/b73d9cf0-1d9e-11e8-b2d9-08e748f892c0_story.html.

90. Emma Kerr. "Income Share Agreements: What to Know." *U.S. News and World Report*. April 13, 2021. Accessed July 2022. https://www.usnews.com/education/best-colleges/paying-for-college/articles/income-share-agreements-what-students-should-know. Also see Sydney Johnson. "Wall Street Wants In on Income Share Agreements." *Edsurge.com*. April 5, 2019. Accessed July 2022. https://www.edsurge.com/news/2019-04-05-wall-street-wants-in-on-income-share-agreements.
91. Marco Rubio. "Press Release: Rubio, Young, Warner, Coons Introduce Innovative Higher Ed Financing Proposal." July 16, 2019. Accessed July 2022. https://www.rubio.senate.gov/public/index.cfm/2019/7/rubio-young-warner-coons-introduce-innovative-higher-ed-financing-proposal.

CONCLUSION

1. Ben H. Bagdikian. *The New Media Monopoly*. Boston: Beacon Press, 2004, p. 3.
2. C. Wright Mills. "Letter to the New Left." *New Left Review*, no. 5, Sept.–Oct. 1960. Accessed July 2022. https://www.marxists.org/subject/humanism/mills-c-wright/letter-new-left.htm.

INDEX

For the benefit of digital users, indexed terms that span two pages (e.g., 52–53) may, on occasion, appear on only one of those pages.